The Frugal Gourmet
On Our Immigrant Ancestors

David Brun and his wife, Grace; grandparents of the author. Norwegian immigrants married on September 11, 1911. Grandma was eighteen years old and Grandpa was twenty-eight.

· The ·
FRUGAL
GOURMET
On Our Immigrant
Ancestors

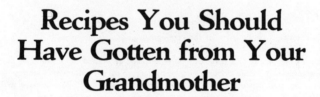

Recipes You Should
Have Gotten from Your
Grandmother

JEFF SMITH

Craig Wollam
Culinary Assistant

Chris Cart
Illustrator

Terrin Haley
D. C. Smith
Research Assistants

William Morrow
and Company, Inc.
New York

Library of Congress Cataloging-in-Publication Data

Smith, Jeff.
    The Frugal Gourmet on our immigrant ancestors: recipes you should
have gotten from your grandmother/Jeff Smith; Craig Wollam,
culinary assistant; Chris Cart, illustrator; Terrin Haley, D. C.
Smith, research assistants.
        p.   cm.
    Includes bibliographical references and index.
    ISBN 0-688-07590-8
    1. Cookery, International. 2. Frugal Gourmet (Television program)
I. Title.
TX725.A1S564   1990
641.59—dc20   90-48368
                                                                      CIP

Printed in the United States of America

First Edition

1 2 3 4 5 6 7 8 9 10

BOOK DESIGN BY RICHARD ORIOLO

TO EMILY GRACE BRUN SMITH
A Frugal Immigrant of Norwegian Blood,
Who Taught Her Son Well

Tusen Takk!
Tusen Takk!

ACKNOWLEDGMENTS

This is the first cookbook that I have written in which the acknowledgments are longer than the book itself. How could it be otherwise? American immigrants and their descendants are all over the country and they seem to have come from every place and every time. And I thank them for their kind help and insight . . . for the dinner parties and the recipes and stories of the earlier days.

The list is long but each name is important.

Vicki Tamoush, Arabian
Vahram Keogian, Armenian
Ron's Supermarket, Los Angeles, Eastern European Foods
The Nugget Hotel, Reno
Louis and Lorraine Erreguible, Louis' Basque Corner, and their
    friends, J. T. Lewkenberry, Jesus Rey, and Mrs. Grace Jaunsaras
The Ly family, Tacoma, Cambodian
Father Kevin Allen, for his ministry
La Teresita Restaurant, Tampa, Cuban
Kokeb Restaurant, Seattle, Ethiopian
The kind members of the Ethiopian Orthodox Church in Seattle
The Mabuhay Café and Elena's, Honolulu, Filipino
Bavarian Meats, Seattle, German
Herman Berghoff of Berghoff's German Restaurant, Chicago
Paulina Sausage Market, Chicago, European
Senator Michael Crozier and Mrs. Lynn Crozier, Hawaii
Ms. Lani Barnet Williams, Hawaii
Laszlo, my Hungarian friend at WTTW, Chicago
The kind people of Budapest

Ms. Julie Sahni, Indian cooking instructor

The Indian shops on Lexington Avenue in New York, and in Vancouver, Canada

Doyle's Irish Restaurant and Bar in Boston

Pepper Pot Restaurant in Kingston, Jamaica

Jamaican Pepper Pot Restaurant in New York, Gary and Yvonne Walters

Endo, Sushi Master at Fujiya Restaurant, Tacoma

Judy Lew, friend and teacher, Uwajimaya, Seattle

Bob's Kosher Treats, Miami

Cantor's Delicatessen, Los Angeles

Mr. Itzhak Perlman, fine Jewish cook . . . also plays violin

Woo Lee Oak restaurants in Los Angeles and New York, Korean

Chun Soo Chang Korean Restaurant, Chicago

Maija Riekstinis, and the women of the Latvian Lutheran Church in Seattle

Victor Abdo, my beloved Lebanese uncle

Grandma Abdo, from Syria. Bless her!

Holy Land Bakery, Chicago

Bezjian's Grocery, Los Angeles

Father Peter, Ann Challan, and the kind people of St. Casimir's Lithuanian Church in Pittston, Pennsylvania

Grand Central Market, Los Angeles, Mexican

Las Palmas Tortillas, San Francisco

Hanna Fields, my young friend in Tacoma

Dominguez Bakery, San Francisco

Ben, the Moroccan chef at the Marrakesh, Seattle

Pasha Moroccan Restaurant in San Francisco

Ebba and Gunner Olsen, Johnsen's Scandinavian Foods, Seattle

Mrs. Emily Smith and Mrs. Inger Blendheim, master *lefse* makers

Finn and Karen Moseid, beloved Norwegian friends in Chicago

Joseph Toulabi, chef at Reza's Persian Restaurant in Chicago

The Polish bunch at WTTW, Chicago, especially Gosha

Gene's Sausage Shop, Chicago, Polish and Heaven!

Sophie Madej of the Busy Bee Polish Cafe, Chicago

Roberto, our fine driver with Carey Limo in San Juan, Puerto Rico

El Coqui Puerto Rican Restaurant in Miami

Ratto's Fine Foods, Oakland

The Monteiro household, San Leandro, Portuguese

Mrs. Pearl Mailath and her grandson John, Indiana, Romanian

Father David and Father John, and the good people of St. Basil's
Russian Orthodox Church in Simpson, Pennsylvania.

Sofia and the M&I International Russian Market in Brighton Beach,
Brooklyn

The Medinah Scottish Pipe and Drum Band, Chicago

Dr. William Campbell, a child of Scotland

El Oso Spanish Restaurant, San Francisco

Rosa Montoya's Bailes Flamencos Dance Company, San Francisco

Columbia Spanish Restaurant, Tampa

Dr. and Mrs. Richard Klein, Swedish friends in Tacoma

Manora's Thai Restaurant, San Francisco

Welcome Market, Seattle

Quoc Huong Vietnamese Restaurant, Seattle

Ms. Kitty Jenkins and Mr. Tom Gable, Welsh friends in Scranton,
Pennsylvania

The kind Welsh people of the United Baptist Church of Scranton,
Pennsylvania

The Cor Meibion Ystradgynlais Male Choir from Wales

The staff at the Coal Mine Museum, Scranton

Chef John Sarich, a Yugoslavian chef and dear friend

Thanks to my wife, Patty, the articles were edited before I gave them
to my editor and dear friend, Maria Guarnaschelli. We were assisted in
the research by Terrin Haley and D. C. Smith. Chris Cart, our illustrator, continues to do with a pen and pencil what I try to do with a
cooking pot. In terms of communication, he is much better than I. And,
thanks to the labors of Al Marchioni, president and chief executive officer of William Morrow and Company, we have a book.

Bill Adler, my book agent, continues to remain a source of strength
when I am worn out, as does Herb Rickman, of PRIDE in New York.
One phone call to Herb and problems are solved.

Special thanks are due to special helpers: to Harriet Fields for her
patience and cookbooks, to Sara Lea of the Lennox House Hotel in
Chicago, and to Peggy Greene at Mutual Travel in Seattle. Such care
these people have given!

Our studio and kitchen staff in Chicago have been more than giving.
Tim Ward and Cynthia Malek, our producers/directors, and Michael
and Roy, on-the-road cameramen, and Harvey and Bob, our sound men.
Troupers, all! Marion Schiewe, our kitchen mom, and Kit Hoover, our

second cook, were blessings. And none of us could have had a good day doing all of these recipes and shows if it were not for the smiling face that met us each morning at 5:45, that of Maurice. The whole of the WTTW production staff have continued to be supportive and skilled. Special thanks to Bosco for always bringing his own fork (at least he claimed it was his!).

The people who take the most weight off my back when I am doing such projects have ceased to be just employees and have become dear friends. Dawn Sparks, our secretary, and Jim Paddleford, our business manager, deserve unusual thanks for putting up with my moods. Maybe they should be canonized!

This book has been the most interesting bit I have ever worked on . . . and it was a joyful effort because of the intense support of my assistant, Mr. Craig Wollam. He deserves much more credit than he will probably ever understand.

Thank you all. Our immigrant ancestors are proud of us, each and every one!

CONTENTS

INTRODUCTION

As you view the Statue of Liberty you may read these words by Emma Lazarus:

"Keep, ancient lands, your storied pomp!" cries she
With silent lips. "Give me your tired, your poor,
Your huddled masses yearning to breathe free,
The wretched refuse of your teeming shore,
Send these, the homeless, tempest-tossed to me:
I lift my lamp beside the golden door."

The great dream of this country was to establish a melting pot, a sort of democratic amalgam resulting from the many peoples who had already come here, and those who were to come.

The first time that the word "melting" was used in reference to this nation was in 1776, the year of the birth of this nation, by Gibbon, in his *Decline and Fall of the Roman Empire*. He claimed that the nations of the empire "melted" away into the Roman name and people. In 1782, in an essay called "Letters from an American Farmer," Michel Guillaume Jean de Crèvecoeur, an immigrant from France, wrote, "Here [in America] individuals of all nations are melted into a new race of men."

Immigrants leaving for the rest of America, Ellis Island, c.1910

The phrase "melting pot" became popular following the publication of a play of 1908 by Israel Zangwill. Woodrow Wilson then used it in a great speech in 1915, and Teddy Roosevelt soon claimed in 1917 that "We Americans are the children of the crucible!"

Thank God the concept of the melting pot has never worked.

That is what this cookbook is all about.

We have traveled all over this great nation eating with immigrants, many of them grandmas, who know that it is terribly important to retain those characteristics of our immigrant ancestry, characteristics that will help us remember who we are. We have not melted together into a common mass, an indistinguishable alloy. Rather, we remain a land of proud immigrants, proud to be from some other place but most proud to be Americans!

While gathering material for these recipes we have learned that the Greek towns, the German towns, the China towns, the Japanese towns, the Lebanese markets, the Basque communities, all point to the fact that we get along best in America not as we are melted down but as we form a sort of stew, in which many traditions and flavors and cultures can each add to the pot, but each can be distinguished. No other nation in the world does this stew as well as we do.

The strangest thing happened when we decided to write this book. The idea grew out of our last book, *The Frugal Gourmet Cooks Three*

Ancient Cuisines. We studied and tasted and wrote about those three ancient cuisines that have most influenced the Western world—the cuisines of China, Greece, and Rome. Then it occurred to us that so many other cultures have contributed to the American stewpot of flavors that we should learn about those as well. My assistant, Craig Wollam, and I traveled to Portugal, Spain, Budapest, the Caribbean, Hawaii, and all over America to see how foods from the old countries had been changed by the immigrant experience. We made out a list of thirty-five different cultures that we wanted to include in the book and in the television shows. We included Germany and Romania, Lithuania and Latvia, and Russia and Hungary. We had already completed visits with immigrant families, we had tested the recipes, and we were ready to begin writing them down for you and showing them on television. And then it happened. Eastern Europe simply blew sky high in a bid for democracy.

As we read the papers and watched the television news we were able to say that we knew about the people who had just torn down the Berlin Wall and those who had demanded freedom from Moscow. Our list of recipes suddenly took on a whole new meaning. Now we want you to be able to cook in order to know these particular immigrant groups. They live here and belong here, and they come from heroic circumstances. What a way to study peace!

During this same time a young friend of mine, Cari Pienta, joined some other high school students on a tour of Eastern Europe. Cari is of Polish ancestry and she thought it would be fun to visit Eastern Europe since she and her parents had never been. They all signed up for the trip and, when they returned, she wrote me, "Between November and June miraculous political changes took place in some of these countries that made my trip one that could never be taken again."

I understood. When we were about to tape the television show on the cooking of Romania, the crew discussed the fact that Ceausescu, the longtime and ruthless dictator in Romania, had just been tried and shot. My director told me not to mention the fact since you must do television shows that can play for several seasons and not be dated. "Evergreen" is the word. Then the Berlin Wall fell while I was cooking German dumplings. Then, Lithuania called for freedom while I was cooking Kugelis.

I cannot tell you how important this collection of recipes is to me. The need for understanding between nations and cultures is more crucial now than it has ever been. Peace is the central problem. Saving the environment will not work unless we save one another. So, I offer a cookbook. Strange political move, isn't it?

Within these pages you will find memories that you can only recall through a particular dish from the old country. One remembers flavor more than dates and times in the memory portion of the brain. Taste and smell and grandma's rolling the dough . . . that's it! And no, I do not

Main hall, U.S. Immigration Station, Ellis Island

expect you to eat this kind of food every day. Old World cooking, for the most part, is heavy, and the healthy-food people of our time will simply reject these recipes in the name of flavorless health. Moderation is the answer to a good diet, moderation and flavor and history.

There is a most serious need to remember who we are so that we may assist other peoples in remembering who they are. Ethnic cooking in our time is not "in" just because it tastes good. It is historical and meaningful on its own. Therefore we have subtitled this collection *Recipes You Should Have Gotten from Your Grandmother.* I know that you are now sorry that you didn't get these recipes when Grandma was around, but perhaps this book will help you catch up with your ethnic background as well as a few others.

This introduction is actually an introduction to an introduction. That is to say, each of the thirty-five ethnic sections of the book is not a full discussion of their culture or cuisines. Your particular history will match only a few of these sections. I want you to study the rest for the sake of understanding and flavor and history. And if your ethnic group is not included in this collection, please forgive me. If I have not already "done" you before, you are up next.

What a wonderful experience we have being Americans. We can shop for just about any kind of food at any time and in most any place. We are a nation of immigrants and we wish to continue to share our great dishes and memories with one another.

Now, to the kitchen. Remember your ancestors and what they had to put up with in order to get here. And, remember that they were convinced that you would never forget them.

—Jeff Smith
*On the opening of Ellis Island as a national museum of our
immigrant ancestors
September 1990*

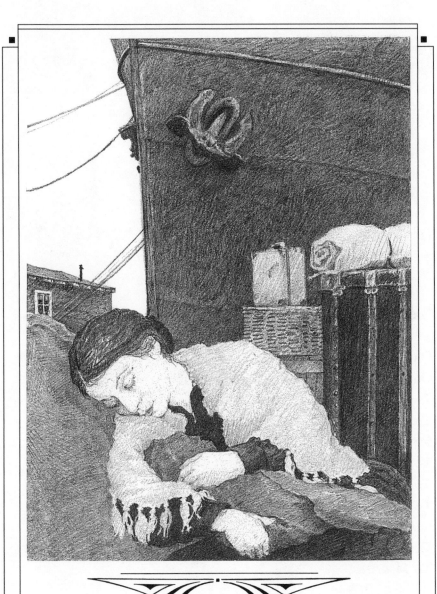

GLOSSARY

HINTS

KITCHEN EQUIPMENT

KNIVES

Knives are the most important pieces of equipment in your kitchen. When purchasing knives you should be mindful of the following points:

1. Please do not buy knives that are cheaply made and designed to go into the dishwasher. (No good knife should ever be put into the dishwasher. Low-quality knives may be made of stainless steel so that they are hard enough to take the dishwasher, but they cannot be sharpened.)
2. I prefer the standard old French chef's knife, not a designer gadget. The old model is hard to improve upon, and I have seen no improvement in function with the new "modern"-looking knives. Form follows function. A knife is for cutting. Buy one that does just that.
3. Buy good-quality knives of high carbon steel. They are now made to be nonstaining but are not stainless steel. Use a sharpening steel on them often to keep a good edge. If a sharpening steel makes you a bit nervous, use a Chantry knife sharpener. It is safe and works very well. Please do not consider buying an electric knife sharpener . . . no matter who tells you to do so. I find that people who use such devices simply sharpen their knives to death. There is no point in doing such a thing.
4. There is no such thing as a knife that never needs to be sharpened, any more than there is a plate that never needs to be washed. Good

knives need sharpening and care, so never just throw them in a drawer. Keep them in a rack, and in good repair. A dull knife is very dangerous since you have to work harder and thus are more apt to let the knife slip and cut yourself.

5. I use the following knives constantly, but you may wish some other sizes. (I have about fifty knives. You don't need that many. Neither do I but I love good knives!)

10-inch-blade chef's knife
8-inch-blade chef's knife
Boning knife
Paring knife
Long slicing knife (thin)
Sharpening steel

Chinese Cleaver: There are several thicknesses available. A thin one is used for slicing and chopping vegetables and a thicker one for cutting meat and hacking poultry. Do not bother buying a stainless-steel cleaver. You cannot sharpen it.

POTS AND PANS

Good pots and pans make good cooking easy. Pans that are thin and flimsy can offer only burning, sticking, and lumps. Buy good equipment that is heavy. You will not be sorry.

TIPS FOR BUYING GOOD EQUIPMENT

1. Don't buy pots and pans with wooden or plastic handles. You can't put them in the oven or under a broiler.
2. Buy pans that fit your life-style, that are appropriate for the way you cook. They should be able to perform a variety of purposes in the kitchen. Avoid pans that can be used for only one dish or one particular style of cooking, such as upside-down crepe pans.
3. I do not buy sets of pans but rather a selection of several different materials that work in different ways. Most of my frying pans are heavy stainless steel or aluminum with SilverStone or Excalibur nonstick lining. I have aluminum stockpots and saucepans. No, I do not worry about cooking in aluminum since I never cook acids such as eggs or tomatoes or lemon juice in that metal . . . and I always keep aluminum well cleaned, remembering never to store anything in aluminum pots or pans.

I have copper saucepans for special sauces and some stainless-steel saucepans as well. These are heavy stainless with plain metal handles, with an aluminum core sandwiched into the bottom. I also have a selection of porcelain-enameled cast-iron pans, Le Creuset being my favorite brand for that type of thing.

4. The pots and pans I use the most:

20-quart aluminum stockpot with lid

12-quart aluminum stockpot with lid

12-quart stainless-steel heavy stockpot with lid

4-quart aluminum *sauteuse,* with lid

10-inch aluminum frying pan, lined with SilverStone, with lid

Several cast-iron porcelain-coated casseroles, with lids

Copper saucepans in varying sizes, with lids

Chinese wok—I own six of them. (See page 24 for descriptions.)

MACHINES AND APPLIANCES

Please do not fill your kitchen with appliances that you will rarely use. I do not own an electric deep-fryer or an electric slow-cooking ceramic pot or an electric egg cooker or . . . you know what I am saying. Other pieces of equipment will work for these jobs, and have other functions as well. But, I do use an electric frying pan often because I can control the surface cooking temperature easily, and it's a versatile appliance.

I also have:

Food mixer: Choose a heavy machine, one that will sit in one spot and, using the different attachments available, make bread dough, grind meat, and mix cake batters. I prefer the KitchenAid and have the large model with the five-quart bowl. For bread-making, you'll need both the paddle-blade and dough-hook attachments. The meat grinder and sausage attachments make for easy and fun sausage-making.

Food processor: While I use this machine less than my mixer, it is helpful.

Food blender: I have a heavy-duty model that will take a beating. Don't skimp on this machine. It should be able to purée solids easily—not make just milk shakes.

Electric coffee grinder, small size: I use this for grinding herbs and spices, not for coffee. It is from Germany.

SPECIAL EQUIPMENT

Pick and choose among these. Most of them are just amazingly helpful:

Garlic press: I cannot abide garlic in any form except fresh. Buy a good garlic press. Be careful in purchase as there are now many cheap ones on the market and they just do not work.

Lemon reamer, wooden: This is a great device, but since I began using it on television many companies have been producing copies that are just not the right size and shape for proper use. Buy a good one, even if you have seen a cheaper model.

Heat diffuser or tamer: This is an inexpensive gadget that you place on your gas or electric burner to even out or reduce the heat. It will save you from a lot of burned sauces.

Tomato shark: This little gadget takes the stem out of a tomato in nothing flat. Be careful—there is a phony one on the market that doesn't work half as well.

Wooden spoons and spatulas: I never put metal spoons or utensils in my frying pans or saucepans. Metal will scratch the surface, causing food to stick. Buy wooden utensils and avoid that problem. I have grown very fond of tools made from olive wood as it is very hard and will last for years, even with regular use and washing. They cost more to start with but they will outlast the others by three times, at least. I have also found some very durable plastic spoons, spatulas, and gadgets. These are made of an extremely high-heat-resistant plastic. They are the only plastic tools that I have ever found durable. Robison makes them and they are called Ultratemp. Do not bother buying cheap plastic.

Wok: I use my Chinese wok constantly. It is an ingenious device that is made of steel. Do not buy an aluminum or copper wok. The idea is to have a "hot spot" at the bottom of the wok, thus quickly cooking small amounts of food by moving them about in the pan. Aluminum and copper woks heat too evenly and the advantage of wok cooking is lost. Electric woks do not heat quickly enough, nor do they cool quickly enough. You can use your steel wok on an electric burner, though I prefer gas. If cooking with electricity, simply keep the burner always on high and control the temperature of the wok by moving it off and on the burner.

Bamboo steamers: These stackable steamers, usually three or four in a set, allow you to steam several dishes at once. The advantage that these have over metal steamers stems from the fact that bamboo will not cause moisture to condense and drip on your food, as metal ones will. I use bamboo steamers for cooking many types of food and for warming up leftovers. I could not run a kitchen without them.

Sand pots: While these are not a necessity, they are fun to have. Great for use in the oven or on top of the stove. Find in most Asian markets.

Stove-top smoker: This is a wonderful device put out by Cameron and it is made entirely of stainless steel. The idea is to place it on top of your stove with a bit of alder or hickory sawdust in the bottom and you can smoke things in just a moment in your kitchen. These are an investment, but you will find yourself smoking all kinds of things. Other sawdusts come with the device and can also be purchased in additional quantities. I remain partial to alder and hickory.

Important: You must have a strong out-of-the-house exhaust fan to use this, or use it outside directly on the barbecue.

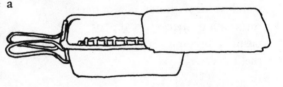

Stove-top grill: This is great for grilling peppers, bread, and other things right on top of the burner. It is called an *asador,* and it works very well.

Grill racks: Choose one or two sizes of these racks for grilling on top of a griddle or on the barbecue. They are especially helpful in holding a fish together while you grill it.

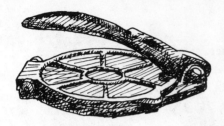

Tortilla press: This is very helpful in rolling out dough for dumplings. Buy a good one that is smoothly polished and you will have less trouble with sticking.

Dumpling maker: This plastic gadget is cheap but clever. Helps you make filled dumplings in nothing flat.

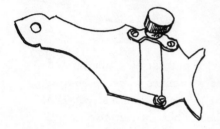

Truffle cutter for cheese: A very fancy gadget . . . but it does a great job on slicing thin bits of hard cheeses. Great for pasta! I also use mine for shaving chocolate.

Cheese grater, hand-held: This little stainless-steel grater is wonderful for grating cheese on top of pasta. I use mine right at the table.

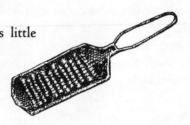

Ginger grater: This little porcelain piece works like a scrub board to grate fresh ginger very quickly and very fine. From Japan.

Chopper/noodle cutter/breadstick maker: An Italian cutting device that I find just great for making noodles and breadsticks. It also works well for cutting fresh herbs such as basil, parsley, et cetera.

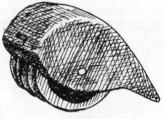

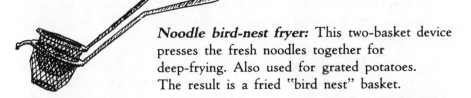

Noodle bird-nest fryer: This two-basket device presses the fresh noodles together for deep-frying. Also used for grated potatoes. The result is a fried "bird nest" basket.

Meat skewers: All kinds are available for making grilled meat cubes. I prefer those made of stainless steel. These are easily found. Wide thick ones for Chelo Kebab (page 355) will probably have to be made for you, but you can certainly use sturdy metal ones.

Apple corer/peeler/slicer: This is a great device for coring, peeling, and slicing apples. I use mine for making the best thin-cut potato fries that you can imagine. Great for shoestring potatoes, as well.

Apple parer/wedger: This little device cores and cuts an apple into wedges. Perfect for desserts, appetizers, or baking.

Pepper mill: The flavor of freshly ground black pepper is very different from that of the preground. Find a good mill and grind your own. I have several mills, but my favorite is a Turkish coffee grinder. These are expensive, but if you are a pepper lover you will love this device. Be careful that the one you buy comes with a guarantee that it can be adjusted for pepper.

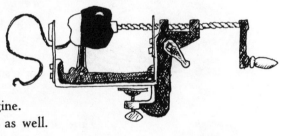

Meat pounder: This malletlike device will flatten out slices of meat so that they are very thin. Great for chicken, beef, and veal dishes.

Plastic sheeting: Sheeting is very helpful when you are pounding meat thin. It is inexpensive and available in most lumberyards or hardware stores. Ask for clear vinyl sheeting 8 millimeters thick. *Do not store food in this sheeting.*

Fire extinguisher: A must for your kitchen. Buy one that will work on electrical fires as well as stove fires. Talk to the salesperson. You will sleep better at night.

Marble pastry board: These can be purchased in several sizes. I could not make pastry, bread, or pasta without one.

Stainless-steel steamer basket: This is a great help. I have two sizes, and they are adjustable for different pan sizes. Great for steaming vegetables and not expensive.

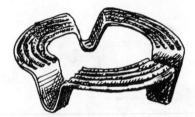

Steamer stand: This aluminum stand sits in the bottom of your kettle. A plate of food is placed on top and the pan becomes a steamer. You can also use this as a rack for a double boiler.

Fine strainer for skimming oil: If you do get into deep-frying, this very thin mesh strainer will help you keep the oil clean. From Japan.

Baking tiles: These will help you get a good crust on your bread. Whether or not you use a pan the tiles keep your oven temperature even. Salday makes these.

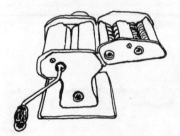

Pasta-rolling machine: This is the easiest way to make pasta. I prefer rolled pasta to extruded, and this machine can also be used for making other thin doughs.

Roasting racks, nonstick: At last a roasting rack for a serious chicken lover. These work very well as the bird or roast does not stick to the rack.

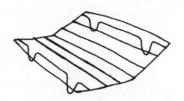

Kitchen scale: Buy something that is fairly accurate. It will be helpful in baking perfect breads and in judging the size of roasts.

Mandoline: This is a wonderful device for cutting vegetables into thin slices or into julienne-style matchstick cuts. Be sure that you get a good one and be careful with it. You can cut yourself unless you use the guards properly. You can also cut french fries with this.

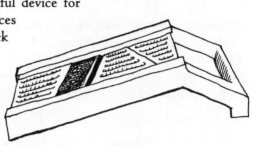

Big dinner and serving plates: A dinner is much more exciting if served on large platters. Loneoak, in California, makes my favorite large white plates and serving platters. You can also find wonderful old serving platters in antique and junk shops.

Big wooden salad bowl: A good one will cost you some money, but if you like salad, you know that the greens will just not taste as good in metal or glass as they will in wood.

Large stainless-steel bowl: All-purpose mixing bowl 15 inches in diameter. Ideal for making bread dough and covering it while it rises.

Couscousier: Special cooking apparatus consisting of three parts: a kettle, a steamer that rests on top, and a lid. This piece of equipment is designed specifically for making Moroccan Couscous (page 324). Find in gourmet shops. Also available by mail order from Dean & DeLuca (page 524). Expensive!

Spaetzle maker: This device rests on top of a pot of boiling water. The round hopper is filled with dumpling batter and slid across the plate consisting of holes. Dumplings are cut off and cook when they fall into the pot. Buy in gourmet shops.

Japanese bamboo mat: Flexible mat made of thin sticks woven together. Necessary equipment for making certain types of *sushi*. Find in many Asian markets.

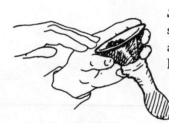

Sausage funnel: Some electric mixers have sausage-making attachments, or you can use a sausage funnel to stuff the casings by hand. Buy in gourmet shops.

Tostone press: This hinged device flattens out slices of plantain. The slices are then fried to make Tostones (page 393). Find in Puerto Rican and Mexican markets.

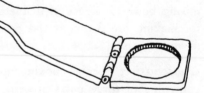

Plastic pouring spouts: Use in wine bottles for oils, vinegars, et cetera. Buy in gourmet shops or restaurant-supply stores. I do not use metal pouring spouts as they corrode when used with soy sauce, wine, or vinegar.

 ***Instant response thermometer:***
Calibrated from 0 degrees to 220 degrees. Use for making yogurt, bread yeast, and cheese, and for testing roasted meats for doneness. These are not designed to stay in the oven during cooking. Buy in gourmet shops and restaurant-supply stores.

Baking sheets: I think the age of burned rolls and cookies is over, and it is about time. Buy insulated or air-cushioned baking sheets and pans. Wilton has a line called Even-Bake. I have tried them and they work! Bagels, rolls, breads of any kind, turn out much better than you could possibly expect. These are first class!

COOKING METHODS
AND TERMS

BLANCHING

Plunging a food product into boiling water for a very few minutes (the time varies and will be explained in each recipe). The food is then removed and generally placed in cold water to stop the cooking process. The purpose is to loosen the skin of a vegetable or fruit, to set the color of a vegetable, or to cook a food partially in preparation for later completion of the dish.

CHOW (STIR-FRY)

A basic cooking method in Oriental kitchens. Generally a wok is used, but you can also do this in a frying pan. The food is tossed about in a hot pan with very little oil, in a process not unlike sautéing.

CORRECT THE SEASONING

When a dish is completed, a cook should always taste it before serving. To correct the seasoning simply means to check for salt, pepper, or herbs to make sure that the dish has turned out as expected. A little correction at the last minute may be necessary.

DASH

Generally means "to taste." Start with less than 1/16 teaspoon.

DEGLAZING A PAN

After meats or vegetables have been browned, wine or stock is added to the pan over high heat, and the rich coloring that remains in the pan is gently scraped with a wooden spoon and combined with the wine or stock.

DEVELOP

Developing a food product means that you have allowed it to sit for a time before serving so that the flavors have a chance to blend or brighten.

DICE

This means to cut into small cubes; the size of the cube is generally stated in the recipe. For instance, a ¼-inch dice means cubes of that size. It is accomplished very easily with a good vegetable knife.

DREDGING IN FLOUR

Meats and fish, generally sliced thin, are rolled in flour in preparation for frying or sautéing. The flour is usually seasoned.

DUSTING WITH FLOUR

Most often a fillet of fish or some type of shellfish (shrimps, scallops, et cetera) is rolled in flour, and the excess flour is patted or shaken off. The idea is to have a very light coating on the food.

GRILLING

An ancient method whereby the food is cooked on a rack or skewer over hot coals or an open flame.

HACK

When cutting up chickens or thin-boned meats, one "hacks" with a cleaver, thus cutting the meat into large bite-size pieces and retaining the bone. The presence of the bone will help keep the meat moist during cooking. Do this hacking carefully.

JULIENNE CUT

Cut vegetables into thin slices, stack the slices, then cut the slices into thin sticks, like matchsticks.

MARINATING

Meats or vegetables are soaked for a time in a flavoring liquid, such as soy sauce, wine, oil, or vinegar. The time of the marinating varies with the recipe.

MINCE

A minced vegetable or herb is one that is chopped very fine. It is fine enough to be of a very coarse, granular nature. This pertains especially to garlic, onion, and herbs. The process is done by hand with a knife, or by a food processor.

PINCH OF HERBS OR SPICES

Usually means "to taste." Start with less than $\frac{1}{16}$ teaspoon, and then increase if you wish.

POACHING

Gently cooking fish, meat, or eggs in stock or water at just below a simmer. The liquid should just barely move during the poaching process. When fish or eggs are poached, a little vinegar or lemon juice is added to the poaching liquid to help keep the food product firm.

PURÉE

When you wish to make a sauce or soup that is free of all lumps of any sort, purée the stock. This means that you put it in a food processor and mill it until it is free of all lumps, or run it through a strainer or sieve.

RECONSTITUTING

A procedure used for preparing dried foods, whereby the product is soaked in fresh water for a time. The food absorbs the water so that its "life" is restored and it can be used properly in a given recipe. The process of drying food concentrates flavor and changes the texture, giving it a unique quality in the dish.

REDUCING

Boiling a sauce or liquid over high heat until it is reduced in volume, generally by half. The result is a very rich concentration of flavors.

ROUX

A blend of flour and oil or butter used to thicken sauces and gravies. The fat and flour are mixed together in equal amounts over heat. If a white *roux* is desired, the melting and blending are done over low heat for a few minutes. If a brown *roux* is desired, the flour is cooked in the fat until it is lightly browned.

RUBBED

When whole-leaf herbs, such as sage or bay leaves, are crushed in the hands so that their oils are released, the herbs are then referred to as having been rubbed.

SAUTÉ

This term comes from the French word that means "to jump." In cooking, sauté means to place food in a very hot pan with a bit of butter or oil and to shake the pan during the cooking process so that the food jumps about. Thus one can cook very quickly over high heat without burning the food. It is not unlike chowing or stir-frying.

SCALDED

Generally this term applies to the milk in a recipe, and it simply means to heat the milk to just under simmering. The milk is scalded when it becomes very hot. It is not a boil at all.

SHOT

A liquid measurement that amounts to very little or to taste. A shot of wine is about an ounce, but a shot of Tabasco is less than 1/16 teaspoon.

STEAMING

Cooking with steam as the heat source. This method is not to be confused with pressure cooking.

STIR-FRY

See Chow (page 32).

SWEAT

To sauté over low heat with a lid on. This method causes steam and expedites the cooking time.

TERRINE

A dish used for the cooking and molding of coarse-ground meat loaves or pâtés. Also the meat itself. The dishes can be found in many styles and materials.

INGREDIENTS,
CONDIMENTS, AND
FOOD DEFINITIONS

ACKEE

A Jamaican fruit with spongy white or yellow flesh. Available fresh or canned. Also called *akee*.

ANAHEIM PEPPER, FRESH

Slightly hot light-green pepper. Found in most supermarkets. There is also a red Anaheim pepper. These are usually found in the dried form, but don't substitute the dried for the fresh.

ANCHOVY FILLETS, SWEET PICKLED

A must for Jansson's Temptation (see page 466), this variety is available in Scandinavian markets. I'm told you can substitute a small amount of well-soaked Mediterranean anchovy fillets, but I recommend you search out this unique-tasting product first.

ANNATTO SEEDS

Small rust-colored seeds used to make annatto oil. The oil is then used as a yellow food coloring. Can be found in Hispanic markets.

ASAFETIDA

A gummy resin derived from a special plant. Also comes in powder form. Used as a flavoring in Persian and Indian cooking. Find in Indian markets.

BACCALÀ

See Salt Cod, Dried (page 45).

BAMBOO LEAVES, DRIED

Used in Asian cooking to wrap ingredients for steaming. They need to be reconstituted before use.

BASMATI RICE

A common but delicious rice used in India and many Middle Eastern countries. Looks like long-grain rice, but has a light nutty flavor. Found in Middle Eastern and Indian markets.

BEAN CURD

Cheeselike product made from soybean milk. Buy fresh in cakes at Oriental markets or in produce sections of most supermarkets. It can also be purchased in cans, but the flavor is far inferior. Fresh bean curd looks very much like a five-inch rectangular block of soft but firmly shaped white cheese.

BEAN SPROUTS

You will find these fresh in most produce sections. The canned variety is so tasteless that you should omit them if you cannot find fresh ones.

BEEF STOCK

Please make your own. Canned consommé or bouillon is little more than salt. Real beef stock is rich in flavor and inexpensive to make from fresh bones. See my recipe on page 78.

BOK CHOY

A vegetable resembling Swiss chard in shape, but much lighter in color and flavor. A member of the mustard family, it can be found fresh in most supermarket produce sections and Oriental markets.

BROWN BEANS

Smaller and rounder than American beans, these are cooked up to make a fantastic Scandinavian dish. Find in specialty stores or Scandinavian markets.

BULGUR WHEAT

Processed wheat for Middle Eastern dishes. Three grinds: fine, medium, and coarse. Find in Middle Eastern stores or in fancy supermarkets or gourmet stores.

CANDIED GINGER

Found in Asian markets.

CELLOPHANE NOODLES

Noodles made from the mung bean, the same bean from which bean sprouts grow. Find in Oriental markets and some supermarkets. Also called glass noodles, *sai fun,* bean threads, and long rice.

CHICKEN STOCK

A chicken soup or stock made from chicken backs and necks, carrots, yellow onions, celery, and a bit of salt and pepper and allowed to simmer for a good hour or so. It is then strained and served. See my recipe on page 74.

CHILES, DRIED

I used ancho and New Mexican dried chiles in this book. While both are considered mildly hot, the New Mexican carries less "heat." Be sure to use both with care, avoiding the fiery seeds and washing your hands with soap and water after handling.

COCONUT MILK

Canned or frozen. Don't confuse this with cream of coconut, which is used solely for making *piña coladas,* a cocktail. Found in Oriental or fancy supermarkets.

COUSCOUS

A fine-grained semolina pasta used in Moroccan cuisine. Buy the regular, non-instant variety for the recipes in this book. Available in most supermarkets.

CREAM

When the term is used in this book, I mean half-and-half or whipping cream. Either may be used or you may dilute whipping cream with milk.

CUBANELLE PEPPER

A mild light-green pepper. Probably the closest thing in flavor to a real Hungarian pepper. Found in a good supermarket or in Caribbean markets. You can substitute fresh green Anaheim peppers. They are just a tiny bit hotter, but nothing serious.

CURING SALT

A salt that has nitrates added and is used as a preservative in sausage making. Available in some supermarkets, specialty shops, and by mail (see page 527).

DAIKON RADISH

Long, white tubular radish eaten in many Asian cultures. Found in Oriental markets and finer supermarkets.

DASHI STOCK

This broth is a basic ingredient in Japanese cooking. The stock is made from dried seaweed or from dried tuna shavings. Instant *dashi* stock is also available. You may find in Japanese markets.

DIJON MUSTARD

A style of mustard from France. A good American brand is Grey Poupon.

DRY-CURD COTTAGE CHEESE AND FARMER CHEESE

Cottage cheese with no cream added. Farmer cheese, like cottage cheese, is curdled milk that has been drained of whey. The major difference is that farmer cheese is a smaller curd. Farmer cheese, like dry-curd cottage cheese, has no cream.

FAVA BEANS, DRIED

A Mediterranean bean similar to our lima beans. Buy the peeled variety.

FISH CAKES, JAPANESE

These are fish paste molded into cakelike shapes and grilled or deep-fried. Available frozen in Japanese markets.

FISH SAUCE

A condiment made from fermented anchovies, salt, and water that is common in Cambodian, Vietnamese, and Thai cooking. The Cambodian version, *nam pla,* is considered the finest and has the richest flavor. The Vietnamese variety, *nuoc mam,* most widely available, is milder. The different varieties are interchangeable, but it is fun to use each country's sauce. Available in any Oriental or Asian market.

FUL

This is an Egyptian dried bean. Buy the small variety in specialty food shops.

GARBANZO FLOUR

Flour ground from dried garbanzo beans. Also called *ceci* flour. Found in fancy delicatessens and Italian specialty shops.

GARLIC AND RED CHILI PASTE

Very hot Chinese sauce made of red peppers and garlic. Good condiment for other Asian cuisines as well. Find in Oriental markets or substitute garlic and Tabasco. It is worth the effort to find this delicious sauce.

GARLIC CHIVES

Light green in color, long thin stalks with a small bud on the tip. Find fresh in some Asian markets.

GARLIC CLOVES, PICKLED

Available in Asian markets.

GLASS NOODLES

See Cellophane Noodles (page 38).

GRAPE LEAVES

The leaves of the grapevine. Find in supermarkets and delicatessens packed in jars in brine. You can also use fresh grape leaves, but blanch them first in boiling water for 1 minute.

HIBISCUS BLOSSOMS

Also called sorrel blossoms, these make a delicious iced tea. Find in Latin and Caribbean markets.

HIJIKI

A form of dried seaweed. Find in Japanese markets.

HOT PEPPER OIL OR CHILI OIL

May be purchased in Oriental markets.

JALAPEÑO PEPPERS, FRESH

Green or red, these little guys pack a wallop. Other hot chiles (serrano, fresh cayenne) can be substituted, but adjust the amounts to your taste. Be sure to wash your hands with soap and water after handling.

KAFFIR LIME LEAVES

Dried leaves from the Kaffir lime tree. Pale green in color, resembling a bay leaf. Purchase in packages from Oriental markets.

KAMPYO

Japanese gourd shavings that are a popular stuffing for sushi. Find in Japanese markets and mail order (see page 525).

KASHA

Buckwheat groats common in Middle Eastern, Russian, and Jewish dishes. Find in any large supermarket or Jewish markets. This is delicious stuff.

KELP

Dried seaweed used for making *dashi* stock (page 39). *Konbu,* a dried rolled kelp, is used as a flavoring in Sushi Rice (page 242). Found in Japanese or Korean markets.

KOREAN PICKLING SALT

A coarse salt used in making Korean delicacies like Kimchee. Substitute kosher salt if necessary.

LEEKS

These look like very large green onions in the produce section. Wash carefully because they are usually full of mud.

LEMONGRASS

Pale green stalk about 18 inches long, resembling a scallion or green onion. While not related to a lemon, it actually imparts a perfumy flavor much like the fruit. Found in Asian markets.

LIQUID SMOKE

Find in the condiment section of the supermarket. I like Wright's.

LOP CHONG

Chinese sweet pork sausage. Find in any Oriental market.

LOTUS LEAVES, DRIED

Very large leaves that, after reconstituting, can be used as wrappers in Asian cuisine. You may have to fold each in half to get it down to a workable size.

LUMPIA

Although these wrappers are a little larger, you can substitute them for egg roll wrappers. Find frozen in Filipino and Asian markets.

MATZO MEAL

Jewish flat bread that has been ground.

MIRIN

Sweet rice vinegar. Find in some supermarkets and in any Japanese market, or add a bit of sugar to regular rice-wine vinegar.

MISO, LIGHT OR DARK (RED)

Fermented soybean paste used as a basic ingredient in many Japanese dishes. Find in any Japanese market.

MUNG BEANS, DRIED

A versatile bean common throughout Asia. This bean or pea is also the source of bean sprouts. Found in Oriental markets.

MUSHROOMS, CHINESE

Find in Oriental markets. Soak in water before cooking. Trim the stems and save for chicken soup.

MUSHROOMS, DRIED EUROPEAN

Cepe, boletus, or porcini. These are delicious, but if they come from Europe they will be terribly expensive. Find an Italian market that brings them in from South America, and you will pay only somewhere between $14.00 and $20.00 a pound. The real Italian dried mushrooms will cost you a fortune! You may also find some that are domestic, or go to an Eastern European market and buy dried Polish mushrooms. In any case keep them in a tightly sealed jar at the back of your refrigerator, where they will keep for a year.

NAM PLA

See Fish Sauce (page 40).

NAPA CABBAGE

Sometimes called Chinese celery cabbage, it can be found in many super-market produce sections and Oriental markets.

NORI

See Seaweed Sheets, Dried (page 45).

NUOC MAM

See Fish Sauce (page 40).

ORANGE-BLOSSOM WATER

This orange-blossom extract can be found in fancy food shops. Common in the Middle East.

OYSTER SAUCE

Classic cooking sauce from China. Also used in other Asian cuisines. While actually made from oysters, it has no strong fishy taste. Found in Oriental markets. Refrigerate after opening.

PANSIT

Wild rice noodles used in Filipino cooking. Soak in warm water for 15 minutes until supple, and drain before using.

PAPPADUM

Flat lentil wafers that puff up when deep-fried. Used in Indian cuisine.

PHYLLO DOUGH (FILLO)

Thin sheets of dough for Middle Eastern baking. Can be found in most delicatessens and supermarkets.

PICKLING SALT

A fine-grain salt without iodine, used in pickled meat dishes. Find in any supermarket.

PINE NUTS

Expensive little treasures that actually come from the large pinecone of Italy. Found in Italian markets, or substitute slivered almonds.

PLANTAINS

Resemble bananas in size and shape but are starchier and not sweet. Both green (hard) and brown (ripe) are used in the cuisines of the Caribbean and South America. Ripe plantains can be peeled like bananas, but green ones pose a problem. Make lengthwise slits through the peel to the flesh. Remove the tough skin by peeling across, not lengthwise. Find them in Hispanic and Caribbean markets.

PORK CRACKLINGS

See **Hint** on freshly rendered lard (page 168).

POTATO STARCH OR FLOUR

Starch made from dried potatoes ground into flour. Find in Scandinavian shops or some delicatessens.

QUICK-RISING YEAST

There are a couple of brands on the market now that will cause the dough to rise in half the time. Both Red Star and Fleischmann's manufacture such a thing. Be sure to follow the manufacturer's instructions on the package for best results. You can find these in any supermarket.

RED CHILI PASTE WITH GARLIC

See Garlic and Red Chili Paste (page 40). Same product.

RED CURRY PASTE

A spicy condiment used in Thai cooking. Rather hot, with its main ingredient being red chile peppers. Found in Oriental markets.

RICE STICKS

Clear noodles made from ground rice. Available in varying widths. May be found in most Asian markets.

RICE WINE

Called *shao hsing* in Chinese markets. A good dry sherry is a fine substitute.

RICE WINE VINEGAR

Delicious vinegar used in Oriental cooking. Find in Oriental markets.

SAKÉ

Japanese rice wine. Necessary to good Japanese cooking. Find in Japanese markets or liquor stores.

SALT COD, DRIED

Codfish that has been cured with salt, common in Mediterranean and Caribbean cooking. Also known as *baccalà*. Must be soaked in water for at least 18 hours, changing the water several times, before you cook it. Buy in good delicatessens and seafood shops.

SALTPETER

A common kitchen chemical used in the preservation of meat or preparing corned beef or pork. May be purchased at a drugstore.

SAUSAGE CASINGS

Made from beef or pork products, these are available by special order from good meat markets or by mail order (see page 527).

SEAWEED SHEETS, DRIED

Also known as *nori* and *laver*. Find in Oriental markets.

SESAME OIL

Used as a flavoring in Oriental cooking, not a cooking oil. Find this at an Oriental market. Used for flavoring a dish at the last minute. The health-food-store version is not made from toasted sesame seeds, so the flavor will be very bland.

SESAME SEEDS, TOASTED

Often used as a garnish in many cuisines. To make: Toast raw sesame seeds in a frying pan over medium heat until golden brown. Shake and stir the seeds over the burner to get even coloring. Ready for use.

SHIITAKE

This dried mushroom can be found in most Oriental markets. It can also be found fresh in better supermarkets.

SHORT-GRAIN RICE

The most common rice in Japanese cooking. It has a short oval shape compared to long-grain rice. Also known as pearl rice.

SHRIMP POWDER, DRIED

Tiny shrimp dried and ground into a fine powder. Found in Oriental markets.

SILVER FOIL (VARK)

Edible silver in ultra-thin sheets. Used for fancy garnishing in Indian cooking.

SOY SAUCE

Light: To be used when you don't want to color a dish with caramel coloring, which is what dark soy contains. Do not confuse this with "Lite" soy sauce, which is lower in salt and flavor. Find in Oriental markets. I prefer Wing Nien brand. It is the very best quality and made by the company founded by my adopted Chinese uncle, Colonel John Young.

Dark: Used in dishes in which you wish to color the meat and sweeten the flavor with caramel sugar. Most common soy sauce. Buy good quality. I prefer Wing Nien brand. See explanation above.

Japanese: Chinese soy is very different from Japanese. Japanese soys contain much more wheat flour and sugar. I like Kikkoman. Buy in larger quantities at a Japanese market. It is cheaper that way and it will keep well if kept sealed.

STRAW MUSHROOMS, CANNED

Small buttonlike mushrooms indigenous to Asia. Fresh ones are so delicate that they aren't shipped. The Green Giant company packs them in glass jars and makes a good product.

TAHINI

A light paste made of toasted sesame seeds and sesame oil—almost like peanut butter. Used in many Middle Eastern dishes, it is to be found in Middle Eastern delicatessens or fancy supermarkets.

TAMARIND

Tamarind paste and concentrate, fresh products, are available in the produce section of many ethnic markets. They keep for 2 to 3 weeks, refrigerated. Both products, made from the pulp of the tamarind pod, need to be reconstituted.

TOMATILLOS

Small green fruits that, although they look like tomatoes, are actually members of the gooseberry family. If using fresh, remove the husks. Canned are a good substitute, but rinse well before using.

WASABI

Japanese green horseradish powder. Turn it into paste by stirring in water, drop by drop.

VIGO COLORING

Common substitute for the yellow color of saffron. Can be found in small envelopes in any Latin American, Mexican, or Cuban market.

HERBS AND SPICES

ALLSPICE

Not a blend of spices at all, but a single one. Buy it whole or already ground.

ANISE SEED

A pungent spice resembling fennel seed. Has a strong licorice flavor. Buy in good spice shops.

BASIL

Basic herb in the Mediterranean. Buy it fresh or dried, whole at the supermarket. Or grow your own. There are also special fresh basils used in some Asian cuisines that can be found in Oriental markets.

BAY LEAVES

Basic to the kitchen for good soups, stews, et cetera. Buy whole or dried or, if your area is not too cold, grow a bay laurel tree. I have one in Tacoma.

CARAWAY SEED

This ancient dried seed is excellent for baking fresh breads. In Eastern Europe it is popular in sauerkraut.

CARDAMOM

Common in Scandinavian, Middle Eastern, and Indian dishes. Rather sweet flavor. Expensive. Buy whole pods, remove the seeds, and grind them as you need them. You can substitute ground cardamom.

CAYENNE PEPPER

Fine-ground red pepper, very hot.

CHILI POWDER

Actually a blend of chile peppers and other ingredients like cumin and oregano. Buy in the can, ground. Usually I use the hot blend.

CILANTRO

See Coriander (below).

CINNAMON

Buy in the stick form or already ground.

CLOVES, WHOLE AND GROUND

I use both. You can grind your own whole cloves.

CORIANDER

The three most common forms are the whole seed, ground seed, and the fresh plant, which resembles Italian flat-leaf parsley in appearance. Any of the above may be found in Middle Eastern, Indian, and Mediterranean cuisines. In Asian cooking the fresh leaves are preferred. Thai cooks sometimes use just the root or stems. Also used in Mexican cooking where it is known as cilantro. Find in supermarkets or in the markets of the above cultures.

CUMIN

Can be purchased by the can in powder form, or buy the whole seed and grind it. The flavor is much brighter with the whole seed. Used extensively in Mexican and Indian cooking.

CURRY POWDER, JAMAICAN

This is very similar to the more common Indian curry powder. If you must substitute, add ¼ teaspoon of ground allspice to every 1 tablespoon of regular curry powder. I like the Madras brand.

DILL

Both fresh and dried are used in many cuisines, especially by Eastern Europeans and Russians.

FENNEL SEED

Resembles anise or licorice in flavor. Buy it whole or grind it as you need it. Common in Indian cooking.

FENUGREEK

A primary ingredient in curry powder. Used in Persian cooking as well as in Indian curries. Find in Middle Eastern and Indian markets.

GALANGAL ROOT, DRIED

A member of the ginger family used especially in Thai cooking. Buy this in small packages in dried slices. It is very hard, so reconstitute in warm water for 1 hour before trying to mince. Find in Oriental markets.

GARLIC

The bulb, of course. Use only fresh. I like mine from the garlic capital of the world, Gilroy, California. Buy garlic braids that can hang in the kitchen for up to a year. Just pull off a bulb as needed. And buy a good garlic press (page 24).

GINGER, FRESH

Buy by the "hand" or whole stem at the supermarket. Keep in the refrigerator, uncovered and unwrapped. Grate when needed. (See the ginger grater, page 26).

JUNIPER BERRIES

These are to be found in good spice shops. They will remind you of the flavor of English gin. There is no substitute.

MACE

The outer covering of the nutmeg. Not as strong as nutmeg, but rich in flavor.

MAHLEB

Small seed that is ground fresh for wonderful Middle Eastern and Greek breads. Often available in Middle Eastern markets, and it is worth the search. There is no exact substitute, but some cookbooks recommend using a little ground fennel seed.

MARJORAM

Common kitchen herb, light in flavor. Buy whole dried.

MINT

Fresh mint can be grown in the backyard; or buy in the supermarket.

MSG

A powder made from seaweed or soybeans. Used as a natural flavor enhancer. Some people seem to be allergic to it and talk about Chinese Restaurant Syndrome, in which they have a light headache or chest pains after eating food containing too much monosodium glutamate (MSG). Very few people, percentagewise, are bothered by this natural chemical and I use it now and then. IT SHOULD BE USED SPARINGLY, JUST AS YOU USE SALT.

MUSTARD, DRY

Ground yellow mustard seeds. I buy Colman's, from Britain.

MUSTARD SEEDS

While most of us are familiar with whole yellow mustard seeds, Indians use black mustard seeds, which are available at Indian markets.

NUTMEG

Basic to the kitchen. Buy in bulk, and grate your own with an old-fashioned nutmeg grater.

OREGANO

Basic to the kitchen. For salads, meats, sauces. You can grow your own, or buy the whole tiny leaves dried.

PAPRIKA

Light, lovely flavor and color. Buy the ground "sweet" variety, imported from Hungary, not "hot."

PARSLEY, DRIED AND FRESH

I rarely use dried because fresh is better. However, dried holds up best in salad dressings. Buy whole bunches. Fresh parsley can be purchased in the supermarket or you can grow your own. I like the Italian flat-leaf variety, which is bright in flavor.

PEPPERCORNS, BLACK

Buy whole, and always grind fresh.

RED PEPPER FLAKES, HOT, CRUSHED

Also labeled "crushed red pepper flakes." Buy in bulk, and use sparingly. The seeds make this a very hot product.

RED PEPPER FLAKES, KOREAN

Ground Korean red peppers. Not as hot as it looks. A must for making Kimchee (page 262). Find in Korean markets and many Asian markets.

RED PEPPERS, HOT, DRIED

There are many different types. The Portuguese and Indian cooks use a specific kind. Some of the Asian cultures have specific types as well. In any case, these are very small and extremely hot. Do not confuse these with fresh hot red peppers you'll find in Hispanic markets. Find in most Asian and Indian markets.

RED PEPPER THREADS, KOREAN

Fine strands of dried Korean red pepper. Find in Korean markets.

ROSEMARY

Basic herb in Mediterranean cooking. Grow your own or buy it whole dried.

SAFFRON

Real saffron is from Spain and is the dried stamens from the saffron crocus. It costs $2,000 a pound. Buy it by the pinch or use Mexican saffron, which includes the whole flower and is very cheap. This works well, but just remember to use much more. Available in threads or powdered.

SAGE

Basic kitchen herb. Grow your own, or buy it whole, dried.

SESAME SEEDS

The white seeds are used in many cuisines and are often toasted (page 46). Black sesame seeds are very popular in Indian cooking. Find in Indian markets.

SUMAC

Herb grown in the Middle East. Burgundy or rust in color and has a wonderful tangy flavor. The Persians sprinkle it on their food and the Lebanese enjoy it as well.

THYME

Common kitchen herb used extensively in soups, stews, and sauces and for seasoning meats. Buy it whole, dried, or grow your own.

TURMERIC

Bitter orange-colored spice that gives the flavor and color to many Indian dishes. Also a main ingredient in curry powder. Buy it ground. Cheaper in Middle Eastern and Indian stores.

ZARTAR BLEND

From Lebanon. Find in Middle Eastern markets. A blend of *zaatar* (a marjoramlike herb), sumac bark, and chick-peas or sesame seeds. Common in foods from the Middle East.

December 17, 1900

THE IMMIGRANT
EXPERIENCE

U.S. Immigration in winter, Ellis Island

In this country all of us are either immigrants or the descendants of immigrants. *All of us*. That holds true even for the Native American Indians, who, while they were here first, probably came across the North Pacific from Siberia. We have always been a nation of immigrants.

When the first colonists from Europe arrived here in the 1600's, our seemingly inevitable attitude of national prejudice had already begun. Those already here looked down upon those who were just arriving, and within a generation or two those same new arrivals were looking down on those who wished to come.

Let's be honest about this. The newly arrived immigrant has always had a difficult time in this country. In the beginning the Founding Fathers declared that becoming an American was a right conferred by God, but later this became a privilege granted by sufferance. This sad change was due to the attitude of the old immigrants toward the new immigrants, namely that the new people were potentially dangerous invaders, a threat to job, home, and the public good. John Adams, Ben Franklin, George Washington, and Thomas Jefferson all expressed serious reservations when it came to immigration. They suspected that newly arrived immigrants would retain all of their native culture, language, and prejudice, never truly becoming "Americanized." Therefore restrictions should be placed on immigration. The attitude seemed to be "America is for the Americans!"

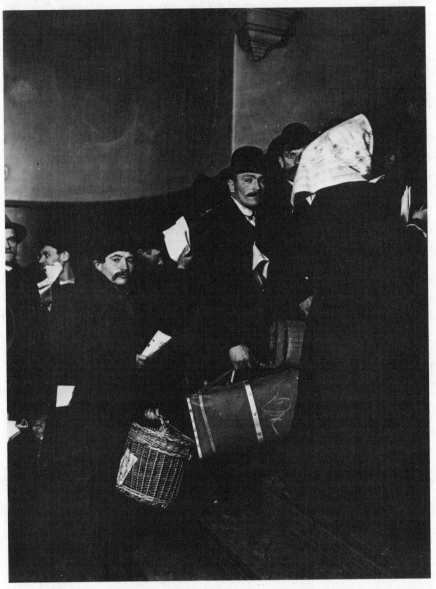

Climbing into America, Ellis Island, 1905

In 1788 the first immigration laws were passed, and they simply stated: "Resolved, that it be and it is hereby recommended to the several states to pass laws for preventing the transportation of convicted malefactors from foreign countries into the United States." This policy was so broad that we achieved the ideal of free immigration in spite of the basic antagonism that was common toward immigrants in those early days. America was off and running!

Later immigration laws seemed to be based on racial prejudices or popular hysteria. Such is seen in the limitation on Chinese immigration, passed in 1875, when American labor groups achieved wide restrictions by claiming that the Chinese would damage the labor market. In 1907 Japanese immigration was limited. Later, in 1921, immigration quotas were set limiting everybody, with set numbers of persons that could come from a particular nation.

Even with all of the limitations placed on free immigration the American population grew at an astounding rate. And the new citizens came from everywhere! Those whom the Founding Fathers would have preferred to keep out have contributed to the development of this nation. No, "contributed" is too weak a term. The immigrants have made this nation! Professor Oscar Handlin, an American historian, said, "Once I thought to write a history of the immigrants in America. Then I discovered that the immigrants *were* American history."

When we look at our contemporary culture we must admit that the foods celebrated in America came along with the immigrants. And, it must have been a long way from the skimpy meals eaten on the boats from Europe to the grand ethnic dinners that the grandmas were able to celebrate thirty years later. The food helped the newly arrived remember something about their homelands, and comforted them as they faced the problems of being in the New World.

The problems that the immigrants faced in this culture cannot be overstated. No one likes to be seen as an immigrant, a foreigner, and that was the first problem that they faced. Once they arrived in the New World they were confronted by the fact that they were "different." Their tongues were different, their customs were different, even their appreciation of food was different. The logical solution to this feeling of being outsiders was to find communities in which they wouldn't feel different at all. Ethnic communities, churches, newspapers, language, all gave the first-generation immigrants comfort, and hope for an understandable future. (For the most part, they were proud of their past.)

The second generation, the children of the immigrants, had an additional problem. When they went to school the other students saw them as foreigners—no matter how carefully they worked on their English. After all, these kids had parents from the old country so they were less "American" than the kids whose parents were born here, even though these parents were born of immigrant ancestors. So, the second generation felt foreign at school. When they went home, they pleaded with their parents to stop speaking Polish around the house. "Mama, we are in America. Speak English!" So, the first-generation immigrant parents began to get the uneasy feeling that their children had become too American, and that they are ashamed of the parents. "You are becoming too American. Don't you respect us anymore?" In short, the second generation felt foreign at school and foreign at home. They wanted to forget about anything that marked them as outsiders; they wanted to forget about their ethnic backgrounds. Many rejected their ethnic churches as another part of the baggage of foreignness.

The third generation, the grandchildren of the immigrants, however, didn't feel foreign at all. They were comfortable at school, and at home; they were comfortable as Americans. But, a question arose—and it seems to be the serious question for the third generation—"What am I?"

"An American" seems to be too simple an answer, and they turn to their grandparents for definitions. The third generation wants to learn about its past and ancestry so that in some way they can be special Americans. They begin attending the family's traditional house of worship with their grandmas . . . and then it happens. To the dismay of second-generation parents who have rejected ethnic identity, their child runs into the kitchen after school and yells, "Mama, guess what. Grandma is going to teach me Polish!" The sociologist Marcus Hansen said it best. "What the son wants to forget, the grandson wants to remember."

Thus the third generation often returns to the religion and customs that the parents have rejected. The third generation realizes that it is through the ethnic community that memories and history will be salvaged. And how do they celebrate these memories? With ethnic food festivals, of course. I have attended such festivals with Greeks, Japanese, Italians, Welsh, Russians, Filipinos, Blacks, Jews, Ethiopians, Latvians, Lithuanians, and countless others. Most often the persons doing the cooking are third generation and are using the recipes of their grandparents. When I begin to eat, the cook runs to my table and yells, "How do you like the food? Isn't it terrific?" In other words, it is not strange at all, is it? It is different, it is ethnic, but *now* it is American! Such is the American immigrant experience.

My wife, Patty, grew up in Brooklyn when it was the center for many ethnic communities. She claims that in Brooklyn, when immigrants talked about their homeland, they never used the term "Old World." Of course they wouldn't since it was not "old" in the sense that Americans mean "old." They talked instead of the "Other Side." And, when Patty was very young, she lived in a very mixed neighborhood. I am sure that she got around a lot because she remembers being "yelled at in six or seven different languages . . . but then, it was Brooklyn!" Those are her affectionate memories of the immigrant experience.

But there is another side to the immigrant experience, and that was the shock of arrival.

Between 1892 and 1954 no fewer than 17 million immigrants came through Ellis Island. I have gotten over the anger and frustration that I felt when reading the accounts offered by some of the immigrants, but I

Getting tagged by an official for a railroad trip, Ellis Island, 1905

have come to believe that most were treated fairly. Only 2 percent or so were turned back after they reached the island. The reasons for rejection generally dealt with health, but often a political reason caused the rejection slip to be given. Thousands of others were turned back due to the limitations placed on particular nationalities. Boats filled with would-be immigrants would wait in the harbor, promising the Americans-to-be that they would get into the country next week since the month was over and the new monthly limit could be filled. As the boats jockeyed for position, the nationality quotas would be filled and unscrupulous agents on the ships would simply ship the hopefuls back home. Those who made it through the exams were considered the lucky ones. However, once here, thousands simply could not take this country, the changes, the attitudes, and they returned home of their own free will.

How would newly arrived immigrants feel upon reaching the island? They had just passed the Statue of Liberty which proclaimed, "Give me your tired, your poor, Your huddled masses yearning to breathe free, The wretched refuse of your teeming shore. . . ." How did it feel to be seen as the "wretched refuse" of another culture?

Mama had packed food for the trip, though it causes me to wonder what a family short on funds might eat during the ten- to fifteen-day trip to the New World. Mama probably had made sausages, had dried fruits and bread. That may have been it. Oh, some things were given out on the boats. I remember reading of a young boy's shock at being given a banana. What was it and what was he to do with it?

Upon arrival at Ellis Island, everyone in the family would be dressed in their very best. After all, one had to pass muster, and it was not easy. The forms to be filled out were confusing, and if the agent at the desk could not figure out the spelling of your name, he would simply give you a new name, based, if you were lucky, on something similar to your name, but much shorter, and much more American. One author at the time claimed that the people filling the reception hall at Ellis Island, each dressed in his or her best, which meant a national costume, of course, made the place look like a "costume party."

The medical exam was frightening. Certain eye diseases, as well as a long list of other diseases, were enough for deportation. And there was the problem of language. Often someone would arrive who spoke a dialect from a tiny village or area, and few could understand him. Can you imagine the fear that you feel when you can speak with no one?

Oh, yes, there were interpreters and most did a fine job. Some rascals charged a fee for a service for which they had already been paid, but I suppose that was to be expected. Some agents also claimed that for a certain fee they could get you through the lines. Many families spent what little money they had just trying to deal with the small but powerful group at the island who were simply corrupt. However, given all of the above, we must remember that only about 2 percent of those who made it to the island were turned back.

The immigrant experience, in terms of Ellis Island, is best described by the immigrants themselves, and by those who worked at the island at the time:

Everybody was sad there. There was not a smile on anybody's face. Here they thought maybe they wouldn't go through. There they thought maybe my child won't go through. There was such a sadness, no smile anyplace. You could see. . . . That's when I came here in 1905. The people had such terrible sad faces. Such a sad place there.

Esther Almgren and her husband encountered one set of officials who let them come in with only $1.50 between them. They were lucky, as it turned out, since other immigration officials on duty later the same day would have turned them away. "They looked at me and my husband and said, 'Let them go through. They are young and they will make it. Don't worry about them.'"

Another little sidelight on how an immigrant got through the lines here. Not all of it was done exactly the way the officials would like it to be, because twenty-five dollars was not available to everybody as they arrived. [The twenty-five dollar sum was necessary proof that an immigrant would not become a public charge.] I can assure you that certain twenty-five dollars were passed along from one passenger to another to help out those who didn't have it, and this was done with a quick motion of the hand so no one would get caught doing this, but I do know that this was a part of the whole procedure. The immigrants help each other in these trying moments, as all want to get off Ellis Island and get to the United States, so I recall this well.

Food was offered to the incoming immigrants, and the dining rooms, or dining halls, must have looked like a great blessing after the trip across the seas. This story causes me tears: One little lad from Eastern Europe sat down at a long table for the free American lunch. A glass of milk was placed in front of him—a whole glass of milk. He looked at his parents as he did not know what to do. He was told it was all right to drink the whole glass, all by himself. He did so, and then the waiter came by and filled the glass again. Now what was he to do? The land of milk and honey. . . . "Lord," he must have thought to himself, "We are going to have a good time here. There is enough to eat!"

A friend in New York, Herb Rickman, told me this story. When his people, Russian Jews, came to this country, there was an uncle, a young boy, in the family who had been mistreated by the Czarist soldiers in the homeland. They had grabbed the boy by the arm and swung him about, thus permanently dislocating his arm. The arm withered in a few years. When the family came to this country, they knew that they would have to pass muster at Ellis Island. A boy with a withered arm would be sent back. So, they gathered clothes and rags and packed the kid's little parka so that he looked puffy and healthy. When the inspector patted him about to be sure that he was in good form, the boy felt firm and whole. He was admitted. Herb and I cried when the story was shared—and, we were on the "Island of Tears," Ellis Island, where it all took place.

Grandma Bess sent me this account. She was born in Krasna, Russia, into a Jewish family who lived in a typical ghetto. Her father went off to America to make his fortune and was then to send for his family. Finally, in 1917, when the Bolsheviks were victorious and mail was again allowed in, a letter from her father in America came and plans were made to travel there. "Mother began planning our trip. She started selling every-thing she possibly could, except for a big pillow that we managed to schlepp all over Europe. With the help of my uncle and aunts Mother spent weeks making dry salamis for the trip and also jams in case we would get sick on the train. Many times I would feign illness so I could get a teaspoon of this wonderful jam."

No one was allowed to leave Russia during this time so Grandma Bess's family's escape had to be very secret . . . but everyone in the tiny

"Uncle Sam, host." Immigrants being served a free meal, Ellis Island

Jewish ghetto knew about the trip. It took them two years to get to America, having been hidden in several countries and finally reaching a boat in Bucharest. They had to hide in holes in the ground several times before they made it to Bucharest, after dealing with thieves, night hunts, and kind Jews operating the underground, and short stays in this city and that. The crossing took ten days, and her mother had to place all of their important belongings in a single wicker trunk—belongings for herself and her six children.

"The day arrived when we saw the Statue of Liberty. The thrill of that moment cannot be conveyed unless you experience it. I have little replicas of the statue and can just sit and look at them and the same surge of feeling comes over me as if I am seeing it again for the first time. My mother gathered my brother and the three younger girls and stood us up on the bench. As we were approaching the Statue of Liberty she signaled for us to start singing the song that my cousin Dave had taught us. (The song had a few English words, such as "sure," "America," and "Columbus," and we thought that we learned an American song!) We were delirious with joy until we docked at Ellis Island. We were taken to tremendous cages where the doctor took one look at us, barely coming close, and we were shoved to one side with new tags pinned which meant that we were not getting off the ship. Little did I dream that I was going to spend eight months there. My mother, Ruchel, Sophie, Ben, and Dora were kept at Castle Garden, which meant that they passed inspection, but had to wait until the proper papers were completed.

To Mr. Wm. Williams: Hearty greetings from the Ellis Island immigrant children. July 12 – '13.

A group of immigrant children, Ellis Island

"Reba and I were sent to Ward Seventeen at Ellis Island. There were about thirty women and children in this ward. After a while I felt very much at home there, as I was sure that this was going to be my permanent home. In the beginning I would look across at the big buildings of New York City and I would fantasize that I could swim across or find a boat to get there. On Sunday many visitors would come to observe the immigrants. We would be dressed up in new uniforms, which were blue dresses with white collars. I didn't like it when one would ask who speaks English because I was told to kind of show off. I always got the same question. 'What do you see out of the window?' and I would answer, 'That is the Statue of Liberty.'"

Bess was kept in the island hospital because she had lice due to the unsanitary conditions of her life and her trip. The cure was inhumane. First, her head was shaved, and then adhesive tape was stuck to her head to form a kind of cap. The tape was ripped off along with the roots of her hair; some salve was applied before her head was finally covered with a gauze handkerchief. After a few weeks, when her hair began to grow back, the procedure was repeated.

Grandma Bess and her sister were finally united with her father, mother, sisters, and brothers, in Brooklyn. It is there that she continues to gaze at her small Statue of Liberty.

The shock of arriving in America was the shock of the new. The shock of a new culture, new sights, sounds, tastes, and smells, was coupled with the shock of scale. Even today it is common to find visitors from other parts of the country staring at the heights of the New York skyscrapers.

Another friend wrote about the imagined experiences of an immigrant of student age:

All sorts of worries came to me even before leaving my village. I was concerned about paying back the one hundred and fifty dollars I had borrowed for my passage. My brother wrote to say he was making good money in America, about five dollars a week.

The week before I left I went to the school in the next village and asked to see America on a map. The master showed it to me, a big yellow shape with strange-sounding towns marked on it, and I found the Atlantic. It seemed small on the map until I asked where our village was, and it was penciled in on a tiny blue patch that was Poland. My heart sank, the ocean was huge and I get sick in boats.

After taking the train to Hamburg I spent the next two weeks in my berth below the deck wishing I could die. During my misery I remember the yellow place on the map. America is much bigger than the ocean, so how will my brother and I find each other in such a huge place?

One morning there is an air of activity on the ship. I stagger up on deck where I see the beautiful city, and the great lady holding up a light to greet me. I forget my seasickness and rejoice. Then a little boat comes up and a doctor and some nurses come on board. I am a little worried because I look so pale, I haven't eaten, and I smell of my sickness. But they don't come to the boat deck so I forget them.

We are at the dock, but a man who knows English tells me that the steerage passengers don't get off here with the first- and second-class passengers. I ask why. He says that we have to go to Ellis Island. I've never heard of it, and I ask why the first- and second-class passengers don't go also. He laughs and says it's because they have money. I still don't understand. Why should money make a difference? I ask what goes on at this Ellis Island. He says that is where they test you to become American. And he walks away. Suddenly I am very afraid, really scared. I didn't know about the test. I failed the exams for Krakow University. Is the test very hard? What happens to me if I don't pass the test?

That was the immigrant experience. It must have been horrifying. Still, most who came here were treated well and remain creative and productive Americans.

What about the future of immigration to this country? Polls show that most Americans are nervous about more immigrants, so little in the way of public attitude concerning immigration has really changed since the days of the Founding Fathers. Today there are some 2 million people who are all qualified for immigration into this country and await visas for entry. Can we take on more people?

All the old fears seem to remain. Americans are worried about jobs, food production, city population, and so forth. Again, I am convinced that in terms of our fears little has changed since colonial times. The truth is that the Chinese never did take anyone's job and the Japanese have certainly become devoted and productive citizens. The Germans, despised and feared during two great wars, did not return to Germany but stayed and made this country their own. The Vietnamese and Koreans, who became citizens due to our warring in their countries, have set up productive and independent communities in America.

Some scholars such as Julian Simon, author of *The Economic Consequences of Immigration,* are convinced that we need not worry about immigration. Simon claims that immigrants take care of themselves, improve the economy, and actually make work within their own communities. He is for open immigration and literally believes in "the more the merrier!"

Are you not sorry that he was not around when your great-grandfather was trying to get through Ellis Island?

Such is the immigrant experience.

One more story. I recently had dinner at the Grand Central Oyster Bar in New York City. The meal was outstanding, and Craig, my assistant, began talking with the waiter about the restaurant and the kitchen. Craig asked the waiter, a man from Puerto Rico, how long the current chef had been there. The waiter replied, "You mean in this kitchen or in this country?" Only in America!

THE RECIPES

THE ARMENIAN
IMMIGRANTS

ARMENIA

I had really never understood Armenian history. I was in Fresno, California, talking with an Armenian Orthodox priest when I was brought to tears with the stories of the tribulations of this wonderful people. During 1915 the Turks caused wholesale massacre. Between one and two million were killed. . . . We don't even know the number. It was like the Jewish Holocaust but few Americans even heard about it. Why? It is hard to say, but I am astounded by this story. It has been said that when Hitler decided to wipe out the Jews in his horrendous program, he announced his plan to his cabinet. "But," asked one officer, "if you wipe out all the Jews, what will history say about you?" Hitler replied, without a moment's hesitation, "Who any longer remembers the extermination of the Armenians?" The cabinet agreed that no one remembered so they decided to go ahead with their diabolical plan.

Such a tragic history. The Turkish occupation lasted for so long, for nearly four hundred years, and the result was the great massacre.

The land itself in Armenia is rugged and stark. Rocks are everywhere, and an old creation story is a favorite among this people. They claim that when God distributed the earth's land nothing was left but rocks by the time He got to the Armenians. Nothing but rocks. And that is what they got. Talk about a tenacious people . . . but their history remains tragic.

Since they were located on the great trade routes, they were invaded and taken over by many peoples, long before the great massacre by the Turks. They were ruled at one time or another by the Persians, the Romans, the Mongols, the Ottoman Turks, and finally by the Soviet Union. Yet in the midst of all of this the Armenians have continued to remember who they are. Fantastic!

Just prior to and following the great massacre, the real immigration to America began. The immigrants who have come to this country have been literate, artistic, and skilled. And the food that they have brought with them as a memory of the Old World is just heaven. We must thank them for the casaba melon, Armenian pilaf, shish kebab and dolmas, as well as Almond Joys and Mounds bars. Delectable breads, including Lavash, and Armenian meat pies, are also a part of their tradition. You can see from the following recipes that lamb and stuffed tomatoes and peppers can provide you with a wonderful table, a table filled with memories from ancient Armenia.

ARMENIAN THIN BREAD

(Lavash)

Makes 8 cracker breads

This crackerlike bread is basic to the Armenian diet. It is not complicated to prepare and it is just delicious. And with a little bit of clever insight you can wet it and roll it up with wonderful fillings . . . for a sandwich you would not believe!

1⅓ cups tepid water (barely warm, about 105°)	2 teaspoons salt
¼ cup olive oil	4 cups all-purpose flour (See Hint, page 423.)
3 tablespoons sugar	½ cup milk for topping
1 package quick-rising yeast	Sesame seeds for topping

Place the tepid water in your electric mixing bowl and add the water, olive oil, sugar, and yeast. Using the batter blade let the electric mixer blend these very well. It will take about 5 minutes on low speed. Stir in the salt.

Gradually add 2 cups of the flour and beat on low speed until a thick and smooth batter forms. Change the blade to a bread dough hook and knead in the additional 2 cups of flour. If you do not have a heavy mixer such as a KitchenAid, incorporate the flour with a wooden spoon and finish the kneading by hand. Kneading should take about 10 minutes in the machine, 20 minutes by hand.

Place the dough on a plastic countertop and cover with a large stainless-steel bowl. Allow the dough to rise until double in bulk, about 1½ hours. Punch the dough down and divide into 8 pieces. Let stand, covered, 15 minutes.

Roll out each piece of dough into a 12-inch-diameter circle. Working with 2 pieces of dough at a time, arrange breads on ungreased baking sheets. Brush with milk and sprinkle sesame seeds over tops. Prick with a fork many times, all over.

Bake on the lowest racks in the oven, at 375°, for 8 to 10 minutes, or until light brown. Rotate the pans in the oven from top to bottom, to insure even browning.

Serve dry or wet. (To wet, hold the cracker under running water until lightly moistened all over, and then wrap in a moist towel for 10 to 15 minutes.) If the cracker is too dry to roll, it will crack. Sprinkle with a little more water and let stand a few minutes. If it is too wet, cover with a dry towel and let it stand.

ARMENIAN STUFFED MEATBALLS

(Kufta)

Serves 6–8

My Armenian friend, Vahram Keogian, must be given credit for his interpretation of this wonderful dish. He is a charming fellow who lives in San Francisco. Vahram and his wife make this often for the sake of family memories. This is a scrumptious dish that is fun to prepare.

THE FILLING (can be made in advance)

1 pound ground lamb or beef	¼ cup pine nuts, toasted and chopped
2 large yellow onions, peeled and finely chopped	1 teaspoon paprika
	½ teaspoon finely chopped mint leaves
½ cup finely chopped green bell pepper	½ teaspoon each of salt, freshly ground black pepper, ground cinnamon, and dried basil
3 tablespoons chopped parsley	

Fry the meat until lightly browned. Add the onions and simmer 30 minutes. Add the green pepper and parsley. Cook 10 minutes. Add the remaining ingredients and stir. Chill completely. Shape into balls the size of a small walnut.

THE KEYMA (the outer meatball)

1½ pounds *extra lean* lamb, finely ground

¾ cup fine bulgur (page 38), soaked 20 minutes in water and drained

2 quarts Chicken Stock (page 74) or use canned

1 medium yellow onion, peeled and finely chopped

1 tablespoon chopped parsley

Salt and freshly ground black pepper to taste

Mix all the Keyma ingredients together. Beat mixture in an electric mixer until light and fluffy, 10 to 15 minutes. Dip hands in cold water, then shape meatballs twice the size of walnuts. Make a dent in the middle of each ball, pressing all around the inside wall to make an opening for the filling—the thinner the wall the better. Place some filling in each hole. Seal and smooth surface with wet fingers.

TO COOK

Place the Kufta, a few at a time, in boiling Chicken Stock. Cover and simmer 8 to 10 minutes. When the Kufta rise to the top, they are done.

Accompany with Homemade Yogurt (page 428).

CHICKEN STOCK

Serves 6–8

There is no way that you can run a proper kitchen without having fresh stocks on hand. If you buy commercially prepared products you are generally getting little more than salt, and in a very expensive form. I know it sounds like lots of work but to tell the truth stocks are very easy to make, and they are not expensive. Cook one day a week and fill the refrigerator and freezer with the blessed liquids that free you to be creative and comforting when cooking. Chicken Stock is one of those necessary and comforting fluids.

3 pounds chicken backs
and necks

3 quarts *cold* water

4 ribs celery, coarsely
chopped

6 carrots, unpeeled, sliced
thick

2 yellow onions, peeled
and quartered

8 black peppercorns

Place the chicken backs and necks in a soup pot and rinse with very hot tap water. Drain and add the cold water to the pot, along with the other ingredients. Bring to a simmer and cook for 2 hours. Be sure to skim the froth that forms when the pot first comes to a simmer.

The stock will taste a bit flat to you since it has no salt. Salt will be added when you use the stock in the preparation of soups, sauces, or stews.

ARMENIAN LAMB STEW

(Tass Kebab)

Serves 4–6

This is simply a spicy lamb stew, but the Armenian name is so beautiful that I think you should try it. Tass Kebab is what an Armenian grandma would call it, that's for sure.

2 pounds boneless lean leg of lamb, cut in 1½-inch cubes

2 tablespoons butter

2 medium yellow onions, peeled and coarsely chopped

1 teaspoon salt

½ teaspoon paprika

½ teaspoon freshly ground black pepper

½ teaspoon ground allspice

¼ teaspoon ground cinnamon

¼ cup tomato paste diluted with ½ cup water

2 tablespoons dry red wine

Heat a large frying pan and add the lamb and butter. Brown the meat and place it in a 6-quart stove-top casserole, leaving the fat in the frying pan. Sauté the onions in the reserved fat and add to the pot, along with the remaining ingredients except the wine. Cover and simmer 45 minutes or until all is tender. Add the wine, cover, and simmer 15 minutes more.

This stew is very thick and rich-tasting. Serve it over rice.

Armenian Hand-Rolled Sausages

(Luleh Kebab)

Makes about 14 sausages

When our Armenian immigrants came to this country they certainly understood our love of hamburger. However, these meat rolls have a flavor that no hamburger could ever match.

2½ pounds lean ground meat, half beef and half lamb

1 tablespoon tomato paste

½ cup (4 ounces) tomato sauce

1 cup bread crumbs

¼ cup (4 tablespoons) evaporated milk

1 teaspoon ground cumin

¼ cup minced parsley

1 tablespoon minced dried onion

1 teaspoon salt

Freshly ground black pepper to taste

GARNISHES

1 cup peeled and minced yellow onion

½ cup minced parsley

Mix the ingredients, except garnishes, together. Roll mixture into balls just smaller than a tennis ball, then form into sausage shapes about 1 inch by 4 inches long. Moisten hands with water to facilitate shaping. Place the kebabs in a shallow baking dish.

Bake 20 minutes in a preheated 400° oven. Transfer to a heated platter and reserve the pan juices to serve separately, first spooning off the excess fat. Garnish the kebabs with the chopped onion and parsley.

ARMENIAN STUFFED TOMATOES AND PEPPERS

When I was a child, my mother used to make stuffed green bell peppers. They were overcooked and my brother, sister, and I called them "gooshy." The Armenians, and other cultures from the Middle East, do not cook vegetables to death as we did during the 1940's. These are delicious, and the recipe is quite versatile. You can use the filling to stuff all kinds of vegetables.

MEAT AND RICE STUFFING

⅓ cup long-grain rice	3 tablespoons tomato paste
⅔ cup water	2 tablespoons minced parsley
½ pound ground beef	1 teaspoon salt
½ pound coarsely ground lamb	½ teaspoon paprika
1 medium ripe tomato, finely chopped	Freshly ground black pepper to taste
2 medium yellow onions, peeled and chopped small	Pinch of ground allspice

To partially cook rice, bring rice and water to a boil, reduce heat to a simmer, cover, and cook for 10 minutes. Drain and cool. Combine with rest of ingredients and mix well.

This filling can be used to stuff an assortment of vegetables. It fills about 8 large-sized tomatoes or green or red bell peppers. It is also enough to fill about 12 to 14 small Japanese eggplants.

STUFFED TOMATOES

8 large firm tomatoes	Juice of ½ lemon
Salt to taste	1 cup Beef Stock (page 78)
1 recipe Meat and Rice Stuffing (page 76)	or water
Iceberg lettuce leaves	2 tablespoons butter, melted

Wash the tomatoes; cut off tops and reserve; scoop out the pulp (centers) and reserve.

Sprinkle salt in the tomato shells and loosely fill them with stuffing. Replace tops.

Line a 4-quart covered heavy stove-top casserole or deep skillet with some lettuce leaves and arrange the tomatoes in one layer over them.

Chop up the reserved tomato pulp, combine with the lemon juice, salt, and broth and pour over the stuffed tomatoes. Spoon butter over each tomato.

Bring to a boil, reduce to a simmer, and cook, covered, for 45 minutes. When they are done, do not uncover for 15 minutes, then serve.

STUFFED PEPPERS

8 medium green bell peppers	1 14½-ounce can tomatoes, drained and crushed
Salt	
1 recipe Meat and Rice Stuffing (page 76)	½ teaspoon salt
Iceberg lettuce leaves	1 cup Beef Stock (page 78) or water
	2 tablespoons butter, melted

Wash the peppers. Cut ½ inch off each stem end. Remove the seeds and membranes. Reserve the tops.

Sprinkle cavities with salt and loosely fill them with stuffing. Replace tops.

Line a 4-quart heavy covered stove-top casserole with lettuce leaves and arrange the peppers over them. Combine the tomatoes, salt, and broth and pour over the peppers. Spoon butter over each pepper.

Bring to a boil, reduce to a simmer and cook covered, for 45 minutes. When they are done, do not uncover for 15 minutes, then serve.

BEEF STOCK

Makes 5 quarts of stock

The Old World has always had basic soup stocks on hand. The frugal cook was not about to throw out anything since he could not afford our luxury of waste. The bones of any and every creature were used for stock, and the stock eventually became the basis of another meal, in the form of either a soup, a sauce, or a gravy. You will need to make a batch of this now and then. It freezes well and it has a much better flavor than the only other possible substitute, canned beef stock. Please do not even think of using a bouillon cube. It is nothing but salt!

5 pounds bare beef
rendering bones, sawed
into 2-inch pieces

1 bunch of carrots,
unpeeled and chopped

1 bunch of celery, chopped

3 yellow onions, unpeeled
and chopped

Tell your butcher that you need bare rendering bones. They should not have any meat on them at all, so they should be cheap. Have him saw them up into 2-inch pieces.

Roast the bones in an uncovered pan at 400° for 2 hours. Be careful with this, because your own oven may be a bit too hot. Watch the bones, which you want to be toasty brown, not black.

Place the roasted bones in a soup pot and add 1 quart water for each pound of bones. For 5 pounds of bones, add 1 bunch of carrots, chopped, 1 bunch of celery, chopped; and 3 yellow onions, chopped with peel and all. (The peel will give lovely color to the stock.)

Bring to a simmer, uncovered, and cook for 12 hours. You may need to add water to keep soup up to the same level. Do not salt the stock.

Strain the stock, and store in the refrigerator. Allow the fat to stay on the top of the stock when you refrigerate it; the fat will seal the stock and allow you to keep it for several days.

ARMENIAN KNOT ROLLS

(Choereg)

Makes about 24 knot rolls

We owe this recipe to my Armenian friends, the Keogians, in San Francisco. I can just see them making these rolls and then offering them to the baby. Mama is proud of the rolls, Papa is proud of the heritage, and the baby is just proud . . . period.

1 cup milk

½ pound butter

⅓ cup sugar

2 teaspoons ground mahleb (page 50)

1 teaspoon salt

1½ teaspoons baking powder

¼ cup orange juice

2 eggs, beaten

¼ cup warm water (about 105°)

1 package quick-rising yeast

4 cups all-purpose flour (See Hint, page 423.)

EGG WASH

1 egg beaten with 1 tablespoon water

GARNISH

2 tablespoons sesame seeds

Place the warm water in the bowl of a heavy-duty electric mixer, such as KitchenAid. Add the yeast. Stir to dissolve.

In a small saucepan, combine the milk, butter, sugar, mahleb, salt, baking powder, and orange juice. Heat and stir to melt the butter and dissolve the sugar and salt. Cool to tepid, barely warm, 105°. Stir in the beaten eggs. Add to the yeast mixture.

Add 2 cups of the flour to the yeast mixture. Beat 5 to 10 minutes or until a soft sponge is formed and the dough begins to pull away from sides of bowl. This can also be done by hand with a wooden spoon.

Using the dough hook on your electric machine or by hand add the remaining 2 cups flour and knead to make a smooth dough. Knead for about 10 minutes by machine or 20 minutes by hand.

Place on the counter under a large stainless-steel bowl. Allow to double in bulk, about 1½ hours. Punch down and form rolls.

TO MAKE KNOT ROLLS

Pinch off a piece of dough the size of a golf ball. Roll into a snake 11 inches long. Tie into a knot and then bring up the ends through the

center of the knot. (See the illustration.) Continue with the rest of the dough until you have 24 knots. Place the knots 2 inches apart on a greased baking sheet. Allow to double in bulk (45 minutes to 1 hour). Brush with the egg wash. Sprinkle with the sesame seeds. Bake at 350° for 25 to 30 minutes or until golden brown.

ARMENIAN LAMB SHANKS

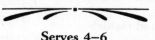

Serves 4–6

I know, everybody makes lamb shanks. But consider the plight of the Armenian immigrants. They arrived with very little money to spend on food . . . yet lamb was the meat that they loved most. So they bought cheap cuts and created marvelous preparations. I love lamb shanks and they are not cheap any longer, but you can see from this recipe what glorious things our immigrant ancestors did with inexpensive cuts of meat.

Incidentally, if you are ever in Fresno, California, you will find a large Armenian community. And in the midst of it you will find George's Restaurant. It is sort of high-tech Armenian, but George's lamb shanks should be declared a national treasure!

4½ pounds lamb shanks,
   sawed in 2-inch pieces
2 medium yellow onions,
   peeled and sliced
8 ripe tomatoes, chopped
1 teaspoon crushed dried
   oregano

1 teaspoon salt
½ teaspoon freshly ground
   black pepper
½ teaspoon ground allspice
¼ teaspoon ground nutmeg

GARNISH

Finely chopped yellow
onion and parsley

Trim shanks of excess fat. Place in an 8-quart stove-top casserole. Add the remaining ingredients except the garnish. Bring to a boil and simmer, covered, until the lamb is tender, about 1½ hours. Partially uncover pot for the last ½ hour. Garnish with onion mixed with parsley.

ARMENIAN MEAT PIES

(Lehmejun)

Makes 12 pies

The argument about the birth of the pizza starts in Greece and moves to Rome . . . then on to the countryside. However, in Armenia—and remember, this is a very old culture—meat pies have been local fare for centuries. Close to a meat-covered pizza, but not with a dripping sauce. You can buy these ready-made in Armenian markets in Los Angeles, New York, and San Francisco. Otherwise, you need to make your own . . . and it is worth the effort.

MEAT PIE FILLING

- 1 pound finely ground lean beef
- 1 14½-ounce can whole tomatoes, drained and crushed
- ½ medium yellow onion, peeled and finely chopped
- ½ medium green bell pepper, cored and finely chopped
- 1 teaspoon peeled and minced or crushed garlic
- ¼ cup finely chopped parsley
- 1 tablespoon finely chopped fresh mint leaves
- 1 tablespoon tomato paste
- ½ teaspoon paprika
- ¼ teaspoon ground allspice
- Salt and freshly ground black pepper to taste
- Pinch of cayenne pepper

Mix all together and set aside.

THE DOUGH

- 1 package quick-rising yeast
- 1 cup warm water (about 105°)
- 1 tablespoon olive oil
- ¾ teaspoon salt
- ½ teaspoon sugar
- 2¾ cups all-purpose flour (See Hint, page 423.)

Dissolve the yeast in the water in the bowl of an electric mixer. Stir in the olive oil, sugar, salt, and 1½ cups of the flour. Mix the dough for about 5 minutes, until smooth. Knead in the remaining 1¼ cups of the flour, using the dough hook, and knead until smooth. If you do not have a powerful machine, such as a KitchenAid, then you should knead in this last bit of flour by hand. Knead until the dough is very smooth and elastic, about 10 minutes by machine, 20 minutes by hand.

Place the dough on a plastic counter and cover with a large stainless-steel bowl. Allow to double in bulk, about 1½ hours.

Punch the dough down and shape into 12 balls. Use 4 balls at a time, placing the remaining balls in the refrigerator. On a lightly floured surface roll each ball into a 6- or 7-inch circle. Do not roll too thin. Arrange circles on two large, lightly greased baking sheets. Allow the dough to rise slightly. Cover the entire surface with a thin layer of the meat mixture, spreading it to about ¼ inch from the edge. Bake at 375° about 25 to 35 minutes. Do the same with the remaining balls.

THE BASQUE
IMMIGRANTS

BASQUE

The background and origins of this unusual ethnic group called the Basques are hidden in history, so that it is difficult to describe them. While they were a nation at one time, they are a nation no more. They don't even have a homeland that is strictly theirs.

They come from the Pyrenees, the beautiful mountains of southwestern France and northern Spain. The border between these two countries goes right through the middle of the Basque region, so some Basques are French and some Basques are Spanish, but no Basque is Basque. There is no longer such a place.

These people are unique in that they have lived in this region since about 200 B.C. and they remain possibly the oldest homogeneous group in Europe. They are a people unto themselves and even the language that they speak, Euskera, has no relationship whatsoever to any other language on the European continent.

The story that they tell of their background is fascinating. They claim that Tubal, a grandson of Noah, came to Europe before the tower of Babel was built. He brought with him the original language spoken by Adam and Eve in the Garden of Eden. And the Basques still speak it. Now, how can you argue with a legend as beautiful as that?

These people have a fierce ethnic pride and have always been known to be ferocious in battle. When Napoleon's soldiers invaded Spain in the early 1800s it is said that when the French troops heard the battle cry of the Basques, these sons of Napoleon shuddered with fright. "Irrintzi!" the Basques would cry . . . and the French would cower or run. In our time you still find Basque nationalist movements that fight for the memory of their homeland in the most dedicated ways. After all, the French and the Spanish simply robbed the Basque people of their homeland. And the Bascos have not forgotten, and they will not.

The first Basque immigrants to this country probably came during the 1400s as sailors. They were the first whalers of Europe and they came to this country before Columbus. As a matter of fact, the largest ethnic contingent of sailors on Columbus's ship was Basque.

During the days of the great Gold Rush in California many immigrants from the Pyrenees came to the New World. They were followed by Basque sheepherders who settled in the great cattle-raising areas in Idaho and Nevada. With the immigrants came a new set of American customs, the Basque boardinghouse being one of the most interesting living arrangements I know of. When a Basco arrived in a town in Nevada, such as Reno, he looked for a Basque boardinghouse. That was to become his address in the New World. Even though he spent weeks at a time in the hills with the sheep he considered his new address to be home. Meals were served family style and most meals consisted of many courses of soup, rice, beans, dried salt cod, and the inevitable course of innards. Tongue, oxtail, and tripe were all favorites since the whole animal was sold at the market, and the innards were left for the herders. That is still the custom in these boardinghouses. Now it is tradition, but the food is plentiful and tasty. Special thanks to the Erreguible family at Louis' Basque Corner in Reno. Such food! Such people! Bascos all!

BASQUE OXTAILS

(Behi Buztanak Anda Goriren Zaltzan)

Serves 8

This dish is from Louis' Basque Corner, a fine but informal restaurant in Reno. Reno? Yes, the Basque sheepherders came to this area generations ago, and they brought their recipes with them. Louis and Lorraine Erreguible have kept up the Basque boardinghouse tradition of dining, and I suggest you go. The place is just terrific.

4 pounds oxtails, rubbed with salt and freshly ground black pepper

2 tablespoons olive oil

1 cup chopped celery

1 medium yellow onion, peeled and chopped

2 carrots, sliced

3 cloves peeled garlic

2 shallots, peeled and chopped

1 tablespoon chopped parsley

1 tablespoon all-purpose flour

2½ cups Beef Stock (page 78) or use canned

1½ cups red wine

2 bay leaves

½ teaspoon dried thyme, whole

Salt and freshly ground black pepper to taste

Using a large black frying pan, brown the seasoned oxtails in the oil. You will need to do this in about 3 batches. Remove the meat to a 6- to 8-quart heavy stove-top pot. Leave the oil in the frying pan and sauté the celery, onion, carrots, garlic, shallots, and parsley. When the onions are clear add the flour and stir in well. Sauté a few minutes longer and add the remaining ingredients, along with the oxtails, except the salt and pepper. Simmer partially covered for 2 hours, or until tender. Stir occasionally. Add salt and pepper to taste as the dish finishes.

Codfish Pil Pil

Serves about 4 as a main dish

I was told by one Basque old-timer that a meal that did not include a salt cod dish was not a Basque dinner. Since the Basques and Spaniards share a love for this fish, it is understandable. The following recipe is typical of Basque cuisine. It is very rich and quite good.

- 1 pound salt cod, skinless and boneless (page 45)
- 3 tablespoons olive oil
- 4 cloves garlic, peeled and crushed
- Pinch of red pepper flakes
- 1 cup Chicken Stock (page 74) (simmered with 1-inch piece lemon peel) or use canned
- 1 egg, beaten

Cut the salt cod into 1-inch-wide serving pieces and rinse well. Soak for 24 hours or more, rinsing with fresh water several times.

Cook the salt cod in fresh water for about 15 minutes, or until it can be easily flaked, but leave the pieces whole. Drain and let cool, discarding the liquid.

Heat a large frying pan and add the oil and crushed garlic. Sauté over medium heat until the garlic barely begins to brown. Add the red pepper flakes, the drained cod, and the Chicken Stock. Bring to a simmer while shaking the pan gently. With a pancake turner, remove the cod to a platter. Turn off the heat, add the beaten egg and return to low heat. Stir the liquid constantly until the sauce begins to thicken. Remove from the heat and immediately pour over the fish and serve.

SHELLFISH AND RICE

Serves 4–6 as a side dish

The Basques have always enjoyed dishes that we usually call *paellas*. The Spanish influence is afoot here, to be sure, but the Basques do not create such flamboyant dishes with meat and rice as the Spanish do. It is more like an everyday and expected course in the meal. And it is delicious.

¼ cup olive oil

3 cloves garlic, peeled and chopped

1 medium yellow onion, peeled and chopped

¼ cup chopped parsley

½ teaspoon dried basil

1 teaspoon paprika

1 cup Uncle Ben's Converted Rice

2 cups Chicken Stock (page 74) or use canned

Salt and freshly ground black pepper to taste

SHELLFISH

½ pound (25–30 size) shrimp, shells removed

2 pounds mixed clams and mussels, shells on

Heat a deep stove-top covered casserole and add the oil, garlic, and onion. Sauté over medium heat for a few minutes and add the parsley, basil, and paprika. Sauté for 5 minutes and add the rice. Stir and cook for a moment. Add the Chicken Stock, bring to a boil, and then turn down to a simmer. Add the salt and pepper, cover the casserole, and cook for 20 minutes on low heat.

Stir in the shellfish, cover, and cook 5 minutes more or until clams and mussels open.

CHICKEN AND RICE

Serves 8 as a rice dish

Another variation on a meat and rice dish. These rice dishes seem to appear at the Basque table in an endless variety, and one can understand how important they were to the immigrant cook. This chicken dish will be a favorite with your household.

2 tablespoons olive oil

1 3-pound chicken, cut into 8 serving pieces

3 cloves garlic, peeled and chopped

1 medium yellow onion, peeled and chopped small

½ medium green bell pepper, cored, seeded, and chopped small

¼ cup water

2 cups Uncle Ben's Converted Rice

4 cups Chicken Stock (page 74) or use canned

1 bay leaf

Salt and freshly ground black pepper to taste

Heat a deep stove-top casserole and add the oil and chicken. Brown the pieces well and then remove to a platter. Leave the oil in the pan. Add to the pan the garlic, yellow onion, and green pepper. Sauté until the onion is clear and then deglaze the pan with ¼ cup water. Return the chicken to the pot and add the remaining ingredients. Bring to a boil, cover the pot, and turn down to a simmer. Cook for 25 minutes, or until the rice is just tender.

Basque Leg of Lamb with Mushroom and Wine Sauce

(Bildotz Istera Anoa Zaltzan Onduekin)

The meat and sauce serve 4–6

This is another dish from Louis and Lorraine at Louis' Basque Corner in Reno (see Basque Oxtails, page 86). In the old days of herding, a roast leg of lamb was a very special event as the herders needed to sell all the meat. This dish is great for any special occasion.

1 5–6 pound leg of lamb

6 cloves garlic, peeled

Salt and freshly ground black pepper to taste

2 tablespoons olive oil

FOR RARE LAMB

Have the lamb at room temperature. Heat the oven to 400°. Using a paring knife, poke 6 small holes in the fat side of the roast and insert the garlic cloves. Rub the roast all over with salt and pepper and a little bit of oil. Insert a meat thermometer in the thickest part of the leg, being careful not to touch the bone. Place in a pan with a roasting rack and roast at 400° for 40 minutes, so the meat can brown. Turn down the oven to 325° and roast for an additional 40 to 50 minutes, or until the thermometer registers 140°.

FOR MEDIUM LAMB

Follow the above instructions but cook a bit longer so that the thermometer registers 145° to 150°.

Remove the meat from the oven and allow it to sit ½ hour before slicing. It will continue to cook during this time.

In the meantime prepare the sauce.

SAUCE

Makes 3 cups

2 cups Beef Stock (page 78) or use canned

1 cup dry red wine

2 tablespoons olive oil

2 cloves garlic, peeled and crushed

¾ pound mushrooms, sliced

1 bay leaf

½ teaspoon dried thyme, whole

4 tablespoons butter

6 tablespoons all-purpose flour

Salt and freshly ground black pepper to taste

½ teaspoon dried mint (optional)

Place the beef stock and wine in a 2-quart saucepan. Bring to a simmer. Heat a 10-inch frying pan and add the oil and garlic. Sauté for a moment and add the mushrooms, bay leaf, and thyme. Sauté until the mushrooms are tender and then remove them from the pan and set aside. Return the pan to the stove and melt the butter. Add the flour and cook a few minutes to form a roux—a paste of butter and flour just barely browned. Add the roux to the stock and wine and whip it with a wire whisk until smooth. Add the mushrooms and simmer for 10 minutes. Add salt and pepper. If you wish to add the optional mint, do so during the last 10 minutes of cooking.

BASQUE SWEETBREADS IN SAUCE

(Choriak)

Serves 4–6 as part of Basque meal

The Basques love innards. That should be understandable when one considers that the animals they had raised and been herding were to be sold, not eaten. They were left with the innards and thus the following wonderful recipes.

Please do try this dish. No, sweetbreads are not "mountain oysters." They are part of the thymus gland of the young calf. They taste a bit like very mild liver but they are far superior.

2 pounds veal sweetbreads

2 quarts water

¼ cup distilled white vinegar

6 cups Chicken Stock (page 74) or use canned

1 bay leaf

1 cup all-purpose flour, seasoned with salt and freshly ground black pepper (See Hint, page 423.)

3 cloves garlic, peeled and crushed

2 tablespoons olive oil

½ cup Basque Tomato Sauce (page 92)

TO PREPARE SWEETBREADS

Wash the sweetbreads and soak in 2 quarts cold water with vinegar for 1½ hours; drain. Poach the sweetbreads in the Chicken Stock and bay leaf for 15 minutes. Remove the sweetbreads and plunge into cold water. Save the poaching liquid for another use. Allow sweetbreads to cool; drain. Carefully pull off the clear membrane that coats the gland. Separate the sweetbreads into 1½-inch pieces, discarding any gristle or fatty parts.

Dust the sweetbreads in the seasoned flour. Heat a large SilverStone-lined frying pan and brown the sweetbreads in the garlic and oil for a few minutes. Add the Basque Tomato Sauce and toss together in the frying pan until all is hot.

BASQUE TOMATO SAUCE

Makes about 6 cups

This is a rather involved tomato sauce, and typical of the cooking of the Basque immigrant. It can be used in many dishes and it will keep several days in the refrigerator.

¼ cup olive oil

8 cloves garlic, peeled and crushed

2 cups peeled and diced yellow onion

1½ cups cored, seeded, and diced green bell pepper

3 cups diced *very* ripe tomatoes

1 4-ounce can whole green chiles, Mexican style, puréed

¼ cup chopped parsley

5 cups Beef Stock (page 78) or use canned

Salt and freshly ground black pepper to taste

In a 6-quart saucepot sauté the garlic, onion, and green pepper in the oil until tender. Add the tomatoes, puréed chiles, and parsley and simmer until very tender. Add Beef Stock. Cover and simmer 1 hour. Uncover and simmer 1 hour more to reduce and thicken the sauce. Stir occasionally. Salt and pepper to taste.

BASQUE SWEETBREADS, FRIED

(Choriak)

Serves 4–6 as part of a Basque meal

I think this is my favorite sweetbread recipe ever. It is fairly close to the great dish that they serve at Louis' Basque Corner (see Basque Sweetbreads in Sauce, page 91).

2 pounds veal sweetbreads (See page 91 for preparing sweetbreads.)

1 cup all-purpose flour, seasoned with salt and freshly ground black pepper to taste (See Hint, page 423.)

6 tablespoons olive oil

3 cloves garlic, peeled and crushed

1 medium yellow onion, peeled and cut into ½-inch dice

1 medium green bell pepper, cored, seeded, and cut into ½-inch dice

1 teaspoon paprika

Salt and freshly ground black pepper to taste

½ cup reserved poaching liquid

¼ cup chopped parsley

Dust the prepared sweetbreads in the seasoned flour. In a large frying pan, pan-fry them in 3 tablespoons of the olive oil until lightly brown. Remove and set aside. Reheat the frying pan and add the remaining oil, the garlic, onion, and bell pepper and sauté until just tender. Return the sweetbreads to the pan and add the paprika, salt, and pepper and sauté all together. Add the reserved poaching liquid, cover, and cook gently for 5 minutes more, tossing about in the pan. Sprinkle with parsley just before serving.

BASQUE TONGUE STEW

Mihia Eskualdun Zaltzan)

Serves 4–6

JT's Bar and Restaurant, an institution in Gardnerville, Nevada, is presided over by a Basque gentleman by the name of Jean Lukumberry. He came to this country in 1947 and worked on a ranch in the area where he lives now. He runs a wonderful Basque restaurant and bar and his tongue stew is just beyond belief. He cooks it forever, and that is the secret to a dish as fine as this one. The following is as close as I could come to his Gardnerville recipe.

1 3½-pound fresh beef tongue

1 medium yellow onion, peeled and quartered

2 carrots, chopped

½ bunch of parsley

2 bay leaves

10 black peppercorns

1 recipe Basque Tomato Sauce (page 92)

In a 6-quart pot place tongue, onion, carrots, parsley, bay leaves, and peppercorns. Add just enough water to cover. Simmer, covered, for 2½ hours. Remove tongue, cool, peel, and slice ¼-inch thick crosswise. Add to the prepared sauce. Simmer covered 1 hour. Then uncover the pot and simmer gently 1½ hours, stirring occasionally.

BASQUE TRIPE STEW

Serves 4–6 as part of Basque meal

I thought that I had a good tripe recipe, but I had not eaten at Louis' Basque Corner. Now, if you have never eaten tripe I do not want to hear you saying, "Never!" If you have not tried this dish you have no idea of what you are missing. You have trusted me before—trust me on this one.

This recipe is as close as I can come to what they serve at Louis'.

2½ pounds beef tripe, washed

6 tablespoons olive oil

8 cloves garlic, peeled and crushed

2 cups peeled and diced yellow onion

1½ cups cored, seeded, and diced green bell pepper

3 cups Beef Stock (page 78) or use canned

2 14½-ounce cans whole tomatoes, puréed

5 canned whole green chiles, Mexican style, puréed

¼ cup chopped parsley

Salt and freshly ground black pepper to taste

In a 12-quart pot simmer tripe in ample water for 1½ hours. Drain and cool. Cut into strips 2 inches long and ½ inch wide.

Heat a 6- to 8-quart pot, add oil, garlic, onion, and bell pepper, and sauté until tender. Add Beef Stock, puréed tomatoes, chiles, and parsley. Simmer covered for 1½ hours. Uncover and simmer ½ hour more. Salt and pepper to taste. Add prepared tripe, cover, and simmer gently 1 hour more, stirring occasionally. Adjust salt and pepper if needed. The stew can be served immediately but it is best if refrigerated overnight and reheated.

BASQUE BREAD

Originally this bread was simply baked in the ground with hot rocks or on top of the fire with coals on top of the pot. The great people at *Sunset Magazine* have worked with some Basque sheepherders and have come up with the following recipe. I really do trust *Sunset* for their authentic recipes from West Coast traditions. They are great!

You'll need a 10-inch cast-iron covered Dutch oven (5-quart size).

3 cups very hot tap water

½ cup butter, margarine, or shortening

½ cup sugar

2½ teaspoons salt

2 packages quick-rising yeast

About 9½ cups all-purpose flour (See Hint, page 423.)

Salad oil for oiling the pan

In a bowl, combine the hot water, butter, sugar, and salt. Stir until the butter melts; let cool to warm (110° to 115°). Stir in the yeast, cover, and set in a warm place until bubbly, about 15 minutes.

Add 5 cups of the flour and beat with a heavy-duty mixer or wooden spoon to form a thick batter. With a spoon, stir in enough of the remaining flour (about 3½ cups) to form a stiff dough. Turn the dough out onto a floured board and knead until smooth, about 10 minutes, adding flour as needed to prevent sticking. Turn the dough into a greased bowl, cover, and let rise in a warm place until doubled in size, about 1½ hours.

Punch down the dough and knead on a floured board to form a smooth ball. Cut a circle of foil to cover the bottom of the Dutch oven. Grease well the inside of the Dutch oven and the underside of the lid with salad oil.

Place the dough in the pot and cover with the lid. Let rise in a warm place until the dough pushes up the lid by about ½ inch, about 1 hour (watch closely).

Bake, covered with the lid, in a 375° oven for 12 minutes. Remove the lid and bake for another 30 to 35 minutes, or until the loaf is golden brown and sounds hollow when tapped. Remove from the oven and turn the loaf out (you'll need a helper) onto a rack to cool.

BASQUE BEANS

(Ezkualdun Itarrak)

Serves 8 as a side dish

One does not eat lightly at noon if one is Basque. The tradition stems from the old days when shepherds in the hills saw the noon meal as the most important. So beans were always on the table, just as a kind of filler in case you had not had enough. I doubt that you will use this as a "filler" since the dish is so very delicious.

1½ pounds dried pink beans or dried light kidney beans, rinsed and drained

3 cups water

2 cups Beef Stock (page 78) or use canned

¾ pound boneless pork, cut in small pieces

¾ pound ham steak, with bone

1 medium yellow onion, peeled and chopped

4 cloves garlic, peeled and chopped

1 bay leaf

½ pound Spanish Chorizo Sausage (page 452) or Mexican chorizo from a good market, cut in ¾-inch pieces

Salt and freshly ground black pepper to taste

In an 8-quart heavy pot, put the beans and at least twice as much water. Cover and bring to a boil. Turn off heat and let sit for 1 hour. Drain the beans and return them to the pot. Add remaining ingredients except the chorizo, salt and pepper. Bring to a boil and simmer for 1 hour. Add the chorizo and simmer uncovered for 20 minutes, stirring occasionally. Beans should be very tender and the liquid will tend to thicken up a bit. Taste to see if it needs salt and pepper.

BASQUE PICON PUNCH

I don't usually give mixed-drink recipes in a cookbook, but after visiting Louis' Basque Corner in Reno I have to tell you about this. The origins go back to the Basque region, of course, and to a French liqueur, heavy with herbs and bitters and caramel coloring, called Picon. The Basques drink it as a before-meal appetizer, and it works as an appetizer if you limit yourself to two. Beyond that, an appetizer it is not! I enjoy these.

For a single drink:

Glass filled with ice

1½ ounces Picon (from France) or Torani Brand Amer (from San Francisco)

Shot of seltzer water

1 teaspoon grenadine

Top with splash of brandy

Lemon twist (peel only)

Both Craig, my assistant, and I are convinced that a better drink is to be made from the Torani Brand Amer. And I tell you that this is what the "boys" drink at Louis' Basque Corner!

THE CAMBODIAN
IMMIGRANTS

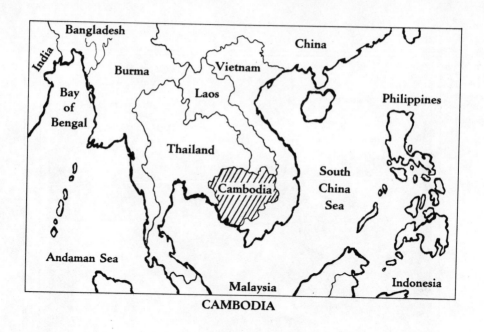

CAMBODIA

Such a beautiful people and such a tragic history!

Cambodia is surrounded by Vietnam, Laos, Thailand, and the Gulf of Thailand. During the first century it was called the Funan Empire. By the fourth century Indian immigrants had introduced Hindu customs and then the Khmer people from the north invaded during the sixth century. Thailand encroached on the western border and Vietnam expanded on the eastern side. Cambodia was drained of the wealth that had been gained from rice production and the luxury caravan trade passing through between India and China. It became a tool of the countries around it.

During the nineteenth century Cambodia fell under the influence of France and it did not gain independence until 1955. Then, when we in the West thought that things might improve for this gentle people, the Khmer Rouge, a Communist regime, took over the government and an estimated three million Cambodians were killed as the government attempted to "reeducate the masses." Most of the well-educated citizens were murdered by the regime. Most of us remember the film *The Killing Fields,* a horrifying account that the Cambodian community said showed a far milder version of events than was actually the case.

It is easy to understand why these lovely people wanted to leave. Many fled to Thailand and thousands came to America. Their Buddhist background somehow gives them a calm and insightful confidence even in the midst of such political and social turmoil. We can learn a great deal from these new Americans.

You will note from the following recipes that the food is very much like the people of Cambodia. It is delicate, not hot or spicy, and it is flavorful and sweet, just like the people. The meals are eaten while sitting on the floor and the host in the house cares for all of your needs while you are eating. One meal with these immigrant Cambodians and you will be charmed forever. I thank the Ly family for being so kind to us. The meal was unforgettable!

CAMBODIAN RAW FISH SALAD

Serves 6

Raw fish salads are common in Cambodia, Thailand, and China. Actually, they should not be called "raw," since the lime sort of cooks the fish and makes it firm and delicious. This dish should be considered no more unusual than Norwegian pickled herring. Kind of the same process, actually.

1 pound fresh cod fillet, skinless and boneless

½ cup fresh lime juice

6 fresh green beans, thinly sliced

4 scallions, thinly sliced

2 cloves garlic, peeled and crushed

1 tablespoon *nuoc mam* (fish sauce) (page 40)

1 small hot red chile, seeded and thinly sliced (optional)

1 head Bibb or iceberg lettuce leaves

GARNISHES

Fresh mint leaves

Fresh coriander (page 49)

Chop the fish very small. Place in a stainless-steel bowl and add lime juice. Allow to marinate 1½ hours in the refrigerator. Drain juice from fish. Add beans, scallions, garlic, *nuoc mam,* and optional red chile. Toss and serve in lettuce leaves with garnishes.

CAMBODIAN FRIED RICE NOODLE WITH BEEF AND BEAN CURD

Serves 6–8

I first tasted this dish at the home of the Ly family, in Tacoma, Washington. I was very taken by the kindness and gentleness of this typical Cambodian immigrant family. They invited us for dinner and taught us this dish. The wife and mother, Ly Lim Shem, was most kind. She claims no secrets as she offers these delicious dishes from her homeland.

1½ pounds boneless beef chuck or round, cut into ½-inch by 1-inch pieces

2 tablespoons peanut oil

1 15-ounce can tomato sauce

1½ teaspoons sugar

¼ cup sliced pickled garlic cloves (page 40)

¼ teaspoon cayenne pepper

1½ cups Chicken Stock (page 74) or use canned

6 cups peanut oil for deep-frying

FOR THE EGG

2 eggs, beaten well

1 teaspoon peanut oil

GARNISHES

½ red bell pepper, cored, seeded, and finely julienned

Egg, julienned

1 cake firm bean curd, cut into ¼-inch by 1-inch pieces (drained and patted dry on paper towels)

2 tablespoons *nuoc mam* (fish sauce) (page 40)

Salt and freshly ground black pepper to taste

6 ounces thin rice sticks (page 45) (found in Oriental and Vietnamese and Thai markets)

1 pound fresh bean sprouts

Fresh coriander sprigs (page 49)

Red and green bell pepper rings

In a stove-top casserole brown the beef in the peanut oil. Add the tomato sauce, 1 teaspoon of the sugar, the pickled garlic, cayenne, and Chicken Stock. Simmer until the beef is tender, about 1 hour.

Place the oil for frying in a wok or heavy pot. Deep-fry the bean curd at 375° until golden brown. Be sure the bean curd pieces have been dried a bit or they will spatter in the wok. Do one third of the pieces at a time. Drain and set aside.

Add the bean curd and *nuoc mam* (fish sauce) to the beef mixture and simmer 10 minutes more. Salt and pepper to taste. Set aside to cool.

In the same wok, deep-fry the rice sticks in small batches at 400° for just a moment as they puff up; remove and drain. Fry again at 400° until golden brown. Drain on paper towels and set aside.

Heat another wok or frying pan on low heat. Rub 1 teaspoon peanut oil on wok with a paper towel to coat the surface. Add the eggs and turn the wok to coat the surface evenly with a thin layer of egg. Cook over low heat until the egg dries out. Remove and chop into a fine julienne.

Toss the beef mixture with the fried rice sticks and bean sprouts. Remove to a large platter and top with garnishes, including the julienned egg.

CAMBODIAN BEEF SALAD

Serves 8

Mrs. Ly, our Cambodian friend in Tacoma, offered this dish at her classic table. I must tell you that the table consists of a very clean tablecloth placed upon the floor of the front room. We then sat on the floor for the feast. That is their custom. I am six feet three and a half inches tall, and it was hard to decide where I was to put my legs. Shoes are to be left at the door. While the head of the body is respected, the feet are seen as a disrespectful part of the body since they touch the dirtiness of the street and the earth. You are therefore never to touch someone else with your feet. You should have seen me trying to move my uncomfortable legs about without touching someone else with my feet! When planning your Cambodian dinner you should plan to eat on the floor . . . unless you invite me. And if you do invite me you must serve this unusually delicious meat salad.

2 pounds sirloin tip or eye of round roast

1 tablespoon light soy sauce (not "Lite"—page 46)

2 cups finely julienned cabbage

½ cup finely julienned carrots

½ cup thinly sliced celery

½ cup cored, seeded, and finely julienned red bell pepper

½ cup cored, seeded, and finely julienned green bell pepper

½ cup coarsely chopped fresh mint leaves

3 tablespoons lime juice

3 tablespoons *nuoc mam* (fish sauce) (page 40)

½ teaspoon peeled and crushed garlic

¼ ounce finely minced dried galangal (page 50) (Soak in water 1 hour; drain.)

1½ teaspoons sugar

Marinate the beef in the soy sauce for 15 minutes. Place in a pan with a roasting rack and roast in a 400° oven until medium rare or 120° on a meat thermometer. Allow the meat to cool. In a large bowl place the cabbage, carrots, celery, peppers, and mint leaves. In a small bowl mix the lime juice, *nuoc mam,* garlic, galangal, and sugar. Slice the cooled beef across the grain in thin slices. Add the beef and the dressing to the vegetables and toss well.

CAMBODIAN BEEF STEAK ON A STICK

Makes 8–10 skewers

The lovely blend of *nuoc mam* and lemongrass does good things for this common but delicious meat course. While you can do these in the electric broiler during the winter, they are really best done on the charcoal barbecue. If you teach your children to make this dish, warn them about poking themselves with the bamboo or wooden sticks. Slivers are painful. You might think about using metal skewers and offering them a good deal of help.

1 pound eye of round or sirloin tip roast

½ teaspoon salt

Pinch of sugar

Freshly ground black pepper to taste

1 stalk lemongrass (page 42), white part only, very thinly sliced

4 tablespoons *nuoc mam* (fish sauce) (page 40)

Slice the beef into long thin strips across the grain. Place the meat in a bowl with the remaining ingredients and marinate for 1 hour.

Place on wooden or bamboo skewers and barbecue to taste. A few minutes on both sides over high heat should do. Don't overcook!

CAMBODIAN SWEET PORK AND EGG

Serves 10–12

The blending of meat with sugar or sweet things is common with our Cambodian immigrant ancestors. Theirs is not a hot cuisine, in terms of spices, but more like the people themselves . . . rather subdued, genteel, and sweet. I love this easily prepared egg and pork dish.

1 quart water

2 pounds pork spareribs, sawed in half crosswise

¾ cup sugar

12 hard-boiled eggs, peeled

3 cups peeled and thinly sliced yellow onion

2 tablespoons peeled and crushed garlic

Salt to taste

Put 1 quart of water in a 4- to 6-quart pot and bring to a boil. Cut the ribs into 1- or 2-bone pieces. Add to boiling water, cover, and simmer gently for 1 hour. Drain the ribs, reserving the liquid. Place the sugar in a small deep pot and melt over medium-high heat. Stir the sugar constantly, until it turns liquid and light brown in color. Set aside and cool a few minutes. Measure out 2¼ cups of the reserved water and slowly stir it into the cooked sugar. Have a lid ready to cover the pot as the sugar will splatter when water is added. When the sugar and water are combined, reheat the syrup to melt any lumps if necessary. Return the ribs to the large pot and add the sugar water, eggs, onion, and garlic. Cover the pot and simmer ½ hour more until the ribs are very tender. Stir occasionally so that eggs color evenly. Salt to taste.

CAMBODIAN SWEET AND SOUR SOUP

Serves 6–8

This delicious soup was another dish offered us by the Ly family. This dish is probably the result of Chinese influence but the gentle touch of *nuoc mam*, or Cambodian fish sauce, changes everything completely.

2 quarts Chicken Stock (page 74) or use canned

½ pound boneless chicken breast or thighs, julienned

1 cup cored and chopped pineapple (Canned unsweetened is fine, but fresh and ripe is better.)

1 medium tomato, cut into wedges

1½ cups zucchini (cut in half lengthwise and sliced ¼ inch thick)

3 tablespoons distilled white vinegar

3 tablespoon *nuoc mam* (fish sauce) (page 40)

1 teaspoon sugar

Salt to taste

½ pound medium prawns, peeled

¼ pound shelled crabmeat

Pinch of ground white pepper (optional)

Place all ingredients, except the prawns, crab, and white pepper, in a 4-quart kettle. Cover and simmer for 1 hour. Add the remaining ingredients and bring just up to serving temperature. Serve immediately.

THE CUBAN
IMMIGRANTS

CUBA

I really think that the Cuban immigrant has been very misunderstood by most other Americans. The images and stereotypes that are common here in the United States simply do not relate properly to the facts. Cuban immigrants have a very low rate of unemployment and a very high median annual income, and at least half of the Cuban Americans have graduated from high school. Yet stereotypes persist, due, I suppose, to the fact that these people are proud of their background and their heritage and therefore continue to speak Spanish at home and within the Cuban business community. In other words, they are often marked as "foreigners" when in reality they are committed Americans.

The relationship of our government with the government in Cuba has been a bit strange. We have liberated the Cubans, occupied the land, invaded, and boycotted, at one time or another. It remains a Communist state in the hands of Castro, and it is only ninety miles off the American coast.

The history of the Cubans is fascinating and tragic. Columbus came to the island in 1492 and found the Arawak tribal people living there. He claimed the whole lot for Spain. After the Spanish invaded by the boatload in 1511 they gradually killed off the natives and then had to bring in black slaves from Africa to keep the sugar-cane business going.

The island had always been important because of its location in the midst of the trade routes. It was for that very reason that the Spanish invaded. In 1898 Teddy Roosevelt and his Rough Riders became famous when they drove out the Spanish at the battle of San Juan Hill. The United States was at first a liberator, but then it became a very unwanted governor of Cuba. In 1909 our troops moved out and in 1933 Batista became dictator. He was overthrown by Fidel Castro in 1959. Americans were optimistic, but it then became apparent that Castro was setting up a Communist state. During the Kennedy administration we sent well-trained Cuban Americans into Cuba to oust Castro . . . and the result was the horrible Bay of Pigs event. The invasion failed and the invaders, Cuban defectors to America, were either killed on the spot or imprisoned for twenty-five years . . . and we did nothing to help them.

What does all this have to do with food? Well, the history of the Cuban immigrant first of all points to ethnic pride. The language and the food of the old country preserve that pride and memory. Many immigrants came to this country during the Castro regime, and most were well educated and very creative. And they brought great cooks with them.

The food of the Cuban immigrant is just wonderful. Black Beans and Rice, Black Bean Soup, Vaca Frita (Fried Beef), Yellow Rice, the famous Cuban Sandwich, and Flan. What a menu and what memories of times in Cuba when things were not as they are. Better to make a new life in America!

CUBAN BLACK BEAN SOUP

A simple version of this dish can be made just by thinning the Cuban Black Bean dish (page 110). Add enough Chicken Stock (page 74) to thin your leftover beans down to the desired consistency and simmer until all is smooth and delicious. It is that simple, and I am sure that this is the method used by immigrant Cuban grandmas who had large families to feed. Who could, or can, afford any waste? Be frugal and use everything.

NOTE: You might wish to add a little more vinegar and black pepper to "soup it up"!

CUBAN BLACK BEANS

Serves 6 as a starch dish

The black bean is as important to the Cuban diet as is the potato to many other immigrant groups. The bean was made into soup, cooked with rice, and cooked as in this dish, where it is more than just a starch. It can be a whole meal. You can imagine how necessary this food product was to the Cuban immigrants—it was cheap, nutritious, and tasted like the Island.

1 pound dried black beans, rinsed

4 cups water

3 cloves garlic, peeled and crushed

1 medium green bell pepper, cored, seeded, and chopped

1 medium yellow onion, peeled and chopped

¼ pound salt pork, chopped

1 pound smoked ham hocks, cut into 1½-inch pieces

2 teaspoons paprika

3 teaspoons ground cumin

2 bay leaves

4 cups Chicken Stock (page 74) or use canned

¼ teaspoon chili powder

1 tablespoon red wine vinegar

Salt and freshly ground black pepper to taste

Wash the beans and place them in a 6-quart stove-top casserole with 4 cups water. Cover and boil 2 minutes; shut off the heat and let stand 1 hour. Add the remaining ingredients, except the vinegar and salt and pepper, cover, and simmer 2 hours until the beans are tender. You may have to add a bit of fresh water to the pot as the beans should be just covered with water when you begin the second cooking stage. At completion, debone the hocks, chop up the meat, and return it to the pot.

Add the vinegar and the salt and pepper to taste. Bring to a simmer and heat all through.

CUBAN BLACK BEANS AND RICE

Serves 3–4

The name for this dish in Spanish, *Moros y Cristianos,* refers to the terrible battles in Spain between the Moors and the Christians, the battle between the blacks and the whites. Thus this blend of black beans and white rice is seen on every Cuban table, and is a reminder of the Spanish influence in Cuban history.

> 2 cups fresh-cooked long-grain rice (1 cup dry rice)
>
> 1 cup cooked Cuban Black Beans (page 110)

Drain the cooked black beans for just a moment in a colander. Combine with fresh-cooked rice. Stir until evenly incorporated.

CUBAN ROPA VIEJA

Serves 8

I love this dish and I love the name. It refers to the fact that the shredded meat looks like "rags," literally, "old clothes." It is tender and delicious, and points to the fact that immigrants from Cuba cooked a cheap cut of beef until it was so tender that you thought it was expensive!

> 1 3½-pound beef chuck or pot roast
>
> Salt and freshly ground black pepper to taste
>
> ⅓ cup olive oil
>
> 1 cup water
>
> 1 large yellow onion, peeled and sliced
>
> 2 cloves garlic, peeled and crushed
>
> 1 green bell pepper, cored, seeded, and chopped
>
> 1 cup tomato sauce
>
> 1 teaspoon salt
>
> 1 bay leaf
>
> ½ cup dry wine

Rub salt and pepper into the meat. Heat a large covered frying pan or stove-top casserole and add a bit of the oil. Brown the meat well on both sides, and then add about 1 cup of water. Cover and simmer until very tender, about 2 hours. If the pan dries out during cooking, add more water. Allow the meat to cool, covered, in the pan juices. Remove the meat from the pan; debone and shred the meat. Set aside in a bowl, along with the pan juices.

Reheat the pan and add the remaining oil. Sauté the onion and garlic, just until clear. Add the green pepper and sauté for a few minutes more. Add the remaining ingredients, including the shredded meat and juices. Cover and simmer on low heat for 15 to 20 minutes more.

Serve with rice or salad.

YELLOW RICE

This sounds like a strange dish for those of us who have been raised on white rice. However, this dish goes back to the times when Spanish immigrants could afford saffron, the most expensive seasoning in the world. In our time very little saffron is used and annatto oil is usually substituted. If you can afford the saffron, use it, of course. But our Cuban immigrant grandmas needed to use this old cheater's method.

2 tablespoons olive oil	1 teaspoon salt
3 cloves garlic, peeled and chopped	1 tablespoon Annatto Oil (page 134)
1 medium yellow onion, peeled and diced	Pinch of saffron (optional)
1 medium red bell pepper, cored, seeded, and diced	2 cups Uncle Ben's Converted Rice
1 cup frozen peas	4 cups water
1 teaspoon paprika	

Heat a 4-quart heavy covered pot and add the oil, garlic, onion, and bell pepper. Sauté for a few minutes until the vegetables are tender. Add the remaining ingredients, cover, and simmer over low heat 20 to 25 minutes until the rice is tender and the liquid is absorbed.

NOTE: You can use the same recipe but omit annatto, saffron, and paprika and use 1 envelope Vigo coloring (page 47). This is common among American Cuban cooks and can be found in Latino markets.

VACA FRITA

Serves 4

I had never seen or heard of this dish until we ran across La Teresita Cuban Restaurant in Tampa, Florida. It is filled with people of Cuban background, and run by Cubans as well. This dish, a simple matter of fried beef, is one of the original owner Max's specials, and a fine dish it is. It is prepared the night before and then grilled at the last minute. Wonderful!

2 pounds flank steak

2 whole bay leaves

6 black peppercorns

2 tablespoons chopped parsley

MARINADE

1 teaspoon garlic powder

½ teaspoon freshly ground black pepper

1 teaspoon ground cumin

1 teaspoon onion powder

2 teaspoons salt

Pinch of MSG (optional)

3 tablespoons dry sherry

2 tablespoons olive oil

GARNISH

2 medium yellow onions, peeled and sliced

Lemon wedges

2 medium green bell peppers, cored, seeded, and sliced

Place the flank steak in a 6-quart covered pot and add just enough water to cover. Add the bay leaves, peppercorns, and parsley. Simmer, covered, until tender, about 1½ hours. Allow to cool in the liquid, covered, as long as overnight in the refrigerator.

Mix the dry spices for the marinade. Cut the meat, across the grain, into serving-size pieces and pound each piece with a wooden or metal meat pounder. This should increase the size of each piece by about half. Rub each piece with a bit of the marinade mixture and then splash each piece with dry sherry. Allow to marinate for a moment.

Heat a flat griddle and add the olive oil. Fry each piece of meat just until it barely browns on each side. Fry the onions and peppers along with the meat, just until they are tender but not mushy. Place all on a plate along with lemon wedge garnish.

YELLOW RICE WITH CHICKEN

Serves 4–5

This dish is exactly what it says it is. Wonderful roasted chicken is served atop yellow rice. It is a common Cuban method of serving and it is great eating!

- 1 3-pound fryer chicken, cut up into 8 serving pieces
- 4 cloves garlic, peeled and crushed
- 1 teaspoon dried oregano
- 1 teaspoon salt

- Freshly ground black pepper to taste
- 1 batch Yellow Rice (page 112)
- 2 tablespoons olive oil

Rub the chicken pieces all over with the garlic, oregano, salt, and pepper. Marinate, covered, 1 hour on the kitchen counter or overnight in the refrigerator.

Heat a large SilverStone-lined frying pan and add the oil. Pan-fry the chicken pieces over medium heat until golden brown, about 15 minutes per side.

Serve on top of Yellow Rice.

CUBAN SANDWICH

This one is so simple that I can only describe it. I do not even know if you can find such a thing in Cuba, but you can certainly find this sandwich in any community where there are lots of Cuban immigrants. In Miami, Tampa, and New York, you must get in line to try this dish.

Tampa's La Teresita restaurant has been called by *USA Today* the home of "the Best Cuban Sandwich in America." Here is their recipe as given us by George Capdevila. He is one of the sons of Max, the fellow who originally opened the place. I will just give George's directions since they are so simple.

"We can seldom find the kind of soft French bread that is necessary for this wonderful dish so I buy a "poor boy" loaf and cut it into sections, place them in a plastic bag, and then zonk them for just a minute or so in the microwave. This makes the bread soft enough so that it can be properly pressed in the sandwich toaster.

"Heat a sandwich toaster . . . the kind you use for toasted cheese. Find one that will open wide enough to take this treasure. I have a Bosch. It works well.

"Slice the bread in half lengthwise and add:
  Butter
  Mustard
  Mayonnaise
  Roast pork, cold and not overcooked, thinly sliced
  Boiled ham, thinly sliced
  Swiss cheese, thinly sliced
  Dill pickle slices, *very optional* (I dislike them!)

"Butter both the inside and the outside of the bread. Construct the sandwich according to your taste and place in a preheated sandwich press. Toast to your taste and serve."

Channing, my son, thinks this is the best use of French bread . . . ever!

CUBAN LAMB SHANKS

Serves 4–5

I know, it looks like almost every immigrant group that came to the New World brought along a recipe for lamb shanks. Well, what would you expect? The shanks were cheap, money was short, and the dish was rich. So try this one. It is rich and it used to be inexpensive. Have your butcher save lamb shanks for you. They freeze well if they are fresh when he gets them.

- 1 tablespoon olive oil
- 3 cloves garlic, peeled and finely chopped
- 1 medium yellow onion, peeled and chopped
- 3 pounds lamb shanks, sawed in 1½-inch pieces (Have your butcher do this.)
- 1 8-ounce can tomato sauce

- 1 tablespoon Annatto Oil (page 134)
- 2 tablespoons chopped parsley
- Salt and freshly ground black pepper to taste
- ¼ teaspoon dried oregano
- ¼ teaspoon ground cumin
- 1 cup Chicken Stock (page 74) *or* use canned

Heat a 4- to 6-quart stove-top covered casserole. Add olive oil, garlic, and onion. Sauté for 5 minutes. Add lamb shanks along with remaining ingredients, cover, and simmer 1 hour and 45 minutes, until lamb is very tender.

These can be served with Yellow Rice (page 112) or white rice.

FRIED PLANTAINS

This is a common dish in Cuba, as it is in Puerto Rico and Jamaica. See page 394 for a recipe.

FLAN

Serves 6–8 as a classic dessert

Tacoma, Washington, has a large and well-educated Cuban community.
They are just terrific, and the parties they throw are beyond belief. They
fled Cuba when Castro adopted the Communist line and they came here.
I am glad they did!

This is a recipe from my friend Rosa Capestany; a more charming
cook you will never find.

THE FLAN MIXTURE

5 eggs, beaten

1 14-ounce can sweetened
condensed milk (I prefer
Eagle Brand.)

1 cup milk

1 teaspoon vanilla

THE CARAMEL

½ cup sugar plus 1
tablespoon water

Blend all the ingredients for the flan, mix well, and set aside.

Heat a very small heavy saucepan and add the sugar and water. Stir
constantly with a wooden spoon over medium-low heat until the sugar
melts and just begins to turn a light tan color. Remove from the heat and
pour the caramel into an oiled 1-quart mold. (A porcelain soufflé mold
will work well, or an enameled-iron saucepan. Be sure the pan is oiled
well!) Allow the caramel to cool for a moment. Pour in the flan mixture
and cover the top with aluminum foil. The foil cover must be very tight!

Place the dish or pan in about 2 inches of water in a cake-baking pan.
The water should be hot and the oven heated to about 350°. Bake about
1 hour or until the tip of an inserted knife comes out clean. Chill the
dish, still covered, overnight. Invert, take from the mold, and serve.

THE ETHIOPIAN
IMMIGRANTS

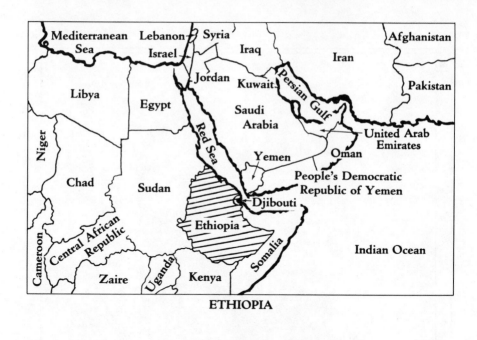

ETHIOPIA

The immigrants who came to these shores from Ethiopia, also called Abyssinia, came from a most ancient and interesting culture. They trace their history back at least two thousand years to the Kingdom of Aksum, the land of the Blue Nile.

The early peoples of this land seem to have come from Arabia, so although they live in the region that is commonly called the Horn of Africa, they are not of the black peoples we normally think of in Africa. Legend claims that for the most part the people in Ethiopia were Jews, members of the household of King Solomon and the Queen of Sheba. You can see from the map how easy it was for them to go up to Israel for the holy celebrations, and, according to the book of Acts in the Bible, an Ethiopian eunuch, a member of the royal household, was converted to Christianity by Saint Philip. The eunuch—we do not know his name—returned to his homeland "rejoicing" and a great conversion took place in Ethiopia.

The son of King Solomon and the Queen of Sheba, Menelik I, was the first in a series of kings and emperors that ended in 1975 with the death of Haile Selassie, "The King of Kings of Ethiopia, Lion of Judah, the Elect of God." From the beginning of this kingdom, the people, often called "Solomids," had 225 emperors. That may sound like a lot but please remember that Rome claims 264 popes for the same period of time. The Ethiopian kingdom appears to have been more stable than the throne of Rome.

In the very early days this was a rich and influential nation. During more recent times it has become the sixth poorest nation in the world, and the problems of starvation and bitter political battles account for the recent immigration to this country. With the immigration came two wonderful Ethiopian treasures, the Ethiopian Orthodox Church and Ethiopian cuisine.

By the fourth century Christianity became the national religion. Most Americans think that the tradition of the Ethiopian Orthodox Church is Coptic, which is an Egyptian tradition. The confusion has come about because in recent times the Church received its archbishops from the Egyptian Church, but this is no longer the case, nor were the Ethiopians ever Coptic themselves. They now have their own Patriarch and the Ethiopian Orthodox Church is quite independent. American Greek Orthodox Christians have stepped forward to support the Ethiopian immigrants and in many cases the Greeks have offered a portion of their church facilities to their Ethiopian Orthodox brothers and sisters. I was asked to preach one morning at the Ethiopian Church here in Seattle, a parish assisted by the Greek Orthodox Church of the Assumption, and I was very taken by the ancient traditions: the color, the chanting, the liturgical movement of the service, all ancient and Ethiopian. So beautiful.

One of the most important functions of ethnic churches in America is that of preserving and teaching the traditions of our ancestors. When the immigrants came to this nation the ethnic church had to come along, for it is in the ethnic church that the children are taught what it means to be Ethiopian, Latvian, Lithuanian, et cetera. These ethnic churches are great gifts to America.

The second wonderful gift that the Ethiopian immigrants have brought to us is their food. I know of no other culture that eats in this manner, and I have become converted to these flavors. And the conversion was not difficult at all.

Everything is eaten communally, so that you always understand that all things are to be shared with those around you. There is no silverware since everything is eaten with a bit of wonderful Injera Bread, a product close to a very thin pancake. Finally, the spices add their particular color to the Ethiopian feast. The following recipes will provide you with a great variety of dishes, and most of these would be served at a single meal. You will love the food, and no, it is not that hot. But I warn you, be prepared to chop onions, onions, and more onions. Our Ethiopian immigrant ancestors brought their love for the onion with them!

INJERA BREAD

Makes 8 breads

This is great fun. The recent immigrants from Ethiopia have opened some fine restaurants in this country and you simply cannot eat the food in a proper manner without this bread. In Ethiopia in earlier days the bread of Ethiopia was made from *teff,* a name which in the native tongue means "lost." The name comes from the fact that the grain is so tiny that when you drop it on the dirt floor of a house it is lost. Too small to retrieve! In modern times wheat flour is more commonly used.

3 cups warm water

3 tablespoons club soda

2½ cups self-rising flour (Gold Medal works best.) (See Hint, page 423.)

Put the warm water into a food blender. Add the flour to the water and blend, slowly at first, and then with rapid speed. You should probably do this in two batches unless you have a very large and powerful blender. A food processor will work too, but you must remember to scrape down the sides of the mixing bowls with a rubber spatula regardless of which machine you use.

Place the batter in a 6-cup bowl and stir in the club soda.

Heat a 12-inch electric frying pan, SilverStone lined, to 400°. Using a ladle pour ¼ cup of batter onto one corner of the hot pan. Immediately tilt the pan about to cover the bottom of the pan evenly with the batter. Cook, uncovered, until the top of the pancakelike bread is filled with holes and no longer wet. The edges should begin to curl just a bit. Remove quickly with your fingers and place the bread on a kitchen towel. Let it cool for 3 or 4 minutes as you prepare the next bread. Place the cooled breads on a plate.

Continue this process until all of the batter is used. Stack the cooled breads one on top of the other and then cover with plastic wrap until dinner.

These wonderful breads can be made up to 3 hours ahead of dinner.

BERBERE SAUCE

Makes 1¼ cups

Here is another ingredient basic to the Ethiopian kitchen that I think is best made by oneself. It is not all that difficult and it keeps well in the refrigerator. There is simply no substitute, and once you have prepared this and the following recipe of Spiced Butter, you are ready to launch an Ethiopian feast. This stuff is delicious beyond belief!

2 teaspoons cumin seeds

4 whole cloves

½ teaspoon cardamom seeds (page 49)

½ teaspoon whole black peppercorns

¼ teaspoon whole allspice

1 teaspoon whole fenugreek seeds (page 50)

½ cup dried onion flakes

3 ounces red New Mexican chiles (page 38), stemmed and seeded

3 small dried long hot red chiles, seeded

½ teaspoon ground ginger

½ teaspoon freshly ground nutmeg

¼ teaspoon ground turmeric

1 teaspoon garlic powder

2 teaspoons salt

½ cup salad or peanut oil

½ cup dry red wine

Cayenne pepper to taste (You may like this a bit hot. I start with 1 teaspoon and go from there.)

Mix together the cumin, cloves, cardamom, black peppercorns, allspice, and fenugreek seeds. Place in a small frying pan over medium heat. Stir constantly until they release their fragrance, about 1 to 2 minutes. Do not burn or discolor the spices. Cool completely.

Combine the toasted spices and all the other ingredients, except the oil and the wine, in a spice grinder or electric coffee grinder (page 23) and grind fine in batches. This may take a few minutes. Keep your face away from the machine as it will release a very spicy aroma that may irritate your eyes or throat.

Place the spice blend in a bowl and add the oil and wine. Add cayenne pepper to taste. Stir until thick and store in a closed plastic container in the refrigerator.

SPICED BUTTER

Makes 3 cups

When you think of the heat of the Ethiopian climate, and the fact that most people do not have refrigeration, you must wonder about this common ingredient. Please understand that this butter is cooked until it becomes a ghee, or clarified butter. It keeps very well since the milk solids that actually cause the butter to go rancid are removed. What remains is a cooking oil of incredible flavor. No, you cannot substitute margarine.

4 teaspoons finely grated fresh ginger

1½ teaspoons ground turmeric

¼ teaspoon cardamom seeds (page 49)

1 stick cinnamon, 1 inch long

⅛ teaspoon freshly ground nutmeg

3 whole cloves

2 pounds salted butter

1 small yellow onion, peeled and coarsely chopped

3 tablespoons peeled and finely chopped garlic

Measure out the spices on a plate.

Melt the butter in a heavy saucepan over moderate heat. Bring the butter up to a light boil. When the surface is covered with a white foam, stir in all remaining ingredients, including the onion and garlic. Reduce the heat to low and cook, uncovered, for about 45 minutes. Do not stir again.

Milk solids will form in the bottom of the pan and they should cook until they are golden brown. The butter will be clear.

Strain the mixture through several layers of cheesecloth placed in a colander. Avoid the milk solids and discard them.

Store the spiced butter in a quart jar, covered, in the refrigerator. It will keep for about 3 months under refrigeration.

LAMB AND CARDAMOM

Serves 8 as part of an Ethiopian meal

The first time I tasted this dish I was at the Kokeb restaurant in Seattle. I have tried it at other Ethiopian restaurants in this country and I have never been satisfied as well as with the Kokeb version. This is as close as I can come to their dish. The secret is lots of cardamom. It is eaten with the fingers with Injera Bread. Wonderful!

3 cups peeled and thinly sliced in onions (Use half yellow and half red onions.)

½ cup Spiced Butter (page 124)

2 pounds lean lamb, cut into ¾-inch cubes

¼ cup Berbere Sauce (page 123)

¼ teaspoon ground cumin

1 teaspoon freshly ground cardamom seeds (page 49)

1 teaspoon grated fresh ginger

2 cloves garlic, peeled and crushed

½ teaspoon freshly ground black pepper

½ cup dry red wine

1 cup water

Salt to taste

Heat a large frying pan and sauté the onion in 1 tablespoon of the butter, covered, until very tender. Use low heat so that the onion and butter are not browned. Remove from the pan and set aside.

Heat the pan again and brown the lamb over high heat with another tablespoon of the butter. You will probably need to do this in two batches. Set aside.

Place the sautéed onions, along with the remaining butter, in a heavy 6-quart saucepan. Add the Berbere Sauce, cumin, cardamom, ginger, garlic, black pepper, and wine. Bring to a simmer and add the lamb. Bring to a simmer again and add the water. Cook, covered, until the lamb is very tender, about 50 minutes. Stir several times.

If the sauce is not thick enough, cook uncovered for a few minutes to reduce and thicken the sauce.

Add salt to taste and serve.

SPICED CHEESE

Serves 6–8 as part of an Ethiopian meal

This is another basic. Remember that the classic Ethiopian meal consists of many small courses . . . and that custom has not changed here with our Ethiopian immigrants.

1 pound dry-curd cottage cheese (page 39) or farmer cheese

2 tablespoons Spiced Butter (page 124), softened

1 teaspoon cayenne pepper

Freshly ground black pepper to taste

Salt to taste

Mix all of the ingredients, being careful not to break up the curds. This is just delicious!

ETHIOPIAN LENTILS

Serves 6–8 as part of an Ethiopian meal

Many cultures enjoy lentils, but few can pack in the flavor that you will find in this Ethiopian classic. It is almost as if meat is unnecessary to the meal.

2 cups dried lentils, picked over and washed

6 cups water

¾ cup seeded and chopped Anaheim green peppers (page 36)

2 cups peeled and chopped red onions

¼ cup Spiced Butter (page 124)

1 tablespoon grated fresh ginger

2 cloves garlic, peeled and crushed

1 tablespoon Berbere Sauce (page 123)

Freshly ground black pepper to taste

Boil the lentils in the water for 5 minutes. Drain, reserving the liquid. In a 4-quart saucepot sauté the Anaheim peppers and onions in the spiced butter until the onions are tender. Add the lentils, 4 cups of the reserved liquid, and the remaining ingredients and bring to a simmer. Cook, covered, over low heat 35 to 40 minutes, stirring occasionally to prevent sticking.

KIFTO RAW BEEF

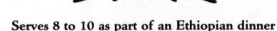

Serves 8 to 10 as part of an Ethiopian dinner

I think that this is my favorite Ethiopian dish. The flavors are so rich that you need put only a small bit on your Injera Bread to enjoy yourself. Please do not be put off by the fact that the beef is not cooked. The spices and peppers would never let you know that!!!

½ cup Spiced Butter (page 124)

½ cup peeled and finely chopped yellow onions

3 tablespoons cored, seeded, and finely chopped green bell peppers

½ teaspoon peeled and finely chopped garlic

2 tablespoons seeded and finely chopped fresh hot green jalapeño peppers

1 teaspoon cayenne pepper

1 teaspoon grated fresh ginger

½ teaspoon freshly ground cardamom seeds (page 49)

1 tablespoon freshly squeezed lemon juice

4 teaspoons Berbere Sauce (page 123)

2 teaspoons salt

2 pounds lean beef sirloin, freshly ground very coarse in your meat grinder

Heat a 10-inch frying pan and add the butter. Sauté the onions, green bell peppers, garlic, jalapeños, cayenne, ginger, and cardamom for about 2 minutes, and then remove the mixture to a bowl. Allow to cool a bit.

Add the lemon juice, Berbere Sauce, and salt to the cooled vegetable mixture.

Mix the ground meat and the spiced vegetable mixture. Mound on a platter or on Injera Bread (page 122) and serve.

DORO WAT CHICKEN

Serves 6–8 as part of an Ethiopian meal

The term "stew" simply does not work with the Ethiopian cook. The concept of simmering a fowl until tender is much more profound in the Ethiopian kitchen than it is in most American kitchens. The spicy flavors just do something to that chicken that normal cooking will not do. I dare you not to fall in love with this dish.

1 whole fryer chicken (about 3 pounds), cut into 8 serving pieces

Juice of 1 lime

5 cups peeled and thinly sliced red onions (Red are preferred for this dish, but yellow will do fine.)

½ cup Spiced Butter (page 124)

½ cup Berbere Sauce (page 123)

½ cup dry red wine

2 cloves garlic, peeled and crushed

2 teaspoons cayenne pepper

½ teaspoon grated fresh ginger

½ cup water

Salt to taste

4 hard-boiled eggs, peeled

½ teaspoon freshly ground black pepper

Place the chicken pieces in a bowl and marinate for 1 hour in the lime juice.

In a heavy saucepan sauté the onions in 2 tablespoons of the Spiced Butter. Cover the pot and cook the onions over low heat until they are very tender, but not browned. Stir them occasionally.

Add the remaining butter to the pot, along with the Berbere Sauce, wine, garlic, cayenne, and ginger. Add ½ cup of water and mix well.

Bring to a simmer and add the chicken pieces. Cook, covered, for 30 to 40 minutes or until the chicken is tender, adding more water if you need to in order to keep the sauce from drying out.

When the chicken is tender, taste for salt. Add the peeled eggs and heat through. Top with the black pepper and serve.

COLLARD GREENS AND SPICED CHEESE

(Yegomen Kitfo)

Serves 6 as part of an Ethiopian meal

This dish looks much more complicated than it really is. When you read the recipe try to taste the ingredients. That will convince you that this dish *must* be present at your Ethiopian feast.

THE CHEESE

- 2 cloves garlic, peeled and finely chopped
- ¼ cup Spiced Butter (page 124)
- ¼ teaspoon freshly ground cardamom seeds (page 49)
- Salt and freshly ground black pepper to taste
- 1 pound dry-curd cottage cheese (page 39) or farmer cheese

Sauté the garlic in the spiced butter for a few moments. Add the cardamom, salt, and pepper. Remove from the burner and allow to cool. Stir into the cheese.

THE GREENS

- 2 pounds collard greens or kale, the stems trimmed off and discarded and the leaves chopped
- ½ cup water
- ½ teaspoon cayenne pepper
- 1 teaspoon freshly ground black pepper
- 1 teaspoon peeled and crushed garlic
- ¼ cup Spiced Butter (page 124)
- 3 tablespoons peeled and coarsely chopped yellow onion
- Salt to taste

Cook the greens, covered, in a 4-quart saucepan along with about ½ cup water. Then add the cayenne, black pepper, garlic, spiced butter, and chopped onion. Cook, covered, until the greens collapse and then allow the dish to cool a bit. Salt to taste.

To serve, drain the greens a bit and place on a platter or on Injera Bread. Spoon the cheese over the greens and serve . . . or you may mix them both together before serving. That is the way I prefer this wonderful dish.

THE FILIPINO
IMMIGRANTS

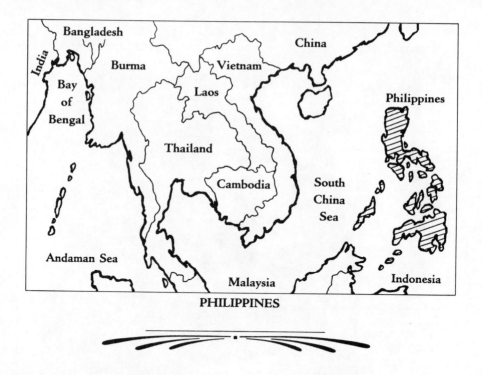

PHILIPPINES

O ur Filipino immigrant ancestors left a most beautiful land to journey here. The Philippine archipelago consists of 7,100 islands, which stretch 1,152 miles! Most of these are mountainous islands surrounded by coral reefs, the largest being Luzon where the capital of Manila is located.

The peoples of the Philippines come from diverse ethnic backgrounds, the result of migration from Malaysia, Indonesia, and China. They had little or no contact with the West.

In 1521 it happened. The Spanish really got around in those days and they took on just about everybody and anybody. Ferdinand Magellan reached the island of Samar and claimed the whole archipelago for Spain and the Roman Catholic Church. When Philip II came to the Spanish throne in 1565 he established a colonial rule that lasted three hundred years. That is a long time for a people to be used for the benefit of another nation. The Spanish and the Roman Church controlled the government, education, and vast estates. All for Spain!

Following the Spanish-American War, control of the islands passed to the United States through the Treaty of Paris in 1898. This relationship lasted for forty-seven years. Eventually the legislative powers were shifted to the Filipino people and the country became a commonwealth. Following World War II the Philippines were declared independent and by 1955 they were seen as a model of democracy in Asia.

During this period one Ferdinand Marcos was elected senator in 1949. In 1966 he was elected president. Marcos increased his power in 1972 by declaring martial law and he ruled on in the midst of extraordinary greed and corruption. Since he was elected to the senate in 1949 I must assume that he was up to his neck in the pork barrel. It was obviously his own disregard for his people that led to his downfall in the eighties. During this time Filipino immigration to the United States was on the increase because many opponents of Marcos felt compelled to flee. Poverty was also a motivator, of course. But these were not the first Filipino visitors to America.

Early in the twentieth century the first American civil governor of the islands, William Howard Taft, encouraged young men to come to the United States for their studies. Some fourteen thousand students had come by 1938, were educated here, and then returned to their homeland. During this same time the largest ethnic immigrant group working in the Hawaiian fields was Filipino. They are still there, though plantation life is not at all what it once was. I have tasted some very fine Filipino food in Honolulu. Later immigration to the United States brought hotel, restaurant, and domestic workers. And in reaction to the Marcos regime many people came here for simple economic reasons. Most were technical workers or professionals, in particular, medical personnel. Their situation was very different from that of their countrymen who preceded them. Professional or otherwise, between 1965 and 1974 only Mexico sent more immigrants to the United States.

The following selection of recipes is about as legitimate as you can get when it comes to Filipino immigrant cooking. Kare Kare, or oxtails cooked with tripe in peanut sauce, is my favorite. You are right, this is not a cuisine that can be called "high class," but it is a cuisine that can be called delicious. The Lumpias are heaven and the Chicken and Pork Adobo is simple and sensational. Make a meal of any or all of these and you will be quite happy. You might even try the Pork Cooked in Pork Blood. Calm down! It is a delicious dish. Now then, enjoy the presence of our wonderful Filipino immigrants.

ANNATTO OIL

Makes 2 cups

Along with the Filipino immigrants came their cooking methods, and their shortcuts. This oil is used in Portuguese, Spanish, Basque, Mexican, Puerto Rican, Cuban, Jamaican, and Filipino cooking. In short, you had better make some. It is used in cooking for the lovely color and bitterness of saffron, but it is much less expensive.

2 cups vegetable oil

1 cup annatto seeds (page 36) (Find these in any Filipino or Latino market. Look for them in bulk as they will be much less expensive than in those little cellophane bags.)

Place the oil in a 2-quart heavy saucepan and heat to about 350°. Add the annatto seeds and remove the pan from the heat. Allow to cool and strain the oil into a glass jar. Store in the refrigerator.

KARE KARE

Serves 4–6

Just the description of this dish will turn some people off, but they are the losers since this mixture of beef tails, tripe, and peanut sauce is just my favorite Filipino dish. It is not strong in flavor and goes great with a bowl of rice.

¼ cup peanut oil

3 pounds oxtails

2 pounds beef tripe

1 yellow onion, peeled and sliced

3 cloves garlic, peeled and crushed

1 tomato, chopped

1¼ cups Beef Stock (page 78) or use canned

1¼ cups water

Salt to taste

2 tablespoons Annatto Oil (page 134)

3 tablespoons peanut butter mixed with ½ cup hot tap water

Several shots of Tabasco, or more to taste

Heat a large frying pan and add 3 tablespoons of the peanut oil. Brown the oxtails well on both sides in 2 or 3 batches. Place them in a 6-quart heavy stove-top covered casserole.

While the oxtails are browning bring 3 quarts of water to a boil and blanch the tripe. Simply boil it for a few minutes, drain, and cool. Cut the tripe into strips ½ inch wide and 3 inches long. Add these to the oxtail pot.

Add the remaining peanut oil to the frying pan and sauté the onion and garlic. Add to the oxtail pot along with the tomato, Beef Stock, water, salt, and annatto oil. Cover and simmer for 1½ hours. Simmer partially covered for another 1½ hours, stirring now and then. At the beginning of the last hour of cooking add the peanut butter mixture and the Tabasco. Taste and add more Tabasco and salt if needed. If all is not very tender, continue to cook a bit longer.

Serve with rice.

MUNG BEANS WITH PORK

Serves 8

This is kind of a Filipino pork and beans dish. It is certainly not expensive and it points to the wisdom of our Filipino immigrant grandmothers who had to feed their families on very little. This is tasty and filling.

2 cups dry mung beans, preferably hulled (page 42) (Find these in a Chinese or Filipino market.)

2 tablespoons peanut oil

1 yellow onion, peeled and sliced

2 cloves garlic, peeled and thinly sliced

4¼ cups Chicken Stock (page 74) or use canned

1 very thin slice of fresh ginger

Salt and white pepper to taste

1 pound Chinese-style roasted side pork, thinly sliced and cut into 1-inch squares (You can find this in a Chinese barbecue shop.) or 1 pound cooked pork roast, cut into small cubes

Soak the beans overnight. If they have not been hulled, make sure the soaking water covers the beans amply. Rub them together with your hands so that most of the hulls float away. They will rise to the top of the water and can be easily removed. Rinse the beans, drain, and set aside.

Heat a 6-quart stove-top covered casserole and add the peanut oil. Sauté the yellow onion and garlic for a moment and add the drained beans, along with the Chicken Stock and ginger. Bring to a boil and then turn to a simmer. Cook for 15 minutes, covered, and then remove the ginger slice. Continue to cook, covered, until the beans are tender and the soup is thick, about 15 more minutes. Add the salt and white pepper to taste, along with the cooked pork. (If you can get Chinese roasted side pork, the dish will be far superior to the plain roast-pork version. In either case you will enjoy it.) Cook the dish until the pork is heated through—and enjoy.

LUMPIA

Makes about 12

This is the Filipino version of the Chinese egg roll, and I like it much better. You can buy these in the streets in Manila and in any Filipino restaurant in this country. It is one of those dishes that made the immigration trip very well.

½ pound pork loin, julienned

½ pound shrimp, peeled, coarsely chopped

2 tablespoons peanut oil

4 cloves garlic, peeled and crushed

1 cup chopped Napa cabbage (page 43)

½ cup chopped green beans, fresh or frozen

½ cup chopped scallions

2 teaspoons salt

½ teaspoon freshly ground black pepper

2 tablespoons light soy sauce (not "Lite"—see page 46)

1 cup fresh bean sprouts

5 cups peanut oil for deep frying

Lumpia wrappers (page 42) (These can be found in many Oriental markets as well as Filipino markets. They come frozen in 8-inch squares, 20 to 30 wrappers per package.)

Heat a large wok and add the oil and garlic. Chow for just a moment and add the pork. Stir-fry for 2 minutes on medium-high heat and add the shrimp. Cook just until they change color and add all remaining ingredients, except the bean sprouts, peanut oil, and wrappers. When all is hot and the cabbage has collapsed, add the bean sprouts. Toss for a moment. Place this filling in a colander, drain completely, and allow to cool.

Roll the Lumpias. Place 2 tablespoons of the cooled filling in one corner of a single wrapper. Roll it up, turning in each end, like a Chinese spring roll. Moisten the last corner just a bit so that it will stick. Place the rolls with the seam side down and cover with plastic as you continue to roll the others.

Place the frying oil in an electric frying pan and set the temperature at 375°.

Deep-fry the rolls in the heated oil, a few at a time, for about 3 minutes, just until golden and crunchy. Keep the fried Lumpias warm in a preheated, warm oven while you prepare the rest.

Serve with Lumpia Sauce (recipe follows).

LUMPIA SAUCE

Makes about 2 cups

4 tablespoons sugar

¼ cup light soy sauce (not
"Lite"—see page 46)

1 cup Chicken Stock (page
74) or use canned

2 tablespoons *nuoc mam*
(fish sauce) (page 40)

2 tablespoons cornstarch,
dissolved in ¼ cup water

1 clove garlic, peeled and
crushed

Put the sugar, soy sauce, Chicken Stock, and fish sauce into a small
saucepan and bring to a simmer. Cook for a few minutes and remove
from the heat. Stir in the cornstarch-water mixture, using a wire whisk.
Stir until smooth and add the garlic. Return to heat and cook for a few
more minutes, stirring all the while. Cool and serve as a dip for the
Lumpia.

PORK COOKED IN PORK BLOOD

Serves 4–5

Now just calm down. You like liver sausage, don't you? And if you are
Norwegian, German, or Swedish you have tasted blood pudding. This is
no different. Even if you refuse to cook this dish, I want you to read
through the recipe. It is a wonderful lightly-liver-tasting pork stew. At
the Filipino restaurants in Hawaii, such as the Mabuhay Café and Elena's Restaurant, this is a very, very popular dish. Now read, please!

3 cups cubed boneless pork
butt with fat (½-inch
cubes)

½ cup vinegar mixed with 1
cup water and 1
tablespoon salt

1½ cups pork blood (Find
this in Vietnamese or
Filipino markets. It is
often frozen and worth
the search.)

3 tablespoons lard or
peanut oil

1 medium yellow onion,
peeled and sliced

3 cloves garlic, peeled and
crushed

2 hot jalapeño peppers,
seeded and chopped

Place the pork in a 4-quart covered stove-top casserole and add the
vinegar mixture. Bring to a boil and reduce the heat. Cook, covered,

until the pork is tender, about 1 hour. Watch that it does not dry out at all. You will need to add a little more water. Heat a frying pan and add the lard or oil. Sauté the onion and garlic until the onion is clear. Add the oil, garlic, and onion to the boiled pork and continue cooking for 5 minutes. Purée the pork blood in a food processor. Add the blood to the pork little by little, stirring the mixture while adding, and bring to a boil. Add the chopped pepper and simmer uncovered to reduce the sauce for a few minutes more. Keep covered and serve hot.

This is most often served over rice.

CHICKEN AND PORK ADOBO

Serves 10

The Filipinos love meat cooked with vinegar. This dish is probably the best example of such a thing and it is unusually delicious. The meat is simmered in a sauce and then pan-fried until dry. Wonderful!

1 cup distilled white vinegar

1 cup water

2 tablespoons peeled and crushed garlic

2 teaspoons salt

2 bay leaves

½ teaspoon freshly ground black pepper

1 3-pound chicken, hacked up (page 33) into small serving pieces

2½ pounds boneless pork butt, cut into 1½-inch cubes

2 tablespoons Kikkoman soy sauce

2 tablespoons peanut oil

Place a 6-quart heavy stove-top covered casserole on the burner and add the vinegar, water, garlic, salt, bay leaves, and pepper. Bring to a boil.

Add the cut-up meat to the casserole, cover, and bring to a boil again. Turn the heat to a simmer and cook, covered, for 30 minutes. Add the soy sauce and cook 10 more minutes. Remove the meat from the pot and reduce the juices by at least half. Remove the sauce to a bowl and reheat the pot. Add the oil and brown the meat in small batches. Brown it well. Drain the oil from the pot, put all of the meat in the pot, and return the sauce to the pot. Heat the adobo to serving temperature.

Serve with rice.

FILIPINO PANSIT

Serves 6–8 as part of a large Filipino meal

This delicious rice noodle dish probably came into the Philippines from China. The Filipino cooks worked their wonders on the dish and brought it with them to Hawaii and finally to the mainland. It is a favorite of mine and easy to prepare.

- 1 8-ounce package thick rice noodles (*bijon*) (page 43) from the Philippines (Find in most Oriental markets.)
- ¼ cup peanut oil
- 2 cloves garlic, peeled and crushed
- ½ pound lean pork loin, julienned
- 3 *lop chong* Chinese sausages (page 42), sliced ⅛ inch thick (available in any Oriental market)
- 1 yellow onion, peeled and chopped
- 1 cup chopped Napa cabbage (page 43)
- 2 tablespoons light soy sauce (not "Lite"—see page 46)
- 1½ cups Chicken Stock (page 74) or use canned
- 2 tablespoons *nuoc mam* (fish sauce) (page 40)
- ¼ cup chopped leeks (Rinse them carefully to avoid mud.)
- 1 tablespoon Annatto Oil (page 134)

GARNISH

Fresh chopped coriander leaves (page 49)

Soak the rice noodles in tepid water (barely warm, about 105°) just until supple, about 10 minutes, while the wok heats.

In a hot wok place 2 tablespoons of the peanut oil along with the garlic and the pork. Chow (page 32) until the pork is done to your taste and add the sausage slices, along with the onion and Napa cabbage. Chow for a few minutes and add the soy sauce, stock, fish sauce, leeks, and annatto oil. Chow until the cabbage is tender and add the *drained* noodles to the pan. Stir-fry over medium heat until the noodles are just tender, not soggy.

Place in a large bowl and top with the garnish.

THE GERMAN
IMMIGRANTS

GERMANY

There is only one other group in America that claims more descendants in this country than do the Germans . . . and that group is the English. At the moment there are some 50 million German immigrants and descendants here, and that amounts to about twenty percent of the entire population.

With so many Germans around, you would think that we would notice them much more, but they are not terribly visible. That is, unless it is Oktoberfest time and you live near a German community. Then, you suddenly feel very German yourself.

Look at the things that German immigrants brought to the New World. They must be credited with the Christmas Tree, the frankfurter (though not the hot dog in a bun—that was invented here), the beer industry, pretzels, Bach, Beethoven, Brahms, Wagner . . . these are signs of German culture. No, they are more than signs. They make up the German culture in this country. What a joy!

German immigration to this country began in 1683, when William Penn invited Germans to establish themselves in his Quaker colony in Pennsylvania. At one point Ben Franklin, our lad from Philadelphia, estimated that one third of all of the Pennsylvania colony was German.

The homeland of Germany suffered two world wars, as did we, and Americans of German descent fought on our side, of course. During the wars Americans of German ancestry were often looked down upon. Many even felt obliged to change their names. I remember feeling sad to learn about such name changes. It was in New York. I had just proposed to Patty Mae Dailey and she had said, "Yes!" A party broke out, a party of two, and the waiter came to see what the fuss was about. We were seated in an old-time German restaurant in the Times Square area of Manhattan. It was 1964 and the restaurant was called The Blue Ribbon. We had a great time and returned often to that wonderful place. The walls were hung with pictures of famous German operatic stars who had played the Metropolitan, pictures of great artists and musicians, all friends of the restaurant. The waiters were just a bit younger than God and all were German. Then, on our last visit, our original waiter came to our table and remembered the night of "the party of two." Patty and I had been married for a few years then and the waiter told us that he had bad news. The old Blue Ribbon was being torn down to make way for a building or parking lot or some other diabolical plot. He then told me the history of the place. It had been there for generations and had always had a long German name. But during World War II the name had to be changed to the Blue Ribbon . . . and now even that was going. A couple of years later Patty and I bought a bottle of May wine and two glasses. We sat on the curb where the old place had been and celebrated our wedding anniversary. It was a party of two, just two. The old Blue Ribbon crowd was all gone.

Do not misunderstand me. The German immigrants who came to this country were not all waiters. Not at all. You must remember names like John Jacob Astor and Frederick Weyerhauser and Henry Steinway and Albert Einstein. There are a thousand other names that we should list.

My admiration for the German people began in 1960 when I was touring Europe as a student. I was in Berlin just a few months prior to the construction of the enormous Berlin Wall. I saw the border guards from both sides as we were allowed to travel between the Western and Eastern zones, though we had to go through a terrifying examination by young guards with tommy guns and dogs, wearing pounds of hero medals. The West Berliners, who were actually living on an island in the midst of Soviet occupation, paid no attention to these Eastern guards.

Then, a few months later, the Wall went up. The East German Communist government called it an "Anti-Imperialist Protective Wall." The West Berliners called it "Schandmauer," the Wall of Shame. Now it is gone and the East and West are one nation again. What an event to witness! And I never did see the Wall.

We owe this particular immigrant group so much. They have been here since the beginning of the Republic. And they brought their food with them, food that now celebrates a wonderful memory, a *Gemütlichkeit*, a feasting without end.

A group of Germans having lunch at Ellis Island, 1926

The following recipes will provide you with an entire meal in the German tradition. Some of the dishes are from the south, some from the north; all are delicious. The Pumpernickel bread is a joy to make, and more than a joy to eat. I am proud of that one. Since this food is a tad heavy (boy, is that an understatement!), you will want to add a green salad to the menu, along with a fine dry white wine, or a beer, of course. *Guten Essen!*

PICKLED PORK HOCKS

(Eisbein)

Serves 8–10

This dish is from Bavaria and it is basic. Believe me, it is basic! What you wind up with here is corned pork, corned just like beef, but the flavor is much richer than beef. When I first made these at the television studio, Marion, my other right hand, was very suspicious. Her husband of some forty years was a German, but she had never tasted *Eisbein*. I pleaded and then I insisted that she try them. She came back for a second helping and took the remains home that night. "I don't know what you are doing to me, Jeff, but these are delicious!"

I ate these often years ago when I was in Germany and you will see them now and then in German restaurants in this country. But your German grandma would have made them this way.

METHOD OF CORNING

2 gallons water

1 pound pickling salt
(page 44)

1 teaspoon saltpeter
(page 45)

Mix this solution well.

10 fresh pork hocks, cut in
half crosswise

Marinate the hocks in the corning solution in the refrigerator for 10 days. Keep a heavy plate on the top of the meat so that all pieces are under the solution at all times. Check them each day to be sure this is still the case.

At the end of the 10 days drain the meat and discard the liquid. Rinse the hocks and place in a large pot. Add:

2 celery stalks, chopped	2 bay leaves
1 carrot, chopped (Don't bother to peel.)	8 whole allspice
1 medium yellow onion, peeled and chopped	8 black peppercorns

Just barely cover with fresh water.

Bring to a boil, cover, and simmer for 2½ hours. You may have to add a bit more water.

When the pork hocks are very tender, remove from the pot and serve over sauerkraut. I must have mine with good German mustard.

This is just a wonderful dish!

GERMAN SAUERKRAUT

Serves 8–9 as part of a full German meal

In the early days in this country this dish was a regular among the German immigrants because it was cheap . . . and it was delicious. It was so widely consumed that many narrow-minded Americans called the new German Americans "Krauts." Will prejudice never end? We have had our fill of it!

Do try this dish. It will give sauerkraut a new image in your house.

5 slices thick lean bacon	1 bay leaf
2 medium yellow onions, peeled and sliced	12 whole juniper berries (page 50) or 2 teaspoons caraway seed
3 quarts sauerkraut in glass jars or fresh, drained and lightly rinsed	
	Freshly ground black pepper to taste
1 tablespoon brown sugar	
1 cup dry white wine	1 cup grated peeled potatoes

Place all of the ingredients in a heavy kettle and cover and simmer gently 2 hours.

NOTE: By fresh sauerkraut I mean just that. Buy it bottled in a glass jar or in plastic bags in the deli section. Canned 'kraut tastes to me just like the can!

GERMAN PICKLED BEEF ROAST

(Sauerbraten)

Serves 5–6

This is one of the most famous German dishes to be found in this country. Why? Because Grandma knew that this method of curing a cheap cut of beef would result in a lovely dinner that tasted of the Old World, that's why!

1 4- to 5-pound beef pot
roast, with bone

MARINADE

1½ cups red wine vinegar	1 stalk celery with leaves, chopped
½ cup water	8 black peppercorns
½ cup dry red wine	4 whole allspice
1 medium onion, peeled and chopped	4 whole cloves
1 medium carrot, chopped	2 bay leaves

TO COOK THE MEAR

3 tablespoons peanut oil	½ cup water
1 medium onion, peeled and finely chopped	½ cup red wine
1 stalk celery, finely chopped	½ cup gingersnap crumbs (Just crush them up!)
1 medium carrot, finely chopped	

GARNISH

Chopped parsley

Place the beef in a deep glass, earthenware, or stainless-steel bowl. Combine the marinade ingredients in a medium saucepan and heat to boiling over high heat. Cool. Pour the cool marinade over the meat, turning to coat all sides. Cover and refrigerate 2 to 3 days, turning the meat several times each day.

Three to 4 hours before serving, drain the meat, reserving the marinade, and pat the meat dry with paper towels. Heat a large saucepan. Add the oil. Add the meat and brown on all sides, turning frequently, about 30 minutes. Remove the meat from the pan and reserve. Pour off all but 2 tablespoons fat. Sauté the onion, celery, and carrot in the fat until tender, about 10 minutes. Return the meat to the pan. Strain into the pan the marinade plus ½ cup water, discarding the marinade vegetables. Reduce the heat to low and simmer, covered, until the meat is tender, 2½ to 3 hours.

Remove the meat and keep warm. Remove the marrow from the bone and stir into the sauce. Purée the liquid in the blender or food processor and strain into pan, adding the red wine. Bring to a simmer and stir in the crumbs. Simmer, stirring frequently, until the sauce is thickened, a few minutes.

Slice and arrange the meat on a heated serving platter. Serve hot with thickened sauce. Garnish with chopped parsley.

This is just great with German Dumplings (page 149). The gravy is perfect for the dumplings.

PUMPERNICKEL

Makes 1 large loaf

This bread is one of the great treasures to come with our grandmas from Germany. Most Americans enjoy pumpernickel but they have no idea of the contents of a recipe. Read this one through first and then try it. It is simple to do and the results are better than those of most bakeries that you know.

2 packages quick-rising yeast

1¼ cups tepid water (about 105°)

1 cup rye flour (See Hint, page 423.)

1 cup whole-wheat flour (See Hint, page 423.)

¼ cup dark molasses

2 tablespoons unsweetened cocoa powder

1 tablespoon caraway seeds

1½ teaspoons salt

1½ cups plus 2 tablespoons all-purpose unsifted flour (See Hint, page 423.)

2 tablespoons cornmeal

In a large bowl, combine the yeast and warm water; let stand until softened, about 5 minutes. Add rye and whole-wheat flours, molasses, cocoa, caraway seeds, and salt. With an electric mixer, or heavy spoon, beat dough until it is mixed very well.

If using a dough hook on a machine such as a KitchenAid, mix in 1 cup all-purpose flour. Knead until the dough is elastic and pulls cleanly from the bowl, about 5 minutes. (If needed, add more all-purpose flour, 1 tablespoon at a time.)

If mixing by hand, stir in 1 cup all-purpose flour with a heavy spoon. Scrape the dough onto a floured board. Knead, adding as little flour as possible, until the dough is smooth and elastic, about 5 minutes. Place the dough on a plastic counter and cover with a large stainless-steel bowl. Allow the dough to rise until double in bulk, about 1 hour.

Sprinkle the cornmeal in the center of a baking sheet; set aside. Punch down the dough. On a lightly floured board, knead the dough to shape into a ball. Place the dough on the cornmeal and press to form a 6-inch round. Let the dough rise in a warm place until almost double, about 30 minutes.

Sprinkle a bit of additional flour on top of the loaf. Bake in a 350° oven until the loaf is a rich, dark brown, about 30 minutes, or until the bottom sounds hollow when tapped. Transfer to a cooling rack. Serve warm or at room temperature.

HINT: FOR A CRUNCHY BREAD CRUST use a water sprayer while baking. Your plant sprayer will do fine, as long as it is clean. Simply spray a bit of water into the oven now and then as the bread bakes. Works great!

GERMAN DUMPLINGS

(Spaetzle)

These are wonderful little noodle-type jewels that are very necessary to the German diet. Grandma brought her *Spaetzle* maker with her from Germany and when things were tough you could always count on *Spaetzle* and brown gravy.

The Hungarians came to appreciate the same dish while the Hapsburgs were in control . . . so I refer you to the Hungarian Dumpling recipe on page 168. It is German in origin, I am sure.

RED CABBAGE

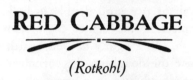

(Rotkohl)

Serves 6–8 as a vegetable course

Red cabbage is a common dish in Germany, and it has become a common dish here in America. It is rich and inexpensive, just the thing for our immigrant German ancestors.

It is served in older German communities as a vegetable or, if you include good German bread, as a main course. It all depends on the amount of money that Grandma had to spend for dinner. It still does!

6 thick slices bacon, diced	4 tablespoons red wine
1 yellow onion, peeled and sliced	4 tablespoons distilled white vinegar
2 heads red cabbage, about 3 pounds total	4 tablespoons brown sugar
3 apples, cored and thinly sliced (do not bother to peel)	1 teaspoon salt
1 cup Chicken Stock (page 74) or use canned	¼ teaspoon freshly ground black pepper

In an 8-quart stove-top covered casserole sauté the bacon until clear. Add the onion and the sliced cabbage to the pot, along with the apples. Sauté, uncovered, until the cabbage begins to collapse a bit.

Add the remaining ingredients and cover. Cook over medium heat, stirring now and then, until all is tender, about 1 hour.

GERMAN ONION PIE

(Zweibelkuchen)

The first time I ever tasted anything like this recipe was at the home of Ingeborg Taylor. She is an immigrant from Bavaria and married a fine scholar in the Pacific Northwest. While I could not get her exact recipe, I think I have come close to something that reminds her of her place of birth. It is the ancestor of the fancy quiches now enjoyed in restaurants aimed at young people. It is German . . . very German.

4 thick slices bacon, diced

2 cups peeled and chopped yellow onions

2 eggs, well beaten

1 cup sour cream

1 tablespoon all-purpose flour

½ teaspoon salt

¼ teaspoon freshly ground black pepper

1 9-inch pie shell (page 501), unbaked

Preheat the oven to 400°.

Sauté the bacon just until clear. Drain most of the fat from the pan. Add the onions and sauté until they are clear. Do not brown them. Set aside to cool.

Beat the eggs and sour cream together in a medium-sized bowl. Sprinkle the flour over the top and beat it in. Stir in the salt and pepper.

Prick the bottom of the pie shell several times with a fork. Spread the onions and bacon over the dough in the pie pan. Pour the sour-cream mixture over the top.

Bake for 15 minutes. Reduce heat to 350° and bake for another 15 minutes or until pie is nicely browned. Serve hot.

POTATO DUMPLINGS

(Semmelknödel)

Makes 12 or more dumplings, enough for 6–8 persons

I have a peasant heart, and I am glad. The things that the German immigrants learned to do with a potato are just amazing. It is true that the potato went from the New World to Germany and it is also true that the Germans learned to raise the tuber to glory. Witness this dish, and I urge you understand that it is very simple to make . . . and far superior to "mashed potatoes."

- 3 quarts water
- 1 tablespoon salt
- 3 pounds russet potatoes, peeled and quartered
- 3–4 eggs, beaten
- 1 cup peeled and grated russet potatoes, squeezed dry

- ½ cup regular farina (Regular Cream of Wheat will be fine.)
- ½ cup all-purpose flour (See Hint, page 423.)
- ¼ teaspoon freshly grated nutmeg
- Additional all-purpose flour for "dusting"

GARNISHES

- 4 tablespoons butter
- 1 cup fine dry bread crumbs

- ¼ cup chopped parsley

Heat the water and 1 teaspoon of the salt to a heavy simmer in a 5-quart Dutch oven over medium-high heat. Add the potatoes and cook until tender, 15 to 20 minutes. Drain very well and put through a potato ricer or food mill. Spread on a platter or baking sheet to dry a bit and cool.

Place the riced potatoes in a mixing bowl and add the eggs, grated fresh potatoes, farina, flour, and nutmeg. Mix all very well. Roll into golf-ball-sized dumplings and roll in the additional flour. If the dumplings do not stick together well, gradually add enough of another beaten egg so that they do.

Bring a large pot of water to a boil. Reduce to a heavy simmer and cook the balls for 15 to 20 minutes. They should all be floating.

While they are cooking, place the butter in a small frying pan and melt it. Toast the bread crumbs in the butter. Use this for a garnish on the dumplings, along with the parsley.

Serve with additional melted butter if you wish or just as they are. I like mine with the gravy from a good *Sauerbraten* (page 147).

THE HAWAIIAN
IMMIGRANTS

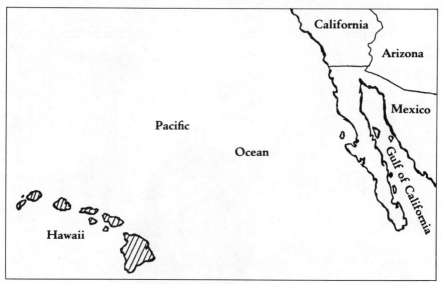

HAWAII

Ⅰt may seem a bit strange to you that I have included the citizens of our fiftieth state in these chapters on our immigrant ancestors. The truth of the matter is that everyone, but everyone, who lives in the beautiful islands is a descendant of immigrants of one sort or another. Even the term "Native Hawaiian" refers to a descendant of people who came from Polynesia and Tahiti some fifteen hundred years ago. They established the wonderful and colorful culture that we now call Hawaii. Take a look at a good map and figure out how they made the trip. These people were incredible sailors! But while they were the first immigrants, they were not the only immigrants.

Through the years people from China, Japan, the Philippines, Korea, Portugal, Puerto Rico, and Europe have also immigrated to these tropical islands. You can still pick out the various cultures in any large city, such as Honolulu. But in this section we are primarily concerned with those who call themselves natives of the land.

The natives came from the great islands to the south and they brought with them a beautiful culture, as well as some interesting food products. The taro root, from which poi is made, was brought to Hawaii along with bananas, coconuts, sugar cane, and pineapples. Breadfruit was brought during the time of the slave trade, a time that gave us stories of the likes of Captain Cook and Captain Bligh. The history of these imports is fascinating and somewhat painful.

In 1778 Captain James Cook, from England, sailed into the islands and the results were disastrous. Missionaries and traders attacked many of the traditional customs and commercialized the economy, having little concern for the natives. In 1848 these European immigrants succeeded in redefining and reallocating the land. The natives lost their own lands and this tragedy was increased with the great decline in the native population due to infection from diseases of the Europeans. Between the loss of their land, the new diseases, and the huge influx of foreign plantation workers in the nineteenth century, the Hawaiians became a minority in their own land.

I had a wonderful time with many native Hawaiians while doing food research and filming the television series. I learned a great deal about Hawaiian history. I am grateful that I was taken under the wing of Senator and Mrs. Michael Crozier. According to the senator, his grandmother, a woman of pure Hawaiian stock, told him that she did not want him to speak the native tongue since she knew that eventually the islands would become a state, and she wanted him to be a good American. So she refused to teach him the language. His son, Dano, on the other hand, is so immersed in the restoration and maintenance of the native culture that he won a statewide contest for high-school students in which the speaking of the native tongue was the goal. So, even in Hawaii, "What the son wants to forget the grandson wants to remember." That is the nature of immigration in this country, and I hope in the future that the sons do not have to forget any of their background in order to feel truly American. Dano is typical of many of his age group, bright young students who want to remember and preserve the ways of their ancestors. What a profound endeavor!

Senator Daniel Inouye, Hawaii's respected Democratic member of the Senate, claims that in Hawaii the concept of the melting pot has never really worked. "We are more of a stewing pot," he claims, "a pot in which you can still distingush the textures and ingredients that make up our culture. It is not a melting pot at all." He is right, of course, and he is one of my heroes. I respect him not just because he is a serious Democrat but because he is also a highly decorated hero from World War II. He was a member of that famous group of Japanese Americans who became the most decorated unit in the American armed forces, the 442nd Regimental Combat Team. He is a serious American, and a child of immigrants, just like most of the rest of us.

The following recipes will provide you with a full luau, or traditional Hawaiian feast. The dishes have been changed a bit so that you can enjoy them on the mainland without going crazy trying to find special ingredients. One word of advice. Poi, the traditional starch dish that is made from taro root, is not terribly popular with those of us who live on the mainland. I personally cannot abide the stuff . . . though I have tried. Craig, my assistant, is of the same opinion. When my wife and I visited the islands recently to celebrate the graduation of our young friend Dano Crozier, we landed in the midst of a poi shortage. I returned to the mainland and told Craig what had happened. "Poor baby!" he replied, and then he broke into fits of laughter. The recipe that we offer below is changed a bit and really quite tasty. Give it a chance in any case. You will love the rest of the dishes.

LAU LAU

This is an ancient dish. In the Islands it is made with the leaves from the ti tree, but in this country we have to use dried leaves. Nevertheless, the result is charming. Everyone is offered a small dinner packet, neatly tied, filled with pork and salted fish.

FOR EACH SERVING

2 ounces butterfish or black cod, freshly salted (This can be prepared by salting the fish fillets with kosher salt and leaving them in the refrigerator for 3 hours before use. Drain well.)

Leaves for wrapping (Dried bamboo or dried lotus leaves, pages 37 and 42, can be found in any Chinese grocery.

You can find frozen banana leaves in many Thai, Chinese, and Vietnamese markets.)

4 ounces boneless pork butt, cut into ¾-inch cubes

2 or 3 spinach leaves

1 tablespoon spinach stems, cut into ½-inch pieces

Prepare the salt fish ahead of time.

Soak the leaves, if dried, in warm water for about 1 hour, then drain. They will be soft and pliable. Set out 1 large banana leaf, 1 soaked and drained lotus leaf, or 4 bamboo leaves. Place the salt fish, pork, and spinach leaves and stems in the center of the leaves. Wrap up into a tight little bundle and tie with string. Place them in a bamboo or metal steamer and steam for 1 hour. It is best to serve them hot though I have enjoyed them lukewarm.

FISH IN COCONUT MILK

Serves 8 as an appetizer course

The Hawaiians eat enormous amounts of fresh fish, and they eat it raw. They seem to have been doing this since the olden days, and the methods of preparation are ingenious. Note that in this recipe the lime juice sort of "cooks" or firms the fish. This is my son Channing's favorite dish from the Islands.

1 pound whitefish, very fresh, skinless and boneless, cut into ½-inch cubes (I suggest cod, snapper, or halibut. It must be fresh!)

1 teaspoon kosher salt

Juice of 2 limes

1 clove garlic, peeled and crushed

3 scallions, chopped

1 cup canned coconut milk (page 38)

¼ cup peeled and chopped white onion

GARNISH

Toasted sesame seeds (page 46)

Place the fish in a stainless-steel or glass bowl. Mix salt and lime juice and toss with the fish. Allow to marinate for 4 hours in the refrigerator. Remove and drain the fish. Add the remaining ingredients and toss well. Chill again before serving. Garnish with sesame seeds.

KALUHA PIG

Serves 8

For the true version of this dish you need a great hole in the backyard lined with volcanic rocks. This is called an *imu* oven. A big fire is started in the *imu* pit and when it is very hot, after a night of burning, the pit is filled with fresh bamboo leaves. A whole pig is salted, filled with hot rocks, and placed in the pit. It is covered with more leaves, then a tarp, and then dirt. The pig cooks during the night and is removed before the luau the next day.

The following method is not quite so complex and the result is really very good.

1 6-pound boneless pork
butt roast, tied

2 tablespoons kosher salt

1 tablespoon liquid smoke
(I like Wright's brand—
found in supermarkets.)

½ pound fresh spinach
leaves, cleaned

Banana, bamboo, or lotus
leaves, reconstituted for
wrapping (See Lau Lau
recipe, page 156, for
instructions.)

Rub the pork with the salt and liquid smoke. Place the spinach in the center of the wrapping leaves, put the pork on top, and tie up the whole bundle with string.

Place a steaming rack or a cake rack in the bottom of a 5- to 6-quart steel-covered oven pot and put in the tied roast. Put ½ cup water in the bottom of the pot and cover with the lid. Bake in a preheated oven at 500° for ½ hour. Turn the heat down to 325° and bake for 5 hours. Add additional water if necessary, but do so very sparingly.

POI

This is a strange food product. It is made from cooked, peeled, and mashed taro root that has been allowed to ferment for a day or two before serving. It is eaten with the fingers with almost every meal. It has a very bland and starchy taste but it has been a major staple in the Islands for hundreds of years.

This root vegetable was common in China as early as 100 B.C. and was probably brought to the Islands from Tahiti. It was a major food source in the old days since the leaves, stems, and tubers are all important in the kitchen. It continues to be very popular in Hawaii. Patty, my wife, and I visited recently and found that we were in the midst of a poi shortage. Everyone was upset but us!

The following recipe is my own variation. Normally the dish would be made with just the taro root, but I find this version to be much more tasty.

The taro can be found in any Chinese market.

Steam and peel fresh taro until tender, about 1¾ hours, reserving steaming water. Break up into chunks and place in a food processor, in small batches. Process just for a moment or two, adding a bit of the reserved water as you go, so that the result is a paste the consistency of sour cream, but much more grainy. Add a bit of salt and coconut milk. Mix well and serve at room temperature.

AKU POKE

Serves 6–8 as an appetizer or as a side-salad course

This dish is raw fish with seaweed. There! Now, calm down and read the recipe. Our Pacific Northwest Indians used to enjoy a similar dish with salmon, but I like this one best with tuna. It is served as an appetizer or first course.

1 **pound raw fish (tuna or salmon), cubed, skinless and boneless**	dried, so soak it for 30 minutes in warm [105°] water. Then drain and rinse well.)
1 **teaspoon Hawaiian or kosher salt**	
1 **cup seaweed (*hijiki* in Japanese markets) (page 41) (The seaweed will be**	1 **small red chile pepper, seeded and chopped, or a shot of hot pepper oil or Tabasco to taste**

Mix all of the ingredients and allow the dish to chill a few hours before serving.

POKE

Serves 8 as an appetizer course

This one can afford to be a little hot. Choose a fiery chile pepper and go at it. Is there some connection here between all of this raw fish and the early Japanese immigrants to the Islands? You bet there is!

1 pound fresh whitefish, skinless, boneless, and cut into ½-inch cubes (I suggest cod, snapper, or halibut . . . but it must be fresh.)

1 cup peeled and chopped white onions

¼ cup chopped scallions

1 teaspoon grated fresh ginger

1 fresh chile pepper, red or green, seeded and finely diced (Choose hot or mild, to taste.)

1 tablespoon light soy sauce (not "Lite"—see page 46)

1 teaspoon sesame oil

Pinch of salt, or to taste

GARNISH

Toasted sesame seeds (page 46)

Mix all the ingredients and chill. Garnish with the sesame seeds and serve cold.

LOMI LOMI SALMON

Serves 10 as a light salad course

This is my favorite! I suppose it is because I live in the Pacific Northwest and adore salmon. In any case, this is like a cold salmon salad, and very good.

1½ pounds moist smoked salmon or salted salmon or lox, skinned, boned, and sliced

3 medium ripe tomatoes, diced

6 scallions, chopped

2 cups peeled and chopped white onions

1 cup crushed ice

Mix all the ingredients together and serve cold.

If the salmon is heavily salted you may wish to soak it first in fresh water for a few hours. This is not necessary with moist smoked salmon nor with lox.

SPINACH AND SQUID

Serves 8

Lynn Crozier, my Hawaiian friend, gave me this recipe following a wonderful luau that she held for us. Traditionally this dish is made of cooked ti leaves and octopus. Her quickie method is delicious and saves you at least a day in preparation.

2 10-ounce boxes frozen whole spinach

1 10¾-ounce can cream of chicken soup

1¼ pounds squid, cleaned and cut in rings (page 480)

Pinch of ground white pepper

Salt to taste

Defrost the spinach and drain. Chop it up just a bit and heat in a large saucepan along with the soup. When all is simmering, add the squid and simmer gently until tender, about 10 minutes. Season with pepper and salt to taste.

This is simply eaten with a spoon or your fingers.

CHICKEN WITH LONG RICE

Serves 8–10 as a noodle course

Long rice is a gift to the Islands from the Chinese immigrants, and perhaps the Filipinos as well. This is a simple chicken and noodle dish, and rice as you normally think of it is not involved at all. Mung bean flour, from the same bean that gives us bean sprouts, is made into a very long and very thin noodle . . . thus the name "long rice."

It is impossible to think of a luau without this dish.

1½ pounds chicken hindquarters (thighs and legs)

2 slices ginger, each the size of a 25-cent piece

1 tablespoon plus 1 teaspoon salt

2 tablespoons oil

2 cloves garlic, peeled and finely chopped

12 ounces Chinese mung bean noodles or *sai fun* noodles (Any Chinese store has these.)

2 tablespoons light soy sauce (not "Lite"—page 46)

1 teaspoon salt

Ground white pepper to taste

½ cup mushrooms (Canned straw mushrooms, page 47, would be great.)

GARNISH

5 scallions, sliced

Place the chicken quarters in a heavy 4-quart lidded pot and add the ginger and 1 tablespoon salt. Cover with water and bring to a simmer. Cook until tender, about 45 minutes. Turn off the heat, cover the pot, and allow the chicken to cool in the broth.

When cool, remove the chicken from the broth, reserving the broth. Debone the chicken and discard the bones and skin. Dice the meat. Discard the ginger slices in the broth. Set both the chicken and the broth aside.

Heat the pot again and add the oil and the garlic. Sauté for just a moment and then add the noodles. Add just enough of the reserved broth to cover. Add the remaining 1 teaspoon salt and all the remaining ingredients, including the chicken, and bring to a simmer. Cook until all is tender, about 5 minutes. Do not overcook the noodles or they will become soft.

Garnish with the scallions and serve.

THE HUNGARIAN
IMMIGRANTS

HUNGARY

Nearly two million Americans claim Hungarian ancestry. More than one third of these people are new immigrants or first-generation Americans. You can find many famous Hungarian-American names in the fields of atomic science, mathematics, computers, music, the arts, the film industry, and philanthropy.

The people of Hungary are Magyars and are more closely related to the Finns and the Estonians than they are to the other ethnic groups of Eastern Europe, who are Slavic.

The Magyars, however, were not the original inhabitants of the area. The Romans established themselves in western Hungary, an area that they called "Pannonia," and built frontier posts along the west banks of the Danube River. This was an important shipping region since it was in the very heart of Europe.

When Rome fell during the fourth century, the Magyars were just one of many tribes who plundered the region. They came from the western corner of the Soviet Union, near the Volga. They had mingled with the Turks for over a thousand years and had taken on many customs of this people. They were great horsemen, having been trained to ride since infancy. In addition, they were wonderful javelin throwers and archers. The Turkic words *On-Ogurs* mean "The People of 10 Arrows." That is how good the Magyars were . . . and it is from this term that we get the word *Hungarians*.

In 955 King Otto the Great of Germany defeated the Magyars, and Christianity was introduced to the Hungarians. By the year 1000 Stephen was crowned king . . . a king so beloved that he was later canonized.

Then the Ottoman Turks invaded and took over. It was not until 1686 that the Hapsburgs of Vienna liberated the Hungarian people, but I cannot say that it was a bargain. New rules and a new language were imposed upon the people, and the result was a reduction of the Hungarians to about 45 percent of the population in their own country.

During the late 1800s many Hungarians immigrated to America. Finally, in 1848 a Hungarian independent state was declared, a state quickly crushed by the Hapsburgs. In 1867 a dual monarchy was established, a governing system that fell with the rest of the Austro-Hungarian Empire after World War I. More Hungarian immigrants came during this period.

Following World War II the Soviets took over the Hungarian government and installed officers "answerable to Moscow." In 1956 the Hungarians revolted but the Soviets crushed the uprising and installed Janos Kadar as premier. Things were liberalized a bit and in 1988 Kadar was replaced by Karoly Grosz. In 1989 a multiparty system was established, so Hungary proudly claims to have been the first nation in the Soviet Bloc to have lifted the Iron Curtain.

The Hungarians are a proud lot, and the immigrants to America certainly have the unquestioned right to be proud of what they brought with them to this land.

The first immigrant to this land from Hungary was probably a fellow by the name of Tryker. He traveled with Leif Ericson, the Norse explorer, who apparently landed in North America around A.D. 1000. There is also good evidence that a Stephen Parmenius of Buda joined an English expedition in 1583 and drowned off Nova Scotia. Then came Jesuit missionaries, Protestant dissenters, and a handful of explorers. One of these, Colonel Michael Kovats, is usually credited with founding the United States Cavalry. He fought in the American Revolution under the Polish immigrant commander Casimir Pulaski. Another Hungarian immigrant, Agoston Haraszthy, was instrumental in founding the California wine industry.

Other names of important Hungarian immigrants and their descendants should be mentioned. There was Joseph Pulitzer, the great newspaper man who established the Pulitzer Prize; he also put comics in the newspapers! Key members of the U.S. team that developed the atom bomb—Leo Szilard and Eugene Wigner—were Hungarian. And Edward Teller was the father of the hydrogen bomb.

In other scientific fields we have Theodor von Karman, the father of supersonic flight; Zolten Bay developed the radio telescope, and Dennis

Gabor the holograph. Long-playing records and color television were the gifts of Peter Goldmark. Most of these Hungarian scientists had two things in common: They were born near the turn of the century in Budapest to well-to-do families, and they were all graduates of the phenomenally successful Hungarian secondary-school system.

The American film industry would not be the same without the work of Adoph Zukor and William Fox, two of Hollywood's first film moguls. And, we can't forget the Gabor sisters, Tony Curtis, Bela Lugosi, and Harry Houdini. In the world of music some of the greatest conductors in the world have Hungarian blood. Fritz Reiner, George Szell, Eugene Ormandy, Antal Dorati, and George Solti are among that special group.

My cook and I went to Budapest to taste the food of the Old World. You *must* find a way to go. The city is beautiful, the Hungarians charming, and the food just outstanding. Avoid the government-run restaurants and you will have a great time. The concierge at your hotel will help you, and I have listed a few restaurants among the following recipes.

You will note the constant use of paprika. Please do not buy cheap paprika in those little tiny jars. It will have no flavor whatsoever. Buy good paprika from Szeged, Hungary. This area grows the best paprika in the world; indeed it is the region that tamed the red pepper to the sweet and lovely thing that we know of as paprika.

I admit that I got a tad carried away with the following selection of recipes. I just could not stop! Many of these dishes I tasted in Budapest, but they are made the same way here in America by our Hungarian immigrant. You can certainly choose several meals from this list typical of the Hungarian table. The Sauerkraut Cooked in Paprika Gravy will probably just do you in. If not, the Pan-fried Pork Steak will finish the job. *Kosonom!*

PAPRIKA GRAVY

Makes about 7 cups

Begin your Hungarian cooking with this basic gravy. It celebrates paprika in a wonderful way. It is used several times in this Hungarian section, so you can see it is both necessary and versatile. You might make a double or triple batch right off the bat. Can you imagine now the amount of paprika that our immigrant Hungarian grandmas had hidden away in their bags on those ships?

- 1 tablespoon freshly rendered lard (See Hint, page 168.) or oil
- 1½ tablespoons Hungarian paprika or more to taste
- 1 clove garlic, peeled and chopped
- 1 cup seeded and chopped Anaheim green peppers (page 36) or chopped but not seeded Cubanelle peppers (page 39)
- 1 cup peeled and chopped yellow onion

- ½ cup chopped ripe tomatoes
- 1 teaspoon chicken base (I prefer Knorr.) or chicken bouillon
- 6 cups Beef Stock (page 78) or use canned
- Salt and freshly ground black pepper to taste
- 1 cup sour cream
- ¾ cup all-purpose flour (See Hint, page 423.)

Heat a 5-quart heavy stove-top casserole and add the lard and paprika. Cook over medium heat for a moment and then add the garlic, green pepper, onion, and tomatoes. Simmer for a few minutes until all is tender. Add the chicken base and Beef Stock, along with the salt and pepper. Cover and simmer for 30 minutes.

In a metal bowl, mix the sour cream and flour together. Mix it well with a wire whip as you do not want lumps. Add a cup of the gravy from the pot and quickly stir it into the cream and flour with the whisk. Remove the gravy from the heat and stir in the cream mixture, whipping it well. Return to the heat and simmer, stirring often, for 15 minutes. Strain the gravy and discard the solids . . . or lumps, if you have any.

HUNGARIAN DUMPLINGS

Serves 4–6

These are similar to German Spaetzle, and I expect that is the background of this dish. The dumplings go well with any kind of meat and gravy. If you have a Spaetzle press or maker, you will find yourself making them often.

2 eggs	2½ cups all-purpose flour (See Hint, page 423.)
2 tablespoons freshly rendered lard (see above) or oil	2½ teaspoons salt
½ cup water	¼ teaspoon baking powder
½ cup milk	4 quarts water

Using an electric mixer, blend the eggs, lard or oil, water, and milk. Stir the flour together with ½ teaspoon of the salt and the baking powder in a dry bowl. Blend this mixture into the liquid. Mix well and set aside for a moment.

Bring 4 quarts of water to a boil and add 2 teaspoons of salt. Using a Spaetzle maker or Spaetzle press (page 30), squeeze the dough into the boiling water (see illustration of the press). Use about ⅓ of the dough for each batch. When the dumplings float to the surface, they are done. Remove them with a slotted spoon and place in a colander. They can be served this way with Paprika Gravy (page 167) or pan-fried with a little butter, just until they are a bit golden, and topped with parsley.

NOTE: These dumplings can also be made by using a piping bag or dropping very small amounts from a spoon. The latter takes much much longer.

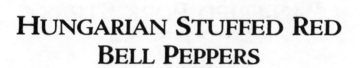

HUNGARIAN STUFFED RED BELL PEPPERS

Serves 6

Everyone in Eastern Europe seems to have a favorite form of this dish. I enjoy it very much, though as a child I thought my mother was trying to kill me with it. Ours were green peppers, of course. She couldn't afford red peppers. Don't overcook the peppers; that's the secret. This version is particularly delicious because of the addition of the Paprika Gravy.

- 6 medium red bell peppers
- 2 tablespoons freshly rendered lard (page 168) or oil
- 3 cloves garlic, peeled and crushed
- 1 medium yellow onion, peeled and finely chopped
- ½ cup chopped parsley
- ¼ cup long-grain rice
- 1½ cups Chicken Stock (page 74) or use canned
- 1 pound finely ground pork, veal, or chicken (A combination is good.)
- 1½ tablespoons Hungarian paprika
- 1 egg
- Salt and freshly ground black pepper to taste
- 2 cups Paprika Gravy (page 167)

Cut off the very top part of the peppers. Chop the pepper tops finely, omitting the stems, and save for the filling. Seed and core the peppers; set aside. Heat a large covered frying pan and add the lard or oil. Sauté the garlic, onion, and reserved chopped pepper tops until tender. Add the parsley and rice, and sauté for a few minutes. Add ½ cup of the Chicken Stock and cover. Simmer for 10 minutes. Allow to cool. In a large bowl combine the ground meat, paprika, egg, salt, and pepper with the rice mixture. Mix very well. Fill the peppers just to the top, but don't pack too firmly because the rice will expand during cooking. Place the filled peppers in a Dutch oven and add the remaining 1 cup Chicken Stock to the bottom of the pot. Cover and simmer very gently for 45 minutes, keeping the temperature very low or the peppers will break. Move the peppers about the pot a few times during cooking to prevent sticking. After 45 minutes pour the Paprika Gravy over the peppers, cover, and simmer for 20 minutes more.

PAN-FRIED PORK STEAK

Serves 4–6

I had this dish in Budapest and I was surprised at the bright flavor. The Hungarians love pork and this treatment is just wonderful. It took Craig, my assistant, and me a minute or two to figure this one out, but we finally realized the key was the celery seeds. Oh boy!

4¾ pound pork steaks, deboned

1½ tablespoons celery seeds

1 cup all-purpose flour (See Hint, page 423.)

Salt and freshly ground black pepper to taste

4 tablespoons freshly rendered lard (page 168) or peanut oil

1½ cups Paprika Gravy (page 167)

Debone the pork steaks and pound out to ⅛-inch thickness. Rub both sides of the steak with the celery seeds. Place the flour in a large bowl and season with salt and pepper. Dredge the pork in the seasoned flour and pan-fry in lard over medium heat until golden brown on both sides. Serve with Paprika Gravy.

HUNGARIAN STUFFED CABBAGE ROLLS

Serves 8

Everyone in Eastern Europe seems to have enjoyed these Stuffed Cabbage Rolls. No wonder, since they're easy to make and fairly inexpensive. You can still smell them cooking in certain sections of Brooklyn. This particular recipe can be adapted to the tongue of the Jewish or Romanian cook very easily.

2 tablespoons freshly rendered lard (page 168) or oil

3 cloves garlic, peeled and crushed

1 medium yellow onion, finely chopped

1 cup seeded and finely chopped Anaheim green peppers or chopped but not seeded Cubanelle peppers (page 39)

½ cup long-grain rice

2½ cups Chicken Stock (page 74) or use canned

1 tablespoon Hungarian paprika

Salt and freshly ground black pepper to taste

1 large head green cabbage

1 24-ounce jar sauerkraut (about 3 cups), drained

1 pound finely ground pork

1 egg

½ pound smoked pork butt, sliced

GARNISH

Paprika Gravy (page 167)

Sauté the garlic, onion, and peppers in the lard until tender. Add the rice, 1 cup of the Chicken Stock, the paprika, and salt and pepper. Cover and simmer for 10 minutes. Set aside and allow to cool.

Core the cabbage and carefully pull the leaves off, keeping them as whole as possible. Blanch the leaves in a large pot of salted water until pliable, about 2 minutes; drain and allow to cool. This should be done in a couple of batches. Cut out the tough white base of each leaf.

In a Dutch oven spread 2 cups of the drained sauerkraut in the bottom of the pot; set aside.

In a large bowl combine the ground pork with the cooled rice mixture, egg, salt, and pepper. Mix very well. Spread out a cabbage leaf on the countertop and roll up into a cylinder, folding in the sides as you roll. Continue with the rest of the leaves; it may be necessary to piece together a couple of leaves to make a nice roll. (See the Romanian version of this dish on page 405 for a clever trick in rolling the cabbage.) Arrange the rolls on the bed of sauerkraut in the pot. Place the pork slices on top of the rolls and spread the remaining 1 cup of sauerkraut over all. Pour in the remaining 1½ cups of Chicken Stock; it should just cover the cabbage rolls. If not, add more stock. Bring to a simmer and cook for 1 hour 15 minutes.

This dish can be served with Paprika Gravy on the side.

SAUERKRAUT AND BEAN SOUP

Serves 6–8

I cannot imagine what our immigrant grandmas from Eastern Europe would have done if sauerkraut had not been available here in the New World. This soup is a great way to stretch a little meat and a lot of beans . . . but it would have been impossible without the wonderful sauerkraut. This is fine eating.

1 cup dried pink beans, rinsed	2 quarts Beef Stock (page 78) or use canned
2 tablespoons freshly rendered lard (page 168) or bacon fat or oil	2 teaspoons Hungarian paprika
½ pound boneless pork butt, diced	3 cups bottled sauerkraut, rinsed and drained
3 cloves garlic, peeled and chopped	Salt and freshly ground black pepper to taste
1 medium yellow onion, peeled and chopped	**GARNISH**
	½ cup sour cream

Place the beans in a 6-quart soup pot, add 3 cups of cold water, cover, and bring to a boil. Turn off the heat and let sit for 1 hour. In a frying pan add the lard and brown the pork. Add the garlic and onion; sauté until the onion is tender. Drain the beans and return to the pot. Add the pork mixture, Beef Stock, and paprika to the beans. Cover and simmer for 1 hour until the beans are tender. Using a slotted spoon, remove about ¾ of the beans to a food processor or blender. Add about 1½ cups of the stock left in the pot to the beans and purée. Return to the pot, adding the sauerkraut. Cover and simmer for 1 hour until the kraut is very tender. Add the salt and pepper, being generous with the pepper. Serve in bowls with a dollop of sour cream.

SMOKED PORK AND BEAN SOUP

Serves 6

This old-fashioned pork and bean soup is given a Hungarian twist with the addition of good paprika. It's hearty winter fare, to say the least.

- 1½ cups dried pink beans
- 2 smoked ham hocks, about 3 pounds total, sawed into 1-inch pieces
- 1 medium yellow onion, peeled and chopped
- 1½ teaspoons Hungarian paprika

- 2 quarts Beef Stock (page 78) or use canned
- 2 teaspoons freshly rendered lard (page 168) or oil
- 4 cloves garlic, peeled and thinly sliced
- Salt and freshly ground pepper to taste

Soak the beans overnight in about 4 cups of water. Drain the beans and place in a 6-quart pot, along with all other ingredients except the lard, garlic, salt, and pepper. Cover and simmer until the hocks are tender, about 1½ hours. Strain the hocks from the pot and cool. Remove the meat and discard the bones. Remove ¼ of the beans and purée with 1 cup of the cooking liquid. Return to the pot. Chop the deboned meat and add to the pot. Stir all together and return the soup to a simmer. Heat a small frying pan, add the lard or oil and garlic, and sauté for a moment. Add to the pot along with the salt and pepper. Be careful with the salt, because the hocks may have provided enough salt already.

PANCAKES BOKOLGNY STYLE

Makes 8–10

This lovely appetizer dish is the Hungarian version of a filled savory crepe or stuffed cannelloni. The serious difference is that this dish is served with Paprika Gravy, of course.

THE PANCAKES

3 eggs

1 cup water

1 cup all-purpose flour
(See Hint, page 423.)

Pinch of salt

Peanut oil for greasing pan

Place the eggs in a blender. Add the water, flour, and salt. Blend until smooth. Over a medium burner, heat a 10-inch Silverstone-lined slope-sided frying pan. This will give you an 8-inch round pancake. Oil the pan with a bit of the peanut oil and pour in about 3 tablespoons of the batter. Do this quickly and tilt the pan so that the batter covers the pan evenly. Cook on one side only, and only until the top is dry. The pancakes should not be at all browned or too dry, so be sure that the heat is not too high. Stack the cooked pancakes as you cook them, separating them with waxed paper.

THE FILLING

½ pound veal stew meat, cut into 1-inch cubes

½ pound boneless skinless chicken breast, cut into 1-inch cubes

2 cups Chicken Stock (page 74) or use canned

3 cups Paprika Gravy (page 167)

Salt and freshly ground black pepper to taste

1 tablespoon freshly rendered lard (page 168)

GARNISH

1 cup sour cream

Simmer the veal and chicken in the Chicken Stock until just cooked, about 15 minutes. Strain the meat and save the stock for another dish. To make the filling, grind the meats fine in a meat grinder. Add ½ cup of the Paprika Gravy and season with salt and pepper. Heat a 10-inch frying pan and add the lard. Add the filling mixture to the pan and warm it over a low flame. In another 10-inch frying pan, warm the pancakes individually over a low flame. Place a warm pancake on a large plate and put about ⅓ cup of filling in the center. Fold in the sides of the pancake and roll it up into a rectangle. Roll all of the pancakes. Place them, 4 at a time, in an oiled frying pan and, with the pan covered, barely toast the bottom of the pancake rolls. Keep cooked pancakes warm while making the rest. Serve on warmed plates topped with the remaining Paprika Gravy, warmed, and a dollop of sour cream.

TOMATO VODKA SOUP

Serves 8

Fresh tomato soup is a glory to all peoples, but especially to the Hungarian immigrants who grew tomatoes in their backyards in the old country . . . and who tried to do the same thing in Brooklyn and Chicago. Our driver in Miami, a man born in Hungary, started to cry when he told of his mother's garden in the old country, and her tomatoes and her fresh bread and the peppers growing outside the back door. She would make a sandwich for him when he came home from school. Bread, crunchy lard pieces, tomato, pepper slices. With tears in his eyes, he said, "How I miss it now!" It was just a sandwich—or was it? No, it was a memory that he brought with him when he came to the New World. A memory of tomatoes and peppers and Mama.

This is a newer version of tomato soup, one that we tasted in Budapest.

2 tablespoons freshly rendered lard (page 168)

6 cloves garlic, peeled and crushed

2 medium yellow onions, peeled and chopped

15 large, very ripe tomatoes, cored and chopped (about 18 cups or a little over 1 gallon)

4 tablespoons Hungarian paprika

4 cups Chicken Stock (page 74) or use canned

6 tablespoons sour cream

4 tablespoons all-purpose flour

Salt and freshly ground black pepper to taste

6 ounces (¾ cup) vodka

In a 10- to 12-quart pot, heat the lard and add the garlic and onion. Sauté until the onion is clear. Add the tomatoes and the paprika, bring to a heavy simmer, turn down the heat, cover, and simmer for 15 minutes. Add the Chicken Stock, cover, and simmer for 45 minutes. Strain the soup into another pot and force through a sieve. Discard the solids.

Return the soup to a simmer. In a small bowl combine the sour cream and the flour, mixing thoroughly. Whip this mixture into the soup until it's smooth and lump free. Simmer uncovered for 15 minutes to reduce and thicken a bit. Add the salt and pepper. When ready to serve, add the vodka and serve immediately.

PAN-FRIED SMOKED TONGUE SLICES

Serves 10–12 as a first course; keeps well in the refrigerator and you can fry more later

This recipe makes a very unusual use of smoked tongue, which is cooked until very tender and then pan-fried and served with Paprika Gravy. This, in my opinion, is one of the best first courses in Hungarian cuisine.

1 corned and smoked beef tongue, about 2 pounds, from your butcher

2 unpeeled carrots, thickly sliced

1 medium yellow onion, peeled and quartered

1 bay leaf

10 black peppercorns

½ bunch of parsley, chopped

1 cup all-purpose flour (See Hint, page 423.)

2 eggs, beaten

3 tablespoons freshly rendered lard (page 168) or oil

GARNISH

3 cups Paprika Gravy (page 167)

Place the tongue in a pot; add everything but the flour, eggs, lard, and Paprika Gravy. Add enough water to cover the contents. Cover and simmer for 3½ hours. Remove the tongue and peel off the skin as soon as you can handle it. Return it to the pot, bring to a boil covered, turn off the heat, and allow to cool in the liquid. Place overnight in the refrigerator. The next day, remove the tongue from the broth and pat dry. Slice the tongue ¼ inch thick. Dredge in flour, then in beaten eggs. Pan-fry in lard.

Serve the hot slices in puddles of Paprika Gravy.

LIPTAUER CHEESE

Makes about 6 cups

This cheese spread is common in the street cafés in Budapest, and it is common in the homes of Hungarian immigrants. It is a very unusual blend that will prove to be good for breakfast, lunch, or dinner. That's how the Hungarians use it.

3 pounds large-curd cottage cheese, drained in cheesecloth overnight

2 pounds cream cheese, at room temperature

1 cup peeled and diced yellow onion (¼-inch dice)

1 teaspoon caraway seeds, ground in a spice grinder

3 cloves garlic, peeled and crushed

1 teaspoon dry mustard

1 teaspoon freshly ground black pepper

½ cup sour cream

3 tablespoons Hungarian paprika

Salt to taste (optional)

Place some cheesecloth in a large colander and pour in the cottage cheese. Tie up the ends of the cloth so that you have a bag you can hang over a bowl overnight. You want to drain the whey from the cheese.

The next morning, mix all ingredients except the cottage cheese, paprika, and optional salt. Mix well and then fold in the paprika and cottage cheese. Do this gently, as you want the spread to have some texture. Taste for salt and add if desired.

CHICKEN PAPRIKAS

Serves 4–6

This is simply a classic. In the Old World, homes in the countryside had chickens and peppers in the backyard. The affection for this dish became widespread in the Hungarian communities in this country, and I think it will remain popular for a long time.

The gravy is very rich and perfect over Hungarian Dumplings.

3–4 tablespoons freshly rendered lard (page 168) or oil

1 tablespoon Hungarian paprika

3 yellow onions, peeled and chopped

1 3½-pound chicken, cut into 8 serving pieces

1 cup Chicken Stock (page 74) or use canned

1 medium tomato, diced

2 Anaheim (page 36) or Cubanelle (page 39) green peppers, seeded and coarsely chopped

1 teaspoon salt

⅛ teaspoon freshly ground black pepper, or more to taste

2 cloves garlic, peeled and crushed

THICKENING

½ cup sour cream

2 tablespoons all-purpose flour

Heat a 6-quart heavy stove-top casserole and add the lard or oil and paprika. Sauté the paprika for about 1 minute and add the onions. Sauté for a few minutes and add the remaining ingredients, except the thickening, to the pot. Bring to a simmer and cool, covered, for about 45 minutes to 1 hour or until all is tender. Remove the chicken pieces and set aside. Mix the sour cream and flour well, using a wire whisk. Add 1 cup of the gravy from the pot to the cream and stir well to avoid lumps. Stir this mixture into the pot and stir while it thickens. Return the chicken to the pot and restore the heat.

Serve over Hungarian Dumplings (page 168).

NOTE: For a very delicious Veal Paprikas, use the above recipe substituting 2½ pounds of veal stew meat for the chicken.

HUNGARIAN SAUSAGE

Makes about 4½ pounds

I have looked for good Hungarian sausage in this country and I have been disappointed. The sausage in Hungary is so rich and delicious, while our attempt at this dish here in America . . . well, it is like most American sausage, rather boring. I finally realized that many immigrant families make their own sausage. I made a batch of this at the television studio and Lazlo, my immigrant Hungarian friend at WTTW in Chicago, yelled, "Where did you get these? They look like they are from Hungary!" What a compliment. Here is the method I use now, but you must have a smoker. Borrow one if you have to, but you will love this sausage.

3 pounds boneless pork
butt, cut into large pieces

1 pound beef chuck, cut
into large pieces

1 pound fresh pork fat, cut
into large pieces

10 cloves garlic, peeled and
crushed (about 2
tablespoons)

1 cup water

2 tablespoons salt

½ tablespoon freshly
ground black pepper

3 tablespoons Hungarian
paprika

1 teaspoon saltpeter
(page 45)

¼ teaspoon ground cloves

Sausage casings, about
10 feet, 1 inch in
diameter as for Polish
sausage (page 45)

In a meat grinder, coarsely grind the pork, beef, and pork fat, in batches. Add all the remaining ingredients except the casings. Mix well and allow to sit while you clean the casings.

Rinse the casings thoroughly in cold water and run fresh water through them. Drain. Using a sausage machine, a KitchenAid with a sausage attachment, or a sausage funnel (page 30), fill the casings and tie them off into about 16-inch lengths. Do not fill them too tightly as they must have room to expand when they cook.

Hang the sausages in a home-style smoker (page 305) and smoke them for about 1 hour. Do not allow the temperature of the smoker to go above 150°.

Remove the sausages and hang over a stick or dowel. Put the stick in a cool place and position an electric fan so that it will blow directly on the sausages. Allow them to dry for 2 days. They are then ready for use. Place them in the refrigerator, where they will keep well for about a week.

HUNGARIAN HAND-ROLLED SAUSAGE WITH ONIONS

Prepare a batch of sausage filling from the preceding recipe. Hand-roll these into pieces about 3 inches long and 1½ inches in diameter. Pan-fry them, grill them over charcoal, or broil them in an electric oven. Serve them with a sauce made of pan-fried onions along with a bit of paprika and sour cream. This is delicious!

PORK ROAST WITH HUNGARIAN DUMPLINGS

Prepare a pork roast using lots of garlic. Serve it with Paprika Gravy (page 167) to which you have added sour cream. Serve the Hungarian Dumplings (page 168) on the side with more of the gravy.

SAUERKRAUT COOKED IN PAPRIKA GRAVY

Drain sauerkraut, fresh or packed in glass, and cook it in a bit of Paprika Gravy (page 167) for about 45 minutes, covered.

SAUSAGE WITH GREEN PEPPERS AND TOMATOES

Pan-fry some smoked Hungarian Sausages (page 179), remembering to poke holes in the casings before placing them in the pan. Top with a bit of *letcho* sauce (below) and cover and simmer until done to taste. You can also do this with Hungarian Hand-Rolled Sausages (page 180).

GREEN PEPPER AND TOMATO SAUCE (Letcho)

Makes 4 cups

6 tablespoons freshly rendered lard (page 168) or oil

1 tablespoon Hungarian paprika

1 teaspoon salt, or more to taste

½ tablespoon sugar

1½ cups peeled and sliced yellow onions

4 cups cored, seeded, and sliced Anaheim green peppers (page 36) or sliced but not seeded Cubanelle peppers (page 39)

1 pound ripe tomatoes, diced

Heat a large frying pan and add the lard or oil. Add the paprika and salt and cook for a moment or two. Add the remaining ingredients, cover, and simmer until all is tender, about 15 minutes. Taste to see if you need additional salt.

This sauce can be served as a side dish as it is, but it's great if you use it with Hungarian Sausage.

ONION SALAD

Serves 4 as a side dish

This is a Hungarian dish that sounds too simple to be really good. You will be surprised.

Take 2 large yellow onions, peel and slice them very thin, then toss with good mayonnaise, salt, and pepper. Chill before serving.

SAUERKRAUT SALAD HUNGARIAN

This needs only a description. It is a common and treasured dish among Hungarian families. Sauerkraut, fresh or packed in glass, is drained and rinsed quickly with fresh water. Drain it well. Put it into a salad bowl along with some slivered fresh cabbage, a few chopped Anaheim (page 36) or Cubanelle peppers (page 39), and 1 or 2 fresh red bell peppers, julienned. A light vinaigrette dressing is added, along with paprika and pepper. Check for salt.

PANCAKES WITH CHOCOLATE SYRUP

I had to tell you about this one. I don't get into desserts much, but this is too much! After an enormous meal in a fine restaurant in Budapest, the Hungarian businessman will order one of these.

Prepare a batch of crepes or Swedish pancakes (page 470).

Heat some Hershey's chocolate syrup and add a dash of whipping cream and a shot of brandy. Simmer until it is smooth and thickened a bit. Fold the warmed pancakes into quarters and place on a serving platter. Top with the syrup and dust with powdered sugar. Whew!

THE INDIAN
IMMIGRANTS

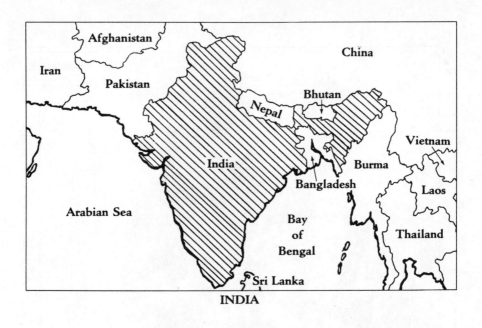

INDIA

India is the seventh largest country in the world and the *largest* democracy. There are 700 million people living in the land of silks and spices. Where did they all come from?

The first significant immigration to that land was by the Aryans, a tall fair-skinned people who came from the shores of the Caspian Sea around 1500 B.C. They had come through the passes in the Himalayas seeking better pastures for their cattle. After some time they mixed with the Dravidians, a dark-skinned people whom the Aryans found living in the south. Thus began the Indian people as we know them.

The important outside influences on this people are fascinating. In 326 B.C. Alexander the Great, the explorer and conqueror from Macedon, entered the land, bringing with him new blood and certainly new customs. Hinduism was already well established in the land and later many were converted to Buddhism. Christianity arrived in the first century and, according to tradition, brought by no less a missionary than Saint Thomas himself. In the fifth century the Huns invaded and in the twelfth, the Muslims. The British were the last to arrive when they became colonial rulers in the eighteenth century and stayed on for two hundred years.

Finally, in 1947 India became an independent state. All three major religions mentioned above still flourish. Indeed, the flag of India has a symbol or color from each of these three groups. In addition, some fifteen major languages and hundreds of local dialects are spoken.

I was amazed to see how many vegetables and cooking methods India shares with China: the wok, bitter melon, eggplant, hairy melon. I could not quite figure out this common ground since the cultures are so very different. I began to think of trade routes, the quest for spices and the intermingling of the two nations. Had I studied my geography when I was in high school I would have remembered that India borders directly on China! There is no mystery here, except why I did not study my geography. Patty, my wife, is right. We must spend more time on geography when trying to educate the citizens of tomorrow.

Now, back to the Indian immigrants. Immigration to the United States is fairly recent. At the turn of the century a severe drought hit the Punjabi region and about 7,000 came here. In 1923 the immigration laws were changed and few Indians were allowed into America. But in 1965 the laws were changed again and thus the 1980 census listed about 200,000 Indian immigrants in this country. There are many more now, of course, and most of them are well-trained professionals. Doctors, scientists, professors, engineers, and businesspeople are all contributing their skills to the American dream. Incidentally, if you wish to find great Indian shopping areas try Lexington Avenue in New York, between Thirty-second and Twenty-eighth streets. You might also take a trip to Vancouver, British Columbia. Many Indians traveled there, since they were British subjects, and the marketing and eating are delightful.

The following recipes will provide you with many possibilities for formal Indian meals. I want you to calm down and not worry about the complexity of the spices; the recipes are really not at all difficult to understand. Once you do a few recipes, all will make sense to you . . . and no, Indian cooking is not necessarily hot, not at all.

I thank my dear friend Julie Sahni for help in this section. An immigrant from India and a true American. And what a cook! You will love her Tandoori Game Hens.

BASMATI RICE WITH GARNISHES

Serves 8

Julie Sahni, author of *Classic Indian Cooking* and other fine books on Indian cooking (page 520), offered us dinner one night. I learned in one short evening that Indian cuisine is not the complicated thing I thought. A basic knowledge of spices is quickly acquired, and then you are on your way to celebrating one of the most profound cooking styles in the world.

The rice that is so favored by this interesting cuisine, basmati rice, really has no substitute as it has a rather rich and nutty flavor. You can find it in any Indian or Middle Eastern market. Please do not buy it in those tiny, fancy boxes. It is much too expensive in that form.

This dish is very exciting!

1½ cups basmati rice (page (37)

Kosher salt to taste, if desired

GARNISHES

½ cup dried onion flakes, toasted in a little oil in a medium-hot frying pan (It will take just a few minutes to get them golden brown.)

½ cup crisp fried okra (page 187)

¼ cup toasted slivered almonds, pan-toasted in a little *ghee* (page 356)

¼ cup toasted cashew nuts, pan-toasted in a little *ghee*

¼ cup currants or raisins (I much prefer currants.)

1 12-inch piece silver foil (*vark*) (optional) (page 46)

Wash the basmati rice thoroughly in several changes of water. Place the rice in a bowl. Add enough water to cover it by at least 1½ inches. Let the rice soak for ½ hour. Drain the rice and reserve.

While the rice is soaking, bring 12 cups of salted water in a deep pot to a boil. Add the drained rice, stir, and bring to a second boil. Cook the rice for exactly 4 minutes. Drain the rice and lightly pack it into a 2-quart greased bowl. Invert on an attractive platter. Lightly press around the rice to shape it into a dome.

Decorate the rice dome with any or all of the garnishes. To adorn with silver foil (*vark*), first peel off the top layer of paper. Lift the bottom sheet, with the silver foil still attached to it, and invert it over the rice at the center. Gently lift away the paper.

CRISP FRIED OKRA

¾ **pound okra**   1 **teaspoon lemon juice**

5 **tablespoons light**
vegetable oil

Wash the okra and wipe dry. Trim both ends and slice into very thin (⅛-inch to 3⁄16-inch) rounds. Heat the oil over high heat in a large frying pan. When it is very hot, add the okra in a single layer. Cook over medium heat, turning and tossing, until it is cooked and crispy brown, about 20 minutes. Sprinkle with lemon juice, mix, remove the okra with a slotted spoon, and drain on paper towels.

HINT: ON SHOPPING IN ETHNIC GROCERY STORES. Do not be intimidated by the wonderful strangeness that you find around you. Simply tell the merchant what you are cooking and he or she will help you find the ingredients. The clerk knows the business . . . so give a professional a chance to help you. You may never find the right thing on your own, but the clerk will find it right away.

CAULIFLOWER AND SCALLIONS WITH BLACK MUSTARD SEEDS

Serves 8

This dish, another one of Julie Sahni's offerings, will show you that you can create the most wonderful Indian flavors with so little work. I have never eaten such wonderful cauliflower in my life . . . and it is a snap to make.

1 head cauliflower, about 1¼ pounds

2 small bunches of scallions

2 teaspoons black mustard seeds (page 51) (found in Indian or Middle Eastern markets or spice shops)

2 teaspoons cumin seeds

1 teaspoon fennel seeds

½ teaspoon turmeric
Kosher salt to taste

⅓ cup warm water (105°)

¼ cup light vegetable oil

⅓ cup chopped fresh coriander (page 49) or 8 fresh curry leaves

Separate and cut the cauliflower into 1-inch florets. Peel the cauliflower stem and cut into thin slices. Set aside.

Trim the scallions and chop them, including the entire green part. Set aside.

Measure out the spices and place them, as well as the water, right next to the stove.

Heat the oil in a wok or a sauté pan over high heat. When the oil is hot, add the mustard, cumin, and fennel. Keep a pot lid handy since the seeds may splatter and sputter when added. When the seeds stop sputtering, add the turmeric and immediately add the cauliflower.

Stir-fry the cauliflower until it's evenly coated with spice-infused oil. Add the scallions, salt, and water; mix and cover with a lid. Cook over medium heat and toss a couple times until the cauliflower is soft, about 10 minutes. Uncover, fold in the coriander, and continue stir-frying until excess moisture evaporates and the cauliflower looks glazed, about 5 minutes. Turn off the heat and serve.

TANDOORI GAME HENS

Serves 8

The *tandoori* oven has traditionally been built in a hole in the ground. Indian immigrant cooks now build such an oven aboveground so that you may stand beside it and reach down inside. The inside looks like that of a great clay urn, and it's covered on the outside with a great deal of insulation. A wood fire is built in one portion of the bottom, and when the temperature hits 900° the oven is ready. Yes, 900°, so you can understand that it takes a long time to heat up this device, and one rarely allows the fire to go out.

Julie Sahni, my Indian friend, has developed this recipe, which comes close to the *tandoori* method in terms of flavor, but it can be done in a household oven or on the grill. An outstanding dish, which can also be made with chicken!

4 Cornish game hens

1 tablespoon red food coloring

2 tablespoons yellow food coloring

MARINADE

1½ cups Homemade Yogurt (page 428) or yogurt from the market

½ cup extra virgin olive oil, plus additional for basting

¼ cup lemon juice

3 tablespoons grated fresh ginger

4 tablespoons ground cumin

1 tablespoon peeled and minced garlic

1 tablespoon Garam Masala (page 199)

2 teaspoons cayenne pepper

2½ teaspoons kosher salt or to taste

With poultry shears or scissors cut the backbones of the hens. Place each hen, open, breast side up, on the kitchen counter. Press down on the breastbones with the heel of your palm to flatten them.

Skin the hens and prick them all over with a fork. Make diagonal slashes, ½ inch deep and 1 inch apart, on the meat, along the grain. Make a slit with a paring knife in the meat between the thigh and the breast. Secure the ends of the legs through the slit. Put the hens in a large shallow dish. Mix the food colorings in a shallow bowl and paint the hens. Remove them to another plate and reserve.

Combine all the ingredients of the marinade with the remaining coloring in the bowl. Mix thoroughly, then coat the hens with the marinade; push it into the slits, to coat them evenly. Cover with plastic wrap and refrigerate overnight (maximum 2 days) or marinate at room temperature for 1 hour. Take the hens from the refrigerator 1 hour before cooking.

Prepare and light a covered charcoal grill or preheat an oven to 550°. Coat the hens lightly with oil. Place them, breast side down, on a rack and barbecue, covered, with the vents open, turning 3 or 4 times, without further basting, for 25 minutes or until the juices run clear when pierced with a knife at the joint. Alternately, roast the hens set on racks in a baking dish for 20 to 25 minutes. Serve immediately, with slices of cucumber, tomatoes, and onions if desired.

FRIED LENTIL WAFERS

(Puppadam)

Makes 8

I see no reason why you should make this dish from scratch. No one in the Indian community in this country does such a thing, as the item is readily available in Indian markets and fancy food shops. Made of lentil or garbanzo flour, the dried wafers puff up when deep-fried. They are a common and delicious first course.

Peanut or corn oil to fill an electric frying pan to a depth of 2 inches	8 store-bought lentil wafers (puppadam) in assorted flavors: garlic, black pepper, cumin, and plain (page 44)

Heat the oil to 375°. Gently slide one wafer into the oil. Push the wafer down and swirl it around using tongs, pressing it gently to keep it submerged at all times during cooking. The wafer will turn light and fluffy and expand enormously in size (about 10 seconds). Remove and drain it on paper towels and continue with the remaining ones in the same way. When slightly cool, the puppadam will turn crisp.

INDIAN SPINACH YOGURT RAITA SALAD

Serves 8

This is not like any salad that is normally served in America. Yogurt, spinach, spices, and nuts blend into a most refreshing and interesting course. You will have no trouble with this one. It is a variation on Julie Sahni's wonderful cooking.

THE DRESSING

- 1½ cups Homemade Yogurt (page 428) or yogurt from the market
- ½ cup sour cream
- 1 teaspoon roasted cumin seeds, ground (See Hint, page 192.)
- 1 teaspoon roasted coriander seeds, ground
- ¼ teaspoon freshly ground black pepper (optional)
- ¼ teaspoon cayenne pepper (optional)
- Kosher salt to taste (optional)

THE SALAD

- 1 10-ounce box frozen chopped spinach, thawed and squeezed dry
- ⅓ cup cucumber, peeled and grated
- 2 tablespoons finely chopped fresh mint leaves
- 2 tablespoons chopped fresh coriander (page 49)
- ¼ cup currants
- ¼ cup roasted walnuts, chopped
- 2 tablespoons other nuts (such as macadamias, almonds, pine nuts, and cashew nuts)
- Paprika to taste

GARNISH

Sprig of mint

Put the yogurt and sour cream in a mixing bowl and mix until thoroughly blended. Add the cumin, coriander, and, if desired, black pepper, cayenne, and salt. Fold in the spinach and any or all of the other ingredients, except the paprika, into the yogurt mixture. If desired, sprinkle with paprika, and serve garnished with a mint sprig.

TOMATO CUCUMBER RAITA

Serves 3–4 as a side dish

This dish will add some color to your Indian table and it is quite easy to prepare.

1½ cups Homemade Yogurt (page 428) or yogurt from the market

1 ripe tomato, chopped

1 peeled, seeded, and shredded cucumber (Use a mandoline, page 29, or grate by hand.)

Dash of chili powder

1 Anaheim green pepper, seeded and chopped

2 teaspoons Garam Masala (page 199)

Salt and freshly ground black pepper to taste

Combine all of the ingredients in a salad bowl. Chill for 1 hour before serving.

LENTIL OR SPLIT PEA DAL
WITH GARLIC BUTTER

Serves 8

A *dal* is a legume of some kind cooked with spices. It is a basic part of the Indian meal and goes back centuries into Indian history. Beans, peas, lentils, and favas all work well with so many foods. This is Julie Sahni's method for making a fine *dal*.

1½ cups yellow split peas *or* yellow or brown lentils

5 cups water

¾ teaspoon turmeric

1½ teaspoons kosher salt or to taste

Freshly ground black pepper to taste

⅓ cup chopped fresh coriander (page 49) (optional)

FOR *TADKA* OF CUMIN-GARLIC

5 tablespoons light vegetable oil or *ghee* (page 356)

1½ teaspoons cumin seeds

5–6 large cloves garlic, peeled and thickly sliced

2–3 dried small red peppers (page 52) (optional)

Pick over, clean, and rinse the split peas. Place them in a deep pot, add the water, turmeric, and salt, and bring to a boil. Boil the peas gently, partially covered, until they are very soft, about 45 minutes, checking and stirring occasionally to ensure they do not stick to the bottom of the pan. Turn off the heat and beat the split peas with a wire whisk or wooden spoon for a minute or until they look thick and creamy. You should have 5 cups of purée; if not, add additional water. Return the purée to the pot, add black pepper, and heat until boiling. Turn off the heat and fold in the chopped coriander; keep the *dal* covered.

Heat the oil in a frying pan over medium heat. When the oil is hot, add the cumin seeds. When the seeds turn several shades darker, add the garlic and optional red peppers. Cook until the garlic is browned and the oil is infused with its flavor. Pour the oil-garlic mixture onto the *dal*. Mix well. Taste for pepper and salt. Serve spooned into small bowls.

PEACH CHUTNEY WITH WALNUTS AND RAISINS

Makes 1 quart

A chutney is a side pickle dish, sometimes sweet, sometimes sour. This one is very easy to make and the results are satisfying to everyone at the table. It will refresh your mouth if you happen to eat something that is a bit spicy.

Julie Sahni makes this with fresh peaches, but I find that you can also use canned or frozen. Fresh ones are best, however.

1½ cups sugar

¼ cup distilled white vinegar

1 teaspoon ground cumin

1 teaspoon red pepper flakes

½ teaspoon black peppercorns

½ teaspoon dried thyme, whole

1 teaspoon fennel seeds

1 teaspoon coriander seeds (page 49)

½ teaspoon kosher salt

½ teaspoon black mustard seeds (page 51)

4 cups fresh peaches, peeled and sliced, *or* unsweetened canned peaches, sliced and drained, *or* frozen peach slices, defrosted and drained

2 tablespoons lemon juice

1 cup roughly chopped walnuts

1 cup dark raisins

Combine all the ingredients, except the peaches, lemon juice, walnuts, and raisins, in a 3-quart saucepan. Boil gently, uncovered, until the syrup is thick and sticks to the bottom of the spoon, about 13 minutes.

Place the drained peaches in a bowl and add lemon juice.

Fold the peaches with the lemon juice and walnuts and raisins into the syrup; simmer for 30 seconds. Spoon into sterilized jars and refrigerate. Let the chutney ripen in the refrigerator for a day before serving.

NAVRATNA CHUTNEY

Makes 1½ cups

This is spicy, sweet, vinegary . . . all at once. The Indians love such blends and you will be surprised at how well this goes with many dishes.

10 black peppercorns

½ teaspoon red pepper flakes

½ teaspoon ground dried ginger

1 tablespoon coriander seeds (page 49)

1½ teaspoons cumin seeds

1½ teaspoons anise seeds (page 48)

2 cloves garlic, peeled

¾ pound golden raisins, soaked in ½ cup warm water for 1 hour, drained

1 tablespoon chopped fresh coriander (page 49)

2 teaspoons salt

1 cup sugar

5 tablespoons distilled white vinegar

Grind the peppercorns, red pepper flakes, ginger, coriander, cumin, and anise seeds in a small electric coffee grinder (page 23) or spice grinder.

Place the garlic in a food processor and chop fine. Add the raisins and chop coarsely by pulsing the machine. Add the remaining ingredients, including the spices and vinegar, and chop to a coarse paste texture.

MINT CHUTNEY

Makes 1½ cups

This bright flavor is great with all roasted meats and with Samosas (page 205). Remember not to touch your eyes after cleaning jalapeño peppers.

1 medium yellow onion, peeled and sliced

1 bunch fresh coriander (page 49), most of the stems removed

1 teaspoon peeled and chopped garlic

½ cup fresh mint leaves

¼ cup lemon juice

1 teaspoon salt

1½ teaspoons sugar

2 small jalapeño peppers, seeded and chopped

1 teaspoon dry-roasted cumin seeds (See Hint, page 192.)

2 tablespoons dry-roasted peanuts

¼ cup water

Blend all the ingredients in a food processor. Refrigerate, covered, for up to 2 weeks.

CORN IN YOGURT

Serves 6–8

This sounds strange to Western ears, but the flavors of this American product, corn, cooked in the Indian kitchen, are unusual and very delicious.

1 teaspoon yellow mustard seeds (page 51)

⅛ teaspoon fenugreek seeds (page 50)

2 tablespoons *ghee* (page 356) or butter

¼ teaspoon red pepper flakes

¼ teaspoon ground dried ginger

½ teaspoon asafetida (page 37) (optional)

2 cloves garlic, peeled and minced

2 medium yellow onions, peeled and chopped

2 tablespoons water

¼ teaspoon turmeric

4 jalapeño peppers, seeded and chopped

20 ounces frozen corn kernels, thawed and drained

2½ cups Homemade Yogurt (page 428) or yogurt from the market

1½ tablespoons butter

GARNISH

1 tablespoon chopped fresh coriander (page 49)

In a small covered frying pan, toast the mustard seeds and fenugreek in 1 teaspoon of the *ghee*. Use a lid on the pan, as the mustard seeds will pop. Place in a mortar and add the red pepper flakes and ginger. Pound into a paste; set aside. Heat a 4-quart saucepan and add the remaining *ghee,* asafetida, and garlic. Sauté for a couple of minutes and add the onion, then sauté until golden brown and tender. Add the water, pounded ingredients, and turmeric. Cook a few minutes longer.

Add the jalapeños, corn, yogurt, and butter. Simmer for 5 minutes. Garnish with chopped coriander.

CHAPATI BREAD

Makes about 24 chapatis

This bread is rolled out and then cooked on a hot pan, like a tortilla. Then, and here is the tricky part, the round loaf is placed over a hot gas burner and it should swell up like a balloon. It looked great when we did it on television, but I will not tell you how many times we tried it before it looked so great. Don't worry about it. Even if it doesn't swell up each time, it's still delicious. Even Julie Sahni can't get it to swell up every time!

2 cups whole-wheat flour (See Hint, page 423.)

1 cup unbleached white flour (See Hint, page 423.)

1¼ cups warm water (105°)

¾ cups additional white flour for dusting

½ cup melted *ghee* (page 356) for brushing

Place the flours in the bowl of an electric mixer such as a KitchenAid. It must be a very strong machine; otherwise this needs to be done by hand. Using a dough hook, stir in the water. Knead the dough in the machine until it is very smooth, about 10 to 15 minutes.

(The dough can be transferred into a Ziploc plastic bag and refrigerated. Bring it to room temperature before using.)

Divide the dough into 2 portions. Roll each portion into a 12-inch-long rope. Cut each into 12 equal parts and roll into smooth balls (or, alternatively, pinch off small portions of dough from the whole and roll each into a smooth 1-inch ball). Dust the balls lightly to prevent sticking. Keep the rest of the dough covered with a metal bowl, upside down, to prevent it from drying out.

Start heating a griddle or a 10-inch frying pan over medium-high heat. Pick up a single ball, dust it with flour, and place it on your work surface. Press firmly to flatten it, turning it once. Roll the patty into a thin round circle with a brisk back-and-forth motion from edge to edge to keep it circular. The circle should be about 8 inches in diameter. Dust often with flour to prevent sticking. Roll at least 6 pieces the same way and keep them on the work surface, covered, to prevent them from drying out. DO NOT STACK, as they will stick together.

Cook each Chapati for a few seconds on each side on the hot griddle. Then place the loaf directly over an open flame to puff it up. This will take only a few seconds. You may wish to turn the loaf once. Stack the loaves on top of each other, after brushing one side with a bit of *ghee*.

NAN

(Indian Bread)

Makes 8 nans

I love this bread, this Nan. I love it so much that I have considered building a *tandoori* oven (page 189) in the backyard in order to make it. The Indian baker prepares this dough and then shapes a bit into a pancake. It is then slapped on the inside wall of the very hot oven. When it is puffy and delicious, it is removed with a metal hook. The following method assumes that you are using a regular oven. It is still very delicious.

½ cup Homemade Yogurt (page 428) or yogurt from the market

½ cup milk

½ teaspoon baking soda

1 teaspoon sugar

4 tablespoons butter, melted and cooled

2 eggs, lightly beaten

2 packages quick-rising yeast

3½ cups unbleached white flour (See Hint, page 423.)

½ teaspoon salt

½ teaspoon poppy seeds or sesame seeds

Warm the yogurt and stir in the milk until thoroughly mixed. Remove from the heat and cool. (This can be done in a microwave.) Place the yogurt mixture in a mixing bowl for a very heavy mixer, such as a KitchenAid. Otherwise do this by hand. Add the baking soda, sugar, 2 tablespoons of the butter, eggs, and yeast. Mix until the yeast dissolves.

Stir in the flour and salt.

Using the dough hook for your electric mixer, knead the dough for 15 to 20 minutes, until smooth and elastic. Place the dough on a plastic counter and cover with a large stainless-steel bowl. Let the dough rise to twice its size, about 2 hours.

Dust your hands with flour. Knead the dough again for a few minutes and divide into 8 balls. Roll each ball into a 10-inch pancake. Pull each pancake gently to give it an oval shape. Cover with plastic wrap for 20 minutes. Do not stack the pancakes as they will stick together. I use plastic trays covered with plastic wrap.

Heat your oven to 450° along with clay tiles for baking bread (page 28) or an upside-down baking sheet. Mix the remaining 2 tablespoons of butter with poppy seeds. Place a bit of flour on a small plywood board and place a loaf on the board. Brush the top with some of the butter and seeds and then slide into the oven. Bake just until the bubbles that form on the dough turn a bit brown, about 4 minutes. Remove from the oven using the plywood board and brush the bottom of the loaf with a bit of water. Stack the loaves and cover with plastic wrap until serving time.

GARAM MASALA

Makes about 2 cups

Indian cooks seem to know more about the use of spices than just about anybody. After all, their ancestors were on the important trade routes in ancient times and began trading spices from the very beginning of such routes.

The following spice blend can be found in a thousand variations, as every family has its own. I like this one and I think it will work well for your Indian cooking.

½ cup coriander seeds (page 49)

¼ cup cinnamon stick pieces

¼ cup black peppercorns

2 bay leaves

¼ cup cumin seeds

3 tablespoons whole cloves

1 teaspoon fenugreek seeds (page 50)

3 teaspoons cardamom seeds (page 49)

1 teaspoon turmeric

¼ teaspoon ground or freshly grated nutmeg

1 tablespoon red pepper flakes

Place all of the spices, except the turmeric, nutmeg, and red pepper flakes, on a baking sheet. Bake at 275° for 10 minutes, or until all smell fragrant. Place in a food processor and grind as fine as you can. You may have to break up the cinnamon stick pieces by hand. Then add ALL the ingredients to a food blender and grind away. Moving the spices from a food processor to a blender will allow you to get a finer grind.

Store in a sealed glass jar.

LAMB VINDALOO

(Gosht Vindaloo)

Serves 4–6

Lamb is very popular with the Indian cooks. Americans are getting better about enjoying this wonderful meat, and I really think this dish will convince you that lamb cooked properly has no "lamby" flavor to it. This is a fine dish, rich in every way.

SPICE MIXTURE

2 tablespoons coriander seeds (page 49)

1 tablespoon turmeric

2 teaspoons red pepper flakes

1 teaspoon ground dried ginger

½ teaspoon cumin seeds

½ teaspoon fenugreek seeds (page 50)

½ teaspoon black mustard seeds (page 51)

THE REMAINING INGREDIENTS

2 pounds lamb stew meat, cut into 1-inch cubes

1 medium yellow onion, peeled

3 cloves garlic, peeled

¼ cup red wine vinegar

¼ cup *ghee* (page 356)

2 cups water

1 teaspoon salt

2 cups peeled and diced potatoes

GARNISH

Chopped fresh coriander (page 49)

Grind the spices in a small electric coffee grinder (page 23) or spice grinder and set aside.

Chop the onion and garlic in a food processor and add the spices. Add the vinegar and make a paste. Put the lamb in a large bowl and rub all the pieces well with the paste. Cover and marinate for 4 hours, unrefrigerated.

Heat a large frying pan (I prefer one that's SilverStone-lined). Brown the lamb, along with the onion, garlic, and vinegar, in 2 batches, using half of the *ghee* for each batch. Place the browned meat in a 4-to 6-quart stove-top covered casserole along with the pan drippings. Add the water and salt, and bring the pot to a boil. Turn to a simmer and cook, covered, for 1 hour. Add the potatoes and simmer for 30 minutes more. Garnish with the coriander and serve.

CHICKEN VINDALOO

Serves 4

This is more than a chicken stew. This is a celebration of the Indian grandma's ability to stretch one chicken, with the aid of many spices, into a dish so rich that you will need very little to be satisfied. Many immigrants to this country realized that it would be necessary to stretch basic food products with methods used during shortages in the Old World. This dish they have never forgotten, and I expect they never will.

1   3½-pound chicken, quartered and skinned
    Salt and freshly ground black pepper to taste
¼   cup *ghee* (page 356) or butter
3   cloves garlic, peeled and minced
2   cups yellow onion, finely chopped
2   tablespoons grated fresh ginger
2   teaspoons ground cumin
2   teaspoons crushed yellow mustard seeds (page 51)
1   teaspoon ground cinnamon
½   teaspoon ground cloves

1   tablespoon turmeric
1½ teaspoons cayenne pepper
1   tablespoon paprika
1   tablespoon tamarind paste (2 tablespoons dried tamarind, page 47, mixed with 2 tablespoons hot water, worked through a sieve, discarding the seeds)
2   teaspoons lemon juice
2   tablespoons distilled white vinegar
1   teaspoon brown sugar
2   teaspoons salt
2   cups water

GARNISHES

Cored and thinly sliced jalapeño peppers

Chopped fresh coriander (page 49)

Salt and pepper the chicken quarters. Heat a large frying pan and brown the chicken in the *ghee*. You will have to do this in 2 batches. Remove the chicken to a 6-quart stove-top covered casserole, leaving the fat in the pan. Add the garlic and onion to the pan and sauté until golden brown. Add to the casserole along with the ginger, cumin, mustard seed, cinnamon, cloves, turmeric, cayenne, and paprika. Sauté all for a few minutes and then add all remaining ingredients except the garnishes. Cover and simmer until the chicken is tender, about 45 minutes. Stir a few times during cooking. Partially remove the lid during the last 10 minutes or so to thicken the sauce.

Top with the garnishes.

MULLIGATAWNY SOUP

Serves 6–8

Someone told me that they thought this name referred to "waste soup." There is such a soup, of course, but this is not it. Julie Sahni explains that some 200 years ago, cooks in the south of India prepared this for their English masters. The name comes from *mullaga* (pepper) and *tanni* (water). This is "pepper water soup," and it is very delicious. There are a thousand variations on this dish and I have tried to put a few of them together in this version.

1¼ pounds chicken thighs

8 cups water

1 tablespoon *ghee* (page 356) or butter

2 cloves garlic, peeled and minced

1 medium yellow onion, peeled and chopped

2 stalks celery, chopped

1½ cups chopped carrots

¼ teaspoon turmeric

½ teaspoon ground coriander seeds (page 49)

¼ teaspoon red pepper flakes

½ teaspoon ground cumin

½ teaspoon ground cardamom (page 49)

½ teaspoon ground dried ginger

2 teaspoons salt

GARNISHES

Chopped fresh coriander (page 49)

Freshly ground black pepper

In a 4-quart pot, simmer the chicken, covered, in 4 cups of water until tender, about 30 minutes. Remove, cool, debone, and chop the meat and skin coarsely. Save the stock in the pot. Set the meat aside.

Heat a large frying pan and add the *ghee,* garlic, onion, celery, and carrot. Sauté just until the onion is tender. Add this to the pot of reserved stock.

Add 4 more cups of water to the pot along with all remaining ingredients except the garnishes and chicken. Cover and simmer for 30 minutes. Add the deboned chicken. Simmer for 5 minutes. Garnish with the fresh coriander and black pepper. I like lots of black pepper in this dish!

PRAWNS MASALA

Serves 4

This dish will be a delight to all seafood lovers. It is terribly rich in flavor, so the shrimp will easily serve 4. The name refers to the spice blend involved.

1 teaspoon yellow mustard seeds (page 51)	2 bay leaves
1 teaspoon coriander seeds (page 49)	2 medium yellow onions, peeled and sliced
5 cloves garlic, peeled	2 cups canned coconut milk (page 38)
1 tablespoon Garam Masala (page 199)	2 tablespoons dried tamarind, page 47, soaked 1 hour in ¼ cup water, worked through a sieve, discarding the seeds
1 tablespoon grated fresh ginger	
1 teaspoon cumin seeds	
¼ teaspoon red pepper flakes	1 pound fresh or frozen prawns, shelled or thawed
3 tablespoons vegetable oil	Salt to taste

Using a small spice grinder or small electric coffee grinder (page 23), grind mustard seeds and coriander seeds.

With a mortar and pestle, mix together the garlic, Garam Masala, ground mustard seeds and coriander seeds, ginger, cumin, and red pepper. Pound it all into a paste.

Heat the vegetable oil in a skillet. Add the bay leaves and onion. Sauté until the onion is translucent. Add the ground paste and cook until the oil separates, about 15 minutes.

Add the coconut milk to the sautéed onion, along with the tamarind paste. Bring to a boil, then simmer over medium-low heat for 15 minutes.

Add the prawns and salt and simmer until done to taste, about 5 minutes.

LEMON PICKLE

Makes plenty

So simple and so delicious. If you like lemons, this pickle will drive you crazy! Just remember that it needs to cure for 2 or 3 weeks before serving.

½ cup salad oil

3 tablespoons salt

1 teaspoon turmeric

1 teaspoon ground fenugreek (page 50)

1 teaspoon yellow mustard seeds (page 51)

1 teaspoon red pepper flakes

½ teaspoon fennel seeds

¼ teaspoon asafetida (page 37) (optional)

6 cloves garlic, peeled and sliced

2 ounces fresh ginger, sliced

18 lemons

Heat a frying pan. Add the oil and all the ingredients except the lemons. Cook over low heat for 45 seconds, but don't brown the garlic. Set aside to cool. Quarter the lemons, do not peel, and place in a large bowl. Add the cooled spiced oil and toss well. Pack into a 1-gallon wide-mouth jar. Seal the jar and leave it on your kitchen counter, near a window. Shake the jar and roll the juices about once every 3 days. You will need to open the jar now and then to allow gas to escape.

After 2 or 3 weeks the pickles are cured. Place in the refrigerator, where they will keep well for a couple of months.

Serve as a pickle course with any of the Indian dishes in this section.

SAMOSAS

Makes 48 small treasures

These stuffed deep-fried pastries are too delicious to be called a snack. I could easily make a whole meal of them. They take a bit of doing, but you will be happy with the results. Get the kids in on the rolling and folding. Either a vegetable filling or a meat filling can be used.

DOUGH

2 cups sifted all-purpose
flour (See Hint, page
423.)

6 tablespoons vegetable oil

1 teaspoon salt

½ cup water

Oil for frying

Using a fork, blend the flour, oil, and salt. Add the water and knead to form smooth dough. Wrap in plastic and refrigerate for 1 hour.

Knead the dough for 1 minute. Cut in half. Cut each half into 12 pieces. Roll each in 7-inch circles using additional flour. Cut each circle in half. Form a "cone." Fill and seal with water into a triangle. (See the illustration.)

Fry in 2 inches of oil at 375° for 2 to 3 minutes per side. Drain.

VEGETABLE FILLING

4 tablespoons *ghee* (page
356)

1 pound potatoes, peeled
and cut into ¼-inch dice

2 cloves garlic, peeled and
minced

1 cup peeled and finely
chopped yellow onion

1 teaspoon grated fresh
ginger

2 teaspoons Garam Masala
(page 199)

1 tablespoon chopped fresh
coriander (page 49)

Pinch of cayenne pepper

½ teaspoon turmeric

2 teaspoons lemon juice

1 cup frozen peas, thawed

Salt to taste

Heat a large frying pan and add the *ghee*, potatoes, garlic, onion, and ginger. Cover and cook on low for 10 minutes, to sweat the potatoes down. Stir a few times. Don't brown. Add the remaining ingredients and continue cooking, covered, until the potatoes and peas are tender, 5 minutes. Set aside to cool.

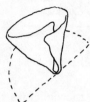

MEAT FILLING

1 tablespoon *ghee* (page 356)

2 cloves garlic, peeled and minced

1 medium yellow onion, peeled and finely chopped

½ pound finely ground lamb

½ pound finely ground beef

1 teaspoon grated fresh ginger

2 teaspoons Garam Masala (page 199)

1 tablespoon chopped fresh coriander (page 49)

½ teaspoon turmeric

Pinch of cayenne pepper

¼ teaspoon ground cinnamon

2 teaspoons fresh lemon juice

Salt to taste

Sauté all ingredients until they are crumbly and most of the liquid is absorbed. Set aside to cool.

THE IRISH
IMMIGRANTS

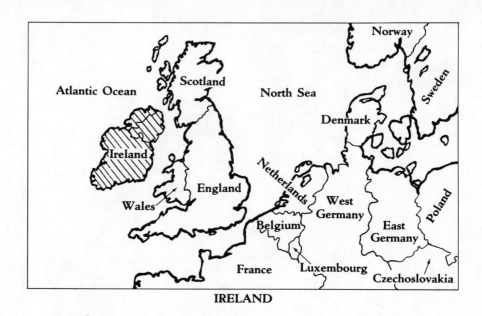

IRELAND

T hey say that there are two kinds of people in this world, "those who
are Irish and those who want to be Irish." Such is the wonderful ar-
rogance of the people from the Emerald Isle. And it must be true. After
all, there are some 40 million Americans who claim Irish ancestry, almost ten times the population of Ireland! This is the third largest immigrant group in America, their number being exceeded only by the
English and the Germans.

The country is no larger than the state of Maine, and it truly is an
Emerald Isle. It derives this name from its green farm and pasture lands.
Certainly it is a wet land, with eight hundred rivers or lakes and a whole
portion of the central plain made up of peat bogs: swampy lands com-
posed of dead plants and mosses built up over the years. (The peat or
turf is one of Irelands's most important resources and a full fourth of the
land's electricity comes from the burning of dried turf at turf power
stations.)

These people have championed the green in America as well, and they
have brought us Waterford crystal, Belleek china, Irish linen, Irish whiskey, Irish stew, racehorses, shamrocks, Leprechauns, and Irish beer. See,
you have always wanted to be Irish!

The original inhabitants of Ireland were the Celts. They came from
Central Europe about 3000 B.C. and moved westward to the land of the

green. Eventually, most other European cultures were absorbed by the Roman Empire, but not the Celts. They were separated by the Irish Sea, and the Romans really didn't think that the trip across would be worth it. So the Celts developed in their own way.

During the fifth century Saint Patrick brought Christianity to Ireland and the island became a major center for Christian learning. Great monasteries were called together and they thrived . . . until the rule of Henry VIII. I really think that the battle between the Catholics and the Protestants was seeded during his reign.

You remember that King Henry broke with the Church of Rome and established himself as the head of the English Church. The Catholics in Ireland who did not join with him in the break began to be severely persecuted. They were not allowed to speak their native tongue, Gaelic, and Catholics were not allowed to buy property. The land was parceled out among all descendants, thus making the holdings too small to support anyone. By 1755 Irish Catholics owned less than 5 percent of their own land. It was during this time that the diet of potatoes began to be a lifesaver.

In 1845 a fungus disease hit the potato crop and millions of people starved to death. Immigration to America became intense, an immigration brought about by famine and landlessness, but many had come before these events. There was even a crewman named William Ayers, from Galway, aboard the ship of Columbus.

The Irish Catholic immigrants who came to the New World during the late 1800s met with a great deal of religious prejudice, even though America was a land founded by religious dissidents. As a result, the Irish wound up in destitute areas and in urban slums. But, typical of the Irish, they were not to be put down and the contributions that they have made to American life have been immense.

The list of names of these influential Irish immigrants, and their descendants, is more than impressive. And it is American. George M. Cohan, Victor Herbert, Eugene O'Neill, Spencer Tracy, James Cagney, Bing Crosby, Gene Kelly, Maureen O'Sullivan, and Grace Kelly all have touched the fields of music and the theater. In the literary field we find James Farrell, John O'Hara, Flannery O'Connor, William Kennedy, Mary Gordon, and Mary McCarthy. One of the most important names in all of American architecture is that of Louis H. Sullivan, of course. In politics the Kennedy family is of utmost importance, as is the name of the beloved former Speaker of the House, Tip O'Neill. The list goes on and on.

I was in Ireland traveling as a student in 1960. The day was gorgeous, the fields green, and the water beautiful. I was on a bicycle pedaling around the Ring of Kerry, one of the most lovely places in all of the Emerald Isle. I came upon a small wooden sign at the side of the road:

MUCKROSS ABBEY—2 KILOMETRES. I stopped and got off my bike and tried to remember where I had heard of this place, and why it had remained in my mind. I had it! Washington Irving, the great American writer, author of such treasures as "Rip Van Winkle" and "The Legend of Sleepy Hollow," said something in his sketchbook . . . something like this: "The reason that America does not have more great writers is because we have no Muckross Abbeys." I turned down the dirt road to learn something about Irving's statement. I found a couple of stone walls still standing and a graveyard. It took some research to fully understand the American writer's remark.

Muckross Abbey was founded in 1448 as a Franciscan monastery. The monks were suppressed by Henry VIII in 1542 and the place was finally burned down by Cromwell in 1652. Here was one of the symbols of the battles between the British Crown and the Irish Catholics . . . and all of this had taken place before we in America had even established the Republic. Irving made it very plain that the reason we do not have more great writers is because we do not have any Muckross Abbey . . . in short, we have a very young history. D. C. Smith, a friend who helps me with research, claims that Irving was not referring just to a short history. "After all," D.C. pointed out, "the graveyard at the abbey is filled with Irish poets and bards. We simply don't have enough dead poets!" He is right, of course, as our history is too short.

I love the Irish. I even married one, Patty Mae Dailey. I shall never forget meeting her very Irish immigrant grandfather. Pop Teehan was such an old curmudgeon that I decided to wear my clerical collar to our first meeting. Since he was a good Irish Catholic I thought perhaps he would be a bit easier on me. When he saw the collar he nearly went crazy. After all, he would not yell and scream at a priest, but this was a Protestant, a Methodist yet, and he was dating his favorite grandaughter. He was stymied, and it was a few years before we became good friends. After all, he was Irish! I miss the old goat.

The following recipes are truly typical of good Irish cuisine. I know you have heard that Irish cooking is bland and boring. This is not so, as you will see from these pages. Yes, there are a few potatoes about, but then that is what the Irish lived on in the old country and that is what the immigrants lived on in this country. However, you will find the food to be really delightful. Give it a chance. The Irish Soda Bread alone should be enough to convert you to some Irish feasts.

POTATO ONION SOUP, IRISH STYLE

Serves 8–10

Yes, it is true that the Irish lived on potatoes for a time. The old country has never been wealthy in food, but the Irish have always been wealthy in humor and spirit. During the great potato famine of 1845, many Irish immigrants came to this country with the hope that they could continue to make this wonderful soup.

- 4 tablespoons butter
- 2 medium yellow onions, peeled and sliced
- 2 pounds potatoes, peeled and sliced
- 3 cups milk
- 5½ cups Chicken Stock (page 74) or use canned

- ¼ cup chopped fresh chives
- ½ teaspoon celery seeds
- ¼ teaspoon dried thyme, whole
- 1 cup light cream
- Salt and freshly ground black pepper to taste

ROUX

- 2 tablespoons butter
- 2 tablespoons all-purpose flour

GARNISHES

- ½ cup chopped fresh chives
- 6 slices lean bacon, crisply fried and chopped

Heat a 6- to 8-quart stockpot, add the butter and onion, and cook gently. Do not let the onion brown. Add the peeled and sliced potatoes, milk, and stock. Add the herbs. Cover and cook gently for about an hour. Prepare a *roux:* Melt the butter in a small saucepan and whisk in the flour. Let the flour and butter mixture (*roux*) bubble for 2 minutes on medium-low heat, stirring constantly. Thicken the soup with the *roux,* whisking carefully to avoid lumps. Cook for 5 to 10 minutes and then purée the soup in a food processor or food blender. Add the cream and gently reheat, but do not boil. Season with the salt and pepper. Serve with chopped fresh chives and the crisply fried bacon as garnishes.

This soup can also be made with the chopped white part of 5 or 6 large leeks instead of onions. Additional garnishes you can use instead of bacon are chopped prawns or a small dice of lobster.

DUBLIN CODDLE

Serves 8

The name is wonderful and the recipe legit. The dish is simply potatoes boiled with ham, onion, and sausage. It is from a wonderful book on Irish cooking by Theodora Fitzgibbon (page 519), a British food authority whom I greatly admire. Nothing complicated about this souplike stew, and it was a source of fond memories for our Irish immigrant ancestors.

1½ pounds pork sausage, cut into 1-inch pieces

1½ pounds smoked ham, cut into 1-inch dice

1 quart boiling water

2 large yellow onions, peeled and thinly sliced

2 pounds potatoes, peeled and thickly sliced

4 tablespoons chopped parsley

Salt and freshly ground black pepper to taste

Place the sausage and ham in the boiling water and boil for 5 minutes. Drain, but reserve the liquid. Put the meat into a large saucepan (or an oven-proof dish) with the onions, potatoes, and parsley. Add enough of the stock to not quite cover the contents. Cover the pot and simmer gently for about 1 hour, or until the liquid is reduced by half and all the ingredients are cooked but not mushy. You may need to remove the lid during the last half of the cooking process. Season with salt and pepper.

Serve hot with the vegetables on top and fresh Irish Soda Bread (page 214) and a glass of stout.

COLCANNON

Serves 6

You may think Irish cuisine is rather boring since it is so filled with potatoes. But please understand that Irish immigrants came to this country willing to work . . . and wishing to maintain their love for the potato. I think the variations on a common theme that they constructed are ingenious. Witness this one!

1¼ pounds kale, tough stems removed, washed (or use green cabbage)

2 cups water

1 tablespoon olive oil

1¼ pounds potatoes, peeled and quartered

1 cup cleaned and chopped leeks (white part only)

1 cup milk

Pinch of ground mace

Salt and freshly ground back pepper to taste

½ cup melted butter

GARNISH (optional)

1 tablespoon chopped parsley

In a large pot, simmer the kale, covered, in 2 cups of water and the oil for 10 minutes. Drain and chop fine; set aside and keep warm. In a small pot, bring the potatoes and water to cover to a boil and simmer until tender. In another small pot, simmer the leeks, covered, in the milk for 10 minutes, and keep warm. Drain the potatoes and purée them, using a potato ricer or masher, into the large pot. Add the leeks with their milk, and the cooked kale. Beat with a wooden spoon until fluffy. Season with mace, salt, and pepper. Mound on a plate and top with melted butter. Garnish with parsley if you are using cabbage.

IRISH SODA BREAD

Makes 2 loaves

No yeast is necessary in this dish . . . never has been in real Irish Soda Bread. Craig, my assistant, and I worked a long time on this recipe to get something that reminded me of the bread that I'd had while touring in Ireland as a student. I really believe that we are very close to the loaves offered the families in this country by our Irish immigrant grandmas.

6 cups all-purpose flour (See Hint, page 423.)	2 teaspoons sugar
2 teaspoons baking soda	1 teaspoon salt
2 teaspoons baking powder	2½ cups buttermilk
3 tablespoons cornstarch	

Preheat oven to 375°.

Add all of the dry ingredients in a large bowl and mix very well. Pour all of the buttermilk into the bowl at once and stir, using a wooden spoon, just until a soft dough is formed. Do not try to make it smooth at this point. Pour the contents of the bowl out onto a plastic counter and knead for a minute or so until everything comes together.

Divide the dough into two portions and shape each into a round loaf, pressing the top down a bit to just barely flatten it. Place the loaves on a large ungreased baking sheet. (I like to use the nonstick kind.) Sprinkle some additional flour on the top of each loaf and, using a sharp paring knife, make the sign of the Cross in slashes on the top of each.

Allow the loaves to rest for 10 minutes and then bake on the middle rack of the oven for 40 minutes, or until the loaves are golden brown and done to taste.

Cool on racks.

IRISH DARK SODA BREAD

Makes 2 loaves

Same story as the bread above. Different flavor due to the addition of whole-wheat flour. This is so simple to prepare and so delicious that I expect you will become famous with your children for the making of this bread. Do it!

3 cups all-purpose flour
(See Hint, page 423.)

2 cups whole-wheat flour
(See Hint, page 423.)

2 teaspoons baking soda

1 tablespoon baking
powder

2 tablespoons brown sugar

2¼ cups buttermilk

Proceed as in the recipe for Irish Soda Bread, being very careful to break up any lumps of brown sugar. Divide the dough into 2 loaves and bake at 400° for about 45 minutes, or until brown and crunchy. Cool on racks just as above.

IRISH BEEF STEW WITH
GUINNESS STOUT

Serves 4–6

Yes, the Irish have traditionally drunk a lot of stout. Stout is a dark and rich beer, and it is often mixed with an equal amount of regular beer in order to produce an "arf and arf." In this beef stew, a very traditional dish both in the old country and here, the stout is a major flavoring. I love it!

2 tablespoons olive oil

3 bay leaves

2 pounds beef stew meat, cut into 1½-inch to 2-inch cubes (with some fat)

1 large yellow onion, peeled and cut into ¼-inch slices

2 cloves garlic, peeled and chopped

1 teaspoon dried thyme, whole

1 teaspoon dried rosemary

2–3 tablespoons all-purpose flour

¾ cup Beef Stock (page 78) or use canned

½ cup Guinness stout

1 tablespoon chopped parsley

½ pound carrots, sliced

Salt and freshly ground black pepper to taste

Heat a 6-quart stove-top casserole and add the oil and the bay leaves. Cook the bay leaves for a moment and then add the meat. Brown the meat on both sides on high heat. Add the sliced onion and cook for a few minutes until it is clear. Reduce the heat to low and add the garlic, thyme, rosemary, and flour, and stir well until smooth.

Add the Beef Stock and stout; simmer, stirring, until the stew thickens a bit. Add the remaining ingredients and cover. Place the pot in a 275° oven for about 2 hours, stirring a couple of times. Check for salt and pepper before serving.

IRISH LAMB STEW

Serves 12

This is not the dish that frightened you as a child. There is a great deal of difference, in terms of flavor, between older lamb and young lamb. Older lamb was less expensive during the Great Immigration . . . and it was less expensive in the old country. Makes this version with lamb from the supermarket or butcher and you will be delighted.

½ pound thickly sliced bacon, diced

6 pounds boneless lamb shoulder, cut into 2-inch pieces

1 teaspoon salt

½ teaspoon freshly ground black pepper

½ cup all-purpose flour (See Hint, page 423.)

2 cloves garlic, peeled and finely chopped

1 large yellow onion, peeled and finely chopped

½ cup water

4 cups Beef Stock (page 78) or use canned

2 teaspoons sugar

4 cups carrots, cut into 1-inch pieces

2 large yellow onions, peeled and sliced

3 pounds potatoes, peeled, quartered, and cut into ½-inch pieces

1 teaspoon dried thyme, whole

1 bay leaf

½ cup dry white wine

GARNISH

Chopped parsley

Using a large frying pan, sauté the bacon. Reserve the fat and the bacon.

In a large mixing bowl place the lamb, salt, pepper, and flour. Toss to coat the meat evenly. Reheat the frying pan. In batches, toss the meat in the flour to coat evenly, then brown in the reserved bacon fat. If you run out of fat, use a little oil. Transfer the browned meat to a 10-quart stove-top casserole, leaving about ¼ cup of fat in the frying pan. Add the garlic and yellow onion to the pan and sauté until the onion begins to color a bit. Deglaze the frying pan with ½ cup of water and add the garlic-onion mixture to the casserole, along with the reserved bacon pieces, Beef Stock, and sugar. Cover and simmer for 1½ hours, or until tender.

Add the remaining ingredients to the pot and simmer, covered, for about 20 minutes until the vegetables are tender. Check for salt and pepper before serving.

Top with the parsley garnish before serving.

NOTE: This keeps well in the refrigerator. I am convinced it is better reheated.

SCALLOP AND MUSHROOM PIE

Serves 4–5

Theodora Fitzgibbon, in her fine book on Irish cooking (page 519), gives us another dish that has always been popular with the Irish immigrant. Yes, it contains potatoes, but it is a pie of seafood and mushrooms. I served this one night at a very formal Irish dinner party and my guests were very delighted. And none of them were Irish!

1½ pounds fresh scallops

1 cup milk

Salt and freshly ground black pepper to taste

1 generous tablespoon butter

1 heaping tablespoon all-purpose flour

¼ pound mushrooms, sliced

¼ cup sweet sherry

3 cups cold mashed potatoes

GARNISH

1 tablespoon chopped parsley

Cut the cleaned scallops in half if they are large and simmer them in the milk, with salt and pepper, for 15 minutes. Strain, but reserve the milk. Melt the butter in a saucepan, add the flour, and mix well, then gradually stir in the warmed milk, seeing that it is free from lumps. Add the mushrooms, sherry, and scallops. Put into an ovenproof dish and cover the top with mashed potatoes. (You may wish to mix the potatoes with a little bit of milk so that they can be spread like an icing over the scallops.) Dot with additional butter and bake in a 350° oven until the top is gently browned, about 20 to 30 minutes. Garnish with parsley.

BOILED CABBAGE WITH SMOKED PORK BUTT

Serves 3–4

I know most Americans figure that the Irish live on corned beef and cabbage. I'm not sure that there's any truth to this. I never did see the dish when I was in Ireland, and the New York Irish community seems to serve it rarely. However, the following dish is just wonderful and I think it can easily replace one Irish myth with another.

2 pounds smoked boneless pork butt, in 1 piece

3 quarts boiling water

½ cup firmly packed light brown sugar

¼ cup fine soft bread crumbs

1 teaspoon dry mustard (I prefer Colman's.)

1 medium green cabbage, 3–3½ pounds

1 tablespoon corn syrup or molasses

1 medium yellow onion, peeled and studded with 4 whole cloves

Salt and freshly ground black pepper to taste

Place the meat in an 8-quart pot. Add the boiling water, cover, and simmer for 1½ hours.

Mix the brown sugar, bread crumbs, and mustard, and set aside.

Remove any limp outer leaves from the cabbage and then cut it into slim wedges. Do not remove the core or the cabbage wedges will fall apart. (Insert toothpicks at strategic points along the cabbage wedges if they won't hold together.)

When the smoked pork butt has cooked for 1½ hours, preheat the oven to 350°. Remove the pork butt from the kettle and set aside, reserving the cooking liquid. Pierce the pork butt in several places with a sharp fork. With a pastry brush, coat the top and sides of the meat with corn syrup. Pat the crumb mixture firmly on the top and sides of the meat. Place it in a shallow baking pan and bake uncovered for 25 to 30 minutes.

Blanch the cabbage and onion in the reserved broth until the cabbage is just tender, about 5 minutes. Discard the onion. Add salt and pepper if desired. Slice the pork butt and serve with the cabbage.

IRISH BOILED DINNER

"Be telling me this serves 6–8"

I believe that it takes a certain amount of gall to be a good cook. You have to be in charge. When Craig, my assistant, and I tasted this dish at a very famous Irish restaurant and bar in Boston, the home of the Irish, he was not impressed. "Smith," he said, "let me at this one!" When he further explained that he had never cooked this particular dish but knew that he could create a variation superior to what we were eating, I told him to hop to it. This simple and delicious version is the result. Craig may not have any Irish blood in him, but he certainly has Irish gall! The beer is his addition, that's for sure. Actually, he has done his research. This is much more common in the Irish-American home than is corned beef and cabbage.

1 3½-pound fresh beef brisket

2 12-ounce bottles lager beer

2 cups water (or enough to just cover)

2 bay leaves

10 black peppercorns

½ cup chopped parsley

2 teaspoons salt

2 tablespoons butter or olive oil

3 cloves garlic, peeled and sliced

2 cups chopped and rinsed leeks (white parts only)

1 medium yellow onion, peeled and sliced

¾ pound large carrots, cut into large pieces

¾ pound small red potatoes

1 pound turnips, peeled and quartered

2 pounds green cabbage, cut in sixths (Secure with toothpicks.)

Salt and freshly ground black pepper to taste

Place an 8- to 10-quart stove-top covered casserole on the burner and add the beef, beer, water, bay leaves, peppercorns, parsley, and salt. Heat a frying pan and add the butter or olive oil. Sauté the garlic, leeks, and yellow onion for a few minutes and add to the casserole. Cover the pot and simmer gently for 3½ hours, or until the meat is very tender. (This will normally take about 1 hour per pound of brisket.) In the last 25 minutes of cooking, add the carrots and red potatoes. In the last 15 minutes of cooking, add the turnips, cabbage, salt, and pepper.

If the vegetables are not done to your liking, cook them longer, but do not overcook.

Remove the toothpicks from the cabbage before serving.

THE JAMAICAN
IMMIGRANTS

JAMAICA

The island from whence our Jamaican immigrants came is strikingly beautiful. The lush trees and surrounding Caribbean waters caused the Arawak Indians, who migrated there from the Guiana and Venezuela areas in the seventh century, to call the area Xaymaca (pronounced "Himaka"), "the land of wood and water." It is also a very mountainous and rugged island, and I can certainly testify to its beauty.

The first Europeans to come to this island were the Spanish. The natives whom Columbus encountered on the island of Cuba told him about Jamaica. Columbus arrived in Jamaica on May 5, 1494, and he was met by no fewer than seventy canoes filled with hostile warriors.

The Spanish always had a method for dealing with such disturbances during the fifteenth century. They simply wiped out the natives. The Spanish settlers who followed put the natives into slavery and the native population fell, in the course of one hundred years, from 100,000 to 74. The practical-minded Spanish colonists then had to bring in black slaves from Africa to work the fields. Some 800,000 African slaves were brought to Jamaica between 1690 and 1820, and they certainly fared no better than the Arawak people. Seventeen out of every hundred black slaves died within nine weeks of capture; only half lived to work the fields. When you wander about this quiet and laid-back island, it is hard to absorb the history. Very hard.

The British began to be jealous of the Spanish-held Caribbean island and in 1655 sent in the troops. The battle dragged on and the Spanish officially ceded Jamaica to the British. The first English governor was appointed in 1661. The slave trade continued.

Sugar was king on Jamaica in the seventh and eighteenth centuries. The slave population was expanded to meet the labor needs of the plantations—plantations that offered sugar, rum, and coffee to the British. Parliament did not end the slave trade in Jamaica until 1838. We find this shocking, but remember that we did not abolish such trade in this country until 1863.

A series of especially devastating hurricanes hit the island between 1910 and 1921, severely damaging the agricultural economy and providing an impetus for migration off the island. By 1920 we had a large Jamaican population in New York City.

The early Jamaican immigrants to this country must have had a hard time of it, given the racial discrimination of the time. Even the American blacks would have little to do with the Jamaicans. They were, and are, however, an industrious lot and in very little time a prosperous community had developed in New York and Miami. At the moment there are about one million Jamaicans in America and it is great fun to be with them. The society is creole, a synthesis of African and European cultures . . . and the food from the island is just wonderful.

You can shop in New York—actually in Brooklyn, on Flatbush Avenue—and find all the things you need for this cuisine. You should have little trouble finding the ingredients in a Latino market, for that matter. The food from the island is very important to the Jamaican immigrant, since it provides one of the most vivid symbols and memories for these charming people. I suspect another important symbol is the distinctive music from the island.

Air Jamaica is one of the few airlines I know of that publishes a travel poster with nothing but food on it. Oh, Air France might do this now and then but the Jamaicans are serious eaters. The poster shows the classics: Curried Goat, Oxtail Stew, Salt Fish and Ackee, Hibiscus Drink, Chicken Fricassee, Beef Patties . . . all on an airline poster. Not a single shot of the land! The food is much more delightful than you can believe.

When you go to Jamaica you can go to the tourist parts of the island, such as Montego Bay, and find nothing but beauty. However, if you go to Kingston, the capital, you will find much lower prices, wonderful food, charming people, and a great deal of poverty. I think you see the real Jamaica in Kingston.

The following recipes will provide you with enough food for a full Jamaican banquet. I warn you. If you start cooking such things as Jamaican Oxtail Stew, you might just not stop.

THE JAMAICAN IMMIGRANTS

JAMAICAN OXTAIL STEW

Serves 4–5

I first tasted this dish in Kingston, Jamaica, at a colorful local restaurant called The Pepperpot. I was really surprised by the brightness of flavor, and for a moment both Craig, my assistant, and I were stumped. The assertive flavor of allspice was so obvious that we missed it. The following recipe is close to what is served at this wonderful restaurant. You will find a similar dish in the Jamaican restaurants of New York.

⅓ cup dried small white beans

1 tablespoon freshly rendered lard (page 168) or vegetable oil

3 pounds beef oxtails

3 cloves garlic, peeled and crushed

1 medium yellow onion, peeled and diced

1 medium tomato, diced

2 cups Beef Stock (page 78) or use canned

2 cups water (approximately)

2 tablespoons freshly ground allspice, or to taste

Salt and freshly ground black pepper to taste

Few shots of Tabasco

Place beans in a small saucepan. Add 1 cup of the water, bring to a boil, covered, and turn off the heat. Allow to sit for 1 hour, covered, and then drain.

Brown the oxtails well in the lard or oil. Place the oxtails in a 6-quart stove-top casserole. Add the garlic, onion, and tomato. Add the Beef Stock and enough water so that it just covers the contents of the pot. Add the allspice, salt, and pepper. Cover and simmer for 3½ hours, adding the drained beans after 1½ hours. Stir occasionally. Remove the lid during the last hour of cooking if you wish a thicker sauce. Be careful that the pot does not dry out. Season with salt, pepper, and Tabasco.

CORNED SPARERIBS WITH BEANS

Serves 4–5

This dish is actually supposed to be made from pickled pigs' tails. I know that this sounds strange to you, but Jamaica has never been a wealthy country, and so every part of the animal is used. The tail is a great delicacy and Jamaican immigrants brought this very dish with them to the States. You can buy them all pickled and ready to go in the Jamaican markets on Flatbush Avenue in Brooklyn. I have substituted pork spareribs for you squeamish ones!

Please note that if you pickle your own ribs, this dish will take 10 days to prepare. It's worth it!

3 pounds pork spareribs, cut in 4 rib sections

½ pound kosher salt

½ teaspoon saltpeter (page 45)

1 gallon water

2 cups dried red kidney beans

4 cups Chicken Stock (page 74) or use canned

3 cloves garlic, peeled and chopped

2 teaspoons dried thyme, whole

1 bay leaf

2 scallions, chopped

Freshly ground black pepper to taste

Corn the ribs by mixing the salt and saltpeter together and dissolving in a gallon of water. Place the ribs in a large plastic or stainless-steel container with a cover. Add the saltwater solution, being careful that the ribs all stay under the surface. You may have to weigh them down with a plate. Cover the container and refrigerate for 10 days—yes, 10! Check a few times to be sure that the ribs stay under the surface. This is very important.

When the ribs are pickled, you may proceed. Place the beans in a heavy saucepan with ample water to cover. Bring them to a boil, turn off the heat, and then let them sit, covered, for 1 hour. Drain.

Rinse the ribs well and soak in fresh water for 1 hour. Drain and blanch in boiling water for 1 to 2 minutes. Drain and cut in 1-rib pieces. Place in a 6-quart pot. Add everything but the beans. Bring to a boil and simmer, covered, for ½ hour. Add the drained beans, cover, and simmer for 1¾ hours.

Uncover during the last 30 minutes to evaporate excess liquid.

SALT FISH AND ACKEE

Serves 4 as a taste of a national treat!

While this is the national dish of Jamaica, you must understand that the fruit from the ackee tree simply does not travel well when fresh. It must be canned. We were in Jamaica just following Hurricane Gilbert. The ackee trees were damaged but we still ate the dish many times. By the time we reached New York, canned ackee sold for $10 a tin. I hope prices have gone down by the time you read this recipe. The dish is very good and it looks very much like scrambled eggs with peppers and fish flakes.

½ pound salt cod (page 45)

¼ cup peanut oil

2 tablespoons butter

1 large yellow onion, peeled and chopped

¼ green bell pepper, cored, seeded, and diced

¼ red bell pepper, cored, seeded, and diced

1 19-ounce can ackee, drained (page 36)

Tabasco or Jamaican yellow hot sauce to taste

Rinse the salt cod several times in cold water. Soak for 24 hours, refreshing the water several times. Drain.

Simmer the drained salt cod in fresh water for about 10 minutes. Drain, cool, and flake the cod.

Heat a large frying pan and add the oil and butter. Sauté the onion until transparent. Add the peppers, drained ackee, and salt cod; sauté and toss until all is hot. Add Tabasco to taste.

JAMAICAN HIBISCUS DRINK

2 quarts

In New York there is a fine restaurant on 7th Avenue and 133rd Street. It's called The Jamaican Hot Pot Restaurant, and the food is terrific. The whole crew, including the owners, Gary and Yvonne Walters, is filled with that delightful charm from the island. When Yvonne told me about this classic drink, I ordered it. She asked if I wanted it with fine Jamaican rum. "Oh, darling," she said, "real Jamaicans always drink it with Jamaican rum!"

Here is the recipe and it's with the rum. It's great during the summer and certainly not bad during the winter.

8 cups water

2 cups dried hibiscus blossoms (page 40) (Find in Jamaican or Mexican markets— sometimes called sorrel blossoms.)

1 tablespoon grated fresh ginger

1 cup sugar or to taste

Jamaican rum (optional)

In a 4-quart stainless-steel or glass pot, bring the water to a boil. Add the hibiscus and ginger. Turn off heat, then cover and steep for 4 hours. Strain and sweeten with sugar to taste. Chill and serve, or serve with good rum, the amount according to your taste. (Isn't that tactful?)

JERK PORK

Serves 4–5

No, the name of this wonderful Jamaican dish does not refer to some degrading remark from one of the neighborhood kids. It refers to a seasoning sauce that is filled with wonderful Jamaican allspice. This is just a great dish for the charcoal grill!

2 jalapeño peppers, seeded and chopped

3 scallions, chopped

4½ tablespoons freshly ground (1 ounce) allspice

½ teaspoon ground cinnamon

½ teaspoon freshly ground nutmeg

1 teaspoon salt

½ teaspoon freshly ground black pepper

2 cloves garlic, peeled and chopped

1 teaspoon grated fresh ginger

4 bay leaves, crumbled

2 tablespoons peanut oil

2 pounds pork chops, pork steaks, or sliced boneless pork butt

Place the peppers, scallions, and all the herbs and spices in a food processor and finely chop to form a paste. Add the oil and purée until smooth. Rub on both sides of the pork and let stand for 30 minutes. Grill on the barbecue.

NOTE: This basic jerk marinade can be used on all kinds of meat. It's terrific on chicken and beef, and I certainly think you should try it on lamb.

CURRIED GOAT

Serves 8

In the streets of Kingston you will see young goats running about. No one bothers them and everyone seems to know to whom each kid belongs. After all, Curried Goat is another one of the great dishes of Jamaica. You can find goat in any Mexican or Jamaican market here in the States. If you cannot find goat, substitute lamb. Just have the butcher cut the meat, bones and all, into 1- or 2-inch pieces. This is a great dish!

4–5 pounds goat, sawed into 2 inch pieces, or lamb shoulder, cut up

2 large yellow onions, peeled and chopped

1 medium green bell pepper, cored, seeded, and chopped

4 scallions, chopped

2 medium tomatoes, chopped

4 tablespoons curry powder (page 49) (Use a Jamaican country-style brand. If you

cannot find that, use Sun brand curry powder and add a bit of allspice.)

2 teaspoons paprika

3 cloves garlic, peeled and crushed

2 tablespoons peanut oil

2 tablespoons butter

4 cups water

Salt and freshly ground black pepper to taste

In a large stainless-steel bowl or pot mix all of the ingredients except the oil, butter, water, salt, and pepper. Let marinate for ½ hour.

Separate the meat from the vegetable mixture, reserving the mixture. Heat a large frying pan and brown the meat, in small batches, in the oil and butter.

Place the browned goat in a 10- to 12-quart stove-top casserole and add the reserved vegetables from the marinade as well as any juice. Add 4 cups of water; cover and simmer until tender, about 3 hours for goat and 2½ hours for lamb. Uncover the pot for the last hour or so in order to thicken the sauce a bit. And salt and pepper to taste.

BEEF PATTIES

Makes 12 patties

We saw these patties in Jamaica but we were not terribly impressed. However, when Yvonne, at the Jamaican Hot Pot Restaurant in New York, made them for us, we were very impressed. Curry remains one of the great flavors of the island, and a curried meat pie is just . . . well, "Hey, mon!"

FILLING

1 tablespoon olive oil

2 cloves garlic, peeled and crushed

½ jalapeño pepper, seeded and minced

1 medium yellow onion, peeled and cut into small dice

2 scallions, finely chopped

1 pound lean ground beef

1 teaspoon dried thyme, whole

1 tablespoon curry powder (page 49)

1 teaspoon paprika

½ cup bread crumbs

½ cup water

Salt and freshly ground black pepper to taste

Heat a large frying pan. Add the oil, garlic, jalapeño, onions, and scallions and sauté for a few minutes. Add the ground beef and cook over medium heat until crumbly. Stir in the thyme, curry powder, paprika, and bread crumbs. Stir in the water and cook over low heat just until the water is absorbed. Add the salt and pepper. Allow to cool.

DOUGH

3 cups all-purpose flour (See Hint, page 423.)

2 teaspoons curry powder (page 49)

1 teaspoon salt

½ cup margarine

½ cup Crisco

1 egg

1 tablespoon distilled white vinegar

3–4 tablespoons ice water

In a large bowl, stir the flour, curry powder, and salt together. Cut in the shortenings using a pastry blender. Keep working the flour and shortenings until the mixture is rather grainy, like coarse cornmeal. Mix the egg and vinegar together and, using a wooden fork, stir the mixture into the flour. Add enough ice water so that the dough barely holds together. Place on a marble pastry slab or a plastic countertop and knead for just a few turns, enough so that the dough holds together and becomes rollable. Keep the remaining dough refrigerated as you work.

Roll out a golf-ball-size piece of dough to at least 6 inches. Use a 6-inch plate as a template to cut out a circle. Put 3 tablespoons of the cooled filling in the middle of dough. Fold the circle over to form a half moon. Seal the pie by pushing down with a fork to crimp the edges. Bake at 400° for 25 to 30 minutes on an ungreased baking sheet. A nonstick baking sheet is best.

RICE AND PEAS

Serves 8–10 as the starch in a Jamaican meal

In Jamaica, and among our Jamaican immigrants, beans are often called peas. This dish is a standard among Jamaicans in America and it should be a winner in your house, too. The combination of beans, rice, and coconut with peppers is sensational. You could practically live on this stuff!

1 cup dried kidney beans, rinsed

5 cups water (approximately)

1 13.5-ounce can coconut milk (page 38)

4 scallions, finely chopped

3 thin slices jalapeño pepper, chopped

3 cloves garlic, peeled and crushed

2 teaspoons dried thyme, whole

2 cups long-grain white rice

1½ teaspoons salt

¼ teaspoon freshly ground black pepper

Place the beans and 4 cups of cold water in a 4-quart pot. Cover, bring to a boil, turn off the heat, and allow to stand for 1 hour. Drain, and return the beans to the pot. Add the coconut milk, onion, jalapeño, garlic, thyme, and 1 cup of cold water. Cover and simmer for 30 minutes until the beans are just tender. Drain the beans and return them to the pot, reserving the liquid. Add the rice, salt, and pepper to the pot. Measure the reserved liquid and add enough cold water to make 4 cups total. Add the liquid to the pot. Cover, bring to a boil, and reduce the heat to low. Simmer for 15 minutes until the liquid is absorbed. Add more salt and pepper if desired.

FRICASSEE CHICKEN

Serves 4

This is another classic from the island. It is served in Jamaica and in Brooklyn with the same degree of pride. It is not overly spicy, but the flavor is rich and reminds Jamaicans of their childhood on the island.

1 4-pound chicken, cut into 8 serving pieces	1½ teaspoons dried thyme, whole
Juice of 1 lime	1 teaspoon salt
2 medium yellow onions, peeled and sliced	½ teaspoon freshly ground black pepper
2 ripe tomatoes, coarsely chopped	2 tablespoons peanut oil
3 cloves garlic, peeled and crushed	½ cup water
3 scallions, chopped	

Toss all the ingredients, except the peanut oil and water, in a large bowl and marinate for ½ hour.

Drain the chicken, reserving the marinade and vegetables. Brown the chicken in a nonstick frying pan, using the oil. You should probably do this in 2 batches. Place the chicken in a 6- to 8-quart stove-top casserole and add the reserved marinade including the vegetables, plus ½ cup of water. Cover and simmer 1 hour.

Add additional salt and pepper to taste.

THE JAPANESE
IMMIGRANTS

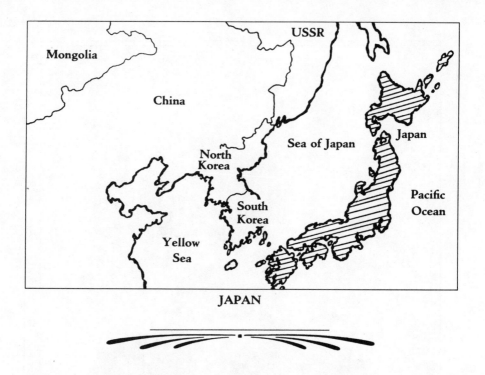

JAPAN

The earliest immigrants to this country from the Land of the Rising Sun came unwillingly and unwittingly. They were sailors washed ashore on the Pacific Coast or rescued at sea during the late eighteenth to mid-nineteenth centuries. From that tiny beginning has developed what is now the largest Asian ethnic group in the United States. They are well educated, hardworking, and instill in their children the desire to achieve. They are one of the most successful immigrant groups in the history of our nation, and the fact that this success was achieved in the face of virulent opposition, prejudice, and legal hurdles designed to prevent it, says much about the character of the Japanese American. The many Japanese American musicians, artists, businesspeople, and scientists in our midst simply attest to their fortitude. The prejudice that they had to put up with during World War II seems, in our time, to be almost insurmountable. But they continued to work.

Many Westerners confuse the Chinese and the Japanese cultures. It is true that the Japanese culture was born of the Chinese and in the beginning the Japanese borrowed some forms of art, agricultural methods, cooking, Buddhism and Confucianism from the Chinese during the fifth century A.D. But by the tenth and eleventh centuries the Japanese had developed a culture uniquely their own.

We actually knew little of this culture since Japan remained isolated from the West as a result of the political system developed by the

Tokugawa dynasty that ruled from 1603 until 1867. They were the people who gave us the concept of the shogun. All foreign contact was banned from the end of the sixteenth century until the mid 1800s. It was not until Commodore Matthew Perry entered Tokyo Bay in 1853 that we began to be aware of the culture of the Japanese. And they began to be aware of the West.

The first real Japanese immigrants were laborers recruited to work on sugar plantations in Hawaii. Today the Japanese American community in Hawaii is the largest in the United States. They are so much a part of the life in the islands, and so integrated, that you cannot actually find a Japanese community in the way that you can find a Filipino or Chinese community.

By the 1890s the Japanese were heading for California in large numbers. California needed cheap labor for the railroads, canneries, logging interests, mines, fisheries, meatpacking houses, and in the expanding agricultural industry. These immigrants were, for the most part, young men, and they were hardworking and efficient. They learned quickly and seized opportunities, all qualities of the good American worker. Ironically, these qualities, which from the beginning marked the Japanese as ideal immigrants, were held against them by the Californians. It is the classic story of prejudice against the immigrant.

A 1910 editorial in the *San Francisco Chronicle* noted: "If the Japanese insisted on progressing beyond servile labor and competing with American workers for better jobs and hours, they would no longer be considered acceptable members of American Society." This attitude was translated into relentlessly discriminatory law. Those Japanese immigrants who had been born in Japan (the Issei) were declared ineligible for United States citizenship, unlike most immigrants, who are eligible to become citizens after a few years. In 1913 California passed the Alien Land Act, which made such aliens also ineligible to own land and limited any lease on land to three years. American civic groups such as the American Legion inflamed anti-Japanese feeling and the Hearst press revived fears of the "yellow peril" that had been directed at Chinese immigrants in the 1870s and 1880s.

The second generation of Japanese in America, the Nisei (those who were born here), fared no better than their parents. Then it happened. At the bombing of Pearl Harbor by the Japanese there arose an extremist call to solve the "Japanese problem." What the press meant by that was simple. Americans were afraid that Japanese American citizens would be loyal to their ancestral land and not to the United States. President Roosevelt signed an evacuation order and by August of 1942 more than 110,000 Japanese Americans, 64 percent of whom were United States citizens, were herded into camps where they were detained for four years. They lost their land, homes, farms . . . everything. This incarceration of an entire ethnic group without any hearing or formal charge being brought against a single member has been described as the worst assault on civil rights in American history.

I must tell you this. Patty, my wife, was studying in a private girls' high school in 1958, the year that Congress was debating the admittance of Hawaii as a state. Patty was assigned a chair at the dinner table next to the head mistress. Patty was in favor of statehood for Hawaii, of course, but the headmistress was upset. "Why," she said, "if Hawaii is admitted as a state we may wind up with a Japanese American senator! Good Heavens . . ." Patty agreed that we could very well have such a person in the Senate and told the headmistress that such a situation would be grand. The headmistress had lived through World War II, and though the Japanese Americans had since been released from the camps, they had not been released from her prejudice. Patty told me this story as Senator Daniel Inouye, Japanese American senator from Hawaii, was walking toward us in a park in the islands. He is a fan of our shows. Inouye was elected to the U.S. House one year after the above conversation between my wife and the headmistress. In 1962 Inouye did indeed become our first Japanese American senator. He was behind the legislation that returned $20,000 to each Japanese American who was locked in the camps—a small remuneration, but a serious apology.

The recipes that follow are easy to prepare, but you must arrange them in a most beautiful manner. The Japanese believe, "Food should feast the eye as well as the stomach."

As I was typing these words my office telephone rang. Channing and Jason, my two sons, were calling from Kobe, Japan. They are there visiting a culture that they have come to love so much. I know that the following recipes will take time to prepare, but you will better understand the Japanese American immigrant, and you will love the culture, just as do Channing and Jason.

MISO SOUP WITH SHRIMP

Serves 5

The Japanese love a soup made with fermented soybean paste. It is a very light soup and is served with just a few delicate ingredients added, so that one may enjoy the flavor of the soup itself. And it is drunk from the bowl; spoons are not offered. Your children will love that aspect of Japanese formality.

- 3 cups *dashi* stock (page 39)
- ½ cup light *miso* (page 42)
- ½ teaspoon sugar
- 2 small cakes deep-fried bean curd, thinly sliced, or 2 small cakes deep-fried fish paste *(kamaboko)*, thinly sliced
- ½ cake fresh bean curd, cut into small cubes
- 2 scallions, chopped
- 10 large shrimp, cooked and peeled

Prepare the stock according to instructions on the package. Bring to a simmer and stir in the *miso,* using a wire whisk. Add the sugar, fried bean curd, and fresh bean curd. Divide into five bowls and add the scallions and shrimp.

SALMON IN MISO

Serves 4

Is there something that the Japanese immigrant will not try with *miso*? Apparently not, since this dish is very popular in Seattle. We have a large and creative Japanese community . . . and lots of salmon.

- 2 pounds fresh salmon steaks or fillets
- ½ cup light *miso* (page 42)
- 1 tablespoon sugar
- Pinch of MSG (optional)
- 3 scallions, chopped
- 1 tablespoon Kikkoman soy sauce
- 1 teaspoon sesame oil
- ¼ cup saké (page 45)

Place the steaks in a bowl large enough for marinating. In another bowl, mix the remaining ingredients. Marinate the steaks in this mixture for about 2 hours at room temperature, or in the refrigerator overnight. Grill or broil until done to your own taste. I never overcook mine.

NOTE: You can make this recipe with any other rich-tasting fish such as black cod (sable).

BEEF MISOYAKI

Serves 4 as part of a Japanese meal

Miso, fermented soybean paste, is used in this dish to provide a beef and soy flavor that is terribly rich. Obviously it will stretch out the meat, but that does not seem to be the concern here. The Japanese have loved beef for the past 100 years or so, and they eat a great deal of it. Still, you will be surprised at how far this dish will go at a meal. Generally it is eaten with boiled rice.

2½ tablespoons sesame seeds
⅓ cup light *miso* (page 42)
1 tablespoon Kikkoman soy sauce
2 tablespoons sugar
½ teaspoon MSG (optional)
¼ cup saké (page 45)
1 pound beef, rib eye roast, very thinly sliced
1 tablespoon peanut oil

Toast the seasame seeds in a frying pan. Cook only until a few pop and the rest turn golden brown. Grind with a mortar and pestle or run through a food blender. Do not grind too fine.

Add the *miso* to the sesame seeds and mix well. Add the soy sauce, sugar, optional MSG, and saké. Spread ½ of the mixture on a platter and place the beef slices in the marinade. Brush the remaining marinade on top.

Let stand for 30 minutes to 1 hour. Remove the beef from the marinade, scrape off the excess marinde, and reserve.

Broil, or pan-fry with a little oil. Heat the leftover marinade and serve with the beef.

CUCUMBER NAMASU

Serves 4 as part of a Japanese meal

The Japanese table must always appeal to the eye as well as the stomach. For this reason several pickle dishes, which can also function as decoration, are often served. This is a good one.

2–3 cucumbers

1 tablespoon plus ¼ teaspoon salt

¼ cup sugar

¼ cup rice wine vinegar (page 45)

1 teaspoon grated fresh ginger

Prepare the cucumbers by slicing them in half. Remove the seeds if they are large. Slice in thin diagonals. Sprinkle with the 1 tablespoon of salt and place in a bowl. Let stand for 20 minutes. Rinse, drain, and remove excess water by putting the cucumbers in a kitchen towel and squeezing out the water. Combine the sugar, vinegar, remaining salt, and ginger. Pour over the cucumbers and chill.

SPINACH WITH SESAME AND MISO

Serves 5 as an appetizer or pickle

I prefer this dish as a cold vegetable side dish. The Japanese immigrants quickly learned to give common American vegetables flavors that reminded them of the old country. I think this is such a dish. I really do love it!

2½ tablespoons sesame seeds

2 tablespoons light *miso* (page 42)

½ teaspoon sugar

¾ pound fresh spinach

1 tablespoon peanut oil

Heat a wok or frying pan and add the sesame seeds. Stir over medium-high heat until they are lightly toasted. Cool the seeds and crush them with a mortar and pestle or food blender. Mix with the *miso* and sugar.

Wash the spinach and drain well. Heat a wok or frying pan and add the oil. Stir-fry the spinach just until it collapses. Remove from the wok. Stir the *miso* and sesame paste into the spinach.

Serve hot or cold.

JAPANESE CUCUMBER AND CRAB SALAD

Serves 6

This is a very delicate and unusual salad. Don't be put off by the salt, as it is used to draw water from the cucumbers, and then the saltwater is drained off. This tasty salad makes a most unusual side dish. It is a gift to us from my dear friend of college days Mrs. Yasuko Wada. She came to this country to study Christian education at my college, and thus our lasting friendship.

4 unpeeled cucumbers, thinly sliced

1 tablespoon salt

1 6-ounce can crab, or use fresh (much better!)

DRESSING

¼ cup light soy sauce (not "Lite"—see page 46)

⅛ cup rice wine vinegar (page 45)

½ tablespoon sesame oil

Pinch of sugar

Mix the cucumbers with the salt. Place in a colander, and let drain for about 45 minutes. Rinse the cucumbers and drain well. Mix with the crab. Make a dressing of the light soy sauce, rice wine vinegar, seasame oil, and sugar. Toss with the crab and drained cucumber, and serve.

TAKUAN

(Pickled Daikon)

Should make about 3 quarts, depending on the size of the *daikon*

This is another pickle that is common on the Japanese table. In earlier days our Japanese immigrant ancestors simply grew the vegetables from the old country here in the new country, and thus the pickles. However, in our time you can purchase these in any Japanese market. I still think it is fun to prepare your own.

5–6 medium *daikon* (page 39), peeled, sliced, and placed in clean canning jars

PICKLING BRINE

¾ cup sugar

1 cup water

¼ cup pickling salt (no iodine)

¼ cup distilled white vinegar

¼ teaspoon yellow food coloring

1 dried red chile pepper, chopped (optional)

Prepare the *daikon*. Boil all the brine ingredients together to dissolve the sugar. Cool the liquid. Pour over the sliced *daikon* and place the sealed jars in the refrigerator. Shake the jars occasionally. The pickle will be ready to eat in 2 days.

SUSHI

The following section is not a list of recipes as much as the statement of a life-style. When Japanese immigrants came to this country, certain dishes were "too exotic" for many Americans, but in the last few years Sushi has become very "in."

The principle is simple, attractive, and clever . . . very Japanese. Warm rice, mixed with vinegar and sugar, is rolled in, around, or with an endless number of possible ingredients. The results can be aesthetically beautiful or just basically delicious. Sushi can be very high class or simple peasant food. In any case, you should learn to make it.

I am thankful to Judy Lew, a fine cook from the famous Uwajimaya Company in Seattle, for instruction in the making of Sushi. She is good . . . and she teaches classes!

SHARI RICE (Sushi Rice)

Makes 6 cups

Really fine Sushi is no better than the Shari Rice, a rice cooked just for this dish. The recipe looks complicated but you will soon learn that it is very simple.

3 cups short-grain Japanese rice (page 46) or pearl rice

1 small bundle dried rolled kelp *(konbu)* (page 41)

SEASONING

⅓ cup rice wine vinegar (page 45)

1 teaspoon salt

1½ tablespoons sugar

Rinse the rice and place it in a colander to drain. Place the rice in a heavy covered saucepan and allow to sit for ½ hour in the pot.

Add 3½ cups of water and the kelp roll. Place the pan on high heat and, when the rice begins to boil, remove the kelp piece and discard. Boil for 2 minutes, lid off. Reduce the heat to low, cover, and cook for 15

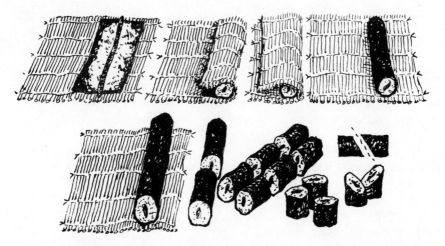

minutes. Remove from the heat and let the rice cool for 10 minutes, lid on.

In the meantime, heat the rice vinegar, sugar, and salt just until everything dissolves. Allow to cool.

Place the rice in a large pan. Pour on the seasoning liquid and stir with a wooden spoon, fanning all the time. (I use an electic fan so that I do not require help. Otherwise, use a hand-held fan, stirring and fanning at the same time for about 3 minutes.) The rice is now complete. Keep it in the pan under a moist towel as you use it.

ROLLED SUSHI (Maki-zushi)

These are the most beautiful little rolls, and they're easy to make. The most common Maki-zushi are made with sheets of seaweed (*nori*, page 43) that have been toasted and cut to the perfect size for the dish. You can find them in any Japanese market. To toast seaweed *(nori)*: Pass the shiny side over a gas flame for 1 or 2 seconds until crisp.

Choose any ingredient for the center of the roll. Using a small bamboo Sushi mat (page 30), place a sheet of toasted seaweed on the mat, the shiny side of the seaweed down. Spread out about ¾ cup of Shari Rice in the middle of the *nori*, making a rectangle of rice that goes from one side of the seaweed to the other, about 3 inches wide. Place your chosen filling in the center and roll up the seaweed over the rice, pulling the bamboo mat back a bit and moving it off as you go. (See the illustration.) Your first one may look a bit crude, but you'll catch on in no time.

Cut each roll into 6 pieces. You might cut them on an angle to change the appearance of your Sushi display. (See the illustration.)

NOTE: Have a little water and vinegar on the side. Always wet your hands in this mixture when you handle the rice—it prevents sticking.

NOTE: Seaweed *(nori)* has 2 sides. The smooth or shiny side goes on the outside, face down on the bamboo mat.

CUCUMBER FILLING

Cut sticks of unpeeled cucumber ½ inch thick, just the length of the *nori*, about 8 inches. Place the cucumber in the center of the Shari Rice and roll and cut.

TUNA FILLING

Cut sticks of very fresh tuna just like the cucumber and prepare in same manner.

EGG FILLING

Prepare the following mixture:

2 tablespoons water	½ teaspoon salt
1 tablespoon cornstarch	5 eggs, well beaten
1 tablespoon sugar	

Mix the water with the cornstarch and then add the remaining ingredients. Heat a square SilverStone-lined griddle pan, about 10×10 inches. Add ½ of the egg mixture at a time and cook over medium heat just until the egg sets and just begins to dry a bit. Remove from the pan and cut into long strips, about ½ inch wide. Place in the middle of the Sushi roll and complete as above.

EGG SHEETS ROLLED WITH SEAWEED

Prepare an egg sheet as above and cut it to the size of a *nori* seaweed sheet. Place the egg sheet on the bamboo mat and top with a sheet of *nori*. Then add the Shari Rice, as above, and roll and cut.

FISH CAKE FILLING

Purchase a colored steamed fish cake *(kamaboko)* at your Japanese market, cut it into long ½-inch-thick strips, and prepare like the cucumber filling above.

MUSHROOM (Shiitake) OR GOURD SHAVINGS (Kampyo) FILLINGS

2 ounces dried *shiitake*
mushrooms (page 46) *or*
1 ounce dried *kampyo*

SAUCE

2 cups *dashi* stock (page 39)	1 tablespoon *mirin* (page 42)
3 tablespoons Kikkoman soy sauce	2 tablespoons sugar

Soak the dried *shiitake* mushrooms in warm water for 1 hour. Drain the mushrooms. Blend all the ingredients for the sauce and simmer the mushrooms over low heat, uncovered, for about 1 hour. The sauce will greatly reduce. Allow to cool and then slice the mushrooms into sticks for Sushi.

Roll into Sushi as above.

GOURD SHAVINGS (Kampyo) FILLING

Soak the *kampyo* shreds in hot tap water until soft, about 10 minutes. Drain them and rub them with a pinch of salt. Rinse well and drain. Place in a saucepan with the sauce ingredients. Simmer, uncovered, over medium heat for ½ hour, and then turn up the heat to reduce the sauce until almost evaporated. Allow the gourd shavings to cool before using.

Cut them into appropriate lengths and use for filling in Sushi.

ASSORTED FILLINGS

Choose any of the above fillings and blend them in the centers of the Maki-zushi rolls. Cucumber, tuna, egg, fish cake, mushrooms, and gourd will all work well, but I think it wise to limit yourself to 3 choices.

SUSHI BALLS IN SESAME

Roll the Shari Rice (page 242) into balls the size of a small golf ball. Roll in salted ground sesame seeds (page 53) and chill before serving. You can use a bit of black sesame (page 53) for garnish. The Sushi Balls are delicious and perfect for picnics since they keep so well.

SUSHI WITH FISH (Nigiri-zushi)

This is my favorite. A thin slice of fish is served over a small hand-formed bit of rice. The result is just spectacular, since the fish and the rice support one another in flavor. No, you should not be upset over the fact that many of these fish slices are served raw. Simply find very fresh fish . . . and if you are nervous about some kind of fish parasite, just freeze the slices for 24 hours before using. Defrost and enjoy.

To prepare this dish, make a batch of Shari Rice (page 242). Gather about 2 tablespoons of Shari in one hand and squeeze it gently into an oblong shape, like a fat sausage. Pick up a small slice of fish, cut to about the size of the bit of the rice, and place a small dab of *wasabi* (page 47) on the fish. Place the fish on the rice in an attractive manner, with the *wasabi* between the fish and the rice, and arrange on a tray.

Any of the following may be used with fine results:

Raw tuna, very thinly sliced
Prawns, steamed and butterflied, or sliced
Squid, fresh or raw
Octopus, cooked and thinly sliced

Raw flounder, very thinly sliced
Broiled fish or eel
Raw sea bass, very thinly sliced
Smoked oysters
Smoked clams
Raw halibut, very thinly sliced
Raw Pacific snapper, very thinly sliced
Lox
Broiled fish with *teriyaki* sauce, thinly sliced

TOKYO-STYLE SUSHI

This is simply a matter of aesthetics. Prepare Sushi with Fish as on page 245, using fresh slices of fish. Cut seaweed *(nori)* into ¼-inch-wide belts and wrap them around the center of the Sushi.

The "jade belt" adds a great deal to the presentation.

TO SERVE SUSHI

Prepare a bit of *wasabi* (page 47) and place it in a small dish, one dish for each person. You may wish to add some Kikkoman soy sauce to the little dish. Each person picks up a piece of Sushi and dips the fish part into the sauce. One is not supposed to dip the rice into the sauce . . . but I always do. So much for tradition. In either case, the result is delicious.

THE JEWISH
IMMIGRANTS

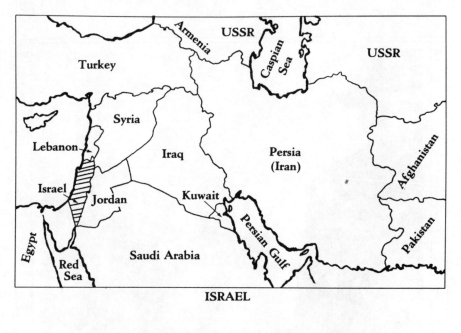

ISRAEL

Jews began immigrating to this country in the 1650s, and they have been coming ever since. While we suspect some Jews came even before that time, we can document the first real Jewish community in America. It was founded by Sephardic Jews from Portugal, in 1654, in New Amsterdam, later to be called New York.

Though the Jews have been in this country since the very beginning of European immigration, we must recognize that they are not the usual immigration group. They came from Russia, Poland, Italy, Germany, Spain, Portugal . . . these were their homelands, yet all were Jews. There is a religious background here as well as an ethnic background, and Jews seem to have always been persecuted for this dual and valid commitment. According to the biblical narratives the Jews were chosen for a very special responsibility, that of speaking to the rest of the world about the Oneness of Yahweh and His Laws, a responsibility not to be taken lightly. As a result many Jews have been persecuted due to their commitment to their religious faith, which must come prior to any commitment to a particular country. Couple this problem with the fact that Jews have always valued education, good business, and the arts, and you have all of the seeds of racial prejudice. Jewish bankers, lawyers, actors, doctors, teachers, musicians, in short, the most educated segment of our society, all have been the victims of prejudice since the Jews feel "called" or chosen in terms of their place in world history. But it has to be under-

Market day in the Jewish quarter of the East Side, New York City, 1912

stood that the Jews have never seen this call as a right to special privilege . . . but rather as a special responsibility. Had the Jewish immigrant not been so bright, so committed to hard work, so determined to celebrate a good education, I doubt that the racial prejudice that they have suffered in America would have been quite so severe.

The roots of this prejudice go back to the ancient world. The Christian community became very arrogant about the place that Jews were to have in the world, and this developed into a Christian hostility toward the Jews that remains one of the great horrors of history. Trials, expulsions, and executions were the norm for hundreds of years.

During the 1600s the situation in Eastern Europe was simply intolerable. Western Europe was not much better, and immigration to America increased. By the 1800s many Jews were coming here as shopkeepers since they were denied secular education in Europe. And in this land of opportunity, they were soon to participate in all areas of American life.

In the 1940s, Hitler set out to exterminate the Jews, claiming that they were at the root of Germany's problems and once they were removed the great new republic could move forward. Isn't it strange how we always seem to need someone else on whom we can place the blame for our own failings? Jean-Paul Sartre, the great French existential writer, said a very profound thing in an essay offered around 1955. He said something like this: "The portrait of an anti-semite is clear. The anti-semite claims that the problems that he is facing are due to another race, another time, another event; in short, he is responsible for nothing. The anti-semite is a man who does not hate the Jews, but since he does not feel in control of things he hates himself!"

Today America is the largest Jewish population center in the world. What they have contributed to the culture can only be hinted at in the following list of names:

Al Jolson, Harry Houdini, Jack Benny, Jascha Heifetz, Arthur Ruben-
stein, Phil Silvers, Lenny Bruce, Lillian Hellman, Jerome Kern, Yehudi
Menuhin, Erich Fromm, Bruno Bettelheim, Louise Nevelson, Florenz
Ziegfeld, Bette Midler, Sid Caesar, Albert Einstein, Benny Goodman,
Bob Dylan, Barbra Streisand, Isaac Stern, Leonard Bernstein, George
Gershwin, The Marx Brothers, Milton Berle, Richard Rodgers, Eddie
Cantor, J. D. Salinger, Isaac Bashevis Singer, Danny Kaye, Zero
Mostel, Arthur Miller, Itzhak Perlman. And Max, who opened the Stage
Delicatessen in New York, years ago.

The following recipes come from the many cultural traditions that
Jews call their own. There is a kind of common thread that runs through
Jewish cuisine, as a result of the kosher food laws, and it has become an
absolutely wonderful tradition. Yes, this stuff is a bit heavy with chicken
fat and sour cream. But, to quote Itzhak Perlman, the greatest violinist
of our time, "So what are you worrying about? This stuff will just bring
on heartburn a little quicker!" Now and then you have to celebrate!

Such is the New York Jewish tradition!

Eat well. L'Chaim!

NOODLE KUGEL

Serves 8

This unusual dish is simply baked noodles with a sweetened cream
cheese sauce. Since there are a million Jewish immigrant grandmas in
this country, there are a million variations on this dish. No, it is not a
dessert, though it can be served as such. Rather, it is a sweet course to
be served along with the main dish. Our Jewish immigrant ancestors
loved sugar . . . a little sweet and a little bitter, and you understand what
life is all about.

1 pound wide egg noodles	1 teaspoon grated lemon peel
1 cup milk	
1 pound cream cheese, cut up	1 teaspoon grated orange peel
½ cup (1 stick) butter	4 eggs
5 tablespoons sugar	1 cup Wheaties
1 tablespoon rendered chicken fat (page 253) or salad oil	3 tablespoons brown sugar

Cook the noodles according to the directions on the package. Drain and
rinse in cold water. Drain again and set aside.

In a 2-quart saucepan, heat the milk and add the cream cheese and ½ stick of butter. Stir until smooth and allow to cool a bit. Add the sugar, fat or oil, and citrus peel. Mix well. Beat the eggs and stir into the cream sauce. Mix the sauce with the drained noodles and place in a greased glass baking dish, 8 inches square. Melt the remaining ½ stick of butter. Top the noodle dish with the Wheaties and the brown sugar. Pour the melted butter over the top and bake in a 350° oven for 1 hour.

KASHA VARNISHKES

Serves 4 as a starch dish

This is a dish that was common among the Russian Jews in the homeland, and it continued to be celebrated on the Lower East Side in New York. It is cheap to make and really quite good, and the flavor reminds one of "the other side." The name literally means "kasha with bow ties."

1 cup kasha buckwheat groats, medium granulation (page 41)	1 yellow onion, peeled and chopped
1 egg, well beaten	2 cups Chicken Stock (page 74) or use canned
2 tablespoons rendered chicken fat (page 253) or vegetable oil	Salt and freshly ground black pepper to taste
	1 cup pasta bow ties

In a small bowl, mix the kasha with the beaten egg. Be sure all the grains are covered with egg. Place a medium SilverStone-lined frying pan on medium-high heat. Add the kasha to the pan and, using a wooden fork, flatten it out a bit, stirring and moving it about the pan until the egg dries and the grains have mostly separated. Set aside.

Place a pot of salted water on to boil for the pasta bow ties. (Do not cook them yet.)

In a 4-quart heavy stove-top covered casserole, heat the chicken fat or oil and sauté the onions until clear. Add the Chicken Stock and bring to a boil. Add the salt and pepper and the reserved kasha. Stir a bit and cover. Cook over low heat, stirring now and then, until the kasha is tender, about 10 minutes. If it is not done to your taste, cook for a few more minutes.

In the meantime, boil the pasta just until tender. Drain well and stir into the kasha. Serve hot.

KNISHES

Makes about 4 dozen

This recipe for classic Jewish baked dumplings is based on information offered me by Pauline Berlin, through the goodness of *Sunset Magazine*. I really think it is one of the best magazines in the country, though it is aimed at west coast living. The recipes are always creative—and they work! I have subscribed for 20 years.

These Knishes are light and delightful, and not difficult to make. Have your chosen filling all prepared before you start the dough.

THE DOUGH

1 egg

¼ cup salad oil

¾ cup water

1 teaspoon distilled white vinegar

2¾ cups all-purpose flour (See Hint, page 423.)

Place all the ingredients in the bowl of a heavy electric mixer, such as a KitchenAid. Mix with the dough hook until the dough is very smooth. Cover and allow the dough to rest for 15 minutes.

Divide the dough into 2 pieces. Roll out 1 piece of the dough into a very thin rectangle. Place a rope of the filling, about ¾ inch in diameter, 1 inch away from the long edge of the dough. Fold the long edge of the dough over to enclose the filling; press to seal. Cut the filled roll away from the rest of the dough. Using the narrow edge of the handle of a table knife, press and cut the roll into individual Knishes, 2 inches long. Place the Knishes on oiled baking sheets. Repeat with the remaining dough and filling. Bake at 425°, uncovered, until lightly browned, about 20 minutes.

POTATO ONION FILLING

4 large yellow onions, peeled and finely chopped

¼ cup butter

¼ cup rendered chicken fat (page 253)

3½ pounds potatoes, peeled

Salt and freshly ground black pepper to taste

Sauté the onions in the butter and chicken fat until golden. Boil the potatoes, drain, and mash. Add the onions, along with any oil that remains in the pan. Season with the salt and pepper.

CHEESE FILLING

2 large yellow onions, peeled and chopped	12 ounces cream cheese, cut up
4 tablespoons butter	2¼ pounds dry-curd cottage cheese or farmer cheese (page 39)

Sauté the onions in the butter until golden. Mix the onions in with the remaining ingredients, including any butter left in the pan, cover, and chill.

HINT: TO RENDER CHICKEN FAT. While chicken fat can be purchased in any Jewish market, it is easy to prepare fresh at home. It is called *schmaltz*. Simply combine chopped fresh chicken fat and skin with a little water in a small frying pan over medium-low heat until the fat is liquid and the solids have shrunk to very small, crunchy bits. This should take about 20 minutes. Strain the bits from the fat and use for other recipes. Watch carefully while rendering so the bits don't burn. Refrigerate the fat.

EGG BARLEY

Serves 6–8 as a side dish

This dish is not made with barley at all but rather with pasta that is cut to look like barley. It is very much like what the Italians call orzo, or pasta that looks like rice. The dish is very rich due to the mushrooms and chicken fat and was always appreciated around the weekend table.

4 cups Chicken Stock (page 74) or use canned	2 medium yellow onions, peeled and chopped
2 cups barley-shaped egg pasta	½ pound fresh mushrooms, sliced
2 tablespoons rendered chicken fat (above) or butter or salad oil	Salt and freshly ground black pepper to taste

Bring the Chicken Stock to a boil and add the pasta. Stir now and then as the pasta cooks. In the meantime, heat a large frying pan and add the chicken fat and the onions. Sauté for a few minutes and add the mushrooms. Sauté for a few minutes more, until the mushrooms are tender.

When the pasta is just tender, drain and add it to the frying pan. Add salt and pepper and serve hot.

CHOPPED LIVER

Makes 2 cups, enough for 4 as a first course

Now we're talking serious eating. Itzhak Perlman, the great violinist, and I once did a show together in which we cooked food from his childhood. He is a Sabra, a Jew born in Israel, but his family lived in Russia. He came to New York as a child, but he still relishes the memories of the food he ate in his youth. I prepared this recipe for him and he announced it to be "almost as good as my mother's!"

1 pound fresh chicken livers

3 tablespoons rendered chicken fat (page 253) or butter or margarine (Chicken fat is best!)

1 yellow onion, peeled and sliced

2 hard-boiled eggs, peeled

Crispy fried chicken skin and fat to taste (optional) (See Hint, page 253.)

Salt and freshly ground black pepper to taste

Sauté the livers in half of the fat until they are no longer pink inside, about 5 minutes. Remove from the pan and add the onion and the remaining fat. Sauté the onion until golden. Grind the liver-onion mixture and the eggs using a coarse blade on your grinder. Add the crispy fried skin and tiny pieces of crunchy fried chicken fat if you wish.

Add salt and pepper. Serve with toast points or crackers.

IRVING'S CUCUMBER SALAD

Serves 4–6 as a side dish

In the early portions of the Bible there is a record of the Jews' love for cucumbers and onions. It seems to have always been this way, and certainly these items had to be celebrated in the New World. The following recipe is typical of many, but this one is a gift to us from Irving Lefferts. He loves to cook and he loves the memories that these dishes offer.

2 cucumbers, thinly sliced	½ cup distilled white vinegar
1 yellow onion, peeled and thinly sliced	½ cup sugar
1 teaspoon salt	½ teaspoon celery seeds
1 cup water	½ teaspoon mustard seeds

In a bowl, put the thinly sliced cucumber and onion.

In a small saucepan combine the salt, water, vinegar, and sugar, heating slightly to dissolve the sugar. Add the celery seeds and mustard seeds.

Pour over the onion and cucumber. Cover and refrigerate for 24 hours before serving.

STUFFED PEPPERS

Serves 6–7

When I was a child and my mother made stuffed peppers, I wanted to put myself up for adoption. They were filled with who knows what and cooked to death . . . but then, that was during World War II and I don't even know where she found the peppers! I realized how I missed them when I saw a fine display of kosher take-out foods at a wonderful shop in North Miami Beach called Kosher Treats. It is a fine operation and Hertzel Notis, the owner, along with Bob Anderson, the manager, convinced me that I should try again. The following recipe is worth the try!

6–7 medium green bell
    peppers

FILLING

2 pounds ground beef	1 large yellow onion, peeled and chopped
3 tablespoons *matzo* meal (page 42)	4 tablespoons rendered chicken fat (page 253)
3 eggs	Salt and freshly ground black pepper to taste
3 cloves garlic, peeled and crushed	3 hard-boiled eggs, peeled and grated

THE SAUCE

1 cup canned tomato sauce	1 tablespoon sugar
2 tablespoons distilled white vinegar	1 cup Chicken Stock (page 74) or use canned

Remove the top of each of the peppers and cut out most of the seeds and core. Reserve the tops but discard the seeds and core. Mix all of the ingredients for the filling together and divide the filling among the peppers. Replace the top on each. Place them in a baking dish.

    Mix all of the ingredients for the sauce and pour into the bottom of the baking pan. Bake in a preheated oven at 350° for 1 hour.

CHEESECAKE, NEW YORK STYLE

Serves 8–12, depending on the size of the slice

This is an old recipe that Patty, my wife, and I used for years when we opened my first restaurant in Tacoma, Washington. Patty tasted many commercial cheesecakes and rejected them all. Since she'd been born and raised in Brooklyn she knew how a New York Jewish cheesecake should taste, and I told her to find the recipe. I have never wavered from my affection for this particular jewel.

1 cup graham cracker crumbs	2 eggs
¾ cup sugar	2 teaspoons vanilla
¼ cup plus 2 tablespoons melted butter	1 pound cream cheese, broken into small pieces
1½ cups sour cream	

Blend the cracker crumbs, ¼ cup of the sugar, and the ¼ cup of melted butter, and line the bottom of an 8- or 9-inch ungreased springform pan.

Blend the sour cream, ½ cup of sugar, the eggs, and vanilla in a food blender for 1 minute. Add the cream cheese. Blend until smooth.

Pour the remaining 2 tablespoons of melted butter through the top of the machine. Pour into the springform pan.

Bake in the lower third of a 325° oven for 45 minutes.

When the baking is finished, remove the cake from the oven, and turn the oven on to broil. Broil the cheesecake just until the top begins to show attractive spots of brown.

Refrigerate for 4 hours, or preferably overnight, before cutting and serving.

This is not a low-calorie version. Cut it into small pieces—it is very rich.

HONEY CAKE

Serves 12

I met Fanny Silverstein and fell in love. She is a very busy Jewish mama who has fed her children well, and her son insisted that she publish a cookbook. She is a Romanian Jewish immigrant and her sense of history in the soup pot is just wonderful. The book is entitled *My Mother's Cookbook,* and the following recipe for an overwhelming cake is included in the book. Thanks, Fanny!

3 cups all-purpose flour
  (See Hint, page 423.)
1½ teaspoons baking powder
¼ teaspoon ground
  cinnamon
½ teaspoon baking soda
1 tablespoon instant coffee
½ cup boiling water
¼ cup vegetable or peanut
  oil

1 cup honey
Grated peel of 1 washed
  orange
2 tablespoons brandy or
  any whiskey
4 eggs
1 cup sugar
1 cup chopped walnuts

Combine the flour, baking powder, cinnamon, and baking soda; set aside. Mix the instant coffee with the water; blend in the oil, honey, orange peel, and brandy. In a large bowl, beat the eggs until frothy; gradually add the sugar and beat until light. Add to the honey mixture.

Combine the flour mixture alternately with the honey mixture, starting with flour and ending with flour. Stir in the walnuts. Pour the batter into an oiled and waxed paper-lined 13 × 9 × 2-inch baking pan. Bake in a 325° oven for about 50 minutes. Test with a toothpick. If moist, continue baking until a toothpick inserted in the center comes out clean.

Invert the cake onto a wire rack. Cool. Peel off the waxed paper and wrap in aluminum foil to maintain freshness.

THE KOREAN
IMMIGRANTS

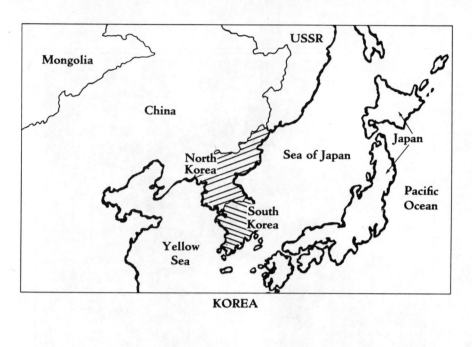

KOREA

Korea is the Land of the Morning Calm. The name actually means "High and Clear" and refers to the mountainous nature of this peninsula which lies between China and Japan. Unless you are at the shore you will see mountains in four directions, from all points of the interior.

The people who live in this lovely peninsula are a very distinct ethnic community. They are descendants of the Tungus tribe, from prehistoric times, and they have remained very homogeneous, with no minority groups except a small contingent of Chinese immigrants. The Koreans speak one language throughout the land and they have one of the highest literacy rates in the world, some 98 percent of the population being able to read and write. Education has always been extremely important to these people.

Seoul, the capital of South Korea, is the ninth largest city in the world. Almost ten million people reside there, but their history has not been easy.

They were an autonomous culture until about 1876 when they set up a trade treaty with Japan. Prior to this time they were called the "Hermit Kingdom" since they had so little communication with the outside. The agreement with Japan proved to be their undoing; it was the first step to complete domination by Japan. At the end of the nineteenth and beginning of the twentieth century Japan emerged as a regional power and sent troops into Korea to protect Japanese interests. Once settled in, the Japanese arranged for the assassination of the Korean queen and by degrees made Korea a protectorate.

Japan occupied Korea until 1945 and the Japanese dominated every aspect of Korean life. Then, following World War II, when the Japanese surrendered, Korea was denied her previous status as a unified nation. It was the only state not responsible for aggression in World War II that was treated in this manner. The land was simply divided along the 38th parallel and the North was placed under the trusteeship of the Soviet Union, the South under that of the United States. There was no communication between the two portions of a formerly united land. In 1950 the North invaded the South. In 1953, after thousands of lives were lost, the battle was declared over. The Korean War proved to be of little help, as is usually the case with wars, and as of this writing the two factions are still staring at one another across a border, a border that represents, it seems to me, two other foreign nations, the Soviet Union and the United States.

In the midst of these battles Korean immigrants came to this country. Actually they had been coming since the turn of the century when approximately seven thousand went to Hawaii as agricultural labor and others went to California as field hands. Following the Korean War many refugees, orphans, war brides, and students came to this country. This immigration led to the transfer of other family members and now we have Korean communities in New York, Chicago, Los Angeles, and my own city, Tacoma, Washington. They are an industrious people and they create more jobs than they could ever take away from the established American community.

The food that the Korean immigrants brought with them is like nothing else you have tasted from the Far East. The principle of the pickle is raised to glory and no one knows more about a properly barbecued bit of pork or beef than do the Koreans. The list of dishes will probably startle most Westerners, but then, you must consider that the Korean table has several courses, the most complicated being the first selection of pickles and snacks. You will note the length of the list of recipes for this section, and then you will understand that Craig, my assistant, and I simply could not stop experimenting on these wonderful dishes. Now Craig and I go into a Korean restaurant and know the difference between good and mediocre Korean food. These recipes represent a great deal of work, and they are legitimate, I promise. You will love this cuisine.

Mung Bean Pancake

Makes about 6 pancakes, enough for 8–10 as a first course

This dish is a classic bit of Korean ingenuity. It is based on dried mung beans, the same beans that give us bean sprouts, and then fried into a most wonderful first course. This looks like a lot of work, but it's not. These pancakes can even be made far ahead of time and refried at the last minute.

- 1 teaspoon peeled and crushed garlic
- 2 teaspoons plus 3 tablespoons peanut oil
- ½ teaspoon grated fresh ginger
- ½ pound boneless loin of pork, julienned
- ½ teaspoon salt
- 1 cup chopped leeks (white parts only)
- ½ cup green beans (fresh or frozen), chopped small

- 2 cups shelled dried mung beans (page 42), soaked in hot tap water overnight
- 1½ cups water
- 2 tablespoons light soy sauce (not "Lite"—see page 46)
- 3 cloves garlic, peeled and crushed
- 2 teaspoons grated fresh ginger
- 1½ teaspoons salt

Heat a wok or frying pan and chow (page 32) or sauté the 1 teaspoon of garlic in 2 tablespoons of peanut oil. Add the ½ teaspoon of ginger, the pork, and salt, and sauté until done to taste. Add the leeks and green beans, and cook until all is hot but not soft. Set the pork mixture aside.

Drain the mung beans, place them in a food processor, and finely chop. Add 1½ cups of water, soy sauce, 3 cloves of garlic, and the 2 teaspoons of ginger. Purée until smooth. Add the pork mixture.

Let the batter stand for 30 minutes. Heat some of the remaining oil in a 9-inch SilverStone-lined skillet. Pour 1 cup of the batter into the pan and cook, turning once, until golden brown. Keep the cooked pancakes warm while making the rest with the remaining batter and oil.

KOREAN BROILED BEEF RIBS

Serves 4–6, about 2 cups sauce

The sauce is simple, the meat is tender, and the result is just great. You can use this sauce on other meats, of course, but I enjoy it on cut beef ribs most.

KOREAN BARBECUE SAUCE

1 cup Kikkoman soy sauce

¼ cup saké (page 45) or
dry sherry

4 slices ginger (about the
size of a 25-cent piece),
julienned

2 cloves garlic, peeled and
very thinly sliced

2 tablespoons sugar

¾ cup apple juice
concentrate (No water
added!)

3 tablespoons sesame oil

Place all the ingredients but the sesame oil in a saucepan and bring to a simmer. Cook 10 minutes, uncovered; then remove from the heat and add the sesame oil. Store in a covered glass or plastic container in the refrigerator.

THE BEEF

Purchase 4 pounds of beef barbecue ribs cut across the grain into 2-inch pieces, Korean or Japanese style. Your butcher will understand. Have the butcher cut them about ¼ inch thick.

Rub each rib with sesame oil and then marinate in a bit of Korean Barbecue Sauce.

Grill the ribs over high heat or charcoal, turning once, until tender. Do not overcook this delicacy.

KOREAN SEASONED RAW BEEF

Serves 4–6 as a first course

The first time I tasted this dish I was in the Woo Lae Oak restaurant in Los Angeles. It was served ice cold, almost with ice flakes in the meat, and I was terribly impressed. Craig, my assistant, shouted, "We've got to study this one!" We did and we have the recipe for you. Keep the meat very cold.

½ pound very lean beef, such as flank steak or sirloin (No fat!)

2 tablespoons Korean Barbecue Sauce (page 263)

1 teaspoon sesame oil

1 teaspoon toasted sesame seeds (page 46)

1 large clove garlic, peeled and crushed

GARNISH

1 egg yolk, cupped in a half shell

Slice the beef across the grain into ⅛-inch slices. Cut the slices into julienne strips. Using a cleaver, chop the meat coarsely. Mix the meat with the remaining ingredients, except the egg yolk. Mound onto a plate and chill very well.

Serve with the egg yolk garnish sitting in its shell on top of the mound. Stir in the egg just as you serve.

NAPA KIMCHEE

Makes about 3 quarts

So many crazy stories have been told about Kimchee that many Americans are reluctant to try the dish. No, it is not buried in the ground in this country, and yes, it is delicious and much milder than you would expect. You can vary the spiciness by varying the amount of red pepper that you put into the dish. Wonderful stuff!

6 pounds Napa cabbage (page 43)

¾ cup Korean pickling salt (page 41) or kosher salt

8 scallions, finely chopped

1½ cups shredded carrot

2 tablespoons grated fresh ginger

2 tablespoons garlic, peeled and finely chopped

2 tablespoons candied ginger (page 38)

2 teaspoons sugar

½ cup Korean red pepper flakes (page 52)

1 tablespoon salt

Remove limp outer leaves from the cabbage. Quarter the cabbage lengthwise, then cut across the quarters into 1½-inch-wide pieces. Put the cabbage in a very large bowl and add the pickling salt. Toss so that the salt coats the cabbage evenly. Allow to stand for 30 minutes. Toss the cabbage a couple of times during that time. Rinse the cabbage with cold water and drain. Toss with the remaining ingredients and pack into a large crock or covered pottery casserole. Add water to cover, about 3 cups. Allow to sit on the counter for 1 to 2 days. Store in the refrigerator, covered, in the crock or in individual glass jars.

Serve as a relish with any Korean dinner or use in cooking meat or soup dishes.

NOTE: This recipe can easily be adjusted for 1 2-pound head of Napa cabbage. Divide the remaining ingredients by one third.

STIR-FRIED PORK WITH KIMCHEE

Serves 4–5 as part of a Korean meal

This dish is so simple that you'll suspect I've made a mistake. No, I haven't. Once you get the pickles prepared, you're in for some very profound but uncomplicated Korean cooking.

1 tablespoon peanut oil

½ pound pork butt, sliced into pieces ⅛-inch thick by 1½-inches long

Salt and freshly ground black pepper to taste

4 scallions, cut into 2-inch pieces

2 cups Napa Kimchee (page 265)

1 teaspoon garlic, peeled and crushed

½ teaspoon Korean red pepper flakes (page 52)

GARNISH

Toasted sesame seeds (page 46)

Heat a wok, add the oil, and chow (page 32) the pork for a couple of minutes, adding salt and pepper. Add the scallions and toss a bit. Add the Napa Kimchee, garlic, and red pepper. Chow for a couple of minutes until all is hot. Remove to a plate and sprinkle with toasted sesame seeds.

NOTE: Be careful with the salt because the Napa Kimchee is already salty.

KOREAN CRISP LAVER

(Seaweed)

Serves 6–8 as an appetizer for a Korean meal

The influence of Japanese cuisine here is quite obvious, though the Koreans have always seemed to enjoy dried seaweed. If you have never tried it, I suggest you calm down and make a batch. It's truly delicious!

10 sheets laver (page 45)
(found in any Japanese
or Korean food store)

1 tablespoon sesame oil
1 tablespoon salt

Spread the sheets one at a time on a board, brush with sesame oil, then sprinkle lightly with salt. Put the sheets on a grill or griddle, or in a skillet over low heat and cook for a few seconds till crisp. Cut each sheet into 4 or 6 pieces, and serve piled on small plates. These laver pieces are usually eaten wrapped around rice, but some people like them as they are.

KOREAN EGGFOLDS WITH SEAWEED

Serves 6–8 as the first course in a Korean meal

This is a great favorite of mine, and you can find a similar dish at a Japanese sushi bar. I could eat this with rice for a whole meal, but the Koreans serve it as a first course.

3 eggs	2 teaspoons sesame oil
3 tablespoons water	2 sheets Korean Crisp
2 tablespoons light soy sauce (not "Lite"—see page 46)	Laver (page 267)
	1 tablespoon Sesame Salt (below)

Whip the eggs with the water and divide the mixture into 2 portions. Make a large, square omelet of each portion by frying the liquid in an oiled SilverStone-lined 11 × 11-inch griddle. Cook on one side only and use medium heat so that the egg does not brown. Cook only until the top side begins to dry.

Mix the light soy sauce and sesame oil and brush half of the mixture over each omelet. Place a sheet of prepared Korean Crisp Laver on top and sprinkle with the Sesame Salt. Roll up and cut like a jelly roll. Place the pieces on a platter with the cut side up.

SESAME SALT

Makes 1 cup

This is an easy-to-prepare Korean condiment that you will find useful in salads and sandwiches, in addition to the recipes in this section.

1 cup white sesame seeds	1 teaspoon salt

Place the sesame seeds in a frying pan over medium heat and toast, stirring constantly, until they just begin to turn a light brown and smell wonderful. Place in a food blender, grind to a coarse texture, and stir in the salt. Keep in a covered jar in the refrigerator.

BEAN SPROUTS SIDE DISH

Serves 6–8 as the first course in a Korean meal

This one is fresh to the taste, and healing with each bite. It does not have to be hot at all to be refreshing to the table, and this recipe should suit you well.

1½ cups water

1 teaspoon salt

2 pounds soybean sprouts

DRESSING

1 tablespoon light soy sauce (not "Lite"—see page 46)

1 teaspoon sesame oil

1 tablespoon Sesame Salt (page 268)

2 scallions, finely chopped

2 teaspoons Korean red pepper flakes (page 52)

In large shallow pot, bring 1½ cups of water to a boil. Add the salt and bean sprouts. Simmer the sprouts for about 5 minutes, tossing them a couple of times to cook evenly. Drain very well. Mix the light soy sauce and sesame oil. Add to the sprouts along with the Sesame Salt, scallions, and red pepper. Toss all and chill.

GREEN PEPPERS AND BEEF

Serves 6–8 as the first course in a Korean meal

The first time I tasted this dish, I was at a Korean restaurant in Chicago that has since closed. The thought that I cannot have it again exactly as the chef prepared it there really pains me . . . but this recipe is very close, and delicious.

Please remember that this dish is no better than the quality of the Korean Broiled Beef Ribs that must be prepared first.

1 tablespoon peanut oil	3 tablespoons Sesame Salt (page 268)
4 ounces hot green peppers such as jalapeños, quartered and seeded	3 ounces Beef Stock (page 78) or use canned
1 pound of the cooked meat from Korean Broiled Beef Ribs (page 263), coarsely chopped	2 teaspoons sugar

Heat a frying pan or wok and add the oil. Sauté or chow (page 32) the peppers in the oil for 1 minute. Add the chopped beef and Sesame Salt, and chow for another minute. Then add the stock and sugar; cook over high heat until the liquid has almost evaporated and the peppers are just tender. Serve from a plate.

SPINACH SIDE DISH

Serves 6–8 as the first course in a Korean meal

We in the West seldom do anything creative with spinach. Here is a cold dish that even spinach-hating children will adore.

3 pounds spinach (about 4 fresh bunches)	1 teaspoon salt

DRESSING

2 tablespoons light soy sauce (not "Lite"—see page 46)	1 tablespoon Sesame Salt (page 268)
2 teaspoons sesame oil	1 tablespoon Korean red pepper threads (page 52)

Remove the tough part of the spinach stems and wash very well. In a large shallow pot bring 1½ cups of water to a boil. Add the salt and spinach. Simmer the spinach for 5 to 10 minutes until it cooks down, stirring occasionally. Drain and cool. Squeeze out excess water and place the spinach in a bowl. Mix the light soy sauce and sesame oil. Add to the spinach along with the remaining ingredients. Toss well and chill.

BEEF BULGOGI

Serves 3–4 as part of a Korean meal

The love that the Korean has for beef surely rivals the affection that we in America share for that meat. However, when the Korean cook prepares beef, the dish is so rich that you eat much less than the normal American serving. This is wonderful eating, I promise.

THE MARINADE

- 2 tablespoons Kikkoman soy sauce
- 1 tablespoon sugar
- 1 tablespoon sesame oil
- 1 tablespoon Sesame Salt (page 268)
- ⅛ teaspoon freshly grated black pepper

- 4 scallions, chopped in 1-inch pieces
- 3 cloves garlic, peeled and crushed
- 1 teaspoon grated fresh ginger
- 1 tablespoons saké (page 45) or dry sherry
- 1 tablespoon Korean red pepper flakes (page 52)

FOR FRYING

- 1 tablespoon peanut oil

GARNISH

Toasted sesame seeds (page 46)

Prepare the beef. Mix the marinade in a medium-size bowl. Add the meat and toss. Allow to marinate for 30 minutes.

The meat can be cooked over medium-high heat in a frying pan or stove-top griddle. Heat the pan or griddle first; make it very hot. Add the oil. Cook the meat for 1 or 2 minutes on each side, browning it nicely. Garnish with sesame seeds.

PORK BULGOGI

I really prefer Pork Bulgogi to the beef version. I will remain a pig fan to the end, I'm sure.

The recipe is the same as that above, but thinly sliced pork butt is used in place of the beef.

TONGUE BULGOGI

This dish is not offered in fine Korean restaurants to the faint of heart. But I am convinced that this is one of the best tongue dishes in the world. And it is not complicated to prepare.

Purchase a fresh beef tongue and carefully slice off the skin. Slice the meat very thin and proceed as in the preceding Bulgogi recipes. Cook it a bit longer on the grill than you would the pork or beef, and you will have a great treasure.

SHREDDED DAIKON KIMCHEE

Makes about 1 quart

This is a very pretty dish, since the lovely white *daikon* radish is cut into very thin strips and then pickled. The result adds both beauty and flavor to the plate.

- 3 pounds *daikon* radish (page 39), peeled and julienned
- 1 tablespoon Korean pickling salt (page 41) or kosher salt
- 3 tablespoons Korean red pepper flakes (page 52)
- ½ cup garlic chives (page 40) or regular chives, cut into 1-inch pieces
- 2 cloves garlic, peeled and crushed
- 1 tablespoon rice wine vinegar (page 45)
- 1 tablespoon light soy sauce (not "Lite"—see page 46)
- 1 tablespoon sesame seeds
- ½ teaspoon salt
- ½ teaspoon sugar

Toss the julienned *daikon* with the pickling salt and let it stand for 5 minutes. Drain well and squeeze out excess water. Toss all the ingredients together. Put in mason jars and put lids on, but not too tight, so gas can escape. Leave them on the counter overnight, then refrigerate.

DAIKON KIMCHEE CUBES

Makes about 2½ quarts

When I say that a dish is common, I do not mean that it isn't delicious. This is a common dish, necessary to the daily diet of the Korean people, and I think it's wonderful. And easy to prepare.

3 pounds *daikon* radish (page 39), peeled and cut into 1-inch cubes

5 tablespoons Korean red pepper flakes (page 52)

2½ tablespoons Korean pickling salt (page 41) or kosher salt

7 cloves garlic, peeled and crushed

2 teaspoons grated fresh ginger

½ cup garlic chives (page 40) or regular chives, cut into 1-inch pieces

1 teaspoon sugar

1 tablespoon Korean red pepper threads (page 52)

½ tablespoon Korean pickling salt or kosher salt

In a large stainless-steel bowl, toss the cut radish with the red pepper flakes. Allow to sit for 30 minutes. Add the remaining ingredients, except the last ½ tablespoon of salt. Place in a crock or stainless-steel bowl, sprinkle with the remaining salt, then cover with a plate along with a weight of a few pounds, such as a pot. Cover with plastic wrap and leave on the counter for 2 days, then refrigerate.

HINT: ON THE USE OF MSG. I am not one to advocate the use of a lot of chemicals or artificial flavorings in food. However, MSG is a very natural derivative of the soybean. In high concentrations it bothers a small group within our population, though it has never bothered the peoples of the Far East. I use it now and then because it has never bothered me or anyone else in my family, and it does impart a richness to the food. So use the same old rule that you use with everything else in the food and wine world: moderation, that's the key, moderation!

STUFFED PEPPERS IN EGG

(Kochu-jang)

Serves 6–8 as the first course in a Korean meal

I cannot help it. I keep going through these Korean recipes and saying to myself, "This is my favorite." It's true, and this one should prove the depth of my dilemma. It only looks complicated. It's really quite simple and astoundingly delicious.

15 medium-hot green
    peppers, such as small
    Cubanelles (page 39)
    or green Anaheims
    (page 36)

½ pound lean ground beef

1 tablespoon Kikkoman
    soy sauce

1 medium scallion,
    chopped

2 cloves garlic, peeled and
    finely chopped

½ teaspoon Sesame Salt
    (page 268)

¼ teaspoon freshly ground
    black pepper

⅛ teaspoon MSG
    (optional)

1 teaspoon sesame oil

½ cup all-purpose flour
    (See Hint, page 423.)

2 eggs, well beaten

Peanut oil for pan-frying

Cut the peppers in half lengthwise and remove the seeds.

Mix the beef with the soy sauce, onion, garlic, Sesame Salt, pepper, optional MSG, and sesame oil.

Stuff each of the pepper halves with the beef mixture. Dip the peppers into the flour and then into the beaten egg.

Fry until golden in a lightly oiled pan.

Serve hot or cold.

THE LATVIAN
IMMIGRANTS

LATVIA

U ntil quite recently I thought the people called Latvians were going
to disappear from Europe, but the events of 1989, in which the Latvians
declared their independence from Moscow, give us all new hope that this
ancient culture will continue to survive.

The Latvians have always been a tenacious bunch. They are part of an
almost extinct Baltic people and speak an especially ancient Indo-Euro-
pean language. They have been under foreign rule since the thirteenth
century, and the fact that the language has survived certainly points to
the commitment that these people have to one another and to their
history.

The area that makes up the nation of Latvia has been known since the
Bronze Age for its large deposits of amber. The amber is considered
precious to the history of these people and every Latvian woman has a
necklace made of amber beads. They call it Latvian Gold.

By the thirteenth century, failure to achieve unity among the local
principalities led to invasion by the aggressive German knights. In 1561
the Poles came in and reduced most of Latvia to serfdom. Over the next
three hundred years Sweden and Poland quarreled over Latvia and by
1795 all of Latvia was absorbed in the Russian Empire. Still, after all of
these centuries of outside rule Latvian culture continued to survive.

In the nineteenth century the serfs were emancipated and by 1940
Latvia had declared itself independent. World War II saw the Nazis

overrunning Latvia and finally, in 1945, the Soviet Union reconquered the nation.

I am telling you all this since it will help us understand the plight of the Latvian immigrant as he looked to this country. A few Latvians came to America during the seventeenth, eighteenth and nineteenth centuries. Tsarist oppression and a desire to avoid service in the Russian army prompted more to immigrate and between 1939 and 1951 people came here to flee Nazi and Soviet suppression. These immigrants were highly educated and multilingual. They established themselves within a decade. Today the culture preserved and celebrated in America combines Germanic, Scandinavian, and Slavic elements.

I first got to know the Latvian community when I was a student in college. Two Latvian brothers were active in the University, and then I found some cousins of theirs and on and on it went. I cherish those memories of Mama Macs, Juris, Andy, Rasa . . . and great food, too.

The following recipes will provide you with ample food for a Latvian buffet, a favorite form for entertaining. The dishes are hearty peasant food, but remember the peasants taught the aristocrats how to eat. In fact, the Latvian women who prepared this buffet for me all had college degrees. Now, enough of this talk about peasant food and let's get on with the party.

Latvian Piragi

Makes about 2 dozen

Latvian immigrants brought it all. The love of education, the Church, the traditions, and the *piragi*. I was first served these little baked jewels by a girlfriend from my college days. Rasa served a great tray of these, along with soup, at the beginning of the meal. They were so delicious that I ate a lot of them, all the time thinking that these made up the meal. I was wrong. Following this dish many other dishes are served . . . and you must be careful to not eat too much.

THE DOUGH

½ cup milk

¼ cup butter

½ teaspoon salt

1 tablespoon sugar

1 package quick-rising yeast

1 egg, lightly beaten

2 cups all-purpose flour (See Hint, page 423.)

In a small saucepan heat the milk, butter, salt, and sugar until the butter is melted and all is blended. Cool to warm, about 105°. If you have a heavy electric mixer that will make bread, such as a KitchenAid, place the liquid mixture in the mixing bowl and proceed as follows. If you do not have such a mixer, simply do the rest by hand. Add the yeast to the warm liquid mixture and stir to dissolve. Mix in the egg.

Add 1 cup of the flour to the warm liquid mixture and mix to form a smooth batter. Or stir the flour into the liquids with a wooden spoon. Cover the bowl and allow the sponge to rise for about ½ hour. Using a dough hook, knead in the remaining cup of flour until the mixture is very smooth. Or add the flour by hand and knead for about 5 minutes on a floured surface.

Place the dough on a plastic counter and cover with a large bowl. Allow to rise until double in bulk, about 1 hour.

THE FILLING

¼ pound bacon, coarsely chopped

½ pound boneless pork butt, coarsely chopped

1 medium yellow onion, peeled and coarsely chopped

Salt and freshly ground black pepper to taste

Heat a frying pan and add the bacon, pork, and onion. Sauté over medium-high heat until the meat browns a bit and the onion is tender. Do not overcook. Drain in a colander until cooled to room temperature. Add salt and pepper to taste.

Form the *piragis* by pulling some of the dough toward you and flattening it out a bit, a little at a time. It should be quite thin. Push it with your fingers until it is. Put 1½ teaspoons of the filling about 1 inch in from the edge of the flattened dough. Be very careful to not spread the oil from the filling around the edge of the dough, as it will prevent the dough from sealing. Fold the outer edge of the dough over the filling and press the edge a bit to seal it. Cut off the dumpling with the edge of a 3-inch-round water glass so that a crescent is formed. (See the illustration.) Pinch the edges a bit and place the *piragi* on a greased baking sheet. Be sure that you pinch each well or they will open during baking and "laugh at you" since they will seem to have their mouths open in great joy. Continue until all of the dough and filling are used. Don't keep kneading the dough, as it will get tough.

THE GLAZE

1 egg	1 tablespoon water

Mix the egg and water well and brush the *piragi* with this.

Let the *piragi* rise for about 15 minutes and then bake at 400° for about 18 minutes, or until a lovely brown.

UNDENS KLINGER

Makes 3 dozen

This is a most delicious Latvian roll that is a cross between a fresh caraway pretzel and a bagel. It will take a few turns to learn to roll them quickly, but the kids will be willing to learn. These are fun to do! The recipe is a gift to us from Maija Riekstinis, a Latvian friend in Seattle.

1 cup milk	1¼ cups water
2 tablespoons butter	1 package quick-rising yeast
2 tablespoons sugar	
2 tablespoons salt	6 cups all-purpose flour (See Hint, page 423.)
2 tablespoons caraway seeds	

In a small saucepan heat the milk, butter, sugar, salt, caraway seeds, and water. When the butter is melted and the sugar and salt dissolved, set the pan aside to cool to warm, about 105°. Place the liquid mixture in a heavy-duty mixer, such as a KitchenAid, and add the yeast to the liquid. Stir to dissolve. Add 5 cups of the flour to the bowl and mix on low until the dough begins to pull away from the side of the bowl, about 10 minutes. Using the dough hook, knead in the remaining cup of flour until the dough is very smooth, another 5 minutes. Place on a plastic counter and cover with a large metal bowl. Allow to rise until double in bulk, about 1 hour, and then punch down.

For each pretzel, cut off a bit of the dough about the size of a golf ball. Roll it into a snake about 10 inches long and form it into a pretzel. (See the illustration.) Place each pretzel on a floured kitchen towel and allow to rise for about 15 minutes.

Bring 8 quarts of salted water to a boil and gradually boil the pretzels, about 5 at a time, until they float. This should take just a minute or so. Remove them carefully with a slotted spoon and place them on a greased baking sheet. Bake at 400° until golden brown, about 20 to 25 minutes.

These can be frozen right after they come out of the oven and re-heated later in a 350° oven for just a few minutes.

ROSOLOS POTATO SALAD

Serves 8–10 as a part of a Latvian meal

This delicious potato and herring salad is a gift from Dr. Bramanis. She is an oral surgeon, retired, and a most charming woman. She arrived from Latvia well educated and ready for work and she is typical of the Latvian immigrant.

Before you begin this dish, understand that everything . . . everything is to be cut by hand into a very small dice. That is how Dr. Bramanis taught us to do it. So, bring in the kids and start cutting. This dish is well worth the work!

THE SALAD

½ cup diced salted herring (Leave the fish whole and soak for 12 hours in fresh water, changing several times. Drain and pat dry. Skin and debone.)

2 pounds baking potatoes, boiled, peeled, and diced

1 cup diced boiled ham

1 cup diced roast pork

4 hard-boiled eggs, peeled and diced

½ cup diced celery

½ cup diced cucumbers (Pickling cukes are preferable here.)

1 medium yellow onion, peeled and diced

1 cup diced pickled beets (Save the juice for the dressing.)

½ cup golden delicious apple, peeled, cored, and diced

½ cup coarsely chopped parsley

THE DRESSING

1 cup sour cream

1 cup mayonnaise (*not* salad dressing!)

1 tablespoon prepared horseradish

2 tablespoons Dijon mustard

Juice of 1 lemon

Salt and freshly ground pepper to taste

Place all of the salad ingredients in a bowl. Mix the dressing, adding a bit of the pickled beet juice to taste, and toss with the salad. This is best served just after it is made, about room temperature.

It is delicious!

LATVIAN HERRING SALAD

Serves 6–8 as an appetizer at a Latvian meal

This seems to be a very necessary part of a Latvian buffet . . . and the buffet seems to be the way Latvians like to entertain. They are an independent lot, those Latvians, so a buffet, where the eater is in charge, is just perfect!

2 salted herring fillets, about ½ pound, boneless and skinless (Soak in fresh water, which is changed often, for 12 hours.)

¼ cup dill pickles, rinsed and diced

4 hard-boiled eggs, diced

1½ cups sour cream

1½ teaspoons prepared horseradish

Freshly ground black pepper to taste

Drain the herring and dice. Toss all the ingredients together and place in a serving dish.

PORK IN GELATIN

Serves 8–10

The peoples of the Eastern European countries all seem to love this jellied pork dish. The Lithuanians make it using only pork feet, while the East Germans use only the shank. The Latvian version is richer than either of these, and worth the work in preparation. Thanks to my friends the Gallerts for this one.

2 pounds fresh pork hocks, sawed into pieces

2 pounds lean, boneless pork butt

3 bay leaves

6 black peppercorns

2 carrots, cut into large pieces

1 small yellow onion, peeled

2 ribs of celery, cut into large pieces

Salt to taste

Mustard (optional)

Vinegar (optional)

Place all the ingredients, except the mustard and the vinegar, in a kettle and just cover with water. Bring to a boil and turn down to a simmer. Cover and cook slowly until the meat is well done, about 1½ to 2 hours.

Remove the meat and vegetables from the liquid. Discard the vegetables, and cut the meat and skin into 1-inch-square pieces. Place the meat in a mold that has been sprayed with Pam. Return the liquid to a boil, reduce by ¼, and then spoon off the fat. Pour enough of the clear liquid over the meat just to cover. Chill until well set, at least 6 hours.

Unmold onto a platter. Slice and serve with mustard and vinegar if desired.

ALEXANDER'S CAKE

Serves 12–16

This is a lovely iced sheet cookielike pastry, with a jam filling, of course, and it points to the fact that Latvian cooks love a few very sweet courses on the buffet table. The kids will love this since it has many flavors all fighting for a stand, but they blend instead into a unique dessert.

THE CAKE

1 pound soft butter

¾ cup sugar

2 eggs

Grated rind of 1 lemon

4 cups all-purpose flour
(See Hint, page 423.)

THE FILLING

1 10-ounce jar red currant
jelly

THE GLAZE

Juice of 2 lemons

1 pound powdered sugar,
sifted

Cream the butter and sugar well in an electric mixer. Add the eggs, one at a time, mixing well. Add the lemon rind and the flour. Mix just until a smooth dough is formed.

Grease two 9 × 13-inch sheet-cake pans and line each with waxed paper. Divide the dough evenly between the two pans. Using a spatula, spread the dough evenly. You may want to put waxed paper on top as well and simply use a rolling pin. Remove the waxed paper on top. Bake at 375° for about 13 to 15 minutes, or until they are just golden brown. Allow the sheets to cool in the pans.

Invert one sheet onto a flat serving platter, and peel off the waxed paper. Whisk the jelly to thin it out, then spread it evenly over the first sheet. Carefully invert the second sheet on top of the first and peel off the waxed paper.

Prepare the glaze by stirring the lemon juice gradually into the powdered sugar with a fork. If it does not spread easily, add enough water, 1 teaspoon at a time, until you get an icing that is easy to work with. Spread the top of the pastry with the icing and allow it to set. Cut into diamonds or 1-inch by 3-inch pieces.

The Lebanese
Immigrants

LEBANON

L
ebanon has a very ancient culture and the battles that these people have been through have been tremendous. I love the history of Lebanon due to my affection for the food, for the life-style, and for my Lebanese uncle, Victor Abdo. Actually his parents came from Syria and Grandma Selma Abdo never called herself Lebanese. She should probably be referred to as a Maronite Christian Syrian American. But when I was a child my uncle told me one day that he was no longer Syrian, he was Lebanese. It has taken me years to figure that one out. Such is the history of this ancient and confusing nation.

Lebanon is one of the smallest nations in the world, only 135 miles long and between 25 and 35 miles wide. It is unique in the Arab world in that it has no desert and no Bedouin population. Syria lies to the north and actually surrounds the nation, while Israel is to the south, and the Mediterranean to the west.

Now, catch this ancient history lesson. In 3000 B.C. the land was ruled by the Phoenicians, so-called because of the wonderful purple dye they had developed and sold about the Mediterranean. These were the original Lebanese, the Phoenicians of the Bible! Not only did these early people provide their famous dye but they also traded wheat, olive oil, wine, and wonderful timber. The wood came from the famous cedars of Lebanon and it was used to construct grand and profound buildings.

King Solomon's Temple used the cedars in construction as did the Egyptian palaces and the Phoenician seafaring galleys.

The Phoenicians were superb sailors and navigators; the first people to use the north star for navigation, they are said to have sailed around the continent of Africa one thousand years before the Portuguese.

In 332 B.C. Alexander the Great, from Greece, conquered this area and brought it under Hellenistic influence. The Greeks ruled until 64 B.C. when the Romans moved in. Under Roman occupation Lebanon did well in terms of business. Wines, raisins, and the famous purple dye of Tyre were sought after all over the Mediterranean.

Christianity came from Palestine. We know that Jesus preached in both Sidon and Tyre, and the Apostle Paul crisscrossed the area often on his teaching missions. In the eighth century an exclusive Christian community developed in the north, a community that followed their patron saint, a fourth-century monk called Saint Maro; thus they called themselves Maronites. This sect came to Lebanon to escape discrimination in Syria by the Muslim majority there. By the twentieth century the Maronite Christians were the majority religious group in Lebanon, and we must remember that they came from Syria. A great deal had gone on during that thousand years that left a legacy of mistrust between the Christians and the Muslims.

I wish I had room in this chapter to talk about these battles and tensions. I wish I understood them! Beirut, one of the most beautiful cities in the world, is in ruins. I cannot conceive of a possible recovery, and every time I speak with Patty, my wife, about this city she becomes terribly sad. She visited there many times when she was a little girl, and her affection for that city is profound. Now the city is gone. You can understand the reasons Lebanese and Syrian immigrants have had for coming to this country.

In 1946 the modern nation of Lebanon became a reality. That was the year when my Uncle Vic, who had always been Syrian, suddenly told me that he was actually Lebanese. His mother and father had come from that portion of Syria that is now Lebanon, so while Grandpa and Grandma Abdo never called themselves Lebanese, the land from which they had come was indeed now called Lebanon. Given the battles going on there, I am afraid that the nation of Lebanon may just disappear.

I remember the dishes that Grandma Abdo prepared for me when I was a child. Please remember that I have no Lebanese blood in me, none at all. I was adopted into this wonderful family because Uncle Vic married my mother's sister, and she was Norwegian, as am I. So their children are half Lebanese and half Norwegian, and they know both cuisines well.

Wheat, olives, and dates are the staples of the Lebanese kitchen. Lamb, garbanzo beans, and yogurt are common. And don't forget hospitality. The Lebanese are really more concerned about hospitality than they are about food, though you will have trouble understanding that after you taste these wonderful recipes.

Most of these are from Uncle Vic . . . actually from Grandma Abdo. Lord, I miss that woman!

TABOULEH

Serves 6 as a salad course

While this dish also appears in the cuisine of other Middle Eastern cultures, I like the flavorings the Lebanese impart best. Perhaps it has something to do with the spices. They remind me of my childhood when my Lebanese Uncle Vic would prepare this for us on a summer evening.

1 cup fine grain bulgur wheat (page 38)	¼ cup olive oil (extra virgin preferable)
2 large bunches of parsley	¼ cup lemon juice
1 small red bell pepper, cored, seeded, and cut into large chunks	¼ teaspoon ground allspice
	¼ teaspoon ground cinnamon
2 stalks celery, cut into large pieces	1 teaspoon salt
2 bunches of scallions, cut into large pieces	¼ teaspoon freshly ground black pepper
2 tablespoons coarsely chopped fresh mint leaves or 1 teaspoon dried mint	4 medium tomatoes, cut into ¼-inch dice

Soak the bulgur wheat in 2 cups cold water for 15 minutes. Squeeze dry.

Pick the parsley leaves from the large stems. Wash at least twice and drain very well. Mix the parsley, bell pepper, celery, scallions, and mint together, and place in a food processor with a metal blade. Pulse-chop until fine and place in a large mixing bowl.

In a separate bowl mix the olive oil, lemon juice, spices, and salt and pepper, and stir with fork or whisk until smooth.

Combine all of the ingredients except the tomatoes thoroughly in the mixing bowl. Then gently blend in tomatoes.

Serve immediately.

NOTE: The amounts of all ingredients can be varied to taste.

KIBBE

(Raw)

Serves 8–10

I cannot remember when Uncle Vic first served this dish of raw lamb . . . but I know I was very young and *very* impressed. Not only was the dish delicious but it had a wonderfully sinister side to it. "Mom," I said, "Uncle Vic is eating raw meat! So am I!" I also remember his eating raw liver, sliced thin, on French bread with salt and pepper. Yes, I prefer the raw lamb. You must try this as it is one of the finest dishes in all of Lebanon.

2 pounds boneless leg of lamb (no fat or gristle), cut into large pieces	½ teaspoon salt
	¼ teaspoon ground allspice
¾ cups fine grain bulgur wheat (page 38)	¼ teaspoon ground cinnamon
2 tablespoons dried onion flakes	2 tablespoons chopped fresh mint or 1 teaspoon dried mint
2 cups water	¼ cup chilled water
2 tablespoons chopped parsley	

GARNISHES

2 white onions, peeled	Chopped parsley
3 tablespoons virgin olive oil	

Grind the lamb coarsely in a meat grinder, keeping it as cold as possible during the process. Uncle Vic even refrigerates the meat-grinding attachment of his mixer before he starts the grinding.

Soak the bulgur wheat and the dried onion flakes in 2 cups of water for about ½ hour. Drain well.

Mix all ingredients thoroughly and run through the grinder using the fine blade a second time.

Mold the kibbe into a mound on a platter and surround it with onion petals. Onion petals are made by cutting an onion into 6 wedges and dividing the wedges into "petals." Place them around the meat. Drizzle a bit of olive oil on the kibbe and garnish with chopped parsley.

To eat, use an onion petal as a sort of spoon to scoop up the meat. Then, eat the meat, onion, spoon, and all. Fantastic!!!!

KIBBE

(Baked)

Serves 8

This baked lamb dish is so filled with flavor . . . so rich . . . I am convinced it will become a favorite dish for entertaining your family. It is served this way in the old country and it is still served this way by immigrant Lebanese, including those that are of fourth and fifth generation. It is probably the most famous lamb dish in Lebanon.

All of the ingredients for raw Kibbe (page 289) with following exceptions: Increase bulgur to 2 cups, dry, and soak in 4 cups water for ½ hour. Drain well. Substitute 2 large yellow onions, peeled, for the dried onion flakes. Omit the garnishes.

Prepare the kibbe mixture as on page 289 and set aside in a bowl.

THE STUFFING

½ pound boneless leg of lamb (no fat or gristle)

2 tablespoons butter

¼ cup pine nuts

1 medium yellow onion, peeled and finely chopped

⅛ teaspoon ground cinnamon

⅛ teaspoon ground allspice

Salt and freshly ground black pepper to taste

5 tablespoons olive oil for oiling the pan and topping the meat

Grind the lamb coarsely in your meat grinder. Sauté the lamb in the butter until the moisture has evaporated, then add all the other ingredients except the oil and continue cooking until the onions are transparent.

Oil a 9 × 13-inch glass baking dish well with 2 tablespoons of the olive oil. Spread a ¼-inch layer of the raw kibbe evenly in the bottom. Keep your hands moist and the kibbe will spread more evenly and smoothly. Next, spread all the stuffing evenly over the bottom layer. Form the remaining raw kibbe into 1-inch-thick patties and lay them over the stuffing. With your hands still moist, join the patties and smooth them into a thick layer to cover the stuffing. Using a paring knife, score lines about ¼ inch deep into the meat, making 1-inch-long diamond patterns all over. Lightly cover with the remaining 3 tablespoons of olive oil.

Bake in a preheated 400° oven for 20 minutes. Reduce heat to 300° and bake for at least 30 minutes, or until golden brown.

To serve, cut the meat into 8 pieces.

EGGS IN OIL WITH SUMAC

Serves 3

This may sound strange to you but the sumac plant produces an herb that is wonderful-tasting when it is ground. Tart and tangy, it is the basis of the Zartar Blend used above and it is useful in many dishes. The Persians love the stuff on rice, but my boys, Channing and Jason, love it on fried eggs for breakfast. The Lebanese word for "sumac" is *semet,* and from the time the boys were tiny they would cheer when they came to the breakfast table and found this dish waiting. They called it "Eggs in Cement"!

4 tablespoons olive oil
6 eggs

1 tablespoon sumac
(page 53)
Salt and freshly ground
black pepper to taste

Heat a 12-inch SilverStone-lined frying pan and add the oil. Break the eggs into the oil, being careful not to break the yolks. Sprinkle the sumac and salt and pepper on top. Cover and slowly cook until done to taste. We like ours soft. These eggs are terrific with pita bread because you can soak up the oil and egg yolk along with the "cement."

LEBANESE BABA GHANOUSH

Serves 4–6 as an appetizer

The eggplant is prized in Asia, the Middle East, Europe—everywhere except America. When our immigrant ancestors came to this country they brought with them their beloved eggplant seeds from the Old World, seeds from their memories. I can't imagine a Lebanese dinner without a dish of mashed eggplant-sesame dip along with pita bread. *Baba Ghanoush* is so good that you will not look for meat . . . not until all of it is eaten.

1 large eggplant, unpeeled, about 1 pound

1 large clove garlic, peeled and crushed

2 tablespoons tahini (sesame paste) (page 47)

Juice of ½ lemon or to taste

Salt to taste

GARNISHES

3 tablespoons olive oil
Pita bread cut into wedges

Chopped parsley

Using a fork, poke the eggplant at least a dozen times. Place on a baking sheet and broil on all sides about 4 to 5 inches from the source of heat. Turn often until the eggplant is browned nicely all over. Total time will be about 45 minutes.

Remove the eggplant from the broiler and allow to cool for a few minutes. Cut the eggplant in half lengthwise, and scoop out the soft insides, discarding the browned peel. In a bowl mash the eggplant and the remaining ingredients, except the garnishes, with a fork. Do not use a food processor or blender as you do not want too smooth a paste.

Serve on a plate with the olive oil and parsley sprinkled over the top. Guests dip the bread wedges into the Baba Ghanoush and go directly to heaven without passing go.

STUFFED GRAPE LEAVES

Serves 6–8 as an appetizer course

I suppose you must wonder about how bad things were in the Old World when they first turned to eating the leaves from grapevines. We think it started in Greece during very difficult times, but so many cultures in the Middle East also enjoy this dish that we must admit that the custom spread quickly. And, it spread to this country. Our immigrant ancestors must have had some explaining to do to the neighbors since this dish is so foreign to American cuisine. But after the neighbors tried the dish, it ceased to be foreign, I am sure.

1 pound ground lean lamb	¼ teaspoon ground allspice
1 cup long-grain rice	Salt and freshly ground black pepper to taste
¼ teaspoon ground cinnamon	Juice of 2 lemons
7 dozen fresh grape leaves or a 1-pound jar of grape leaves (available in any fancy food shop)	GARNISH
	Homemade Yogurt (page 428) or yogurt from the market

Mix the lamb, rice, spices, and salt and pepper. Set aside.

If using fresh grape leaves, be sure to pick those that are still shiny and new. Blanch them in boiling water until they change color, just a moment. Drain and cool. If using bottled leaves, simply remove them from the jar and sort the small ones from the large.

Place a layer of the smaller leaves in the bottom of a large heavy-bottomed kettle or saucepot, with a cover.

Lay each large grape leaf on a flat surface, vein side up, and trim away the stem. Place enough of the lamb mixture on the stem end of the leaf to form a cylindrical shape of ½ inch by 2 to 3 inches, about 1 tablespoon. Fold the stem end over the filling, fold the sides over to secure the filling, then roll the leaf toward its tip. (See the illustration.)

Carefully place each rolled leaf in the kettle or pot, seam side down, close together so that the leaves will not unroll during cooking. You will have about 3 or 4 layers. Place a plate over the rolled grape leaves and cover with water. Bring to a boil, then turn down to a simmer and cook, covered, for 1 hour. After the first 30 minutes of cooking, add the lemon juice. Do not take the lid off the pot again until the leaves are done.

Serve with a tart yogurt garnish. (See **Hint**, page 360.)

NOTE: I recommend that you make your own yogurt. It is really quite simple and the results are much more flavorful than supermarket yogurt. Uncle Vic has been doing it since before I was born.

LEBANESE YOGURT AND CUCUMBER SALAD

(Leban)

Serves 6–8 as a salad or dip

This is a favorite from the old country. I just this minute realized that I have never had a Lebanese dinner at Uncle Vic's house without this dish!

3 cups Homemade Yogurt
(page 428) or yogurt
from the market

12 fresh mint leaves

2 cloves garlic, peeled

Salt to taste

2 or 3 cucumbers, peeled and
thinly sliced

Drain the yogurt in a cheesecloth-lined colander for several hours, discarding the liquid that has collected. Place the mint and garlic together in a salad bowl and crush with a little salt. Add the drained yogurt and cucumbers. Mix and chill before serving.

LEBANESE SHISH KEBAB

Serves 9–10

I remember when Uncle Vic first bought a charcoal grill. I had never seen such a thing, nor had anyone else in the neighborhood. (Boy, that was a while back!) I now realize that grilling was an everyday method of cooking in old Lebanon. His mother, my dear Grandma Selma, must have somehow built such a device when she came to this country. Vic would proudly grill chicken for me, and I had never seen such a dish. I was about seven or eight years old. But, when he made lamb shish kebab I stood back. This was too good to be true . . . and it still is.

Note that Uncle Vic does not mess around with phony bottled marinades . . . never has . . . and never will.

2 large red bell peppers
2 large green bell peppers
2 large yellow onions
1 tablespoon finely chopped fresh mint leaves

3 large cloves garlic, peeled and crushed
½ cup olive oil
3 pounds lean boneless leg of lamb, all excess fat trimmed, cut into 1½-inch cubes
Salt and freshly ground black pepper to taste

Quarter the bell peppers lengthwise. Remove the cores and seeds and cut into 1-inch pieces. Peel the onions and cut lengthwise into 6 wedges. Separate the wedges into "leaves" and set aside.

Make a marinade of the mint, garlic, and olive oil.

Place the lamb cubes alternately with the onion and pepper pieces on skewers. Paint with the marinade and let stand for 1 hour before broiling. Sprinkle with salt and pepper to taste. Broil on the grill or cook under the broiler in your oven. Cook strictly to taste . . . but do not overcook, about 8 minutes for rare, 12 for well done.

OKRA AND LAMB STEW

Serves 6

Grandma Abdo, Uncle Vic's mother, brought this dish with her from Syria . . . an area later called Lebanon. When I was a small boy she would prepare this for us and I was in heaven. One day we were to have a picnic at the beach in Seattle and it rained. I was terribly hurt, but Grandma Abdo and my aunt Tessie said they had a surprise! They spread out our beach blanket in the front room of the house and we ate on the floor. Grandma Abdo had cooked this dish especially for our "picnic"!

No, okra is not gooshy! Cook it for a few extra minutes if you like . . . but I love the texture of okra, as did our immigrant ancestors.

1 pound boneless leg of lamb, cut into long strips, 1½ to 2 inches wide, about ½ inch thick

3 tablespoons olive oil

1 large yellow onion, peeled and minced

3 large cloves garlic, peeled and crushed

½ teaspoon ground allspice

½ teaspoon ground cinnamon

1 2-pound can crushed tomatoes

Juice of 1 lemon

Salt and freshly ground black pepper to taste

1 pound frozen whole okra, thawed

Quickly brown the lamb strips in the olive oil. Add the onion and garlic and cook until transparent. Add the spices, tomato, and lemon juice, and salt and pepper. Simmer until the lamb is tender. Add the thawed okra, and cook 5 minutes. This dish is better if cooked a few hours ahead and reheated.

Lebanese serve over Rice Pilaf (page 297).

NOTE: This dish is also terrific cooked with green beans instead of okra.

LEBANESE RICE PILAF

Serves 6–8

The addition of something as simple as toasted egg noodles gives a whole new dimension to this rice pilaf. And you thought this side dish was an instant job invented in San Francisco! Brought there by Lebanese and Armenian immigrants, it is tasty and versatile.

¼ cup Chinese egg noodles or thin spaghetti, broken into ½-inch pieces

3 tablespoons olive oil

2 cups long-grain rice

4 cups cold water

Salt to taste

In a small frying pan, sauté the noodle pieces in the olive oil until they are golden brown. Careful, they burn easily!

Wash the rice, drain it, and place it in a small pan with a tight-fitting lid. Add the water and the toasted noodles and oil. Add the salt. Bring to a boil, reduce the heat to low, and cook, covered, for 20 minutes.

BREAD WITH ZARTAR

(Man'oushi)

Serves 4–6 as a snack

Zaartar is a Middle Eastern herb blend consisting of a type of wild marjoram, sumac, thyme, and salt. Sprinkled on store-bought pita bread, it is a quick and delicious snack. (I do not expect you to start making your own pita bread.)

4 tablespoons olive oil

2 tablespoons sesame seeds

2 tablespoons Zartar Blend (page 53)

⅛ teaspoon salt

Blend all the ingredients together. Spread this on the top of 2 or 3 circles of pita bread and pop them under the broiler for just a few minutes. Then cut them into wedges and serve.

THE LITHUANIAN
IMMIGRANTS

LITHUANIA

Modern history is so strange. Two years ago if you mentioned Lithuania, the average American would have displayed a very hazy knowledge. Today if you bring up the subject, the average American will start talking about the morning news and the courageous efforts of the Lithuanian people to declare their independence from the Soviets. Lithuanians have been a little-known immigrant group in America . . . but now that Eastern Europe is changing so much, Lithuanians have become heroes in this country.

There are over 1.6 million Americans who claim Lithuanian ancestry and the history of their motherland is fascinating and tragic. The language that has been spoken in the old country seems to be a descendant of Sanskrit, marking it as a very distinct language in the midst of other Eastern European tongues. It is one of the oldest languages still alive in Europe.

The land along the Baltic is hilly, once covered by primeval forests that protected the early tribes from foreign invaders. These tribes were united for the first time in 1251 when Mindaugas was crowned the first and only king of Lithuania. During the 1500s a Polish-Lithuanian Commonwealth was established, and this lasted until 1795.

The Russian Empire took over the Lithuanian people in 1795 and immediately began dismantling the society in order to undermine the

A Lithuanian woman with a colorful shawl, Ellis Island, 1926

power of the Lithuanian-Polish nobility. The country was primarily Catholic at the time and a program of conversion to Orthodoxy was begun. Lithuanian literature was banned and the Lithuanian language outlawed. But the obstinate and courageous Lithuanian peasant would not budge in terms of traditional loyalties and language. The more the Russian Empire attempted to suppress the culture the more spirited and nationalistic the Lithuanians became. It was a sad but proud time for this nation.

In 1915 the Germans invaded and ended tsarist rule and at the end of World War I an independent Lithuanian state was proclaimed. This nation lasted only until Russia's Red Army reestablished Russian rule in 1945.

It was not until 1989, when glasnost, a new attitude of openness on the part of Moscow, began that Lithuanians could fly their national flag, a flag declared illegal since 1945. That same year the Lithuanian parliament declared December 25 to be Christmas! This holiday had been illegal for generations.

Migration to America from Lithuania began in the 1600s, but increased greatly during the 1860s. A great famine hit the land and hundreds were compelled to go begging. Thus, the trek to America.

Today Lithuanian Americans still have a fierce pride in their history and a devotion to the meaning of Lithuania. They are hardworking, well educated, and proud of their American heritage as well. Early in 1989 we visited a Lithuanian Catholic parish, Saint Casimir's in Pittston, Pennsylvania. Good Father Peter told us of his dismay during his last trip to Lithuania. A young woman knocked on his hotel door in the middle of the night. "Father," she said, "please baptize my baby." When Father Peter asked her why she did not go to a local parish, the young woman explained that if she did she would be marked. She would lose her apartment, possibly her job. I need not tell you that Father Peter put on his stole, blessed the water, and baptized the child. That is the kind of situation that these people have had to put up with for generations. Now that the Lithuanian flag is flying we must all hold this nation in our prayers, along with the whole of the rest of Eastern Europe. They are a courageous lot.

The recipes that we offer in this section are gifts to us from this wonderful parish, Saint Casimir's. The Cold Beet Soup is terrific, and the Pressed Cheese delicious. But the Kugelis, the Potato Pudding, will just delight you and your children.

PRESSED CHEESE

(Suris)

Makes about 2 pounds

This is a delicious form of cheese that can be used in cooking or just spread on bread. Father Peter at Saint Casimir's likes to broil a slice of toast with this cheese on it for his breakfast. It is from the Old World and just wonderful!

2 pound small-curd cottage cheese	½ cup sour cream
1 pound dry-curd cottage cheese or farmer cheese (page 39)	Pinch of salt

In a large bowl, combine all the ingredients and mix well. Drain in a cotton muslin bag or in a colander lined with several layers of cheese-cloth, 1 to 2 days. I use a colander for this but Ann, the cook, uses a sewn muslin bag and hangs it, tied with string, from a knob on her kitchen cabinet. Place a bowl beneath to catch the whey.

After 1 or 2 days of draining, place the cheese, bag or cheesecloth and all, in a cheese press, or between 2 boards or plates, topped with a weight. Let stand overnight. Remove the cheese from the bag and place it in a plastic bag in the refrigerator.

KUGELIS POTATO PUDDING

Serves 8–10

Eastern Europe seems to have survived on the potato, a product, unbelievably, from the New World! This dish was given to us by Ann Challan, who works at the Lithuanian Church of Saint Casimir. She is a terrific cook, and you will have to admit that, in comparison with this recipe, most Americans are very uncreative when it comes to cooking the potato.

6 ounces thick-cut bacon, cut into ⅛-inch pieces	1 5-ounce can evaporated milk
6 pounds russet potatoes, peeled and finely grated	5 eggs, beaten
1 medium yellow onion, peeled and finely grated	2 teaspoons salt
	Freshly ground black pepper to taste
	1 tablespoon butter, melted

Fry the bacon until crisp and set aside. Run the grated potato and onion through a meat grinder on coarse. Add the bacon with its drippings and the remaining ingredients except the butter. Mix well and pour into a 13 × 8 × 2-inch buttered glass baking dish. Bake at 425° for ½ hour, then reduce the heat to 375° for 25 minutes more.

NOTE: For best results the pudding should be at least 2 inches deep in the pan.

FRESH SAUSAGE

(Kielbasa)

Makes 5 pounds

Everyone in Eastern Europe seems to have a variation on this sausage. Poland is most famous for their version, but I think this Lithuanian recipe from Bill Daileda of Saint Casimir's will keep all of Eastern Europe happy. It is the best that I have come across.

1½ tablespoons salt	1 pound beef chuck, cut into large pieces
½ teaspoon freshly ground black pepper	1¼ pounds fresh pork fatback, cut into large pieces
½ tablespoon ground allspice	
¼ teaspoon garlic powder	½ cup cold water
½ teaspoon MSG (optional)	Sausage casings, about 14 feet, 1 inch in diameter (page 45)
4 pounds pork butt, cut into large pieces	

Mix all the spices in a small jar. Shake well to mix them.

Grind the meats and the fatback coarsely in a meat grinder or food processor. Place the mixture in a bowl. Add the seasonings and mix thoroughly through the meat. Mix in the cold water, which will make the meat easier to stuff.

Stuff the mixture into casings (see **Hint,** page 453).

SMOKED SAUSAGES

(Kielbasa)

This is Bill Daileda's version of smoked sausage, and it is a bit closer to what most Americans know as Polish sausage. It is Lithuanian in origin, however, and not as fatty as that stuff you get from the supermarket.

- 4 pounds pork butt, coarsely ground
- 1 pound beef, coarsely ground
- 1½ tablespoons salt
- 1 teaspoon freshly ground black pepper
- ½ tablespoon ground allspice
- ½ teaspoon garlic powder

- ½ teaspoon MSG (optional)
- ½ teaspoon mustard seeds
- ¾ tablespoon curing salt (page 39) (made by Morton's and available in specialty shops or supermarkets)
- ½ cup cold water

To prepare, follow the directions on page 304, but then tie the stuffed casings into rings and smoke them. (See **Hint** that follows.)

HINT: TO MAKE A SMOKER BOX find a large sturdy cardboard box. In the upper part of the box, make holes for half-inch wooden dowels to hang the sausages on. Place a small hot plate, one that has a fully variable temperature control, in the center of the box and run its electric cord out through a very small hole in the lower part of the box. It is a good idea to put the hot plate on a wooden board. Place a metal pie tin filled with sawdust such as that of hickory or alder on the burner. Hang the sausages on the dowels. Turn the burner on to medium and close up the box. Smoke the sausages for 2 hours, adding more sawdust as needed. Then refrigerate them.

Needless to say, it can be dangerous if you do not watch the smoker. The hot plate must not be near any of the walls of the box and someone must be on duty to watch, always. The smoker can be used only outside on concrete bricks in an open area with nothing overhead.

COLD BEET SOUP

(Saltibarsciai)

Serves at least 10 for a wonderful dinner soup

This is an unusual version of the traditional Eastern Europe beet soup. This one is chilled, then served very cold with a garnish of hot potatoes cooked with onions and dill. When the garnish goes into the soup, the result is stupendous. Only the Lithuanians!

10 beets, about 3–3½ pounds, with greens

3½ quarts water

2 medium cucumbers, peeled and coarsely julienned

¼ cup finely chopped fresh dill

¼ cup distilled white vinegar

Salt and freshly ground black pepper to taste

1 pint sour cream

GARNISH

2 russet potatoes, boiled until just tender

1 medium yellow onion, peeled and finely chopped

4 tablespoons butter

4 tablespoons vegetable oil

2 tablespoons chopped fresh dill

Remove and save the beet greens for another use. Leave 1 inch of the stem on the beets to prevent excess bleeding. Scrub the beets clean and place them in a 5- to 6-quart pot. Cover with 3½ quarts of water, bring to a boil, and simmer, uncovered, for 20 minutes or until just tender.

Drain the beets, reserving the beet water, and allow to cool. Strain the water, making sure to remove any dirt that may have clung to the beets. Set it aside.

Trim and peel the beets and cut 8 of them into short julienne. Grate the remaining 2 beets on the coarse side of a hand grater.

In a 6- to 8-quart stainless steel pot, combine 3 quarts of the reserved beet water, the beets, cucumbers, dill, vinegar, and salt and pepper. In a separate bowl, whip the sour cream with 1 cup of the reserved water. Mix until smooth, add to the pot, and stir in. Chill several hours.

Peel and dice the potatoes.

Sauté the onion in the butter and oil until clear. Add the potatoes and dill, and toss until hot.

Serve the potato mixture on the side as a garnish for the cold soup.

NOTE: Use a mandoline (page 29) for best results with the julienned beets and cucumbers.

PORK IN GELATIN

(Koseliena Saltiena)

Give one and take one! That seems to have been the motto among our immigrants from Eastern Europe. When in Europe, Lithuanians and Latvians might criticize one another, but once in this country, they united as a group in the midst of the Americanization process. What I am saying is the Lithuanians love jellied pork, and they generally made it from just pig's feet. The Latvian method, however, is not much different but it has a little more meat and a little less fat (page 283).

RAW SAUERKRAUT WITH CARAWAY

To complete your Lithuanian dinner party, buy some fresh sauerkraut in plastic bags or bottled—both are much better than canned. Drain it and add a bit of whole caraway seeds. Store it in the refrigerator overnight and serve as a wonderful and very Lithuanian side dish.

The Mexican
Immigrants

MEXICO

It is predicted that by the middle of the next century the largest ethnic group in America will be the Latinos, the Spanish-speaking people, and most of them will have come from Mexico. They will more than likely remain as the most visible and well-known component of America's Latino population. The current Mexican population in this country is estimated at somewhere between eight and ten million people. I think we had all better start studying our Spanish!

The generally preferred term for these people is "Chicano," which comes from the Aztec pronunciation of *Mexicano* ("Meshicano"), which was corrupted to *xicano* ("shicano") and finally to Chicano. It refers specifically to a multiracial group with principally Spanish and native Mexican roots.

Our American Chicano population continues to celebrate an ethnic pride, a pride that comes from an awareness of the great civilizations that their homeland nourished, the Toltec and the Aztec. The Aztecs are the best known. Their civilization arose around A.D. 1350 in southern Mexico and lasted until conquest by Spain in the sixteenth century. Sixty cities, connected by paved roads, drew together their empire, which spread from southern Mexico and the Yucatán Peninsula through parts of what are now Guatemala and Nicaragua. In the north the Toltecs ruled from A.D. 900 to 1200 controlling much of what is now Mexico.

The Aztecs' most famous emperor, Montezuma II, was the ruler when the Spanish explorer, Hernán Cortés, landed in 1519.

The Spanish wasted no time in taking over the whole of the land. The Aztecs were conquered by 1521, and by 1540 most of Mexico was a viceroyalty of Spain. Heavy taxation for the natives and a land-distribution scheme that greatly favored Spanish colonists gave rise, of course, to discontent and decades of revolutionary activity. However, it was not until 1820 that Mexico gained independence from Spain. We are talking three hundred years of Spanish rule here!

In 1846 the United States went to war with Mexico in order to gain lands that belonged to Mexico. Texas had been under Mexican rule but had already joined the United States in 1845. The Mexicans living in Texas at the time became the first large group of Mexican Americans— but not by choice, by annexation! The other lands that we were eyeing consisted of a bit more of Texas, New Mexico, Arizona, and parts of Colorado, Nevada, and California. We paid Mexico $15 million and the Treaty of Guadalupe Hidalgo gave us these territories.

Consider the plight of the Mexican American who suddenly became a second-class citizen in his own land. Mexicans who owned property in the above-mentioned territory got into all kinds of trouble over new American taxes imposed on their land, failure to file proper title claims, and on and on. These people became unwilling immigrants on their own lands! Soon the Anglo-Americans outnumbered the indigenous Mexicans in these areas and quickly acquired political and economic control. This inferior status afforded Chicanos did not really change substantially until the civil rights movement of the 1960s and 1970s, and even then the changes did not go far enough.

Even with the pain the Chicanos have suffered, they are a very proud people who have remained culturally intact despite their journey northward. They want to keep their ethnic awareness, from the first generation on.

The food that has come to our culture through the Chicano population is at once delectable and embarrassing. The delectable part comes from first-class Mexican kitchens. The embarrassing part comes from taco drive-ins that serve something that most Chicanos have never seen. The following recipes are about as close as I can come to genuine Mexican cooking, and while these dishes take some time to prepare (all real ethnic cooking does), you will be happy with the results. I hope I can steer you away from such North American sins as the crispy-fried taco shell, the cheaply prepared "Spanish" rice, in short, Dinner No. 2 at the Mexican American restaurant. The following soft taco filled with tongue will just do you in. If not, call me and we will add more garlic and coriander!

HOMEMADE SALSA

Makes about 1½ quarts

A fresh salsa is surprisingly easy to make and so much better than what you find in the supermarket. It will keep several days in your refrigerator.

4 cups ripe tomatoes, cored and chopped

5 jalapeño peppers, seeded, cored, and chopped

2 medium yellow onions, peeled and chopped

½ green bell pepper, cored, seeded, and chopped

1 cup canned tomato sauce

1 teaspoon salt

1 teaspoon peeled and finely chopped or crushed garlic

2 tablespoons chopped fresh coriander (page 49)

1½ tablespoons red wine vinegar

Salsa jalapeña (La Victoria brand) to taste

Do not cook. Simply mix all the ingredients well and add enough salsa jalapeña to suit your taste. Careful, the stuff is hot! Store in the refrigerator, covered, in plastic.

Use this salsa in the following recipes. It is great in a salad and on top of fried or scrambled eggs.

HANNA'S GUACAMOLE

Makes about 1½ cups

Hanna Fields is a special friend. She started tasting recipes for me when she was a tiny girl, and now she is a young woman and working out her own recipes. I have taken the liberty of suggesting the use of my own salsa in her excellent and very straightforward guacamole. I hope she agrees with me.

2 ripe avocados, peeled and mashed

Juice of ½ lime

4 tablespoons Homemade Salsa (page 312)

Pinch of ground cumin

½ teaspoon salt

¼ teaspoon freshly ground black pepper

2 scallions, chopped

1 tablespoon chopped fresh coriander (page 49)

The secret to this dish is avocados that are ripe. Place all the ingredients in a bowl and mash with a fork until chunky. Do not let the guacamole get too smooth. Hanna leaves the avocado pit in the guacamole while storing it covered in the refrigerator, to keep it from turning brown. Best made fresh!

This can be used on salads or as a wonderful dip. I like some sour cream on the side.

ENCHILADAS SALSA ROJA

Makes 8 enchiladas

I love these and they are far more legitimate than a lot of enchiladas found on most American Mexican restaurant menus.

1 recipe Salsa Roja (page 315)

1 cup peanut oil for frying

8 corn tortillas

1 medium yellow onion, peeled and finely chopped

¾ pound white Cheddar cheese, grated

Place Salsa Roja in a large shallow bowl. Heat the oil in a frying pan and fry each tortilla until pliable, just a few seconds. Dredge each tortilla in the salsa, coating both sides. Fill each with some of the onion and cheese and roll up. Spread a little of the salsa in a 9 × 9-inch baking dish and add the enchiladas as you go along. Be sure that you put them seam side down so that they do not unroll during baking.

Top the dish with more sauce and the remaining cheese. Bake at 350° for 15 to 20 minutes.

SALSA ROJA

Makes about 3 cups

The bright flavor that comes from preparing this sauce from dried chiles is far superior to any you will get in a can. Find the large, whole chiles in any Mexican or Latino market and talk with the merchant about the strength and heat of the various kinds. Don't be intimidated by this recipe. It is just excellent.

2 ounces large whole dried red chiles (page 38)

1½ cups hot water

2 cloves garlic, peeled and chopped

1½ teaspoons salt

¼ cup peanut oil

1 medium yellow onion, peeled and finely chopped

1 teaspoon ground cumin

2 tablespoons browned all-purpose flour (Spread on a baking sheet and baked in a 400° oven 5 to 7 minutes or until brown.)

1 ripe medium tomato, cored and chopped

¾ cup Chicken Stock (page 74) or use canned

1 tablespoon red wine vinegar

Clean the dried chiles by removing the stem and seeds. Careful, use rubber gloves for this! Soak the chile pieces in 1½ cups hot water, covered, for 1 hour. Place them in a blender along with the water, garlic, and salt. Purée and set aside.

Heat a medium frying pan and add the oil and onion. Sauté until the onion is clear and then add the cumin and browned flour. Stir for a moment and add the tomato. Sauté until all is tender, about 5 to 6 minutes. Add the chile mixture, Chicken Stock, and red wine vinegar. Simmer, uncovered, for 5 minutes, stirring until the sauce thickens.

Enchiladas Verde con Queso

Makes 8 enchiladas

Channing and Jason, my sons, will each eat a pan of these by himself. They are not especially hot and the flavor is fresh and filling.

1 recipe Salsa Verde (page 317)

8 flour tortillas

1 cup peanut oil for pan frying

2 cups cooked and shredded chicken

¾ pound Jack cheese, coarsely grated

½ cup sour cream

GARNISHES

Additional Jack cheese

Additional sour cream

Chopped fresh coriander (page 49)

Place a bit of the sauce in a 9 × 9-inch baking dish. Heat the oil in a frying pan and fry each tortilla in the oil until pliable, just a few seconds. Fill them with the chicken, Jack cheese, and sour cream, then roll them up. Top with more sauce and the rest of the cheese. Bake at 350° for 15 to 20 minutes. Garnish with additional Jack cheese, coriander, and more sour cream.

SALSA VERDE

Makes about 3 cups

1 clove garlic, peeled and minced

2 small yellow onions, peeled and chopped

8 fresh tomatillos, husked, or 8 canned tomatillos, chopped finely

3 tablespoons peanut oil

2 tablespoons all-purpose flour

1¾ cups Chicken Stock (page 74) or use canned

1 7-ounce can green chiles, finely chopped

2 tablespoons salsa jalapeña (I like La Victoria brand.)

Salt to taste

In a medium saucepan, sauté the garlic, onion, and tomatillos in the oil. Stir in the flour and sauté for a few minutes more. Add the Chicken Stock and stir until smooth. Add the chiles and simmer 30 minutes. Add the salsa jalapeña and simmer 10 more minutes. Add salt to taste.

HINT: TO TEST FOR LEAD CONTENT IN CERAMIC POTS you must purchase a lead-testing kit. It will cost you about $40 but it will test at least three hundred different styles of cooking pottery. This is very important if you love Mexican or Spanish cooking pieces since many that have a high-lead-content glaze get by the American government. And, if you have pieces that you bought years ago in Mexico, I am sure that they are filled with lead. This is murder!

You can buy a testing kit from the Frandon people to test all of your stuff. You will be surprised at what you find and comforted by what you learn. The kit is approved by the government, the health department people, the whole works. You probably need one. Write to: Frandon Enterprises, Inc., 511 North Forty-eighth Street, Seattle, WA 98103.

REAL TACOS, MEXICAN STYLE

The deep-fried, dried, and rather tasteless item called a taco by American Mexican restaurants and taco stands is nothing like what is to be had in Chicano communities. The following recipes for the different meats are very typical of such places as the Antojitos Mexicanos stall in the Grand Central Market in Los Angeles.

BEEF TACO FILLING

Prepare a beef pot roast as in Cuban Ropa Vieja (page 111), adding to the recipe ½ teaspoon ground cumin and 1 teaspoon chili powder.

Cook the meat, covered, then debone and shred it. Return it to the sauce and keep warm.

PORK TACO FILLING

Prepare a boneless pork roast as above. Shred the meat and keep it warm in the sauce.

CHICKEN TACO FILLING

Prepare a cut-up chicken as in the above recipes. Debone, shred, and keep the meat warm in the sauce.

TONGUE TACO FILLING

This one is a bit unusual but well worth the effort. It is my favorite taco!

Simmer a whole beef tongue, covered with water, along with 2 ribs of celery and a couple of chopped carrots. Add a chopped yellow onion and 2 bay leaves. Add 2 teaspoons salt and 8 whole peppercorns. Cook, at a low simmer, for 3 hours. Allow the meat to cool in the liquid. Peel the tongue and cut into ¼-inch dice.

Heat a large frying pan and add:

2 tablespoons peanut oil	1 green bell pepper, cored, seeded, and sliced
½ yellow onion, peeled and sliced	2 cloves garlic, peeled and chopped

Sauté for a moment and add the diced tongue to the pan along with:

¼ teaspoon ground cumin	Salt to taste
¼ teaspoon dried oregano	2 tablespoons dry sherry

Sauté the meat until all is hot.

TO PREPARE THE TACOS

Choose any of these meat fillings and place some in the center of a *warm* wheat tortilla. I prefer the large ones.

Garnish with:

Chopped scallions	Sour cream (optional)
Thinly sliced lettuce	Chopped fresh coriander
Homemade Salsa	(page 49) (optional)
(page 312)	

Roll up and enjoy!

MEXICAN CABRITO

Serves 4–6

You can make this with a leg of lamb but young goat is much more flavorful. No, it is not strong. It is mild and just a delightful change from the run-of-the-mill chicken and pork roast. You can find young goat (kid) in most large cities that have a Chicano or Latino population.

The recipe is simple. Buy a shoulder of goat that weighs about 5 to 6 pounds. Allow it to come to room temperature and then rub it with olive oil, crushed garlic, salt and freshly ground black pepper, and ground cumin.

FOR RARE CABRITO

In a preheated 400° oven, bake the roast, uncovered on a roasting rack, for 40 minutes, so the meat can brown. Turn the oven down to 325° and bake for an additional 40 to 50 minutes, or until a meat thermometer registers 140°. Remember to insert the thermometer in the thickest part of the roast, being careful not to touch the bone.

Remove the meat from the oven and allow it to sit for ½ hour before slicing. It will continue to cook during this time. Slice and serve with the pan juices.

Follow the instructions for rare but cook a bit longer so that the thermometer registers 145° to 150°.

Slice and serve with pan juices.

REFRIED BEANS

Serves 6–8

These are so easy to make that I cannot understand anyone buying them in the can, where they taste just like that—a can! These are much better and go with any Mexican meal.

1 pound dried pinto beans, soaked overnight then drained

1 quart water

½ pound Spanish Chorizo Sausage (page 452) or Mexican chorizo from a good market

¼ cup olive oil

3 cloves garlic, peeled and crushed

1 large yellow onion, peeled and chopped

1 teaspoon cumin seeds

½ cup chopped fresh coriander (page 49)

¼ cup freshly rendered lard (page 168) (optional)

1 cup white cheese, grated (Mexican or Jack cheese)

½ cup chopped pork cracklings (page 44) (optional)

Salt and freshly ground black pepper to taste

Place the soaked and drained beans in a heavy 3-quart saucepan and add 1 quart of water. Simmer, covered, until they can be mashed with a potato masher, about 45 minutes. You may have to add more water. Don't make them mushy.

In the meantime, pan-fry the chorizo and set it aside. Heat the olive oil in a frying pan and sauté the garlic, onion, and cumin seeds. Add the rest of the ingredients to the mashed beans and cook over medium heat for about 15 minutes.

THE MOROCCAN
IMMIGRANTS

MOROCCO

Although immigrants from Morocco are a relatively small group, their food is so delicious, and the restaurants so marvelous, that I had to include them in this discussion of our immigrant ancestors.

Morocco is very unusual: Geographically it is African, but since it is part of the world of Islam, it is also an indirect part of the Middle East. And its history links it also to Europe since Morocco, Tunisia, and Algeria together are often referred to as the "fourth shore of Europe."

I think it is fascinating that there is one part of the Arab world that is only nine miles from Spain. Look at the map! This is a most unusual nation. It is a part of the Mediterranean but it is also on the Atlantic Ocean. It is part of Africa but it almost touches Europe. It is the gateway to the Sahara Desert but it is also a land of beautiful beaches.

The indigenous people of Morocco were the Berbers, whom the Greeks and Romans called barbarians and for whom the Barbary Coast is named. We really do not know where the Berbers came from but they could have come from the Middle East and they were Caucasian.

The name "Berber" refers to their language and also their fierce sense of independence. Their name means "free and noble spirit."

Everybody seems to have tried to invade Morocco. The Phoenicians, who came from present-day Lebanon, were the first outsiders, followed by the Carthaginians, who came from what we now call Tunis. The

Romans conquered the Carthaginians in 146 B.C. and ruled for two hundred years. By the third century A.D. the Romans needed to call their men home to defend Rome, so the Berbers attacked the few remaining troops and by 429 Roman authority was destroyed in Morocco.

In 700 the Arabs moved in and used the region to launch attacks on Spain. They converted the Berbers to Islam and the Berbers assisted in the Spanish invasions. One can still see a great deal of Moroccan influence in Spain, in the architecture, especially.

During the sixteenth and seventeenth centuries Morocco was invaded by both Spain and Portugal. In the eighteenth century pirate raids along the Atlantic shores became common. Finally, in the nineteenth century, the empire-hungry French moved in and battles between the Moroccan Muslims and the French continued until 1930 when 300,000 French troops, aided by 100,000 Spaniards, completely defeated the Moroccans.

Morocco remained a French protectorate until around 1956 when it emerged as a constitutional monarchy. Today the land is ruled by King Hassan II, a direct descendant of the prophet Muhammad. The king explains the temperament of contemporary Morocco by likening it to the desert palm tree: rooted in Africa, watered by Islam, and rustled by the winds of Europe.

The food of the region is considered by many to be among the great cuisines of the world. Its complexity derives from Morocco's history, of course, its relationships with Spain, France, and the Arab world. No wonder the food is so wonderful.

The most common dish, here not using *common* to mean "mundane," is Couscous. This wonderful wheat pilaf became a favorite with the French and you can find it in many Parisian restaurants. The stews, or *tagines,* of Morocco are so filled with sweet fruits and spices that they take on a romantic aura. You will enjoy all of the following dishes, and you will have no difficulty in picking out a delicious menu. Remember that the Preserved Lemons will add a heavenly flavor to your table, but they must be made a week or so in advance. Make the lemons first and then make out the guest list.

COUSCOUS

Serves 4–5 when served with a stew or tagine

Morocco has offered some of the most wonderful food imaginable . . . and it would take quite an imagination to come up with something as clever as couscous. This is a processed wheat dish not unlike bulgur wheat. But it is a finer grain, light in flavor and texture, and it absorbs the flavor of the foods with which it is served, stews being the usual accompaniment. This dish is also fun for the kids to eat since it is to be eaten with the fingers . . . not with silverware.

If you wish to purchase a special pot for making this dish, you will find a couscousier (page 29) in any Middle Eastern market or in fancy gourmet shops. It consists of a cooking pot with a steaming section that fits on the top, then a lid. You can also find a stainless-steel vegetable steaming pot that will do a good job on couscous, and it will be less expensive than the French aluminum or copper versions. Le Creuset now has a steamer that fits on Le Creuset heavy pots and it works very well.

METHOD 1 (Couscous in a couscousier)

2½ cups water	Salt to taste
1 pound couscous, not quick-cooking	3 tablespoons melted butter or *ghee* (page 356)

Bring the water to a boil in a 4-quart pot. Add the couscous and salt. Remove from the heat and let sit 5 minutes, covered.

Add the melted butter or *ghee,* then place the buttered grain in a large bowl and roll it in your hands to separate the kernels.

Steam the couscous in the top of a couscousier for 20 minutes, then put it in the bowl again and break it up. Return it to steamer for 15 minutes longer.

METHOD 2 (Couscous without a couscousier)

1 pound couscous, not quick-cooking	Salt to taste
2½ cups boiling water	2 tablespoons butter or ghee (page 356)

Place the couscous in a large bowl and add the boiling water and salt. Let the couscous rest a few minutes to expand. In a 12-inch frying pan, heat the butter or *ghee* and couscous. Cover and cook over medium heat, about 5 minutes, stirring occasionally. Be careful not to burn the couscous. Turn off the heat and let stand covered a few minutes.

MOROCCAN RED PEPPER SAUCE

(Harissa)

Makes 1 cup

For those who love hot things here is a sauce that is traditionally served with couscous. You just spoon it on and enjoy. This recipe is from Eva Zane's fine book *Middle Eastern Cookery* (page 521).

2 tablespoons cayenne pepper	½ teaspoon salt
1 tablespoon ground cumin	1 cup olive oil
2 garlic cloves, peeled	

Using a mortar and pestle, crush the spices, garlic, and salt together to form a paste. Heat a frying pan, add the olive oil and spice mixture. Cook, stirring constantly over medium heat, for 5 minutes. Serve with couscous dishes.

KEFTA TAGINE

(Meatball Stew Moroccan)

Serves 6

T*agine* simply refers to a fine stew spiced with the flavors of Morocco. Since one is to eat it with the fingers, these meatballs are convenient . . . and the sauce is great with Couscous (page 324).

THE KEFTA (MEATBALLS)

1 pound ground lamb

2 tablespoons chopped parsley

1 tablespoon chopped fresh coriander (page 49)

½ teaspoon ground cumin

½ cup onion, peeled and finely chopped

¼ teaspoon cayenne pepper

Salt to taste

2 tablespoons olive oil for pan-frying

THE SAUCE

2 cloves garlic, peeled and chopped

2 medium onions, peeled and finely chopped

1 green bell pepper, cored, seeded, and chopped

1 small bunch of parsley, chopped

2 pounds tomatoes, chopped

1 teaspoon ground cumin

1 teaspoon freshly ground black pepper

½ teaspoon ground cinnamon

2 tablespoons fresh lemon juice

¼ teaspoon cayenne pepper

1½ teaspoons salt or to taste

GARNISH

6 eggs

Combine all the ingredients for the kefta and form into 1-inch balls with wet hands. Heat a 6- to 8-quart stove-top casserole and add the olive oil. Brown the meatballs in the oil, then remove, leaving the oil in the pot. Set the meatballs aside, covered.

Add the garlic, onion, and bell pepper to the reserved oil and sauté until the onion is clear. Add the remaining ingredients for the sauce and simmer, covered, 30 minutes until the sauce has cooked down to a thick gravy.

Return the meatballs to the sauce and simmer uncovered 10 minutes more. Carefully break the eggs into the sauce and poach for a few minutes (don't overcook the eggs). Serve at once directly from the pan.

CHICKEN TAGINE WITH SEVEN VEGETABLES

Serves 4–6

I first tasted this dish at my friend Ben's Marrakesh Restaurant in Seattle. He does a fine job with his food and the place is a delight with all of its formal Moroccan trappings. A dish similar to this one is served with couscous and is very popular on his menu.

1 chicken, about 3½ pounds, cut into 8 serving pieces, with the breasts cut in half (Remove the backs and wings and save for soup.)

3 tablespoons olive oil

1 cup peeled and diced yellow onion

3 cloves garlic, peeled and finely chopped

1 ¾-pound eggplant, cut into 1-inch cubes, unpeeled, salted, and drained for 20 minutes, then rinsed

3 cups Chicken Stock (page 74) or use canned

1½ cinnamon sticks, about 3 inches long

1 teaspoon curry powder (page 49)

1 teaspoon ground cumin

¼ teaspoon turmeric

¼ teaspoon freshly ground black pepper

1 large carrot, cut into ½-inch dice

1 medium zucchini, cut into ½-inch dice

1 medium white turnip, peeled and cut into ½-inch dice

½ medium red bell pepper, cored, seeded, and cut into ½-inch dice

2 cups medium ripe tomatoes, cut into ½-inch dice

½ cup golden raisins

2 tablespoons chopped fresh coriander (page 49) or chopped parsley

Remove all the skin and fat from the chicken pieces. Heat a large frying pan and add 1 tablespoon of the oil. Sauté the chicken in 2 batches until opaque on both sides (a few minutes). Set aside.

Heat a 6- to 8-quart casserole and add the remaining 2 tablespoons of oil. Add the onion, garlic, and eggplant. Sauté over low heat until the onion is just tender, about 5 to 10 minutes. Add the Chicken Stock, cinnamon sticks, curry powder, cumin, turmeric, and black pepper. Stir, bring to a boil, reduce heat, and simmer for 10 minutes.

Add the dark meat along with the carrot, zucchini, turnip, and red pepper. Simmer, uncovered, for 10 minutes.

Add the chicken breasts, tomato, raisins, and 1 tablespoon of the coriander, pushing down lightly to be sure the ingredients are covered by the liquid. Simmer, covered, for 10 minutes more. Salt and pepper to taste.

Serve hot in deep soup bowls on top of rice, noodles, or couscous, garnishing the top with the remaining coriander.

MOROCCAN ROASTED LAMB

Serves 8

This recipe is frequently the specialty of the house at many Moroccan restaurants. After one taste you will understand why. The cumin and salt that is sprinkled on the meat at the table just make this dish!

2 tablespoons ground coriander seeds (page 49)	2 teaspoons freshly ground black pepper
4 cloves garlic, peeled and crushed	1 teaspoon salt
1½ teaspoons ground cumin	¼ cup olive oil or *ghee* (page 356)
1½ teaspoons paprika	1 5-pound leg of lamb

GARNISH

1 tablespoon ground cumin mixed with 1 tablespoon salt

Mix all the ingredients except the garnish and rub on the leg of lamb. Let sit 10 minutes.

Roast the lamb according to the instructions for Basque Leg of Lamb (page 89). Allow it to sit a few minutes before slicing.

Place the cumin and salt garnish in a small dish and let each guest sprinkle a bit on his or her sliced lamb.

LAMB TAGINE

(Lamb Stew Moroccan)

Serves 4–6

This is every bit as good as the lamb tagines you will find in Moroccan restaurants. To get your Moroccan kitchen going you will have to prepare some preserved lemons . . . and this takes ten days. Though you might be able to buy them in a Middle Eastern grocery. But, the lemon adds an authentically wonderful flavor to this dish.

2 pounds boneless lamb shoulder, cut into 1-inch cubes

1 teaspoon salt

2 teaspoons freshly ground black pepper

½ teaspoon saffron threads, crushed (page 52), or ½ teaspoon saffron-colored powder

1 teaspoon ground ginger

2 garlic cloves, peeled and crushed

1 large yellow onion, peeled and finely chopped

Small bunch of parsley, finely chopped (optional)

4 tablespoons *ghee* (page 356) or oil

½ preserved lemon, diced, no pulp (page 333)

2 teaspoons ground cinnamon

¼ cup honey

2 tablespoons orange-blossom water (page 43) (available at Middle Eastern markets)

GARNISH (optional)

1 tablespoon sesame seeds

6 ounces blanched slivered almonds

In a 6-quart pot, put the lamb, salt, pepper, saffron, ginger, garlic, onion, optional parsley, and 3 tablespoons of the oil or *ghee*. Add 2½ cups water, enough to just barely cover. Simmer, covered, for 1½ hours or until the meat is very tender.

Add the preserved lemon and cinnamon and cook, uncovered, for another 15 minutes, then add the honey and the orange blossom water and cook for a few minutes more until the sauce is quite thick and reduced. Salt and pepper to taste.

Just before serving, toast the sesame seeds and almonds in a frying pan in the remaining tablespoon of oil or *ghee,* then sprinkle them over the meat.

This is delicious served over Couscous (page 324).

CHICKEN AND OLIVES

Serves 4

Paula Wolfert, in her wonderful classic book entitled *Couscous and Other Good Food from Morocco,* talks lovingly of this dish, and of couscous in general. Her book is in paperback and if you get into this cuisine I think that you will want to buy a copy. While the following is not her recipe it certainly shows her influence. Very delicious influence!

¼ cup olive oil

1 3½-pound chicken, quartered

3 cloves garlic, peeled and chopped

1 large yellow onion, peeled and chopped

1 teaspoon ground ginger

½ teaspoon turmeric

½ teaspoon paprika

1 teaspoon salt

½ teaspoon freshly ground black pepper

2 cups chopped tomatoes

1 tablespoon chopped parsley

1 tablespoon chopped fresh coriander (page 49)

1 preserved lemon, rinsed and chopped (page 333)

1 7½-ounce bottle cracked green olives, drained (available in fancy food shops)

Salt to taste

In a large frying pan, heat 1 tablespoon of the oil and sauté the chicken in two batches until brown on both sides. Set aside.

Heat a 6- to 8-quart casserole and add the remaining 3 tablespoons of oil. Add the garlic, onion, ginger, turmeric, paprika, salt and pepper and cook for about 5 minutes until the onion is softened. Add the chicken, tomatoes, parsley, coriander, and lemon and bring to a simmer. Cover and simmer over low heat for about 30 minutes, or until the chicken is cooked. Add the olives and cook for 5 minutes longer. Salt to taste.

LAMB BREWATS

Makes about 2 dozen

These little pillows of thin pastry filled with meat, eggs, and spices can be served as a snack, an appetizer course, or a meal. They are unusually tasty and easier to prepare than the classic Bastilla, or phyllo dough pie. The filling here is similar but takes less work.

2 tablespoons olive oil

½ cup peeled and chopped yellow onion

2 cloves garlic, peeled and crushed

½ pound lean lamb, coarsely ground

¼ teaspoon ground cumin

¼ teaspoon turmeric

¼ teaspoon ground cinnamon

½ teaspoon freshly ground black pepper

Salt to taste

1 tablespoon chopped fresh coriander (page 49)

2 tablespoons chopped parsley

¾ cup Chicken Stock (page 74) or use canned

4 eggs, beaten

1 teaspoon powdered sugar, for dusting

THE DOUGH

½ pound butter, melted

8 12-inch by 17-inch sheets of phyllo dough (See Hint, page 507.)

Heat a frying pan and add the olive oil, onion, garlic, and lamb. Sauté until the onion is clear. Add the cumin, turmeric, cinnamon, pepper, and salt. Simmer for 5 minutes. Add the coriander, parsley, and Chicken Stock, and simmer for about 2 minutes.

Drain the meat, reserving as much broth as possible. Set the meat aside and return the broth to the pan. Bring the broth to a simmer and add the beaten eggs, stirring them into the broth. Cook and stir the eggs until scrambled but not at all dry. Return the meat to the pan and mix it with the eggs. Allow to cool.

TO FORM THE BREWATS

Using a pastry brush, butter a 12-inch by 17-inch sheet of phyllo dough and cut it into thirds lengthwise. Place 1 tablespoon of filling on a piece of dough and roll it into a triangle, like folding the flag. Repeat with the remaining dough and filling. (See the illustration on page 332.)

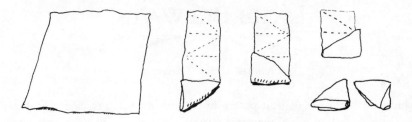

TO BAKE

Place the brewats on a nonstick baking sheet and brush butter on the top of each. Bake at 400° for 15 minutes or until golden brown.

TO PAN-FRY

Heat a SilverStone-lined frying pan. Add a little butter. Pan-fry on medium heat until golden brown on both sides.

Sift the powdered sugar over the Brewats before serving.

BASTILLA

If you have ever been to a Moroccan restaurant you know of this phyllo pie filled with fowl, eggs, sugar, and spices. The recipe is so complicated that I do not have room for it here . . . and I like Brewats (page 331) just as well. However, you can find a good recipe for a Bastilla in *Middle Eastern Cookery*, an excellent paperback by Eva Zane. Paula Wolfert also has a fine recipe in her book *Couscous and Other Good Food from Morocco*.

MOROCCAN PRESERVED LEMONS

1 quart-jar or 5 preserved lemons

These are fun to make and they add a very cleansing flavor to Moroccan dishes. You may be able to buy these in a Middle Eastern market, but do not confuse them with Indian Lemon Pickles (page 204). They are quite different.

> 5 lemons, quartered but still attached at one end (Don't cut them all the way through.)
>
> ¼ cup kosher salt
>
> Juice of about 8 additional lemons

Rub a little bit of salt inside each of the quartered lemons. Pack them tightly inside of a 1-quart glass jar. Add any remaining salt and enough lemon juice to completely cover the lemons. Seal the jar. Let stand 14 days at room temperature, inverting the jar every day. Before using, rinse each lemon in water. Store covered in the refrigerator. Will keep indefinitely.

VARIATION

You might wish to add some spices to the above recipe. Try adding a stick or two of whole cinnamon and a few cloves. These give the lemons a little extra kick.

MOROCCAN BUREK

(Cheese or Meat)

Makes 3

I tasted this dish for the first time in an excellent restaurant in San Francisco called the Pasha. These make a great appetizer course and are a bit different from the Yugoslavian dish by the same name.

> CHEESE FILLING
>
> 1½ cups coarsely grated Jack or brick cheese
>
> 1 cup ricotta cheese
>
> ½ tablespoon chopped fresh dill
>
> 1½ tablespoons lemon juice
>
> Salt and ground white pepper to taste

Mix all ingredients well, adding ½ cup of the Jack cheese. You will be using the remaining 1 cup of Jack cheese when you assemble the pastry. Set aside.

THE PASTRY

5 12-inch by 17-inch sheets of phyllo dough (See Hint, page 507.)

1 stick of butter, melted and cooled a bit

Cut each of the phyllo sheets in half the short way across so that you have 10 sheets, 6 inches by 8½ inches. Brush an 8-inch SilverStone-lined frying pan with a bit of the butter. Brush 3 of the half sheets of dough with some of the butter and place them in the bottom of the frying pan. Spread ⅓ of the filling and ⅓ cup of the grated Jack cheese over the sheets. Repeat the process twice more, ending with the remaining sheet of dough. Tuck the edges down and around. Cook over medium heat about 2 minutes, and then place in a preheated 375° oven for 15 to 20 minutes, or until the bottom is golden brown.

MEAT FILLING

1 tablespoon olive oil

2 cloves garlic, peeled and crushed

1 pound ground lamb

¼ cup pine nuts

⅓ cup tomato sauce

1½ teaspoons ground allspice

½ teaspoon ground cinnamon

Salt and freshly ground black pepper to taste

Heat a frying pan. Add the oil, lamb, and garlic and sauté until the lamb is no longer pink. Stir in the remaining ingredients and simmer 5 minutes until thickened.

Fill the pastry using the same procedure as for Cheese Burek.

THE NORWEGIAN
IMMIGRANTS

NORWAY

Between 1820 and 1975, 855,000 Norwegians immigrated to this country. This number almost equals Norway's whole population in 1820. In other words, the equivalent of an entire nation moved here. And I am glad they did since I am half Norwegian and my grandfather came here in 1889. I have placed a picture of the old boy, along with my grandmother, as the frontispiece of this book.

The Norwegians who came in the early days reflected a centuries-old history of exploration and travel. They also had the usual immigrant desire for economic betterment, but we must also understand that there was a fervent desire among the peasant class in Norway to achieve social equality. During the nineteenth century every village in Norway got a letter from someone in America. "Here," stated the letter, "it is not asked what or who was your father but the question is, what are you?" Nothing could hold back the Norske in this country. They were hardworking and frugal, and they were obstinate. They still are! I learned the whole concept of frugality from my Norwegian mother.

Norway is a land of the sea. This is so absolutely true that the Norskes call their land "The Blue Meadow." Because inland Norway is so mountainous (only 4 percent of the land is tillable), travel by sea was considered safer than by land. Three fourths of the population lives within sight of the coast, and the cuisine centers on fish, of course. The nation is a major shipping power and the North Sea a source of oil and gas.

From very early times Norway has been a nation of seafarers, explorers, and colonizers. By A.D. 1000 the Vikings had settled in Iceland, the Faroe Islands, and Greenland. In addition, they had established communities in France, Ireland, Scotland, the Isle of Man, and parts of England. More and more evidence points to the fact that Leif Ericson, a Norseman born in the Viking colony of Iceland, voyaged to North America during the year 1000. He called the new land "Vinland" since it had so many grapevines. And while a few scholars argue the point (they are certainly not Norwegians!), Norse scholars have long claimed that there were Norse settlements on the east coast of North America and as far inland as Minnesota and North Dakota as early as the thirteenth and fourteenth centuries.

While Norwegian immigration to this country began in the seventeenth century it was not until the nineteenth century that Norwegians came to this country in large numbers. Norway had fallen under Swedish rule during the late eighteenth century and there followed a time of great intellectual ferment, not only in Norway but throughout Europe. On May 17, 1814, Norwegians rejected Swedish rule and declared Norway to be an independent kingdom. That seems not to have been enough, however, since the ideas of liberty, human rights, and self-determination, ideas that captured the minds of the Norwegians decades before, called for a new life and understanding of the worth of the person. Off to America they went. And they have been coming ever since.

Large numbers of Norskes came to the Pacific Northwest, my part of America. My Grandfather Brun came at the end of the last century, and after traveling in Norway myself, I can understand why he came. The Pacific Northwest, with its many mountains that go right down in to the sea, is very much like Norway. Immigrants similar to my grandfather came here and became involved in fishing, shipbuilding, and the timber industry, just as he did, and by the turn of the century Seattle had one of the largest groups of urban Norwegians in the country.

The recipes that I have chosen for this section are very typical of the Norwegian diet. Some of these recipes belong in my family and some have come from Norski friends. You will note that some dishes sound a bit colorless and boring, such as Fish Pudding, but once you make Fiskegrot and fry it with a few onions, you will understand my affection for the cuisine. No, I have not included *lutefisk* in this section. I really doubt that you would want to get into it.

FISH PUDDING

(Fiskegrot)

Serves 6–8

Molded into balls this is called *fiskeboller*. Baked in a loaf it is called *fiskegrot*. The Norwegian table would not be without this basic form of fish, and my Norwegian background becomes a little clearer each time I make this. The Norski (Norwegian) immigrants brought their eating habits from the old country with them to the New World, and this is a perfect example.

2½ pounds lingcod fillets, skinless and boneless, or any other fresh cod

2 tablespoons potato starch (page 44)

2 teaspoons salt

White pepper to taste

Dash of ground nutmeg

2 eggs

⅓ cup butter (room temperature)

½ cup warm cream (Use a microwave.)

1 cup warm milk (Use a microwave.)

Place the fish in a food processor and process until smooth. You may have to do this in 2 batches. Remove it to the bowl of your electric mixer. Add the potato starch, seasonings, and eggs, 1 at a time, beating in thoroughly. Add the butter and then the cream and milk, beating until light and fluffy.

Place the mixture in a buttered loaf pan, cover with foil, then place the pan in a large pan of hot water. The water should come 2 inches up the side of the fish pan. Bake in a 350° oven for about 1 hour.

Slice and serve with a Cream Sauce (page 339). Or you can serve it with fried onions instead. I love it sliced and lightly fried with onions. You can also mold the fish batter into small balls and poach them in fish stock.

CREAM SAUCE

Makes 2½ cups

This is another basic sauce for the frugal kitchen. It is easy to make and offers many possibilities in terms of creamed meat dishes, fish, vegetables . . . on all kinds of things. I know that there is a canned white sauce out there. It is terrible stuff but people buy it because they don't know how to make a lumpless sauce. This one will be lumpless and you will never buy that canned white paste again.

2 cups milk

3 tablespoons peeled and chopped yellow onion

1 bay leaf

Cayenne pepper to taste

4 tablespoons butter

3 tablespoons all-purpose flour

Salt to taste

Bring the milk to a simmer. Add the onion, bay leaf, and cayenne pepper. Simmer for a few minutes, and strain the milk stock. Return to the stove. In another pan, melt the butter and stir in the flour. Remove the milk from its burner and stir in the flour/butter mixture (*roux*). Continue to simmer, stirring until thick, about 10 minutes. Add salt to taste.

VARIATION

Try adding a dash or two of dry sherry to this sauce. It is great on vegetables. I stir cooked onions into this sauce and eat the whole dish by myself!

LAMB AND CABBAGE STEW

Serves 6–8

This is so Norski (Norwegian) that when I made a batch and offered it to my Norwegian mother, she ate the whole works—over the course of a couple of days, of course. It is delicious and the recipe is the gift of Northwest Orient Airlines' magazine. Whoever would have thought that I would ask an airline for a recipe! No, they don't serve it on the plane. You will have to make it.

1 medium head cabbage, about 3 pounds

3 pounds boned lean lamb shoulder, cut into 1-inch cubes

2 teaspoons salt

¾ teaspoon freshly ground black pepper

⅓ cup all-purpose flour (See Hint, page 423.)

5 cups Beef Stock (page 78) or use canned

½ cup sour cream or heavy cream

THE ROUX

4 tablespoons (½ stick) butter

5 tablespoons all-purpose flour

Preheat the oven to 300°. Trim the cabbage of any discolored outer leaves. Core it and slice it into slim wedges.

In a large Dutch oven or kettle, layer ⅓ of the lamb, generous sprinklings of salt and pepper, and ⅓ each of the flour and cabbage. Repeat twice more.

Pour in the Beef Stock, and set the Dutch oven over moderate heat. Bring the broth to a simmer.

Cover the Dutch oven and transfer it to the oven. Bake for 2 hours, until the lamb is tender.

In the meantime, prepare the *roux* by melting the butter in a frying pan and stirring in the flour. Cook for a few minutes over medium heat.

Remove the Dutch oven from the oven. Drain the juices into a medium saucepan, skimming off the fat. Quickly whisk in the *roux,* and simmer until thickened. Whisk in the sour or heavy cream and season to taste. Pour the gravy back into the Dutch oven.

Serve with cooked unpeeled new potatoes if you wish.

RULLESPULSE

Makes 2 rolls and serves 16 as a Norwegian sandwich snack

Grandma Brun used to make this spiced lamb and veal roll for us when I was a child. I have tasted many versions since but my memory was not satisfactorily fed. I began to fiddle with the recipe that got handed down and I think I have it here. I finally figured out that Grandma Brun used more spice, better lamb, and pickled the rascal for days. Even my mother teared up when she tasted this, so it is well worth your trouble, I promise.

4 pounds lean lamb breast and flank (Have your butcher bone it and cut out the extra fat. Tell him you need 4 pounds total of meat after boning . . . and take the bones home for soup stock. Also, tell him that you are going to roll and tie the meat. He will understand.)

4 heaping teaspoons kosher or pickling salt, no iodine

1½ teaspoons freshly ground black pepper

½ teaspoon ground allspice

2 pinches of saltpeter (page 45)

1 medium yellow onion, peeled and chopped

1 pound boneless veal shoulder, cut into 1-inch cubes

THE BRINE

½ pound pickling salt, no iodine

¼ cup sugar

2 quarts water

TO COOK

2 whole allspice

2 bay leaves

1 yellow onion, peeled and chopped

2 carrots, chopped

Lay out the breast of lamb on a counter or tray. Mix the 4 heaping teaspoons of salt, the pepper, allspice, and saltpeter together and spread over the meat. Top with the chopped onion and veal cubes. Roll the whole works up like a jelly roll and tie it with good string so that it will not come undone.

Make 2 rolls from this meat. Mix the brine and soak the rolls in the brine for 3 days, refrigerated. Be sure that the whole rolls are submerged in the brine. I use a plate and a weight for this.

At the end of the 3 days, rinse the rolls in fresh water, quickly. Place them in a tight-fitting pot and add the whole allspice, bay leaves, yellow onion, and carrots. Barely cover with water and simmer, covered, for 2 hours.

Remove the rolls from the pot, and while still hot, place the rolls on a plate. Cover them with another plate. Place a weight on top plate then put the whole works in the refrigerator. Chill for 2 days.

This should be sliced very thinly for a classic Norwegian buffet. Serve with bread and butter . . . and enjoy.

SYLTE

Serves 8–10 as a first course

This is another dish my Grandma Brun used to prepare when I was a child. The mixture of veal and pork is wonderful and the spices perfect. No, I did not get this recipe from her. I was too young and too dumb to ask. I had to figure this one out on my own. Please, don't you make the same mistake. Call your grandma and get those recipes!

10 whole allspice

15 black peppercorns

2 tablespoons salt

2 bay leaves

1 yellow onion, peeled and cut up

Pinch of saltpeter (page 45)

4 fresh pigs' feet, sawed in half

2 fresh pork hocks, sawed in half

1½ pounds meaty pork neck bones

2 pounds boneless veal shoulder, cut into 1-inch cubes

Place all but the veal in a very large pot and barely cover with water. Bring to a boil, skim the top, and turn the heat down to a simmer. Cover and simmer for 1½ hours, then add the veal to the pot. Cook an additional hour.

Remove the meat and bones from the pot, reserving the juices. Remove all bones and discard, being sure to get the meat off of the pork bones. Chop the meat up very coarsely and divide it between 2 loaf pans or pâté molds.

Strain the broth and discard the spices and onion. Remove the fat from the broth. Press the meat tightly into the molds and add enough broth just to cover. Cover the molds with plastic wrap and refrigerate for 24 hours.

Slice and serve as a first course.

POTATO LEFSE

Makes 24

So many of our immigrant ancestor groups have always enjoyed a pancake type of bread. The Mexican tortilla, the French crepe, the German pancake, the Ethiopian *injera,* the Indian *chapati,* the Middle Eastern pita bread, the Russian blini, the Armenian *lavosh,* and the Welsh *ffrois* all are now common in America. Add to these the gift from the Norwegians, this wonderful potato bread pancake that is eaten in the hills of the old country, and has been an American favorite for at least one hundred years.

There are two kinds of *lefse.* The first is thin and dry and must be moistened before eating. The second is made with potato and served fresh and moist. I love them both but the dry one is too much work for me. My mother is teaching Jason, my youngest son, to make it. I give you the easier, and I think, tastier, version. When Jason reads this he will accuse me of family heresy!

2½ **pounds russet potatoes,
peeled and cut in half**

2 **tablespoons butter (room
temperature)**

¼ **cup milk**

1 **teaspoon salt**

2 **cups all-purpose flour
plus additional flour for
rolling and dusting (See
Hint, page 423.)**

Boil the potatoes until tender. Drain them well, return them to the pot, and stir over low heat, a few minutes, to dry the potatoes, being careful not to brown them.

Mash the potatoes, using a potato ricer, in a heavy-duty electric mixer bowl. Add the remaining ingredients, except for the flour for rolling and dusting, and mix well. Blend together to form a nonsticky dough. Knead and form into a smooth log. Divide it in 24 pieces. When you are ready to prepare the *lefse,* roll each into an 8-inch to 10-inch circle. Turn the *lefse* as you roll it and keep it well coated with flour to prevent sticking. The dough is soft, but try to use as little flour as possible.

Preheat an electric griddle or frying pan to 375°, or use a griddle or frying pan over medium heat. Lightly grease it with oil.

Shake excess flour off each circle of *lefse* and place it in the pan. It will start to bubble; cook until the bubbles are lightly browned, about 1½ minutes. With a spatula, turn and cook the other side. Stack the *lefse* on a wire rack as they are cooked, or wrap them in foil and keep warm in a 200° oven.

They can be frozen and quickly reheated in the frying pan or on the griddle.

RICE PUDDING

Serves 4

My mother used to make rice pudding for me when I was a child. I always thought it to be a great treat, and now I realize that her love for this dish came from her own Norwegian upbringing. Like all good desserts, this takes some time to make but it can be made well ahead and chilled. I prefer it warm.

¾ cup long-grain rice

6 cups boiling water

1 quart milk

1 teaspoon salt

2 tablespoons butter, melted

2 tablespoons sugar

½ teaspoon almond extract

Freshly ground nutmeg to taste

½ cup coarsely ground blanched almonds

GARNISH

1 cup heavy cream, whipped

Place the rice in a strainer and pour the boiling water over the rice. Drain well. Place the rice, milk, and salt in a double boiler and cook, covered, for 1 to 1½ hours, or until all is thick and creamy. Stir in the butter, sugar, almond extract, nutmeg, and almonds.

Serve warm or chilled, with whipped cream.

ROMMEGROT

Serves 8–10

When I was very young Grandma Brun would make this pudding for us on Christmas Eve. The flavor of this is so associated with that winter holiday that when I make *rommegrot* in July I begin singing Christmas carols. I am sure you understand.

Grandma Brun used to drink straight Scotch as she cooked this dish and by the time she was finished she would be crying great tears into the pot. As a child I thought this to be a bit odd, but now I cannot get *rommegrot* that tastes as good as hers. It finally dawned on me that this dish needs a grandma's tears.

2 pints sour cream, the richest (with the highest butterfat) you can find

11–12 tablespoons all-purpose flour to thicken

2–3 cups hot milk

½ teaspoon salt, or to taste

1 teaspoon sugar, or to taste

GARNISHES

Melted butter

Sugar

Ground cinnamon

Place the sour cream in a heavy-bottomed saucepan and bring to a simmer over medium heat, stirring constantly. Turn down the heat and allow to barely simmer for 1 hour, uncovered, to reduce slightly. It must not boil. Use a heat diffuser (page 24) for this process.

Using a flour sifter or strainer, slowly add enough flour to thicken the cream. I use about 11 or 12 tablespoons for a very thick pudding. Using a wire whisk, whip in the flour 1 tablespoon at a time. The cream will thicken and begin to pull away from the sides of the pan. If the sour cream is very rich, butter will now begin to form and rise to the top. Remove this with a spoon and set aside. Stir in enough hot milk to obtain a porridgelike consistency. Add sugar and salt to taste.

Serve in bowls with melted butter, sugar, and cinnamon on top.

THE PERSIAN
IMMIGRANTS

PERSIA

T he land that we used to call Persia is now called Iran. You knew that. But I have chosen to use the old name of Persia since the contemporary Middle Eastern situation is so tense and confusing that I feel that Iranian-American immigrants will not be understood fairly if we use the more recent name. So, Persian immigrants it is. This is also the name that they seem to prefer.

Now, after explaining all this I must go back to the name of the nation. Originally it was called "Aryana," land of the Aryans. The Aryans were the first people to invade the region that we now know as Iran. They entered during the first millennium B.C. These people, and later the Medes and the Persians, were among the first in the world to move to lower land, to form villages, to cultivate crops, and to domesticate animals. I think only the Chinese predate this profound change in human habitat, so we are talking about a very old culture.

The land of the Aryans came to be called Persia. In the sixth century B.C. the Persian Empire brought together all of the old cultures and lands, from the valleys of Egypt and Mesopotamia to the coasts of Palestine and Asia Minor to the mounts of Elam and the Iranian plateau.

Cyrus the Great established the Persian Empire. He was the first ruler in the ancient world to introduce mercy into warfare, a change in human behavior that needs to be respected, even though warfare continues to be barbaric under any conditions. In any case Cyrus was busy conquering and he captured Babylon. In a famous act of clemency he freed the captive Jews who had been carried off to Babylonia as slaves by Nebuchadnezzar in 586 B.C. Cyrus decreed that they be allowed to return to Jerusalem. You don't have to believe me when I tell this story. You can read about it in the Bible. The book of Isaiah.

The Islamic conquest of Persia occurred in the seventh century A.D. and most of the inhabitants converted to the Muslim faith. In the thirteenth century, when Genghis Khan invaded, many of his troops converted to Islam. This really began the golden age in terms of Persian arts. Poetry flourished and the art of illuminating texts was perfected. Wonderful buildings arose, as we can see from the Taj Mahal; though in India, it was designed by Persian architects. The sixteenth and seventeenth centuries saw the creation of the most famous Persian carpets and the art of painting miniatures.

Following 1935 Persia was called Iran. The wealth of its oil resources caused the Western nations to begin jostling for influence there and in 1953 Shah Muhammad Riza Pahlavi was seated on the throne. This was done with the full approval, indeed the help, of the United States. Under the Shah's direction oil revenues were used to develop Iran, but the rapid spending resulted in high inflation and by the mid-1970s ownership of a house or a car was well beyond the means of a middle-class family. During this period the Shah created a rigid atmosphere of repression and a secret police force developed, some four thousand strong, to root out those who opposed the Shah. The Shiite Muslims were among this group.

Now the plot thickens. The Shiite religious leaders opposed the Shah's leadership and began to organize protests. Previously the Shah had exiled the Shiite leader, the Ayatollah Khomeini, and the protests from the people became too great for the Shah to handle. In January 1979 he fled the country and on February 1, 1979, the Ayatollah Ruhollah Khomeini returned after fifteen years in exile. His revolutionary government took over and began a rule no more patient nor more democratic then that of the Shah. It is very easy to understand why so many Iranians, no, let us call them Persians, came to this country seeking political asylum and an opportunity to raise a family without the intervention of either the Shah's spies or the revolutionary tactics of the Ayatollah.

Most of the Persian American immigrants whom you meet now came during the reign of the Shah. Most are well educated and many had come here as students in the first place. Following the events of 1979 they realized that they could not return home. This posed a serious brain drain for Iran, especially with respect to doctors.

The cuisine that the Persians have brought us is unusually beautiful, and they are most gracious about sharing these delights. Their method of cooking rice brings the grain to a state of glory, and then it is served with wonderful ground sumac. The Kebabs drip with clarified butter and the baked omelettes, called Kuku, are more flavorful than anything you have tasted in either France or Spain. When you come to my favorite dish, Persian Lamb Tongues, think of me. No, better yet, call me and we'll find a time to share this terribly sophisticated food.

KUKU SABZI

Serves 4–6

The Persians are fond of broiled omelets called "Kuku." This one is very tasty and since it contains no meat it is inexpensive to prepare. This would be a normal portion of a fine Persian dinner.

- 2 cups washed and finely chopped fresh spinach
- 1½ cups finely chopped scallions, including green tops
- ½ cup finely chopped parsley
- ½ cup finely chopped fresh coriander (page 49)
- 1 tablespoon chopped dill
- 2 tablespoons chopped garlic chives (page 40) or regular chives

- 1 tablespoon all-purpose flour
- 1½ teaspoons salt
- ½ teaspoon ground fenugreek (page 50)
- 1 teaspoon freshly ground black pepper
- Ground cumin to taste
- 8 eggs
- 1 tablespoon *ghee* (page 356) or butter

In a bowl, combine the spinach with the scallions and green herbs. In another bowl, mix the flour with the salt, fenugreek, pepper, and cumin to taste. Toss well and sprinkle over the greens.

Beat the eggs until frothy and pour over the greens. Mix well.

Heat the *ghee* or butter in a 10-inch SilverStone-lined frying pan and swirl to coat the sides. Pour in the egg mixture, and cook over medium-low heat for about 5 minutes. Then place it under a hot broiler. Cook until the center sets up, about 5 minutes, and is lightly browned. Tilt and slide onto a serving platter.

Serve hot, cut in wedges, with yogurt and flat bread. Also good served cold.

NOTE: Vegetables and herbs must be well washed and dried before chopping and measuring. Chopping can be done very speedily and efficiently in food processor. Accurate measuring of the greens is not essential to success of the dish.

KUKU EGGPLANT

Serves 4

The eggplant has a wonderful history all over the Middle East. Why we have not given it its due in this country is beyond me. The Persian love for the Kuku, or broiled omelet, is plain in this one made with the eggplant. It is excellent.

2 large eggplants, about 2 pounds

1½ tablespoons salt

½ cup olive oil

2 medium yellow onions, peeled and thinly sliced

2 cloves garlic, peeled and crushed

5 tablespoons *ghee* (page 356)

6 eggs

Juice of 1 lemon

1 teaspoon salt, or more to taste

¼ teaspoon freshly ground black pepper

¼ teaspoon saffron threads (page 52), crushed and dissolved in 1 tablespoon hot water (1 teaspoon if lower grade of saffron is used)

Peel the eggplants and slice in ⅛-inch slices lengthwise. Place them in a colander, sprinkle with the salt, and allow to drain for 20 minutes. Rinse and pat dry.

In a skillet, brown the eggplant slices in 4 batches, using a portion of the oil each time. Remove from the skillet, cool, and mash with a fork.

In the same skillet, brown the onion and garlic in 4 tablespoons of the *ghee*.

Break the eggs into a bowl. Add the lemon juice, salt and pepper, and saffron. Beat thoroughly with a fork.

Add the mashed eggplant, onion, and garlic to the beaten egg mixture. Taste and adjust seasoning.

Follow the instructions in Kuku Sabzi (page 350) to cook the omelet, using the 1 tablespoon of *ghee* for the pan.

Serve with yogurt, bread, and a dish of raw vegetables and fresh herbs.

VARIATION

Zucchini may be substituted for eggplant.

CHELO

(Persian Rice)

Serves 6

The Persians take their rice very seriously, and they cook it very carefully. Only basmati rice is used . . . that wonderful rice that comes from India and tastes of nuts.

This recipe looks like a bit much but rice is basic to the meal, absolutely basic. Always has been.

2 cups basmati rice (page 37)	2 teaspoons salt
8¼ cups water	¼ cup *ghee* (page 356) or butter

Pick over the rice and remove discolored grains and stones. Place it in a sieve and wash well under running water until water is clear. Drain.

Bring 8 cups water to the boil in a covered heavy 4-quart stove-top casserole. Add the salt and rice, and stir until the water returns to the boil.

Boil the rice for 5 minutes. Pour immediately into a large sieve or colander and drain.

In a small pan heat the *ghee* or butter with ¼ cup water until bubbling. Pour half of this into the pan in which the rice was cooked and swirl to coat the bottom and sides.

Spread half of the partly cooked rice in the bottom of the pan, and even it out with the back of a spoon. Spoon the remainder of the rice on top in a mound. Make a hole in the center with the end of a wooden spoon and pour the remaining *ghee* mixture on top.

Cover the rim of the pan with a cloth towel and place the lid on firmly. Place an upside-down coffee cup on the towel and pan handle to weigh the towel in place.

Using a heat diffuser (page 24), cook the rice over medium-low heat for 10 minutes, reduce the heat to very low, and cook for a further 35 minutes. The cloth absorbs the steam and makes the rice fluffy and light. During cooking a lightly browned crust will have formed on the bottom of the pan. Stir the rice gently with a fork to distribute the *ghee* evenly.

Serve this with kebabs and stews, with its bottom crust.

STEAMED PLAIN RICE

(Persian)

Serves 6

This is a bit less complex than the previous recipe but the results are just about the same.

2 cups basmati rice (page 37)	**4 quarts water**
2 teaspoons salt	**3 tablespoons butter**

Place 4 quarts of water in a heavy 6-quart stove-top covered casserole and bring to a boil. Add the rice and salt and boil hard, uncovered, for 10 minutes. Drain the rice in a colander and rinse well with cold water. Drain.

In the same pan, melt the butter over medium heat. Return the rice to the pan. Place a dish towel over the inside of the lid, bring the overlapping edges up over the top of the lid, and place a coffee cup over the towel and handle to keep in place. (The towel will absorb any moisture from dripping back onto the rice.)

Steam over medium-low heat for 30 to 35 minutes. The rice will be ready when a cloud of steam emerges from the pan when the lid is lifted.

The heat can then be turned very low, and the rice kept warm until ready to serve.

Always dish out the rice with a slotted spoon, fluffing it as you place it in a serving dish. A crust of tah-dig (literally, bottom-of-the-pan) will have formed on the bottom of the pan. To serve this in one unbroken piece, immerse the exterior of the pan in cold water for a few minutes, then pry the tah-dig loose with a spatula.

KATEH RICE CAKE

Serves 6

Now, this is serious stuff. You must watch this pan very carefully as it cooks as you want a light brown crust to form on the bottom of the pan. It can burn, so be careful. This is served as a very special treat.

2 cups basmati rice   2 teaspoons salt
  (page 37)   ¼ cup *ghee* (page 356)
3½ cups water

Pick over the rice, wash it very well, and drain. Place it in a 10-inch SilverStone-lined frying pan and add the water and salt.

Bring to the boil over medium heat, stirring occasionally. Cover, reduce heat a little, and cook for 15 minutes until all the water is absorbed.

Add the *ghee* and stir with a wooden spoon. Even out the top of rice, pressing lightly.

Cover the pan and return it to medium-low heat for 30 minutes. Move the pan over the burner from time to time so that bottom of the rice becomes evenly browned.

Remove from the heat and place the bottom of the pan in cold water for 10 seconds. Dry the bottom of the pan off with a towel. Run a spatula around the sides to loosen the rice, then place a plate on top of the pan. Holding the plate and pan firmly, turn them upside down so that rice cake comes out cleanly.

Serve this cut in wedges with kebabs or stews. This is often served cold in summer.

CHELO KEBAB

Serves 6–8

The chef at Reza's Persian Restaurant in Chicago, a charming fellow named Joseph Toulabi, makes a wonderful kebab and serves it in a traditional style over heaps of Chelo rice. This is as close as I can come to the superb dishes that he makes. You must stop by the place.

Craig, my assistant, and I were surprised by the flavor the sumac imparted to the rice. This is a popular seasoning in the Middle East but I had never tried it simply sprinkled on hot rice. It was so good, now we are sprinkling the stuff all over everything!

THE KEBAB

1 3-pound boneless leg of lamb

THE MARINADE

1 cup yellow onion, peeled and chopped

½ teaspoon crushed saffron threads (page 52)

¾ cup lemon juice

Freshly ground black pepper to taste

TO COOK

½ cup *ghee* (page 356) or butter, melted

Salt to taste

THE DINNER PLATE

6 to 8 tomatoes

Chelo rice (page 352)

GARNISHES

6 to 8 egg yolks in half shells

Butter pats

Sumac (page 53)

Salt and freshly ground pepper to taste

Homemade Yogurt (page 428) or yogurt from the market

Trim off all the fat and fine sinew from the lamb. Slice it with the grain into ⅜-inch thick slices. Cut the slices into pieces about 8 inches long and 3 inches wide. Lightly hammer them with a metal meat pounder to tenderize and flatted them out a bit. Place the lamb in a stainless-steel or porcelain bowl and set aside.

Prepare the marinade by blending the onion, saffron, lemon juice, and pepper in a food blender. Add the marinade to the bowl of lamb and toss to coat it evenly. Cover and refrigerate 12 hours. Turn the meat occasionally.

Pass a flat, swordlike skewer through the length of each strip of lamb. Brush the lamb lightly with melted *ghee* or butter and cook over a glowing charcoal fire for about 5 minutes, turning frequently, until the lamb is lightly browned and just cooked through. (The meat will flop somewhat at the beginning of cooking. As it cooks it flattens out—a good indication that it is ready. Add salt to taste as you go.)

Cut a cross on the rounded end of each tomato, place the tomatoes on a skewer, and brush them with *ghee*. Cook on the fire until their skins blister, about 4 minutes.

Slide the lamb off the skewers and serve on hot Chelo (page 352) on individual plates, with a tomato as garnish for each serving.

Each diner places an egg yolk in center of the hot Chelo and stirs it in. Butter, sumac, and salt and pepper are then stirred into the rice. Yogurt can be added if desired.

Speed is the essence of a good Chelo Kebab meal, as it is most enjoyable when very hot.

GHEE

Makes 1 pound

Ghee is butter that is cooked to separate the clear butter fat from the milk solids and moisture, an ingenious method that allows butter to keep for long periods . . . and it also gives the butter a marvelous nutty flavor. This is a basic necessity in Persian, Indian, and Moroccan kitchens.

1 pound unsalted butter

Bring the butter to a simmer and cook, partly covered, 10 to 15 minutes until most of the froth has subsided and the milk solids on the bottom of the pan are brown but not burned. Turn it off and allow it to cool a bit and separate. Strain it through several layers of cheesecloth. Seal it in plastic containers. It will keep for several weeks in your refrigerator.

This recipe can be doubled or tripled.

EGGPLANT SALAD

Serves 6–8

This is a lovely and flavorful eggplant salad . . . with walnuts yet. So very Persian.

2 large oval eggplants, each about ¾ pound

Salt for the eggplant

½ cup olive oil

2 cups Homemade Yogurt (page 428) or yogurt from the market, drained in cheesecloth in a colander for 4 hours

2 cloves garlic, peeled and crushed

Salt to taste

Freshly ground black pepper to taste

GARNISH

1 cup chopped walnuts

Cut the eggplants in half lengthwise, then slice lengthwise ¼ inch thick. Sprinkle the slices liberally with salt (stack them if necessary) and leave for 30 minutes. Rinse and dry with paper towels.

Heat half the oil in a large frying pan and fry the eggplant in 4 batches until golden brown on each side. Drain on paper towels. Add more oil to pan as required.

Blend the yogurt with the garlic and salt to taste.

Place a layer of cooled eggplant in a serving dish, overlapping the slices a little. Season with pepper and spread with some of the yogurt. Finish all the layers ending with yogurt. Cover and chill.

When serving, garnish with chopped walnuts.

PERSIAN LAMB TONGUES

Serves 4

This dish is so rich and so very beautiful . . . and I hate to think that you might not try it thinking that you dislike lamb tongues. You are missing out on one of the most glorious dishes of Persian cuisine. Read through the recipe, catching the ingredients in the *advieh* spice mix, and then give me a chance.

You may have to call about to find lamb tongues. They will probably be frozen, but that is just fine.

- 2 pounds lamb tongue, cooked and peeled (Just barely cover with water, simmer, covered, for 2 hours, cool in broth, peel. Reserve the broth.)
- 2 tablespoons olive oil
- 3 cloves garlic, peeled and crushed
- 1 medium yellow onion, peeled and finely chopped

Tongue broth
- 2 tablespoons lemon juice
- 1 cup Homemade Yogurt (page 428) or yogurt from the market
- 2 teaspoons turmeric
- 2 tablespoons Advieh (page 359)

Salt and freshly ground black pepper to taste

Trim any cartilage and fat from the base of the tongues. Cut into 1-inch cubes.

Heat a frying pan, add the oil, garlic, and onion, and sauté until clear. Add 1 cup of the reserved cooking broth and the lemon juice, and simmer 1 minute. Add the yogurt, turmeric, and *advieh,* and simmer to make a smooth sauce. Salt and pepper to taste. Add the tongue cubes and simmer all a couple minutes.

This is great with Persian rice (page 352).

ADVIEH

Makes ⅔ cup

Just read through the list of ingredients and you will understand why I think this is the most romantic cooking imaginable. Its fragrance is reminiscent of Persian nights, temples, and flying carpets. I found this recipe in an excellent Persian cookbook called *Food for Life*.

- 2 tablespoons ground dried rose petals (Available in spice shops. Be sure they are edible!)
- 2 tablespoons ground cinnamon
- ½ teaspoon cardamom seeds (page 49)
- ½ teaspoon black peppercorns
- ¼ teaspoon turmeric
- 1 teaspoon freshly grated nutmeg
- 1 teaspoon cumin seeds
- ½ teaspoon coriander seeds (page 49)

Grind all the spices and mix together in a blender. Store in an airtight container to preserve freshness.

SPINACH BORANI

Serves 4–6 as an appetizer or side dish

This is a popular dish at Reza's Persian Restaurant in Chicago. Joseph, the chef, does not put any garlic or sesame tahini in his *borani* but I enjoy a bit of both. See what you think of this scrumptious appetizer or side dish.

2 cups Homemade Yogurt (page 428) or yogurt from the market (See Hint.)

2 tablespoons olive oil

1 clove garlic, peeled and crushed

1 medium yellow onion, peeled and thinly sliced

1½ pounds fresh spinach, stemmed, washed, drained well, and coarsely chopped

1 tablespoon tahini (sesame paste) (page 47)

2 teaspoons lemon juice

Salt and freshly ground black pepper to taste

Place the yogurt in cheesecloth in a colander and allow it to drain for 3 hours. Set aside.

Heat a large frying pan and add the oil, garlic, and onion. Sauté until the onion is clear. Add the spinach and sauté over medium heat until the spinach cooks down, about 10 to 15 minutes. Remove the pan from the heat and stir in the yogurt and the remaining ingredients. Mix well and serve warm.

HINT: TO IMPROVE FLAVOR OF MARKET YOGURT simply leave it out on the counter overnight; refrigerate it the next day. This results in a richer, tangier flavor in the yogurt. Use in any recipe.

PERSIAN LENTIL AND RICE SOUP

Serves 10

I have taken some liberties with this dish, but I was so inspired by what Joseph, the chef at Reza's Persian Restaurant in Chicago, serves for the house soup that I had to begin experimenting. Is that not what the immigrant experience is all about? And I am not even Persian!

This is a great soup. Craig, my assistant, and I worked hard on it. Just great stuff, if I say so myself.

2 tablespoons olive oil

1 medium yellow onion, peeled and thinly sliced

3 tablespoons chopped parsley

4 cups chopped ripe tomatoes

10 cups Chicken Stock (page 74) or use canned

2 tablespoons chopped fresh mint leaves or 1 teaspoon crushed dried mint

1 cup lentils

Juice of 1½ lemons

¼ cup basmati rice (page 37), broken up very coarsely in a blender

½ cup bulgur wheat (page 38), medium grind

2 tablespoons tomato paste

½ teaspoon of sugar

2 teaspoons sumac (page 53)

2 teaspoons Advieh (page 359)

Salt and freshly ground black pepper to taste

Heat a six-quart stove-top covered casserole and add the oil, onion, and parsley. Sauté until the onion is tender and then add the tomatoes. Sauté a few minutes and add the Chicken Stock, mint, lentils, and lemon juice. Bring to a boil, cover, reduce the heat, and simmer for 30 minutes.

Add the broken rice and bulgur wheat, and simmer, covered, for an additional 1 hour and 15 minutes.

Add the remaining ingredients, taste for salt and pepper, bring to a simmer for a few minutes, and serve hot.

PERSIAN SALAD

This one I am just going to describe. Joseph Toulabi, the chef at Reza's Persian Restaurant in Chicago, claims this is legit. However, I think it is the clever invention of fine Persian immigrant chefs who know how much Americans love salad. Note that he uses no garlic in his dressing. Can you imagine? The result is delicious, I must admit, even without my beloved garlic.

Cucumbers, tomatoes, onions, and parsley are chopped. The dressing consists of olive oil, fresh lime juice, and salt and freshly ground black pepper to taste. That's it!

THE POLISH
IMMIGRANTS

POLAND

The Poles make up one of our largest immigrant groups, and their fellow Americans were made especially aware of their presence when John Paul II was elected to the throne of Saint Peter. He was the first non-Italian to be elected to the papacy during the last 450 years. And he was Polish! Then America began to hear about the Poles. It was recognition that was a long time in coming.

Poland has always had to struggle to maintain its existence. But even a long history of domination by neighboring nations has not succeeded in erasing Polish pride. The nation itself may have disappeared from the map of Europe at different times, but the Polish people have held tenaciously to their culture and ethnic identity no matter who has controlled them. As of the writing of this article, Poland is finally becoming that independent nation that so many have waited for so long.

Approximately six million Americans are of Polish heritage, descendants for the most part of the many thousands who came here as part of the immense wave of immigration from southern and eastern Europe at the turn of the century. They formed the third largest immigration group at the time, after the Italians and the Jews.

The people we now call Poles are members of that large Slavic group that has been in Europe since the sixth century. The term "Slav" refers to a group of people using related languages. The Polish-speaking Roman Catholic majority in the nation now known as Poland originated with a tribe of western Slavs whose king converted to Christianity in 966.

The sixteenth century is generally regarded as the golden age in Poland. The Polish empire stretched from the Baltic Sea to the Black Sea, and arts and sciences flourished. This was a time of political union with Lithuania, a union that was to have great impact on Lithuanian culture for many years.

During the seventeenth through the nineteenth centuries Poland's influence gradually declined. This was true in large part to the geography of Poland. The word *Pole* derives from a local word for "field." Much of the country lies on the great plain of northern Europe and there are no major natural barriers to the east and west of Poland. Unfortunately for Poland, powerful nations lay in both directions. To the west was Prussia, to the east Russia. In addition, Austria lay to the south. All of these nations took a share of Poland. By the end of the eighteenth century Poland as a political entity had almost disappeared from the map.

At the end of World War I a reconstituted Polish nation arose. It lasted only twenty years. Hitler invaded Poland in September 1939; it was one of the early victims of the Nazis. The Allies did not come to Poland's rescue and Nazi tanks mowed down the famous Polish cavalry. The Nazis simply ran over them! Hitler's troops retreated in 1945 and Poland fell under Soviet control. As the Nazi troops left, Hitler gave orders to destroy Warsaw; 90 percent of the city was left in ruins; only Hiroshima suffered more than Warsaw in World War II. Eight hundred thousand Poles died there, 200,000 of them during a nine-week uprising against occupying Nazi troops in 1945.

Poles have been coming to America for a long time. If legend is to be believed, they actually came to North America before most other immigrants. The Poles claim that a Polish sailor, Jan Kolmar, acting as the captain of a Danish ship, reached Canada sixteen years before Columbus arrived in the New World. We do know for sure that there were Poles at Jamestown, founded in 1608. They were artisans in the community and they staged the first labor strike in America when the English would not let them vote on Jamestown's laws. Leave it to the Polish!

More Poles came here during the American Revolution, as many wished to obtain the same rights for the Polish people that the Americans were seeking in the war for independence from England. Ben Franklin recruited several Poles during these efforts, the most famous being Count Casimir Pulaski, who had been ordered to leave Poland because of his opposition to the Polish king. He is credited with establishing the United States Cavlary. The Poles have always been great horsemen.

It is hard to say enough about the Poles as "Freedom Fighters," considering what has gone on in the past decade. When in 1978 John

Paul II was elected Pope, the Poles gained a new pride in themselves. Then, in 1981, Lech Walesa stood against the Communist party in Poland through a strike at the Gdansk shipyards, a strike that grew into a national movement called Solidarity. He was given the Nobel Peace Prize in 1983. In 1989 the Chinese students in Tianamen Square stood against the Chinese Communist party, and in 1990 all of Eastern Europe was demanding freedom from the Communist regimes that ruled them. We must credit the Hungarians and the Poles with giving birth to this whole movement.

The list of Poles who have added so much to our lives is long. Copernicus, the seventeenth-century astronomer, was Polish. Marie Curie was Polish. Frédéric Chopin was Polish. Among Polish American immigrants we find Ernestine Potowski-Rose who persuaded the New York State legislature to pass a law that gave married women the right to own land without their husbands' permission. Elizbieta Zakrzewska, one of the first women doctors in America, founded two hospitals where female doctors could learn and work. These two women did this long before the Women's Liberation movement in this country. And we must thank the Polish American composers, Leopold Stokowski, Artur Rodzinski, and Stanislaw Skrowaczewski. And keyboard artists, pianists Paderewski and Arthur Rubenstein, along with harpsichordist Wanda Landowska. In television we must point to Loretta Swit, "Hotlips" on M*A*S*H, and Ted Knight, who played Ted Baxter on The Mary Tyler Moore Show. Even the Warner Brothers were Polish Americans, as are Edmund Muskie, former governor of Maine, and Zbigniew Brzezinski, political adviser to both President Johnson and President Carter.

All of the above share a common heritage and the land from which their ancestors came has a rich food tradition. That tradition came with the grandmas and grandpas, a tradition that was dictated by what could be grown in a climate that was often cold and damp. Potatoes, beans, cabbage, beets, eggs, dairy products, pork, beef, apples, rye, wheat, and barley are all typical Polish foods.

The following recipes are typical and not complex in preparation. The Pierogi are wonderful and the Tripe Soup is just one of my favorite soups in the world. Some of the basic dishes—or we can call them peasant dishes—such as the Noodles and Cabbage will surprise you with their flavor. So I don't want to hear any more of your stupid Polish jokes. These people are heroic, ingenious, and FRUGAL!

POLISH SAUSAGE

(Kielbasa)

It is hard to think of a Polish meal without wonderful sausage. And, please remember that there are many types of sausage popular in Poland. That which we call *kielbasa,* the simple Polish word for sausage, is actually closer to the kind of sausage that is popular in Kraków, the home of Pope John Paul II.

There is no point in writing out two recipes when only one is needed. For a sausage that is very close to that of Kraków, see Lithuanian Smoked Sausage (page 305).

Serve with the following Sauerkraut recipe.

POLISH SAUERKRAUT

(Kapusta)

Serves 4–6

This dish is so rich and wonderful that it will convert anyone who has ever said, "I hate the smell of sauerkraut cooking!" If you just open a can and heat it then I am with you. The Poles would never do such a thing. Buy fresh sauerkraut if you can get it, or at least buy it in plastic bags or bottled. Then this dish will become a family favorite.

1 ounce dried mushrooms (page 42), soaked for ½ hour in ½ cup warm water (Reserve the water.)

3 tablespoons butter

1 large yellow onion, peeled and diced

1 medium tomato, chopped

2 pounds fresh sauerkraut, in plastic, or bottled, rinsed and drained well

1 cup dry white wine

½ cup Beef Stock (page 78) or use canned

⅛ teaspoon freshly ground black pepper

2 tablespoons all-purpose flour

Pinch of sugar (optional)

Drain the mushrooms, reserving the soaking water. Pour water through a fine strainer and set aside. Coarsely chop the mushrooms and sauté them in the butter. Add the onion and tomato and sauté until the onion is clear. Add the sauerkraut, wine, Beef Stock, reserved mushroom water, and pepper, and bring to a simmer. Sprinkle the flour over the top of the sauerkraut and then stir in well. Simmer, covered, stirring occasionally, for 30 minutes.

You may need to add a pinch of sugar.

POLISH LAZY DUMPLINGS

(Pierogi Leniwe)

Makes about 40 dumplings

The name for this thick and delicious noodle stems from the fact that you mix the filling right into the dough. You don't even stuff the dumplings! It is an easy dish and very tasty.

2 pounds dry-curd cottage
   cheese or farmer cheese
   (page 39)

4 large eggs, beaten

1½ teaspoons salt

2 cups all-purpose flour
   plus more for rolling
   (See Hint, page 423.)

10 quarts water

GARNISH

1 cup bread crumbs, lightly
   toasted in 3 tablespoons
   butter in a frying pan

In a medium bowl mash the cheese with a fork. Stir in the eggs, ½ teaspoon of the salt, and the flour, all at once.

Turn the dough out onto a floured board and divide it into 4 pieces. Roll each piece out into a rectangle 12 inches long and 2 inches wide. Cut each piece on the diagonal into about 10 pieces.

Bring 10 quarts of water to a boil and add 1 teaspoon salt. Reduce the water to a lightly rolling simmer and add ⅓ of the dumplings to the pot. Simmer, uncovered, until they float to the top. Remove them with a slotted spoon and drain. Continue until all dumplings are cooked.

Serve with a garnish of toasted bread crumbs.

POLISH NOODLES AND CABBAGE

(Kluski z Kapusta po Polski)

Serves 4–6

This sort of dish is prevalent in most of the splendid cuisines of Eastern Europe. It looks like peasant food, and it is, but it is delicious and warming food, food that comforts you when you remember your childhood.

¼ cup butter

½ cup peeled and chopped
  yellow onion

4 cups chopped or thinly
  sliced cabbage

1 teaspoon caraway seeds

½ teaspoon salt

⅛ teaspoon freshly ground
  black pepper

1 8-ounce package egg
  noodles

½ cup sour cream
  (optional)

Melt the butter in a large skillet. Add the onion and sauté until transparent. Add the cabbage and sauté 5 minutes, or until tender but still crisp. Stir in the caraway seeds, salt, and pepper.

Meanwhile, cook the noodles in salted water as directed on package. Do not overcook. Drain well.

Stir the noodles into the cabbage and add the sour cream. Cook 5 minutes longer, stirring frequently.

POLISH MUSHROOM AND BARLEY SOUP

(Krupnik Polski)

Serves 8–10 as a soup course

The Poles love to use mushrooms in all sorts of dishes. The following soup is thick and rich with the flavor of this forest delicacy . . . and the dried mushrooms are a lot less expensive if you buy them in bulk in an Italian or Polish shop.

1 ounce dried mushrooms (page 42), soaked for ½ hour in 1 cup of warm water (Reserve the water.)

10 cups Beef Stock (page 78) or use canned

2 cups water

1 cup pearl barley

¼ cup butter

2 carrots, diced

2 potatoes, peeled and diced, about 1 pound

1 stalk celery, chopped

½ cup green beans, fresh or frozen, cut in ½-inch pieces

1 tablespoon chopped parsley

Salt and freshly ground black pepper to taste

GARNISH

½ cup sour cream

Soak the mushrooms and drain them, reserving the soaking water. Chop the mushrooms into ½-inch dice. Pour the mushroom water through a fine strainer into the Beef Stock, avoiding any sand or grit that may be in the bottom of the bowl.

Bring the 2 cups of water to a boil in a medium saucepan. Add the barley and simmer, covered, until all the moisture is absorbed, about 15 minutes. Stir the butter into the barley. Set aside.

Heat the Beef Stock in a large pot and add all the remaining ingredients, except the garnish. Bring to a simmer and add the barley/butter mixture, stirring well to separate the grains. Cook, covered, until the barley is tender, about 1 hour. Add salt and pepper to taste.

Garnish with a dollop of sour cream as a garnish.

POLISH CHICKEN WITH MUSHROOMS

(Potrawka z Kurczaka Polska)

Serves 4

When I first tried this dish the kitchen was filled with a marvelous smell. It made me think of my Polish grandmother . . . and then I remembered that I didn't have a Polish grandmother. This chicken will make you wish you did have such a lady in your background.

1 fryer chicken, about 3½ pounds, quartered

2 cups water

1 stalk celery, chopped

1 carrot, chopped

1 tablespoon chopped parsley

1 ounce dried mushrooms (page 42), soaked for ½ hour in 1 cup warm water (Reserve the water.)

Salt and freshly ground black pepper to taste

2 tablespoons *each* butter and flour cooked together to form a *roux* (page 34)

½ cup dry white wine

2 egg yolks

Place the chicken pieces in a stove-top covered casserole and add the 2 cups of water. Bring to a boil. Soak the mushrooms and drain them through a fine strainer, reserving the soaking water. Chop the mushrooms. Add the celery, carrot, parsley, mushrooms, along with the strained soaking water. Add a bit of salt and pepper to taste and simmer the whole, covered, for about 1 hour.

Remove the chicken to a heated platter and thicken the pan liquid with the *roux*. Add the wine and bring the sauce to a simmer. Remove the pan from the heat. Place the egg yolks in a 2-cup glass measuring cup and add about ½ cup of the sauce, stirring all the time. Blend this mixture into the sauce in the pot, then return the chicken to the pot. Test for salt and pepper. Heat the dish to serving temperature but not to a simmer or the eggs will curdle.

POLISH FIRST COURSES

(Zakaski)

The Poles love a first-course table of snacks that provide a bit of time to nibble and talk with other guests before being seated at the table. Set up a snack buffet using any or all of the following items. I prefer dry sherry at such a function.

Pickled mushrooms	Cold smoked whitefish
Sardines	Olives
Pickled vegetable salad	Sliced cold tongue or chicken
Smoked oysters, clams, or mussels	
Assorted sliced cheese	Sliced pumpernickel or rye bread
	Small Polish sausages

You can make it much more elaborate, of course, but the above should be enough before a dinner party.

POLISH DUMPLINGS

(Pierogi)

Serves 10–12

While filled dumplings are popular all over Eastern Europe it seems to me that the Poles have got them down to a science . . . no, a life-form. When I did my first cookbook and show on Polish cooking I received letters containing hundreds of varieties of this wonderful culinary invention. This is a new recipe, and much better than my old one.

2 cups (1 pint) sour cream	2 eggs plus 1 egg yolk
4½ cups all-purpose flour (See Hint, page 423.)	2 teaspoons salt
2 tablespoons melted butter	2 tablespoons vegetable oil

In a large bowl, mix all the ingredients and knead into a soft, pliable dough. Cut in half and let rest, covered, for 10 minutes. Roll out each half into a thin circle. Using a drinking glass, cut the dough into round circles and fill them with desired filling (recipes follow). Place less than a tablespoon of filling in the center of each circle and fold over. Press and seal into a half moon. You may want to rub a bit of water on the edges in order to get a great seal. Cook for 10 minutes in boiling salted water.

Drain. They can be pan-fried in butter at this point, if you wish, for a really tasty finish.

CHEESE PIEROGI FILLING

1 cup dry-curd cottage cheese (page 39)	2 tablespoons sugar
1 teaspoon butter, melted	1 tablespoon fresh lemon juice
1 egg, beaten	

Run the cheese through a ricer, or a coarse sieve. Then mix well with everything else.

SAUERKRAUT AND MUSHROOM PIEROGI FILLING

1 small yellow onion, peeled and finely chopped	2 cups fresh sauerkraut, rinsed, drained, and finely chopped
1 ounce dried mushrooms (page 42), soaked for ½ hour in 1 cup of warm water	Salt and freshly ground black pepper to taste
2 tablespoons butter	

Soak the mushrooms and drain them through a fine sieve. Chop the mushrooms finely. Pan-fry the onion and mushrooms in the butter until the onion is clear. Add the sauerkraut and salt and pepper. Cook for about 15 minutes and cool.

CABBAGE AND MUSHROOM PIEROGI FILLING

The same as the filling above but use two cups finely shredded cabbage instead of sauerkraut.

POTATO AND CHEESE PIEROGI FILLING

See the Pegach Potato and Cheese Filling in the Russian section (page 424).

MEAT PIEROGI FILLINGS

Various cooked meats may be used such as turkey, beef, pork, etc. Simply grind the meat, add raw egg, salt and pepper, and any additional desired seasonings, such as dill, parsley, or chives.

HINT: FOR LOW-FAT PIEROGI DOUGH this recipe works great with yogurt instead of sour cream. Simply add ½ cup additional flour to the recipe along with the yogurt instead of the sour cream. Substitute vegetable oil for the butter.

POLISH STUFFED CABBAGE

(Galumkis)

Makes about 2 dozen

Every Polish immigrant grandmother who reads this recipe will probably turn to her grandson and say, "Well, it looks like a good recipe but it is not the way your great-grandmother made it!" That is the glory of ethnic cooking. A recipe can go back for generations and yet still help everyone remember.

Actually, this is a very good recipe for the Polish classic.

THE FILLING

1¼ cups Uncle Ben's Converted Rice	2 tablespoons chopped parsley
¾ cup olive oil	1¾ pounds lean ground beef
4 cloves garlic, peeled and crushed	¾ pound ground pork
1 large yellow onion, peeled and chopped small	Salt and freshly ground black pepper to taste (I like lots of pepper in this dish!)

THE CABBAGE LEAVES

3 medium heads winter cabbage	Salt

THE COOKING SAUCE

3 cups tomato sauce	¼ cup distilled white vinegar

Place the rice in a small pot and cover with 2 cups of water. Simmer, covered, for 10 minutes. Allow to cool and then drain the excess water.

Heat a frying pan and add the oil, garlic, and onion. Sauté until the onion is transparent. Stir in the parsley and allow the mixture to cool.

In a large bowl, combine the ground meat with the cooled rice and onion mixture. Add salt and pepper to taste.

Cut out the cores of the cabbages with a paring knife. Bring a large pot of water to boil and add a bit of salt. Add the cored cabbages, one head at a time, and blanch for 5 minutes. Place in a colander and carefully pull off 24 of the largest, best-looking leaves, 1 at a time. Rinse with cold water, just as soon as you pull each one from the head. Place

⅓ cup of filling in the center of each leaf and roll it up, folding in the ends so that you have a nice bundle. (See the illustration.)

Place the stuffed leaves in a 10- to 12-quart stove-top covered casserole. Be sure that they are packed rather tightly together. Place some of the leftover leaves on the top. Mix the tomato sauce and vinegar together and pour over the contents of the pot. Add boiling water to just barely cover the rolled leaves. Bring to a boil slowly over medium-low heat. Simmer, covered, for about 50 minutes, or until all is tender. Do not overcook.

NOTE: You may wish to remove the cooked rolls from the pot and thicken the juices with a *roux* (page 34).

POLISH POTATO PANCAKES

Use the recipe for Russian Potato Pancakes (page 418) but add a bit of grated onion.

POLISH TRIPE SOUP

(Flaki)

Serves 10 as a soup course

This dish causes many people to just tune out . . . before they even taste it! It is the best tripe soup recipe I know and it was given us by Sophie Madej of the Busy Bee Cafe in Chicago. She serves extraordinary Polish dishes, such as great potato pancakes, duck, lovely light pierogi, and this tripe soup. It is on the menu every day, and if I were not typing this recipe I would be in Chicago eating at her table.

You must try this. It is wonderful. Just remember to cook it for a long time so that all is very tender.

3½ pounds tripe

3 beef shanks, 1½ to 2 pounds

2 stalks celery, chopped small

2 cups chopped leeks (white parts only)

4 cloves garlic, peeled and chopped

2 bay leaves

½ teaspoon freshly ground black pepper

4 cups Beef Stock (page 78) or use canned

6 cups water

½ teaspoon dried marjoram or more to taste

½ teaspoon dried oregano or more to taste

2 tablespoons tomato paste

Salt to taste

Freshly ground black pepper to taste (I like lots!)

PAPRIKA ROUX

2 tablespoons butter

3 tablespoons all-purpose flour

1 teaspoon paprika

Blanch the tripe in several quarts of water. Boil it for about 5 minutes, then drain and cool. Cut into 1½-inch by ¼-inch pieces.

In a heavy 8- to 10-quart soup pot place the tripe, beef shanks, celery, leek, garlic, bay leaves, ½ teaspoon black pepper, Beef Stock, and water. Simmer for 2 hours and 45 minutes, the pot only partly covered for the first ½ hour. Cover completely for the remaining cooking time. Remove the beef shanks and chop the meat, discarding the bone. Return the meat to the simmering pot.

Add the marjoram, oregano, tomato paste, and salt to taste. Add additional pepper if you wish. I like lots! Simmer for an additional ½ hour, covered.

Prepare the *roux* by melting the butter in a small frying pan and stirring in the flour and paprika. Cook until it is a light brown. Whisk the *roux* into the pot, stirring carefully as it thickens.

NOTE: This soup is even better the second day.

DUCK WITH RED CABBAGE

(Kaczka Duszona z Czerwona Kapusta)

Serves 4

Polish people are very fond of duck. One of the old classic dishes is soup made with duck blood. Yes, I like it but I eat it rarely since it is so rich. The following recipe is very traditional, and it will increase your affection for duck, without the soup.

1 duck, about 5 pounds	½ pound salt pork, diced
1 medium head red cabbage, cored and coarsely shredded	½ cup dry red wine
	Juice of 1 lemon
1 yellow onion, peeled and chopped	1 teaspoon sugar
	1 teaspoon caraway seeds
2 teaspoons salt	

Place the duck in a roasting pan and roast at 425° for 30 minutes. Drain off the fat.

In the meantime, place the cabbage and onion in a bowl and sprinkle with about 2 teaspoons salt. Let stand for 10 minutes, rinse, and then squeeze out the moisture, discarding the salty liquid. In a frying pan, sauté the salt pork until just golden. Add the cabbage and onion to the pan along with the wine, lemon juice, sugar, and caraway seeds. Simmer, covered, for 20 minutes.

Spoon the cabbage mixture over the top of the duck and bake the duck a second time at 350° for about 1 hour and 15 minutes, or until tender. Baste several times during the roasting.

Serve the cabbage in a separate bowl alongside the duck.

THE PORTUGUESE
IMMIGRANTS

PORTUGAL

The Portuguese Americans are a complex ethnic group with a complex immigration history. For instance, the oldest Jewish congregation in the United States was founded by twenty-three Portuguese Jews who came to New Amsterdam (New York) from Brazil in September 1654. Congregation Shearith Israel held services in Portuguese until the mid-eighteenth century. The Portuguese have always been great sailors, so the above story may surprise some of us, but it would never surprise a person of Portuguese heritage.

The Portuguese may have been here even earlier than the New Amsterdam Congregation. Most Portuguese believe that a Portuguese explorer, Miguel Corte Real, and his crew lived among the Native Americans in the vicinity of Narragansett Bay a century before the English landed at Plymouth. Some scholars have interpreted markings on Dighton Rock, on the Taunton River, to be inscriptions made by Portuguese sailors in 1511.

Most of the early Portuguese settlers in America came to New England from the Azores, the islands in the Atlantic claimed by Portugal. These were men who signed up with Pacific-bound American whalers who landed in the Azores to build up their crews. The Azores, along with the Cape Verde Islands, were favorite sources for seamen. Harsh working conditions would then move them to sign off in New Bedford where they became a permanent part of the fishing industry in New England.

Other Portuguese immigrants came during the California gold rush of 1849 and later many were recruited to go to Hawaii to work on the sugar plantations. In 1910 the Portuguese monarchy fell and large numbers of conservative Roman Catholics came to New England. Others came later in order to escape adverse social and economic conditions.

Since 1958 Portuguese have come to the United States in record numbers, providing a higher percentage of new arrivals than any other ethnic group of European origin as of 1980. The Azores Islands experienced a series of submarine volcanic eruptions and the United States responded with special legislation that allowed victims of this disaster to enter on an expedited basis.

People with Portuguese ancestry come to America now from all over the world. This simply attests to the widespread influence the Portuguese sailors had in the old days. Incidentally, I visited Lisbon, the capital of Portugal, not long ago. The nation is certainly not wealthy but these people are charming. I remember stepping off the curb one day in an effort to cross through the heavy traffic. "Don't get hit," my driver shouted. "We can't afford the lumber to build you a casket!"

To further convince you that these are unusually creative people, I must tell you that the Portuguese who went to Hawaii to work on the plantations gave the Hawaiians the ukulele. No, it is not Hawaiian. It is Portuguese! And did you know that John Philip Sousa, first director of the United States Marine Band and author of "Stars and Stripes Forever," was Portuguese American? I didn't think you did.

The menu that follows is a cross between what my assistant, Craig, and I found in Lisbon and what we found in the kitchens of Portuguese immigrants here. Bread Soups are common, garlic is a must, and hot pepper oil, called Piri Piri, is everywhere. The Pork and Clams dish will surprise you; it sounds strange to most people in this country but it is extraordinarily delicious. Finally, few Portuguese meals are celebrated without the old dried salt cod. In this case I have prepared Codfish Cakes for you. Have a good time cooking and don't forget the Portuguese Jews from Brazil who first came to New Amsterdam. You should thank them during your meal.

PIRI PIRI

Makes 1 quart, which will last you a while, I promise. Store, covered, at room temperature. This recipe can be easily halved.

We must begin our Portuguese cooking with this hot oil sauce. It is served everywhere in Portugal and was brought here by our immigrant ancestors. I have made it with several different kinds of peppers, and the strength varies. Buy tiny dried hot red peppers in a Chinese, Thai, or Vietnamese grocery. This sauce is worth the pepper hunt!

Fill a 1-quart glass canning jar ⅓ full of tiny hot dried red peppers. Add ½ cup whiskey and fill jar with a mixture of ½ olive oil and ½ vegetable oil. Cap the jar and let sit 1 month. Shake now and then during the curing process.

You can add more oil as you use up the sauce.

ROAST CHICKEN WITH PIRI PIRI

Serves 4

This is a great dish that will get you into Piri Piri. Every Portuguese-American immigrant knows this dish too.

In the old country the oil is kept in little cups with something like a pastry brush so that each person can brush on as much hot oil, or as little, as he or she likes.

Careful with this stuff . . . it is hot!

Split a frying chicken and rub it with olive oil, halved garlic, and salt. Grill the chicken over charcoal until done to taste, and then serve with Piri Piri on the side. The hot oil on the mild chicken is just wonderful.

PORK AND CLAMS

(Cataplana)

Serves 5–6

When I first heard of this dish in Portugal I was surprised. Clams and pork together? It sounds like something the Chinese would do! This dish makes perfect sense once you taste it, and it is not difficult to prepare. We tasted it in Portugal, and in the charming Monteiro household in San Leandro, just south of Oakland, California. Carmen Silvera, a charming woman of Portuguese ancestry, prepared it for us. I have made "some variations on a common theme." I think you will really like this dish.

2 pounds boneless pork butt, cut into 1-inch cubes

1½ cups dry white wine

2 cloves garlic, peeled and finely chopped

Dash of Piri Piri (page 382) (Try about 2 teaspoons to start; more can be added later to taste.)

1½ teaspoons salt

½ teaspoon freshly ground black pepper

2 bay leaves

¼ cup olive oil

4 teaspoons paprika

2 medium onions, peeled and thinly sliced

2 pounds small clams, in the shell

Place the pork cubes in a large bowl. Mix the wine, garlic, Piri Piri, 1 teaspoon of the salt, ¼ teaspoon of the pepper, and the bay leaves, and pour the mixture over the meat. Allow to marinate for 2 hours. Drain the meat well, reserving the marinade.

Heat a heavy frying pan and brown the pork in 2 tablespoons of the olive oil. Place the meat and oil in an 8-quart heavy stove-top casserole and add the reserved marinade and the paprika. Simmer the meat in the juices, uncovered, until the juices almost evaporate, about 45 minutes. Skim the fat and discard the bay leaves.

Meanwhile, in another deep saucepan, sauté the onions in the remaining olive oil until they are tender but not discolored. Add the clams, the remaining ½ teaspoon salt, and the remaining ¼ teaspoon pepper. Cook over high heat, covered, for 5 minutes, or until the clams open. Add the clams and juice to the pork and heat through.

BIFANA PORK

Serves 4

I love this dish, and pork has never been expensive here. The Portuguese immigrant grandma must have cooked this often for the family. It is the Piri Piri that does it!

1 teaspoon salt	2 tablespoons olive oil
1 tablespoon peeled and finely chopped garlic	1 cup Chicken Stock (page 74) or use canned
½ cup white wine	2 teaspoons Piri Piri (page 382)
2 tablespoons pork fat, rendered (See Hint, page 168.)	2 bay leaves
	1½ pounds boneless pork butt, sliced ⅛ inch thick

Crush the garlic with the salt and mix with the wine. Marinate the pork in this mixture for 1 hour.

Heat a large frying pan and add the lard and oil. Add the Chicken Stock, Piri Piri, bay leaves, and any remaining marinade. Bring to a simmer. Add the pork. Cover and cook until the pork is tender, about 20 minutes.

BREAD SOUP

(Asordo)

Serves 8

The Portuguese love bread soup, or *Asordo*. Of course it was a peasant dish in the old country, and when the Portuguese came to this country, it continued to be a favorite way of using up old bread. Our immigrant ancestors wasted very little. They were frugal!

1 1-pound loaf French bread, dry, broken up into small pieces

5 cloves garlic, peeled and finely chopped

3 tablespoons olive oil

2 quarts Chicken Stock (page 74) or used canned

½ pound shrimp, peeled

Salt to taste

Piri Piri (page 382) to taste

GARNISH

Chopped parsley

4 whole eggs

Soak the bread in water until soft. Squeeze out the water and set the bread aside. In a soup pot toast the garlic in the olive oil, just until it begins to barely brown. Add the Chicken Stock to the pot and bring to a simmer. Add the bread to the pot and simmer, making a thick soup. Add the shrimp, salt, and Piri Piri. Cook for a moment. Place the soup in a tureen and garnish with the parsley. Break the eggs on top of the soup. Bring to the table and stir the eggs into the soup before serving.

PORTUGUESE CALDO VERDE

Serves 10–12

When Craig, my assistant, and I were in the public market in Lisbon, Portugal, we were confused by great piles of a very finely shredded leafy green vegetable. We could not figure out what it was, and few persons spoke enough English to explain. Finally, our driver, Big John, who seemed to be a fine cook, began almost to cry about the beauty of *Caldo Verde,* or Green Soup. The vegetable was shredded kale, a basic ingredient for the favorite soup of the Portuguese. They brought the recipe with them to America.

1 pound kale or collard greens (Kale is preferred for this dish.)

⅓ pound dried small white beans, soaked in water overnight and drained

½ cup olive oil

3 medium yellow onions, peeled and thinly sliced

3 quarts Chicken Stock (page 74) or use canned

½ pound linguica (Portuguese sausage) or kielbasa (Polish sausage, page 367), sliced

½ pound potatoes, peeled and grated

Salt and freshly ground black pepper to taste

Remove the large ribs of the kale and slice the vegetable into very thin strips, as thin as possible. Place in a bowl of cold water for 1 hour. Drain well.

In an 8-quart soup pot sauté the onions in the olive oil. Add the kale, Chicken Stock, and remaining ingredients, including the drained beans. Simmer for 1½ hours, covered.

Taste for salt and pepper before serving.

CODFISH CAKES

(Bacalhau)

Serves 6

The Portuguese, like the Spanish and the Basques, have always had salted cod to fall back on during tough times. This fish became very popular with immigrants from these ethnic groups for two reasons. First, the fish tasted like the old country, and second, they could afford little else.

½ pound salt cod (page 45)

½ cup olive oil, plus more for pan-frying

2 cups coarse bread crumbs (use day-old bread)

1 cup yellow onion, peeled and chopped fine

½ teaspoon chopped fresh mint leaves

¼ cup chopped fresh coriander (page 49)

1 tablespoon chopped parsley

2 cloves garlic, peeled and crushed

2 teaspoons paprika

2 shots of Tabasco

Salt and freshly ground black pepper to taste

GARNISH

6 poached eggs, not overcooked

Rinse the cod several times in cold water. Place it in a large stainless-steel bowl and soak it for 18 to 24 hours in plenty of cold water. Change the water several times. Drain the cod and place it in a saucepan and just cover it with fresh water. Bring to a boil and simmer uncovered for 20 minutes. Drain, debone, and flake the cod.

In a large bowl beat together the olive oil and bread crumbs. Mix very well and then add the cod and the remaining ingredients, except the eggs. Mix until well blended and then form into 6 patties, ½ inch by 3½ inches. Pan-fry in a little olive oil until golden brown on both sides. Keep warm in the oven while you poach the eggs.

Serve each fish cake topped with a poached egg.

SNAILS AND SAUCE

Serves 4–5 as an appetizer

The open markets in Portugal sell fresh snails by the bagful! Huge gunnysacks filled with crawling snails, all kept wet, sit about in the stalls. I was anxious to taste them, and off we went to a tiny shop where the snails were kept in cabinets on the wall. The preparation is easy and the recipe remains a favorite with Portuguese immigrants. You will have the best luck finding snails in Chinese fish markets. You want medium-to-large-size snails, very fresh and very much alive! These are just delicious.

THE SNAILS

2 pounds fresh snails, in the shell, rinsed well

½ cup yellow cornmeal

3 cups Chicken Stock (page 74) or use canned

3 cloves garlic, peeled and crushed

½ cup dry white wine

1 teaspoon dried marjoram or oregano

Salt and freshly ground black pepper to taste

Place the snails in a large bowl, cover with fresh water, and stir the cornmeal into the water. This will help to clean the snails of mud and dirt in their system. Let them sit in this for 1 hour and then drain and rinse them.

Bring the Chicken Stock to a simmer and add the remaining ingredients. Add the drained snails and bring to a boil. Reduce to a simmer and cook, covered, for about 15 minutes, no longer.

Serve with the broth and good crusty bread. I also like to offer a special sauce with the snails for dipping. This recipe comes from a little shop in Lisbon.

THE SAUCE

½ pound butter

Juice of 1 lemon

2 teaspoons Piri Piri (page 382)

¼ teaspoon instant chicken bouillon (Knorr)

Melt the butter and add the remaining ingredients. Heat for a few minutes and serve in little cups along with the snails.

PORTUGUESE CORNBREAD

Makes 3 or 4 loaves

The Portuguese make a wonderful bread that is a cross between French bread and cornbread. I have developed a recipe based on that very combination, and it comes close to the great bread of Lisbon. If you can find a Portuguese bakery in this country, you are all set. Otherwise, try this.

2 packages quick-rising yeast

2½ cups warm water (105°)

2 pounds 3 ounces hard wheat flour mixed half and half with unbleached white flour or 2 pounds

3 ounces unbleached white flour (See Note.)

1 cup cornmeal, preferably stone-ground

½ cup water

1½ teaspoons salt mixed in 1 teaspoon water

Place the yeast in the warm water, about 105°. Let stand for 5 minutes. Stir to dissolve.

Place the yeast mixture in the mixing bowl of a heavy-duty electric mixer, such as KitchenAid. Beat in 4 cups of flour and beat until the dough pulls away from the sides of the mixing bowl, about 10 minutes on medium speed. If mixing by hand, beat vigorously with a wooden spoon, about 15 minutes.

Meanwhile, soak the cornmeal in the ½ cup of water for a few minutes. Add to the dough, using a dough hook on the mixer. Mix well. Add the salted water. Beat in the remaining flour and knead for 5 minutes, or knead 15 minutes by hand.

Place on a plastic countertop, or on a piece of plastic wrap, and cover with a large stainless-steel bowl. Let rise until double in bulk, about 2 hours. Punch down and let rise for another 1½ hours.

Punch down again and mold into 3 or 4 circular loaves. Place on 2 lightly greased baking sheets that have been dusted with cornmeal. Cover and let rise until almost double. I use an extra oven with a pan of hot water in the bottom to create steam, perfect for raising dough.

Preheat the oven to 450°. When the loaves have risen to double their original bulk, place them in the upper third of the oven. **IMPORTANT:** Place a pan of hot water on the bottom shelf. This will assure you of a great crust. Bake in the oven for about 25 minutes, or until the bread is nicely browned and the loaves sound hollow when you thump the bottom with your finger.

NOTE: Place a small paper sack on your scale and weigh out 2 pounds 3 ounces of flour. (Unless you can get hard wheat flour, use good unbleached white flour.)

THE PUERTO RICAN
IMMIGRANTS

PUERTO RICO

Some may find it a bit strange that I have included the people of Puerto Rico in a book on immigrant ancestors. While it is true that many citizens of Puerto Rico have migrated to the mainland United States, they are technically not immigrants. Puerto Rico is a commonwealth of the United States, so its people can travel back and forth between the mainland and the island anytime they wish. They are actually U.S. citizens and they are subject to all federal laws, including the draft. However, they cannot vote in federal elections and they have no elected representative in Congress. But they do have to pay federal taxes! The history of the island helps only a little in understanding the strange relationship that these people have with the mainland.

Columbus claimed Puerto Rico for Spain in November 1493. In 1508 Juan Ponce de León sailed there and the story goes that as he came into port he exclaimed, *"¡Qué puerto rico!"* "What a wonderful port!" So the island came to be named. The marks of Spanish rule are evident throughout the island, especially in the architecture, the language, and the food.

Spain used the colony of Puerto Rico both to provide resources and as a military outpost. Following the Spanish-American War in 1898 the small land became a protectorate of the United States. In 1952 it was declared a "free liberated state," or a commonwealth. The island has moved from being called the "poorhouse of the Caribbean" in 1939 to being recognized as having achieved the highest per capita income in the Caribbean by 1968. The difference between life in Puerto Rico and life in another independent country such as Jamaica is very dramatic. However, as improvements in public health and sanitation have resulted in a healthier population, they have also resulted in a much larger population. This population increase has led to a great deal of unemployment.

The combination of high unemployment at home, unrestricted travel to and from the mainland United States, and the availability of cheap and fast air travel have made off-island immigration inevitable. Today a full *one third* of the ethnic Puerto Rican population lives on the mainland and the number of Puerto Ricans in New York City alone is estimated to be about 925,000, or twice the number living in San Juan, the capital of Puerto Rico.

While persistent poverty seems to plague many Puerto Ricans in the larger urban areas such as New York and Miami, their culture remains richly vibrant. They are charming people who maintain regular contact with the home island and travel there as often as they can, in contrast to other immigrant groups who come here and seldom return to the homeland more than once or twice in a lifetime. This ability to maintain close contact with old roots have given us a "Little San Juan" in New York that is almost as exciting as the original. I have been to both and I urge you to take a trip to Puerto Rico yourself. You will be treated well and there are no customs to pass through and no restrictions on what you can bring back. After all, these people are American citizens.

The recipes that follow are legitimate. You can find plantains, a must for a good Puerto Rican meal, in most large American cities, and all else can be found in any Latino market. Learn to cook this food properly, and do it soon. I expect that Puerto Rico will become a full state in the not too distant future. You want to be ready with a party when this happens!

CHICKEN ASOPAO

Serves 4 as a main course

This is not quite a stew, and more moist than a paella. It is thicker than a soup and unusually delicious. This is one of the great dishes that Puerto Rican grandmas brought with them to the mainland.

1 3½-pound chicken (fryer), cut into 8 serving pieces, the breast cut in half

2 teaspoons dried oregano

¼ teaspoon freshly ground black pepper

2 teaspoons paprika

½ teaspoon salt

4 tablespoons olive oil

3 cloves garlic, peeled and crushed

1 ounce salt pork, coarsely chopped

2 ounces ham, coarsely chopped (Use real ham, not that boiled stuff from the deli!)

1 medium yellow onion, peeled and chopped

1 medium green bell pepper, cored, seeded, and chopped

1 medium tomato, chopped

½ pound Spanish Chorizo Sausage (page 452) or Mexican chorizo from a good market, cut in ½-inch pieces,

¼ cup pimento-stuffed olives (small ones)

1 tablespoon capers

1 tablespoon Annatto Oil (page 134)

2 cups Uncle Ben's Converted Rice

3 cups water

½ cup frozen peas

Salt and freshly ground black pepper to taste

Put the cut-up chicken in a large bowl. Add the oregano, pepper, paprika, salt, and 2 tablespoons of the oil. Toss to coat the chicken evenly. Heat a large nonstick frying pan and brown the chicken over medium-high heat.

Heat a large stove-top casserole. Add the remaining 2 tablespoons of olive oil and sauté the garlic, salt pork, and ham a few minutes. Add the onion and pepper, and sauté for 5 minutes over medium heat. Add the tomato, cover, and simmer for 10 minutes until the tomato collapses. Add the browned chicken and chorizo, and simmer over low heat for another 10 minutes. Add the stuffed olives, capers, annatto oil, rice, and water, then cover and simmer for 15 minutes. Add the frozen peas, cover, and simmer for 5 minutes more. Add salt and pepper.

Serve right away. This dish should be a little bit soupy and the rice tender.

MONFONGO CON CALDO

Makes 6 servings as a starch

This is a very unusual dish. It is akin, I suppose, to mashed potatoes, but it has a much more interesting flavor. In order to make this properly, you must have a large wooden mortar and pestle called a *pelon*. You can use a food processor if you do not grind the ingredients too long. The finished dish must have a rather crunchy texture.

4 firm, ripe plantains (page 44)

Oil for deep-frying (I prefer peanut oil.)

½ pound pork cracklings (page 44) (optional)

1 clove garlic, peeled and crushed

½ cup Chicken Stock (page 74) or use canned

Salt to taste

Cut the plantains as for Tostones (below) and deep-fry them. Grind the tostones in a mortar, adding the cracklings a few at a time, and mix well. Add the garlic and mix well. Serve hot in the mortar along with the heated broth, or place in a small bowl and serve. Check for salt.

The dish is eaten directly from the mortar or bowl.

TOSTONES

Makes about 40 tostones, enough for 5–6

When Roberto, our friend in Puerto Rico, told me that I had to eat tostones I was confused. I had heard about these fried plantain chips, but they certainly did not sound exciting. Roberto set us straight. Plantain is close to a banana, but in Puerto Rico it is served as a vegetable, a fruit, and a starch in a salad. Just like our potato! Try this and you will gain an understanding of the Puerto Rican culture. Yes, you can buy plantains in most large cities in America.

3 firm, ripe plantains (page 44)

2 teaspoons salt

Oil for deep-frying (I prefer peanut oil.)

Peel the plantains. Cut crosswise in slices about ½ inch wide. Slant the knife while cutting so slices will have an oval shape. Place in salted water to cover and soak for 1 hour. Drain, reserving the water, and pat dry.

Deep-fry at about 375° until the plantains are tender but not crusty. Remove from the oil, drain well, and flatten by pressing evenly with the bottom of a glass, or you can use a tostone press, a gadget available in any Latino market. (See the illustration on page 30.) After frying dip each slice in the salted water, pat dry, and fry again until crusty. Drain on absorbent paper.

GREEN BANANA SALAD

Serves 6 as a side dish

Craig, my assistant, and I were very surprised to see this salad on the menu of a delightful Puerto Rican restaurant in Miami, called El Coqui, or The Little Frog. They fed us very well, and we finally realized that plantains and green bananas are just as versatile as potatoes. This a perfect example, and a delicious one at that.

½ cup vegetable oil

2 medium yellow onions, peeled and thinly sliced

2¼ pounds green bananas, peeled and sliced ¼ inch thick

2 tablespoons white wine vinegar

Salt and freshly ground black pepper to taste

Juice of 1 lime

Mix all of the ingredients as for potato salad. Let them sit for 1 hour or so before serving. You will startle the kids with this most unusual dish.

NOTE: When buying the green bananas, be sure they are just a tiny bit soft. If they are too hard, the salad will be dry.

FRIED PLANTAINS

This dish is easy to prepare and makes a great change from potatoes. Choose medium-ripe plantains and peel them. Slice them lengthwise and pan-fry them in butter or oil over medium-low heat so that they brown lightly and are tender. Some people deep-fry plantains, but I much prefer them pan-fried.

SMOKED PORK HOCKS
WITH CHORIZO

Serves 4–6 as an appetizer

This dish is served as a first course, but I find it so delicious that I would be content to have it for lunch. We found it in a fine restaurant in Puerto Rico, and have learned it is popular in the States as well.

2 pounds smoked ham hocks, sawed in 1½-inch pieces

3 cups water

1 pound Spanish Chorizo Sausage (page 452) or Mexican chorizo from a good market, cut into 1-inch pieces

1 medium yellow onion, peeled and very thinly sliced

GARNISH
Chopped parsley (optional)

Place the ham hocks in a 4- to 6-quart pot, simmer, covered, in 3 cups of water until the hocks are tender, about 1½ hours. Meanwhile, pan-fry the chorizo. Add the chorizo to the pot, cover, and simmer for 30 minutes longer.

Remove to a platter. Top with onion and pour the pan juices over all. The parsley garnish is nice.

PUERTO RICAN CALDO GALLEGO

Serves 6–8

This spicy, hearty soup is a gift to the island by the Spanish. In fact, a similar dish is still popular in both Spain and Portugal, but the Puerto Rican grandma's version features a more interesting blend of spices.

½ pound dried white beans, soaked overnight in ample water and drained

1 pound chicken thighs

½ pound Spanish Chorizo Sausage (page 452) or Mexican chorizo from a good market, cut in ½-inch pieces

½ pound ham, chopped

¼ pound salt pork, diced

1 medium yellow onion, peeled and chopped

3 cloves garlic, peeled and chopped

2 teaspoons Worcestershire sauce

Few shots of Tabasco

2½ quarts water

½ pound potatoes, peeled, quartered, and sliced

½ pound green cabbage, sliced thin

2 cups kale (tough stems removed), sliced thin

½ pound turnips, peeled, quartered, and sliced

Salt and freshly ground black pepper to taste

GARNISH

Chopped fresh dill (optional)

Place the beans, chicken, chorizo, ham, pork, onion, garlic, Worcestershire sauce, Tabasco, and water in a 6- to 8-quart soup pot. Bring to a boil, then turn down to a simmer. Cook, covered, for 45 minutes. Remove the chicken pieces from the pot and debone. Set the meat aside and discard the bones.

Add the remaining ingredients except the salt, pepper and chicken to the pot. Simmer, covered, for 25 minutes, and then add salt and pepper. Return the chicken meat to the pot and simmer for a few more minutes. Top with the optional dill.

PUERTO RICAN RICE WITH PIGEON PEAS

Serves 8 as a side dish

This substantial dish is a staple in the Puerto Rican household, found at the dinner table as often as potatoes are in our country. The Cubans have a similar dish with black beans and the Jamaicans use red beans. But, most of us seem stuck with boring mashed potatoes. Try this, as it is versatile and very good. I think your kids would love it.

Please note that if you cannot find pigeon peas, also called gandules, try dried black-eyed peas. Gandules, or pigeon peas, can be found in Latino or Mexican markets.

½ pound dried gandules, rinsed

3 cups water

1 ounce salt pork, chopped small

2 ounces ham, chopped small

2 cloves garlic, peeled and crushed

1 tablespoon olive oil

1 medium red bell pepper, cored, seeded, and chopped small

1 medium green bell pepper, cored, seeded, and chopped small

1 medium yellow onion, peeled and chopped small

1 medium tomato, chopped small

1 tablespoon Annatto Oil (page 134)

1 cup Uncle Ben's Converted Rice

Freshly ground black pepper to taste

2 cups cold water

Salt to taste

In a small pot bring the gandules and 3 cups of water to a boil. Cover, turn off the heat, and allow to stand for 1 hour. Drain the peas, reserving the water. In a 6-quart pot sauté the salt pork, ham, and garlic in the olive oil for a few minutes. Add both bell peppers and the onion, cover, and cook over medium heat until the onion begins to turn transparent. Add the tomato, drained gandules, and 1½ cups of the reserved water. Simmer, covered, over low heat for 15 minutes until the peas are almost tender and most of the liquid is gone.

Stir in the annatto oil, rice, black pepper, and 2 cups of cold water. Bring to a boil and simmer covered for 15 to 20 minutes until liquid is absorbed and rice is tender. Add salt if needed.

PUERTO RICAN CODFISH WITH SCRAMBLED EGGS

Serves 4

Dried salt cod was terribly important to our immigrant ancestors. It would keep for a year and it was not expensive. Many ethnic groups used it, and you will note a bit of similarity between this dish and the Salt Fish and Ackee enjoyed by the Jamaicans. Be sure to rinse the dried cod often as it soaks. Otherwise its taste will be too salty.

¼ **pound salt cod (page 45) (Soak 18–24 hours; change water several times.)**

4 **cups cold water**

2 **tablespoons freshly rendered lard (page 168) or peanut oil**

3 **medium yellow onions, peeled and finely chopped**

2 **tablespoons Annatto Oil (page 134)**

8 **eggs, beaten**
Salt and freshly ground black pepper to taste

Place the soaked and drained cod in 4 cups of fresh water and bring to a simmer, covered. Cook for 15 minutes and drain. Cool and flake the fish. Set aside. Heat the lard or oil in a large frying pan and sauté the onion until very light brown. Add the salt cod and achiote oil. Stir together for a moment over medium heat and then add the eggs. Cook, stirring now and then, until the eggs are done to your taste. Season with salt and pepper.

PUERTO RICAN BLACK BEAN SOUP

The Puerto Ricans share this dish with the Cubans. For a good version, see Cuban Black Bean Soup, page 109.

THE ROMANIAN
IMMIGRANTS

ROMANIA

Romania has always been somewhat isolated from the rest of Europe, located as it is at the extreme eastern end of the European continent. It edges on the Black Sea and has the Ukraine of Russia to the north and Hungary, Yugoslavia, and Bulgaria on its borders.

The ancestors of the contemporary Romanians were the Dacians, called by Herodotus "very brave and honest fighters." The Dacians lived in southeastern Europe where they farmed, bred cattle, and mined for gold and silver. This mining activity led to lively trade and an urge to expand the borders of Dacian authority. By the first century A.D. the Romans were nervous about this group and took them on in battle, a battle that the Romans won.

In A.D. 129 the Emperor Hadrian divided Dacia into two provinces. Marcus Aurelius divided it further. Remember the phrase "divide and conquer"? Old Roman tactic! Colonists arrived from Rome and called the colony Roma Nea, or New Rome, from which is derived Romania. The Romans left two main legacies: Christianity and the Latin language, which is the basis of the Romance language spoken today in Romania, the only Romance language spoken in Eastern Europe.

By the third century the Goths from the east invaded and then the Huns and the Slavs. In the seventh century the Bulgars came from the south. At this point the Romanians changed their religious allegiance from Roman Catholicism to the Eastern Orthodox Church. Then, in the ninth century the Magyars from Hungary came as did the Mongols in 1241.

Some scholars claim that this chain of invasions destroyed the original Daco-Roman population, while other historians believe that the remnants of the Daco-Roman peoples escaped to the mountains in the northeast and that these survivors are the ancestors of today's Romanians. But there is more.

In the fourteenth century the Ottoman Empire absorbed Romania and it remained under Turkish rule for a long time. The Turks and the Russians quarreled over this territory in the eighteenth century and in 1829 the land fell under the protection of Russia. Eventually the Stalinists took over and in 1969 Ceausescu became the head of government. He ruled with extraordinary harshness until 1989 when the people rose up against him and at last claimed freedom. He and his wife were shot after a trial of a few hours. It seemed to me that the anger of many generations was compressed into that moment. We hope now for real freedom for the peoples of Romania.

The first immigrants from Romania came here between 1870 and 1895. Most of these people were Jews, with the peasant farmers coming after this time. Today, the Romanian Americans are so assimilated that it is hard to find them. Some communities do still have Romanian Orthodox Churches, and these places would be a great source for recipes, ethnic festivals, and insight.

You will enjoy the Romanian Sausages in this section, as well as the baked Cornmeal Mush with Cheese. The Stuffed Cabbage is so easy that you will be surprised and the Mashed Beans are going to become a favorite of your children. Kids will love all these dishes.

Most of the following recipes were given us by a woman in a Romanian ethnic community in Indiana, Mrs. Pearl Mailath. When we last talked with her she seemed convinced that Romania was never going to get its act together and oppose Soviet oppression. A few weeks after we shared a meal, Romania stood firm. I eat these dishes now and cheer her on, and her people, and their future.

ROMANIAN SAUSAGES

(Mititei)

Makes 12 sausages

Pearl Mailath, a Romanian friend in Indiana, invited us into her home for a real Romanian meal. This was before Romania erupted into what we hope will be independence. As she cooked these delicious sausages, we talked politics. I think the discussion made the sausages taste even better. These are great cooked on the outdoor grill.

4–5 cloves garlic, peeled

¼ cup water

1 pound ground chuck

⅔ pound coarsely ground pork

1 teaspoon baking soda

1½ teaspoons salt

1 teaspoon freshly ground black pepper

½ teaspoon dried thyme, whole

½ teaspoon dried basil

½ cup Beef Stock (page 78) or use canned

Crush the garlic well in the water, using a fork. Stir in the meat, baking soda, seasonings, and garlic purée together. Add Beef Stock and mix well.

For each sausage, take ⅓ cup of the meat mixture, and roll between the palms of your hands into a sausage shape about 4 inches long. Place sausages side by side in a container and cover. Refrigerate overnight so the flavors can blend.

These are excellent on the grill. They may also be broiled or baked in the oven.

Broil the sausages about 3 minutes per side until cooked through and browned.

HINT: WHEN HAND ROLLING SAUSAGES or meatballs of any kind, keep a small bowl of water near you so that you can keep your hands a bit wet. This way, the meat will not stick to your hands.

CORNMEAL MUSH WITH CHEESE

(Mamaliga)

Serves 6

This dish threw me. Since corn was not seen in Europe until after the discovery of the New World (corn is *ours!*), I was confused as to how the Romanians became so fond of cornmeal mush. Then I remembered that the ancient Romans, who had great influence on Romania, loved pulses or cooked grains. That is why cornmeal mush, or polenta in Italy, became so popular. And so it is with the Romanians.

Everyone in your household will love this dish. There will be no exceptions. Tell them I told you that! (Sounds like the old Romanian political regime, doesn't it?)

1½ quarts water

1½ teaspoons salt

1½ cups fine yellow cornmeal (must be yellow)

4 tablespoons butter

1 cup sour cream

⅓ pound white cheese, such as brick or Muenster, grated

⅓ pound yellow cheese, such as Colby or Cheddar, grated

In a 4-quart heavy stove-top casserole, bring 1½ quarts of water to a boil. Add the salt and move the pan off the stove. Stirring constantly, slowly sprinkle in the cornmeal. Stir well so that you have no lumps. Return to the burner and bring to a boil. Turn down to a simmer and let the mush cook slowly for 20 minutes or more, or until it is thick. Stir often during this process. The final product should be the consistency of thick cake batter. If it is too thick, stir in a little more water.

In an 8 × 8-inch glass baking dish melt the butter for a moment in the oven preheated to 350°. Spoon in one half of the cornmeal mush and cover the bottom of the dish. Add one half of the sour cream, spreading it over the mush. Then add half of the cheeses, spreading evenly. Make two layers: in a 8 × 8-inch glass dish. Place another layer of mush, sour cream, and cheese on top of the first layer. Place in the oven until the cheeses are melted and slightly browned on top. Serve immediately.

FRIED CORNMEAL MUSH

(Mamaliga)

Leftover cooked Mamaliga (page 403) is perfect for this. Cool Mamaliga and cut it into ¼-inch-thick slices. Dip each slice in beaten egg. Sprinkle generously on each side with grated yellow cheese. Using a nonstick skillet, fry in hot butter on both sides until golden. Serve with sour cream or yogurt.

MASHED BEANS ROMANIAN

(Fasole Frecata)

Serves 5–6

I expect that this dish goes back to ancient Rome, and to the Romans' love for cooked grains and beans. Here the Romanian cook does some very creative things with an old dish of mashed beans. It is still popular with Romanian immigrants and their families, of course. Our friend Grandma Pearl gave us this one.

½ pound dried Northern beans, rinsed and drained

1 medium yellow onion, peeled and coarsely chopped

1 medium parsnip, peeled and coarsely chopped (1½ cups)

3 cloves garlic, peeled and crushed

1½ teaspoons salt, or more to taste

GARNISH

½ pound bacon, cut into small dice

1 medium yellow onion, peeled and chopped

Salt and freshly ground black pepper to taste

Place the beans in a 6-quart pot and cover them with 2 inches of water above them. Set the pot on the stove and bring to a boil. Cook for about 2 minutes, then turn off the heat. Skim off any foam, cover, and let stand for 1 to 2 hours.

Add enough water to cover the beans about 1 inch above them. Add the onion, parsnip, garlic, and salt. Cover and bring to a simmer. Cook, covered, for 1 hour, or until beans are tender. Do not let the water boil away completely. Add more if needed.

When the beans are fully cooked, pour off some of the broth if too soupy and reserve it. Place the beans in a blender with the vegetables and enough of the broth to purée. Beans should be the consistency of pudding. Add more of the broth as needed to purée, but do not make it too soupy. The beans will thicken a little as they cool. Set aside, covered, in a warming oven.

For the garnish place the bacon in a frying pan with the chopped onion, and fry until the bacon is crisp and the onion is soft. Drain off excess grease. Add the bacon and onion to the beans and serve. Add salt and pepper if needed.

ANOTHER VERSION

The beans are puréed and left plain. No bacon is used. Instead slice an onion thinly for frying. Place 3 to 4 tablespoons of oil in a frying pan, add 1 teaspoon sweet paprika, and sauté slightly. Add the sliced onion and sauté until soft.

Place the beans in a serving dish, spoon the onion over the top, and serve. Or place the sautéed onion-paprika mixture in a separate dish and let guests serve themselves. Do not drain off the oil. The dish should be a little greasy.

ROMANIAN STUFFED CABBAGE

I must give Pearl Mailath credit for teaching me to roll stuffed cabbage properly. It is a snap if you use her method, which she claims is the Old World way.

Prepare a batch of Hungarian Stuffed Cabbage Rolls according to the recipe on page 169. It is so close to the dish Pearl makes. Now, forget about the paprika gravy and make the rolls without that very Hungarian garnish. It is the rolling procedure that I want you to experience. When Pearl rolls up a cabbage roll, she does not tie it, she does not clamp it, she does not stick a toothpick in it. She stuffs the cabbage leaf, folding one end over, and then *she stuffs in the other end to make a solid sausage-type roll.* (See the illustration for stuffing cabbage Polish style, page 375.) Can you believe it? It is *so* simple. Pearl cooks the rolls with smoked ham hocks and cabbage, just as in this recipe. They are delicious and not a one will fall apart on you. Thanks, Pearl!

MIXED VEGETABLES AND VEAL STEW

(Ghiveciu)

Serves the neighborhood

This has got to be one of the most involved recipes I have ever published. It has twenty-eight ingredients in it, so you are not going to throw it together after work some night. This is a dish that reminds us of the affection that the Romanian immigrant has always had for vegetables . . . and of his/her willingness to cook all day for the sake of a memory.

⅓ cup all-purpose flour (See Hint, page 423.)

2½ teaspoons salt

¾ teaspoon freshly ground black pepper

2 pounds boneless veal shoulder, cut into 1-inch cubes

2½ tablespoons butter

¼ cup olive oil

2 medium yellow onions, peeled and sliced

3 cloves garlic, peeled and finely chopped

1 cup Beef Stock (page 78) or use canned

1 cup dry red wine

3 tablespoons finely chopped parsley

2 tablespoons tomato paste

1 cup sliced carrots

2 cups coarsely chopped tomatoes, fresh or canned

1½ cups green bell pepper, cored, seeded, and cut into ¼-inch strips

4 cups cubed eggplant (½-inch cubes)

2 cups cubed zucchini (½-inch cubes)

2 cups cleaned and thinly sliced leeks (white parts only)

2 cups peeled and chopped turnips

2 cups peeled and chopped celery root

2 cups peeled and chopped parsnips

3 cups thinly sliced green cabbage

1 cup trimmed and julienned string beans

½ cup seedless green grapes

½ teaspoon dried marjoram

½ teaspoon dried thyme, whole

Salt and freshly ground pepper to taste

GARNISH

Plain yogurt or sour cream

In a bowl combine the flour, ½ teaspoon of the salt and ½ teaspoon of the pepper, or more to taste. Add the veal and toss until the cubes are completely coated. Remove the meat from the flour, sifting it through your hands to shake off the excess flour. Sauté the veal in the butter and oil in an 8- to 10-quart Dutch oven over medium-high heat, stirring frequently, until brown on all sides, about 5 minutes.

Add the onions and garlic and cook, stirring frequently, until the onions are soft, about 5 minutes. Add all of the remaining ingredients, except the yogurt or sour cream, and stir until well mixed. Cook, covered, over high heat until the liquid boils. Season with salt and pepper to taste.

Place in a preheated 350° oven. Bake, stirring several times during cooking, until the vegetables are very tender, about 1 hour. Serve hot. Garnish each serving with yogurt or sour cream.

CIORBA OF VEAL

Serves 8–10

This dish is a sour soup. In the old days in Romania it was made sour through the use of a fermented sour wheat bran . . . but in our time, sauerkraut juice is more commonly used. This is a lovely and filling dish . . . and very Romanian.

1¼ pounds veal shank, sawed into 1-inch pieces

2 quarts water

2 teaspoons salt and freshly ground black pepper to taste

¼ pound (1 stick) butter

3 medium yellow onions, peeled and chopped

1½ cups diced carrots (½-inch dice)

1 cup diced potatoes (½-inch dice)

1 cup chopped celery

2 shallots, peeled and finely chopped

½ cup chopped parsley

1¼ cups sauerkraut juice (Canned is fine.)

Additional salt and pepper to taste, if necessary

Juice of ½ lemon

½ cup chopped fresh dill

GARNISH

½ pint sour cream

In a 6- to 8-quart stove-top covered casserole or soup pot, place the veal shank, water, and salt and pepper, cover and simmer for 2 hours. Remove the shank pieces and allow them to cool for a moment. Debone the shank pieces and chop the meat coarsely and return it to the pot.

Heat a large frying pan and add the butter, onion, carrots, potatoes, celery, shallots, and parsley. Sauté until the onions are clear and tender. Add the vegetables to the soup pot along with the sauerkraut juice. Simmer for 25 more minutes or so, and taste for salt and pepper. Add the lemon juice and dill. Simmer for a few more minutes and place in a soup tureen. Garnish with the sour cream and serve.

WALNUT CRESCENTS

Makes enough for 3 visits from grandson John, no more! About 100
cookies

DOUGH

1 8-ounce package
Philadelphia cream
cheese, room
temperature

16 tablespoons (2 sticks)
butter or margarine,
room temperature

1 egg

1 tablespoon sugar

6 cups all-purpose flour
(See Hint, page 423.)

½ teaspoon salt

½ cup plus 3 tablespoons
cold water

FILLING

4 tablespoons (½ stick)
stick butter or margarine

½ pound walnuts, ground

½ cup sugar

½ cup milk

1 teaspoon vanilla

Confectioners' sugar for
dusting

TO MAKE THE DOUGH

Place the cream cheese and butter in a bowl with the egg, sugar, flour,
salt, and water. Mix well (you can also mix by hand). Roll the dough into
a log, 10 inches long. Wrap in plastic wrap and refrigerate the dough for
at least 1 hour.

Working with ¼ of the dough at a time, place it on a floured countertop, turning it over to coat well so that it does not stick. Roll the dough
out very thin.

Using a fluted pastry cutter (a pizza cutter works too), cut the dough
into strips 2 inches wide. Then cut the dough across again to make 2-
inch squares. Place ½ teaspoon filling on each square, using the back of
a teaspoon to spread it. Roll up the square diagonally, from one corner
to the opposite corner, or from one side to the opposite side. Form
either into a crescent shape, or leave it straight, and place the filled
dough on an ungreased cookie sheet. Bake for 15 or 20 minutes in a
preheated 350° oven until the cookies are light brown.

Sprinkle with confectioners' sugar immediately. Let cool. More powdered sugar can be added when serving. Store in a covered container.
These freeze well.

TO MAKE THE FILLING

In a saucepan, place the butter, ground nuts, sugar, and milk and cook until thick, stirring to prevent sticking. Add the vanilla. Cool slightly before using on the dough. Sugar may be increased according to taste but do not make the filling too sweet.

NOTE: If all the dough is not used at one time, it can be stored in the refrigerator for several days. Do not freeze the dough.

THE RUSSIAN
IMMIGRANTS

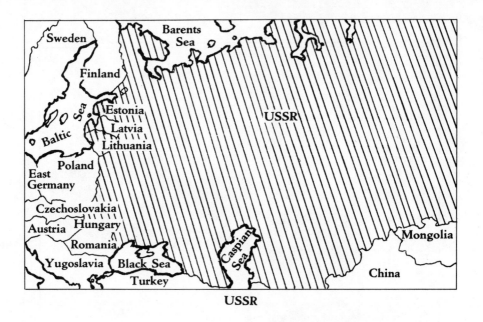

USSR

Russia, or rather, the Soviet Union, is a vast nation forged out of many peoples. Within its borders you will encounter one hundred different ethnic groups, eighty languages, five alphabets, Islam, Judaism, Buddhism, and Christianity. Despite the fact that it is so close to the rest of Europe it remains somewhat separate from it. Historically Russia has regarded foreigners and foreign influences with ambivalence if not outright mistrust.

The first Russian immigrants to the United States came through the Pacific Coast and they did not really come as immigrants but rather as part of the steady eastward expansion of the Russian Empire across Siberia and on to Alaska and the West Coast. Russians were in the Aleutians by the 1760s, mostly fur traders and missionaries. The first actual Russian settlement was at Three Saints Bay on Kodiak Island in Alaska, about 1784. Russian colonists continued to move to the Alaska territory until about 1867 when Russia decided that this far-flung colony was not profitable enough and sold Alaska to the United States. Half of the settlers returned home. Many of those remaining moved to California, and one may still find large Russian communities in both Los Angeles and San Francisco.

Russian migration to the East Coast of America began in earnest between 1880 and 1914 when thousands of impoverished peasants came over. The second wave of Russian immigrants came between 1920 and 1940, fleeing the Russian Revolution. Many Soviet Jews came during this time. Unlike their predecessors these immigrants were relatively well educated, often with professional backgrounds. Following World War II Russians came as refugees displaced by the war. Many more have continued to come in recent years and we now have a Russian American community in this country of about three million. They are a leading ethnic group in terms of income and education.

The Russian American community has had difficulties maintaining itself as a distinct ethnic unit. The most obvious reason is that these people come from so many different cultures and traditions within the Soviet Union. Another reason for keeping a low profile in terms of background stems from the nature of U.S.-Soviet relations in the past. Things are much better today than they have been in years, and we can only hope that good relations will continue. The Russians are charming and creative and seem to need little more than a kitchen table for generating Russian warmth and hospitality. You can spend a great deal of time enjoying this human warmth at the Russian nightclubs in Brighton Beach in Brooklyn. And don't miss the wonderful M&I International Market. You have never seen such beautiful Russian sausages and fish and breads and pastries and . . . well, Russians!

You will have no trouble drawing together a fine Russian meal from the following recipes. Basic foods for the Russian include potatoes, beans, cabbage, beets, eggs, rye, wheat, and barley. Kasha, or buckwheat groats, is popular and the breads and dumplings basic to the diet. Throw a Russian party very soon. The world is looking better every minute!

RUSSIAN BEEF STROGANOFF

Serves 4–6

This recipe is a gift to us from Grandma Nedzel, a friend who lives near our studios in Chicago. She came from Russia as a young woman and still loves to cook. The text is by her proud and well-fed grandson:

"This is not at all the same dish we think of when we envision a cafeteria special, which is essentially a goopy, creamy stew. In old Russia, stroganoff was haute cuisine, made with the finest ingredients. There is not a lot of seasoning because nothing should distract from the flavor of the beef and mushrooms. It is *not* served on noodles, but on buckwheat kasha, a real Russian favorite. The amounts of ingredients can be varied to serve different numbers of people.

1 recipe Russian Kasha
(page 416)

2 pounds tenderloin, top sirloin, or other fine steak, cut into thin strips

2 large yellow onions, peeled and chopped

4 tablespoons olive oil or butter (The latter is traditional and preferred.)

Salt and freshly ground black pepper to taste

½ pound mushrooms, sliced (Russia, particularly southern Russia, is famed for its variety of readily picked fancy mushrooms—somewhat like the Pacific Northwest. This dish is best made with morels, chanterelles, oyster mushrooms or any other delicate mushroom. Button mushrooms will do, as will dried fancy mushrooms.)

¼–½ cup sour cream

GARNISH

Parsley or, preferably, fresh dill

The preparation of this dish is almost like Chinese stir-fry. Everything happens very quickly, so have plates and all the ingredients ready to go! Cook the kasha first, according to the directions on page 416 (use raw egg—it really makes the kasha taste better). Keep the kasha warm in a covered pot. Slice the tenderloin into thin strips and have ready a large skillet (or even a wok!).

Brown the tenderloin strips in the skillet or wok over fairly high heat (not as high as in wok cooking, because you are using butter or olive oil). The steak may have to be cooked in two batches to avoid getting too wet and overcooked. In a separate pot or large skillet, brown the onion in the remaining olive oil or butter (traditional), salt, and pepper until the onion is slightly clear but not soggy.

When the tenderloin strips are nearly finished, add the mushrooms to the onion and cook briefly until heated but not soggy. Set aside the cooked tenderloin and cover for a moment to keep warm. With the heat on low, slowly add dollops of sour cream to the onion-mushroom mixture until a thick, creamy mix is achieved. Watch the heat to avoid curdling the sour cream. The sour cream should be heated just long enough to warm it. Pour any beef juices from the beef skillet or wok into the mixture and stir to a creamy consistency.

Serve immediately on a plate in three separate piles, beef, kasha, and mushroom-onion sauce for diners to mix or eat separately. Add more salt and pepper, if desired. Garnish with parsley or dill. An alternative to frying the tenderloin is to broil the beef whole, then slice before serving."

RUSSIAN KASHA

Makes 3 cups

This traditional Russian dish is made from buckwheat groats, a very nutty-flavored grain. Groats can be purchased under the brand name of Wolff's Kasha—Roasted Buckwheat Kernels. I like the medium granulation, though Wolff's also makes a fine grind. You may also find this grain in bulk in Russian or Jewish markets. It is simple to prepare, and you will find yourself serving it often in the place of rice or potatoes. This recipe comes right off the back of the Wolff's box, and it is the traditional way of preparing this grain.

2 cups Chicken Stock,
  (page 74) or use canned
  (Please avoid bouillon
  cubes.)

1 teaspoon salt

½ teaspoon freshly ground
  black pepper

2 tablespoons butter

1 cup kasha buckwheat
  groats, medium grain
  (page 41)

1 egg, beaten

Place the Chicken Stock, salt, pepper, and butter in a 2-quart heavy covered saucepan. Bring to a simmer. In a small bowl stir the kasha and egg together. Heat a SilverStone-lined frying pan and add the kasha-egg mixture. On medium-high heat flatten, stir, and chop the kasha with a wooden fork for 2 to 4 minutes, or until the egg has cooked and the kernels are hot and mostly separated.

Bring the stock to a boil and add the kasha to the broth. Cover and turn the heat to low. Cook for 10 minutes. Remove the cover, stir, and check that the kernels are tender and the liquid is absorbed. If not, cover and continue to cook another 3 to 5 minutes. Stir and fluff with fork and serve.

HALUSKI

Serves 4–6 as a starch

While dining with members of St. Basil's Russian Orthodox Church in Simpson, Pennsylvania, we tasted this delicious dish. It comes from the Ukraine in southwestern Russia, an area where traditionally there was little meat in the diet. The Russian immigrants who came to Pennsylvania brought the old-country dishes with them, and this is the entire recipe that was given us. It is delicious and terribly easy to make.

Cook noodles (the wide or bow-tie kind may be used) according to package directions. I use an 8-ounce package of bow ties. Do not overcook them. Add cooked sweet Cabbage Filling, as for Pagach (page 424), and mix gently. Add salt and pepper to taste.

NOTE: Homemade noodles are best.

CAULIFLOWER FRIED IN BUTTER

Serves 4–6

Cauliflower is a common winter dish in a large part of Russia. This method of cooking the vegetable is tasty and very different, and because it is Russian it is very hearty.

1 large head of cauliflower	2 tablespoons butter
2 tablespoons all-purpose flour	Salt and freshly ground black pepper to taste

GARNISH

Melted butter	Finely chopped parsley

Separate the cauliflower into flowerets. Break the flowerets up into little pieces. Place the cauliflower in boiling salted water and cook just until barely tender. Drain the cauliflower and rinse with cold water. Drain again and dredge with the flour seasoned with salt and pepper, and pan-fry in the butter until lightly browned. Serve with melted butter and finely chopped parsley.

RADISH AND EGG SALAD

Serves 4–6

1 pound red radishes, cleaned, trimmed, and sliced	½ cup sour cream
	1 bunch of scallions, trimmed and chopped
3 hard-boiled eggs, peeled and coarsely chopped	Salt and freshly ground black pepper, to taste

GARNISH

2 sprigs fresh dill, chopped

Mix all the ingredients, except the dill, and place in a serving bowl. Garnish with the dill.

RUSSIAN POTATO PANCAKES

Makes about 1 dozen

This dish is Russian, it is Jewish, it is peasant, it is delicious. When Russian immigrants came to these shores, they found potatoes were even more plentiful here than in the homeland. So, what do you eat? Potatoes!

1 pound russet potatoes, peeled and soaked in salted water (This will prevent discoloration.)	Salt and ground white pepper to taste
	2 tablespoons oil
1 egg	Peanut oil for frying
½ cup plus 4 tablespoons all-purpose flour (See Hint, page 423.)	

Grate the potatoes and then grind them fine in a food grinder like a KitchenAid. Combine the potatoes with the egg, flour, salt and pepper, and oil. Mix well. In ⅛ inch of oil pan-fry a few at a time until they are golden brown and crisp on both sides, 3 to 4 minutes per side. Remove to paper towels to drain. Serve warm with sour cream and applesauce.

NOTE: Use a mounded tablespoon to measure out the batter and flatten into a 4-inch circle in the hot oil. These pancakes should be thin and crispy. If you do not have a KitchenAid to grind the potatoes, you will have to grate it by hand.

BLINIS AND CAVIAR

Makes 3½ dozen

You are going to think that there are two Russias. In the old days that was true, and that was what the revolution was all about. This is a dish that was popular with the upper classes in the old days, along with Beef Stroganoff. However, it is eaten in this country by hard-working Russian immigrants who can afford things here that they could not afford "on the other side."

THE BLINIS

2 cups milk, scalded and cooled

2 packages quick-rising yeast

½ cup warm water (105°)

1 teaspoon sugar

½ cup buckwheat flour (Find in specialty or health food stores.)

2 cups all-purpose flour (See Hint, page 423.)

3 eggs, separated

½ teaspoon salt

3 tablespoons sour cream

3 tablespoons melted butter, cooled, plus additional for cooking

1½ cups additional milk

Scald the milk and cool to warm (105°). Put the yeast in the water and add the sugar. Let sit for 5 minutes, then stir to dissolve the yeast.

In an electric mixer combine the milk, yeast mixture, both flours, the egg yolks only, salt, sour cream, and melted butter. Mix thoroughly. Beat the egg whites until they form soft peaks and gently fold into the batter. Allow to rise for 30 minutes.

Stir in the additional milk.

Heat an electric SilverStone-lined frying pan to 400°. Brush the pan with a bit of butter and fry the pancakes using 3 tablespoons of batter for each. They should be about 3 to 4 inches in diameter. Cook until golden and turn. Keep blinis covered in a preheated 200° oven until serving.

NOTE: You can cook these ahead of time and refrigerate them in sealed plastic bags. Reheat them on a medium-hot griddle just before serving.

TO SERVE THE BLINIS
Place the following garnishes alongside the blinis:

Melted butter

Sour cream

Chopped, grated hard-
boiled egg

Chopped onion

Caviar (Black caviar is
best with these. Black
lumpfish caviar from
Iceland or Denmark is
just fine if you do not
wish to spend a fortune
on Russian caviar.)

Each person may add a bit of the garnishes to their blinis. This makes
just a great first course.

RUSSIAN BORSCHT

Serves about 12 people a very hearty bowl

This recipe is from Father John, a Russian Orthodox priest whose parish is in Simpson, Pennsylvania. He and Father David, who entertained
us, are great friends, and it was just hilarious listening to the two priests
humorously kid Craig, my assistant. They kept trying to convert him!
Craig could learn a lot from the priests about theology, and we both
learned a great deal about Russian cooking. This recipe is from Father
John, and it is just about the best soup imaginable.

3 tablespoons olive oil

3 cloves garlic, peeled and
chopped

1 pound lamb stew meat,
chopped into ½-inch
pieces

1 medium yellow onion,
peeled and chopped

1¼ pounds green cabbage,
cored and chopped

1½ pounds ripe tomatoes,
diced

2 pounds red beets, peeled
and diced (Save the beet
greens and rinse well!!)

3½ quarts Beef Stock (page
78) or use canned

¼ cup red wine vinegar

2 bay leaves

Juice of ½ lemon

1 teaspoon salt

½ teaspoon freshly ground
black pepper

GARNISH

1 pint sour cream

1 bunch of fresh dill

Heat a 12-quart heavy stockpot and add the oil, garlic, and lamb. Brown
the lamb and add the onion. Sauté until the onion is tender, and then add

the cabbage, tomato, beets, Beef Stock, vinegar, bay leaves, lemon juice, salt, and pepper. Bring to a boil, then turn down to a simmer. Cook covered for 2 hours. Chop the reserved beet greens, add to the soup, and simmer for 15 more minutes. Add additional salt and pepper to taste.

Dish the soup into bowls and pass the garnishes to each guest. A good tablespoon or 2 of sour cream is placed in each bowl with a bit of fresh dill on top. Heaven!

DILL AND ONION BREAD

Makes 2 large loaves

My Russian immigrant grandma friend, Mrs. Nedzel, gave me this recipe. It is rich with memories of her homeland and rich with flavor for the New World.

Please get into making your own bread. *No* bakery shop is going to give you something of this quality! It is easy if you have a heavy-duty mixer. And you can imagine the bread that was cooked by the first-generation immigrants.

- 2 envelopes quick-rising yeast
- ½ cup warm water (105°)
- 2 tablespoons melted butter
- 4 tablespoons sugar
- 2 cups warmed small-curd creamed cottage cheese (Put it in the microwave for a moment, just to take the chill off it. It must not be hot.)

- 2 tablespoons dried minced onion flakes
- 2 tablespoons dried dill, or 4 tablespoons finely chopped fresh dill
- ½ teaspoon baking soda
- 2 teaspoons salt
- 2 eggs
- 4½–5 cups all-purpose flour (See Hint, page 423.)

FOR BAKING

Cornmeal for the baking sheets

1 egg yolk, beaten with 2 tablespoons water

Dissolve the yeast in the warm water (105°). Combine the yeast and water with all the ingredients except the flour and mix well in a heavy-duty electric mixer fitted with the batter blade. Add 2 cups of the flour and blend well. Change to the dough hook on your machine, and mix in the remaining flour. Add the last ½ cup of flour only if you feel that the dough is too wet and it will not pull away from the sides of the bowl after kneading it for about 10 minutes. If you do not have a heavy-duty electric mixer, like a KitchenAid, you must knead in the last 2½ to 3 cups of flour by hand.

Place the dough on a plastic countertop and cover it with a large stainless-steel bowl. Let the dough rise until double in bulk; punch down and let rise again. Finally, knead the dough again until it is smooth and elastic. Shape into 2 loaves and place on baking sheets sprinkled with cornmeal. Let the loaves rise until they double in size. Paint with the diluted egg yolk. Bake in preheated 350° oven for 45 to 50 minutes, or until golden. The bottoms will sound hollow when tapped with your finger.

RUSSIAN ROUND BREAD

Makes 1 large loaf

This is another great recipe from Father John, my Russian Orthodox priest friend in Pennsylvania. Any man who can cook bread like this certainly can be trusted as a priest! It is easy and delicious.

2 cups warm milk (105°)	2 packages quick-rising
½ cup sugar	yeast
2 teaspoons salt	7½ cups all-purpose flour
	(See Hint, page 423.)

WASH

1 egg beaten with 1
tablespoon water

In the bowl of an electric mixer, mix the warm milk, sugar, salt, and yeast. Stir until dissolved. Using a heavy-duty mixing machine fitted with the batter blade, add 3 cups of the flour to the liquid and beat well. Beat in the eggs and the melted shortening. Beat well again. Attach the dough hook and knead in the remaining flour until the dough is smooth and elastic, about 10 minutes. If doing the whole process by hand, simply pour yourself a glass of dry sherry and be prepared to knead for a while. Good bread cannot be hurried.

Place the dough on a plastic countertop and cover it with a stainless-steel bowl. Allow to rise until double in bulk, about 1 hour, punch down and allow to rise again, until double in bulk.

Punch the dough down again and knead for a moment. Remove one-fourth of the dough and set it aside. Mold the large piece of dough into a ball and place it in a well-oiled round metal baking pot such as a 4- to 5-quart black cast-iron kettle or a Le Creuset pot. Be sure to oil the sides of the pot as well as the bottom. Push the dough down just a bit so that when it rises it will fill the bottom of the pot.

Divide the remaining piece of dough into three parts and roll each into a long snake, about 18 inches long. Braid the three pieces together. Place the braid in a circle on the top of the loaf, and brush the braid and loaf with the beaten egg mixture. (See the illustration.)

Allow the loaf to rise until double in bulk, and bake in a preheated 350° oven for about 55 minutes, or until the loaf is golden brown. Allow the pot to cool for a few minutes before attempting to remove the bread. Cool on a wire rack.

HINT: TO MEASURE FLOUR, simply scoop the metal measuring cup to overflowing in the flour and then tap on the edges of the cup with a table knife. This is to remove excess air and bubbles. Level off the cup with the back of the table knife and go on with the recipe. All bread recipes in this book use this method of measurement.

PAGACH

Makes 1 large loaf, enough for 8 servings

This recipe certainly points to the cleverness of the cooks from the Ukraine. The dish is a bread and potato or cabbage pie. That's it; no meat at all. The results are unusually delicious.

THE DOUGH

2½–3 cups all-purpose flour (See Hint, page 423.)

1 cup warm water (105°)

1 package quick-rising yeast

½ teaspoon salt

TOPPING

Salad oil

Additional salt or garlic salt

Dissolve the yeast in the warm water (105°). Add the salt and 2½ cups flour. Knead until smooth, adding more flour as needed if the dough is still too sticky. Place the dough on a plastic countertop and cover it with a stainless-steel bowl. Allow it to rise until double in bulk. Meanwhile, make the filling (recipes follow).

Punch down the dough. Divide it into 2 parts. Roll the dough out into a rectangle, 18 inches long by 12 inches wide. Place the filling on one side of the rectangle, being careful to leave a margin of about 2 inches from the edges. Fold the other half of the dough over the filling so that you now have a turnover, 9 inches by 12 inches. Pat the top of the dough down lightly into the filling. Carefully pinch the edges together. Spread the salad oil on top and sprinkle generously with the salt or garlic salt. Place on a greased baking sheet. Let rise until double in bulk. Bake in a preheated 400° oven for 30 minutes, or until golden brown.

PAGACH AND CHEESE POTATO FILLING

Boil peeled potatoes, about 1½ pounds, drain and mash with a little butter and milk. Add grated sharp Cheddar cheese to the potatoes and cool (the more cheese, the tastier). Taste for salt and black pepper. This is a great filling for Pierogi (page 370) or Pagach.

PAGACH CABBAGE FILLING (Sweet Cabbage Filling)

Cook 1 large peeled and sliced onion in ½ to ¾ cup oil until soft. Add shredded green cabbage (medium head) and salt and freshly ground black pepper to taste. Cover and cook until the cabbage is soft. Drain the excess oil. This makes a good filling for Pagach or Haluski (page 417).

THE
SAUDI ARABIAN
IMMIGRANTS

SAUDI ARABIA

While there are relatively few Saudi Arabians living in this country we must admit that they have had a great impact on American culture. The lives of all Americans and those of the Saudi Arabians have become entangled due to a liquid necessary to Western life . . . oil.

Since Saudi Arabia is so rich in fossil fuels, the ruling family, the House of Saud, is one of the richest families the world has ever seen. Currently more than ten million barrels of oil are produced daily, thus generating a *daily* income of more than $315 million. This nation is also part of an ancient culture, the first Arabs being mentioned around 1000 B.C., and the ruling family continues to take care of its land and its subjects according to practices that date back to the beginning.

The rule of the land is placed in the hands of the king. There is no congress or legislature. One day a week subjects are allowed to bring practical and legal problems before the king, and he alone makes the decisions. The Saudi princes and other high officials may also conduct such hearings. The only other law that is recognized is, of course, the Law of Islam, and that law is with you at all times. Before eating, for instance, you must always say, "In the name of Allah." After eating you say, "Thanks be to Allah." Always.

In earlier days the Bedouin tribesmen were all nomadic, which meant that they shared all things, including their normal diet of dates and camel's milk. The rule of hospitality, which was common on the desert, stemmed from the fact that water and food meant life and therefore were to be shared with all, even one's enemies. Thus hospitality was elevated to a supreme virtue.

The history of this desert people is fascinating. They trace their language and lineage back to Noah and Abraham. During the 1500s the Turks seized the area and it was not until 1916 that they were expelled from Arabia. That was the time of the colorful Englishman who was called Lawrence of Arabia. In 1932 the Saud family established the Kingdom of Saudi Arabia and a great change came over the land. Most Westerners have forgotten the impoverished state that existed in Arabia in the year of the establishment of the Saudi nation. Things were so bad that the minister of the treasury kept the nation's money in an old tin box under his bed! But in 1938 oil was discovered and the life of the people changed, indeed, it changed very much.

I can remember Saudi Arabian students who enrolled in the University of Puget Sound when I was chaplain there. They were all somehow related to the royal family and money seemed to be no problem whatsoever. What a difference from the days when the nation's cash was kept in a box.

We should note that while we are influenced every day by this ancient culture, the influence has not come primarily through immigrants. Our English language is filled with Arabic terms such as alcohol, alcove, algebra, cotton, giraffe, lime, mummy, sherbet, sofa, sugar, sash, monsoon, and who knows what else. And some ten thousand Arabian students come here to study each year.

The food that is enjoyed in the Saudi Arabian home can be found in this land as well. We must thank them for coffee, yogurt, bulgur wheat, and wonderful desert breads, including pita. The meal is a communal one, and the table—or in this culture, the floor or rug—is the proper place to celebrate and discuss all things.

The following recipes will form a fine meal and none are complex. You will note the preference for stuffed vegetables and grains and legumes and sesame. I adore this form of food. And don't forget to say "In the name of God" when you begin the meal and "Thanks be to God" when you end the feast.

HOMEMADE YOGURT

Makes 4 quarts

The home of yogurt is the desert, as it is the home of wine, bread, and cheese. Commercial yogurt isn't tangy enough for me, so I offer the following suggestions for making your own authentic variety. Homemade yogurt is much cheaper, and you can control the tartness.

EQUIPMENT NEEDED:

6-quart stainless-steel kettle

Cheese or yeast thermometer (Needs to go from about 100° to 220°.) An instant-response meat thermometer (page 31) will do fine.

4 quarts fresh whole milk (Skimmed may be used.)

Heat diffuser or flame tamer (page 24)

4 1-quart wide-mouthed canning jars, with lids, sterilized

Electric heating pad

Yogurt starter (Health food stores can provide you with a Bulgarian yogurt starter. I prefer that kind.)

Place the milk in a large stainless-steel pot and gently heat to 180°, using the flame tamer and the thermometer. Remove from the heat and cool the milk to 115°. Have all other equipment ready as this temperature is important. Have the jars ready. Have the heating pad set at low heat on the counter. Use a glass 2-cup measuring cup and remove 1 cup of the milk from the pan. Stir about 1 tablespoon of the yogurt starter into the milk. Stir this mixture into the milk in the pot. Stir well so that you will produce a smooth yogurt. Quickly fill and seal the jars and then place all four on the heating pad. Cover with a large bath towel so that the jars stay warm for the night. After 8 hours, you will have a thick and usable yogurt. If you let it sit longer, however, up to 16 hours, you will have a much more tangy yogurt. Refrigerate.

NOTE: When you make your next batch of yogurt, you will not need a powdered starter. Remember to leave 2 cups of yogurt from the previous batch. Stir this into the 115° milk as your starter. Of course you will need to heat only 3 quarts plus 2 cups of milk. You can keep making your own yogurt like this forever!

BABA GHANOUSH WITH
ACORN SQUASH

Serves 6 as an appetizer

Baba Ghanoush is a rich creamy paste, a combination of two strong flavors: roasted eggplant and tahini sharpened by lemon and garlic. I had always assumed it could be made with eggplant, and eggplant alone. Leave it to a second-generation American Arab to teach me new tricks. Vicki Tamoush, a gorgeous woman of Arabian descent, who lives in Los Angeles, prepared this recipe for me. I tell you, it set me free to re-create this dish with almost any kind of squash or heavy vegetable.

1 1½-pounds acorn squash	Juice of ½ lemon, or more to taste
2 tablespoons olive oil	
1 clove garlic, peeled and crushed, or more to taste	2 tablespoons tahini (sesame paste) (page 47)
	Salt to taste

GARNISH

Olive oil   Chopped parsley

Cut the squash in half and remove the seeds. Brush with the olive oil and bake, uncovered, at 325° for 1½ hours, or until very tender. You want the pulp to brown a bit.

Allow to cool and dig out the pulp with a metal soup spoon. Discard the skins.

Place the meat in a mixing bowl and add the remaining ingredients, except the garnishes. Mix well with a wooden spoon. Place on a plate and top with the garnishes.

This is best served with pita bread or French or Italian bread.

ARABIAN BEAN SALAD

(Ful Madammas)

Serves 4 as a salad

This is another of Vicki Tamoush's recipes. She feeds me so well and has a very creative twist to the way she handles these traditional dishes from the desert.

1 cup dried *ful,* small-size bean (page 40), rinsed and drained

8 cups water

1 medium ripe tomato, chopped

1 clove garlic, peeled and crushed

¼ cup chopped parsley

1 cup peeled and thinly sliced yellow onion

DRESSING

½ cup olive oil

Juice of 1 lemon

Salt and freshly ground black pepper to taste

Place the beans (*ful*) in a medium pot and add 4 cups of water. Bring to a boil, turn off the heat, and let stand 1 hour, covered. Drain.

Return the *ful* to the pot and add 4 cups of fresh water. Bring to a boil, covered, and reduce to a simmer. Cook 15 minutes or until the beans are tender. Drain.

Mix the beans with the tomato, garlic, parsley, and onion. Prepare the dressing and toss with the vegetables. Chill before serving.

FRAYKEE WITH PINE NUTS

(Fried Coarse Bulgur)

Serves 4 as a starch dish

My Arabian friend Vicki Tamoush was somewhat surprised that I didn't know what fraykee was. Vicki explained that it is green wheat that is cut and processed just as in bulgur wheat . . . but it is toasted before it is used. The result is a delicious pilaf. You can find fraykee in many Middle Eastern stores, or you can do as I have done: Substitute bulgur and toast it before using it in the recipe.

1 cup coarse bulgur (page 38)	Pinch of ground cinnamon
2 cups cold water	Salt to taste

GARNISH

¼ cup pine nuts, pan-toasted in 2 tablespoons butter

Heat a dry wok or heavy frying pan and stir the bulgur wheat until toasty and fragrant, just a few minutes.

In a 2-quart covered pot place the bulgur, water, cinnamon, and salt. Bring to a boil with the lid off. Reduce heat and simmer, covered for minutes. Turn off the heat. Allow to sit in the pot for 5 minutes before removing the lid.

Serve in a large bowl, topped with the toasted pine nuts.

LENTILS AND RICE

(Mujadarra)

Serves 8

Here is a modern version of a very old dish. Lentils and rice have been common among desert communities for generations, and the dish varies with every family. This recipe is easy to prepare and surprisingly flavorful.

4 medium yellow onions, peeled

3 tablespoons olive oil

1 cup lentils

3½ cups cold water

1 cup long-grain rice

2 teaspoons salt

Dice 3 of the onions. Heat a large frying pan and add 2 tablespoons of the olive oil and the diced onions. Sauté until quite brown and set aside. In a 4-quart covered pot place the lentils and water. Bring to a boil, covered, and then turn down to a simmer. Cook for 15 minutes.

Add the cooked onion to the lentils, along with the rice and salt.

Cover and simmer 20 minutes until rice and lentils are soft. If a bit of water remains unabsorbed, remove from heat and let stand 5 minutes and it will soak in.

Slice the remaining onion into rings. Heat the frying pan again and sauté the rings in the remaining olive oil.

To serve, top the lentils with the sautéed onion rings. Accompany with plain yogurt and a lemony green salad, with tomato wedges on the side.

SESAME CANDY

This is an Old World candy that will be very popular with your children, and it contains no processed sugar. Although it takes some time to make, the effort is worth it. In the Old World, Grandma didn't mind, but that's why we should make it today. *Do not* make this candy on a hot or humid day.

3 cups honey

2 cups sesame seeds

Peanut oil

In a deep, medium-size saucepan slowly heat honey over medium-low heat, using a heat diffuser (page 24), to the hard-crack stage (about

305° to 310° on a candy thermometer). Stir down often to prevent boiling over, about 45 minutes. Stir in sesame seeds. Set aside for a few minutes to cool slightly.

Lightly grease a 9 × 13-inch baking sheet with peanut oil. Do not use waxed paper. Pour honey mixture onto it. Set baking sheet on a cooling rack. When cooled, but not hard, score into diamond shapes. When cooled completely, remove candy and separate into pieces.

WARNING: Be sure to alert friends and family to the danger of burning themselves on the extremely hot caramelized sugar.

TAHINI SALAD

Serves 4

The sesame seed appears in most of the desert cultures, and it is highly prized in China as well. During biblical times the oil from the seed was commonly used in cooking. A paste was ground from the roasted seeds and used as a flavoring in many dishes, sometimes as a meat substitute. Arabic immigrants have not ceased using this wonderful food product, and my friend Vicki has created a salad that is tasty and refreshing.

½ cup Homemade Yogurt (page 428) or yogurt from the market

2 tablespoons tahini (sesame paste) (page 47)

1 medium tomato, chopped

1 cucumber, peeled and chopped

1 green bell pepper, cored, seeded, and chopped

⅔ cup finely chopped parsley

Salt to taste

Gently mix the yogurt and tahini, then fold in the vegetables, along with the parsley and salt. Serve with red meat or fish dishes.

ARABIAN STUFFED VEGETABLES

(Hashwe)

Serves 4

Everyone in the Middle East loves stuffed vegetables. I believe they are a desert invention. This recipe, another from my friend Vicki Tamoush, is not difficult to prepare and the results are redolent of the Arabian Nights!

2 cups water

1 cup long-grain rice

THE STUFFING

½ pound lamb, finely ground

½ pound beef, finely ground

Pinch of ground cinnamon

¼ teaspoon freshly grated nutmeg

¾ teaspoon ground allspice

Salt and freshly ground pepper to taste

3 tablespoons butter, melted

VEGETABLES FOR STUFFING

Choose any of the following or any combination. The mixture will fill:

4 medium tomatoes, tops cut off and hollowed for stuffing *or*

6 medium zucchini, cut into 3-inch lengths, hollowed out with a corer, placed on end for stuffing *or*

4 medium bell peppers, tops cut off and cored and seeded for stuffing

COOKING SAUCE

½ cup water

¼ cup canned tomato sauce

Juice of 1 lemon

In a 2-quart covered saucepan bring 2 cups of water to boil. Add the rice, return to the boil, cover, and turn off the heat. Let stand for 5 minutes. Drain and cool before proceeding with the recipe.

Mix cooked rice thoroughly with the stuffing ingredients.

Fill the vegetables loosely with the rice mixture. It will expand during cooking, so do not pack; leave room at the top or the sides. Arrange the vegetables in a covered, deep skillet. Simmer, covered, along with the water, tomato sauce, and lemon juice on low flame (30 minutes for bell peppers and zucchini; 20 minutes for tomatoes). Check water to see that it is not evaporating. If it gets low, add more hot water.

VARIATION

Use the same Hashwe to stuff a chicken or a turkey. Or wrap in partially cooked fresh grape leaves, Swiss chard, cabbage, or slices of eggplant. Cloves of garlic added to the cooking liquid impart authentic flavor.

Serve accompanied with Leban Sauce (below), if desired.

LEBAN SAUCE

Makes 3 cups

I find that commercial yogurt is a bit flat. I suggest you make your own for this common desert sauce; your Homemade Yogurt will give the dish a wonderful tartness. If you need to use commercial yogurt, let it sit out on the counter overnight in order to increase its flavor. No, it will not sour. My friend Vicki even gives stirring instructions for this one.

3 cups Homemade Yogurt (page 428) or yogurt from the market

2 tablespoons cornstarch

1 large clove garlic, peeled and crushed

Salt to taste

Heat the yogurt in a 2-quart saucepan over low flame, always stirring in the same direction, using a wire whisk, until smooth. Keep stirring for 5 minutes or more. Place a couple of tablespoons of the yogurt in a glass, and dissolve 2 tablespoons of cornstarch in it. Add the mixture back to the yogurt. Keep stirring. Add the garlic and salt to taste. You may sauté the garlic first for slightly more flavor. Serve over stuffed squash or any stuffed vegetable.

FALAFEL

Makes about 24 patties, enough for 6 sandwiches

This dish is a favorite among Arab immigrants. I remember eating it with Arab students years ago when I was a college chaplain. They often made it from scratch, but more often bought a prepared mix. I developed my own recipe, which has a much brighter flavor than those mixes. Falafel or *ta'amia* are patties made from dried beans, splendidly spiced, deep-fried, and then eaten as a snack. These are traditionally served as a meat substitute and make a great sandwich. Fill pita bread with Falafel, sliced tomatoes, sliced onion, lettuce, and yogurt. Delicious!

1 cup dried garbanzo beans, soaked in water to cover overnight and drained

1 cup dried shelled fava beans, soaked overnight and drained (page 39)

½ cup peeled and finely chopped yellow onions

3 cloves garlic, peeled and crushed

1 cup water

½ cup sesame seeds

½ cup garbanzo flour (page 40)

¼ cup fine bulgur (page 38)

¼ cup finely chopped parsley

¾ tablespoon salt

2 teaspoons ground cumin

2 teaspoons ground coriander

2 teaspoons baking powder

½ teaspoon cayenne pepper

¼ teaspoon freshly ground black pepper

Oil for deep-frying

Run the drained garbanzo beans and fava beans through the fine blade on your meat grinder or in your food processor. Blend in all the remaining ingredients and let the mixture stand for 1 hour. Form into little patties ⅓ inch thick and 1½ inches round. Or, you can form them into balls the size of walnuts. Deep-fry in 375° oil until toasty brown and crunchy on the outside, about 4 minutes.

THE SCOTTISH
IMMIGRANTS

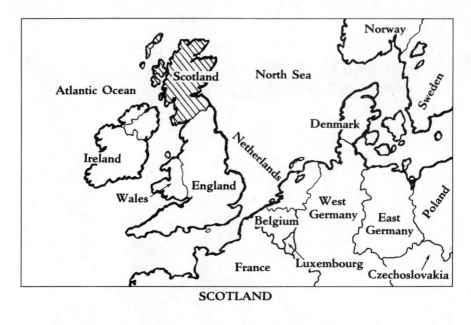

SCOTLAND

The fact that a map of the United States shows eight Aberdeens; eight Edinburghs, eight Glasgows, eight Scotlands, ten Campbells, sixteen Camerons, nine Douglases, thirty Crawfords, and more than a hundred places whose names begin with "Mac" or "Mc" attests to the presence of over ten million Americans of Scottish ancestry. The first Scottish settlers came in the earliest colonial days and they have been coming ever since.

The first Scots entered their land from Ireland during the Bronze Age, making the water passage in boats made of branches plastered with clay. The Roman invasion of southern Britain in A.D. 55 encouraged the tribes of Caledonia to unite in an effort to drive back the invaders. These tribes fought so fiercely that the Romans were forced to construct walls to hold them back (Hadrian's Wall is the best remembered). The Romans called the people of Caledonia the Picti or Picts. This word means "painted people" and is thought to indicate that like certain Native American tribes, they painted or tattooed themselves. These Pictish tribes were the forerunners of the famous clans of Scotland.

The thirteenth to the fifteenth centuries saw a continued effort to maintain a Scotland independent of England. After many battles James IV of Scotland was defeated by the English at the Battle of Flodden. From that point on, Scotland came more and more under the influence of England, a process that led to the Union of the Crowns in 1603.

Following the Union of the Crowns, it took many years for all the clan chiefs to swear allegiance to the British monarch. The Macdonalds of Glencoe delayed so long that they missed the deadline: the last day of 1691. In February of 1692 the Campbell clan came calling on the Macdonalds. It seemed they came in friendship and indeed they allowed themselves to be wined and dined for twelve days and twelve nights. On that twelfth night, however, in the earliest hours of the morning, the Campbells rose up and slaughtered the sleeping Macdonalds, killing men, women, and children—the Massacre of Glencoe.

My dear friend Dr. William Campbell translated the Scottish national motto for me. The National emblem is the prickly thistle and it helps explain the motto. "Nemo Me Impune Lacessit" means "No one bothers me without being hurt!"

Scottish immigrants came to America at the time of the thirteen colonies and they have been coming ever since. From 1921 to 1931 there was severe economic depression in Scotland and some 391,000 came from the Land of the Highlands to join us here. Today there are over ten million Scottish Americans in this country. Incidentally, Alexander Graham Bell, the inventor of the telephone, was a Scottish immigrant.

Scottish cooking has been maligned in America . . . and it should not have been. Oh, it is true that the early Scottish immigrants lived on a lean and frugal diet but the history of the cuisine shows that they should not bow to the English table, not in the least. Cock-a-leekie, Cullen Skink, and Finnan Haddie will make my point. I have worked hard to make even the traditional Haggis most enjoyable, and the Scottish Broth and Scottish Shortbread will win you over for sure. So, get out the tartans, bring on the pipers, and let us raise a glass to Robbie Burns!

COCK-A-LEEKIE

Serves 5–6

The kids will wonder about you when you tell them the name of this very traditional Scottish soup. The name simply refers to chicken and leeks. However, it was no small matter to the immigrant Scottish grandmas who offered this dish to their now-American households. The soup is delicious, and it certainly stretches a chicken. The blending of beef and chicken will surprise you.

1 3½-pound frying chicken, cut into 8 serving pieces

1 pound beef shanks, sawed into 1-inch cubes

6 cups Chicken Stock (page 74) or use canned

3 slices thick-cut bacon, diced

1 tablespoon dried thyme, whole

1 bay leaf

¾ cup pearl barley

1½ cups rinsed and chopped leeks (white part only)

Salt and freshly ground black pepper to taste

GARNISH

2 tablespoons chopped parsley

Heat an 8-quart stove-top casserole and bring all ingredients, except the barley, leeks, salt, pepper, and parsley, to a boil. Cover and simmer 30 minutes.

In the meantime, boil the barley in 1½ cups water for 10 minutes. Drain and set aside.

Remove the chicken from the pot, cool, and debone. Set the chicken aside. Add the leeks to the pot, along with the drained barley, and simmer for 15 minutes. Remove the beef shank and debone. Chop the meat coarsely, and add the beef and deboned chicken to the pot, restore the heat, and simmer, covered, for 5 minutes.

Add salt and pepper to taste. Garnish with the parsley and serve.

CULLEN SKINK

Serves 6

Another wonderful Scottish name that will wow the kids. The term *skink* comes from the Gaelic and means "essence." I think it is also the background of our word "stink." This soup, however, is a joy.

1 pound smoked haddock (Finnan Haddie, page 444) (Find it frozen in your fish store.)

1 quart cold water

1 medium yellow onion, peeled and diced

3 cups milk

2¼ cups cooked mashed potatoes

1 tablespoon butter

Salt and freshly ground black pepper to taste

Tiny pinch of ground mace

GARNISH

Butter

Chopped parsley

Place the fish in a 4-quart shallow pan along with 1 quart of water. Bring to a boil and reduce the heat. Simmer, partly covered, for 10 minutes. Remove the cod, reserving the broth, and allow it to cool. Debone and flake the fish. Return it to the pan. Add the onion, cover, and simmer for 20 minutes.

In a small saucepan heat the milk to a boil and add to the broth and flaked fish. Simmer 4 minutes, partly covered.

Stir in the remaining ingredients, except the garnish, and bring to serving temperature. Salt and pepper to taste. Top with the butter and parsley and serve hot.

HAGGIS

**Makes 3 Haggis, enough for 8–10 if the guests are Scottish.
Enough for 50 if your guests are Norwegian!**

It is truly amazing how a food product born in the midst of utter necessity has come to be a national classic. We see this happening in almost every culture. Our immigrant ancestors brought such dishes, created in destitution, with them to the New World, not because they had to but because they wanted to. These recipes are necessary to our collective memory, to a vision of where we have been and where we have come from. Such a one is Haggis.

Traditionally, a Haggis is made from the lung, liver, and heart of the sheep. These are mixed with oatmeal and a few spices and stuffed into the sheep's stomach. After being boiled, the Haggis is brought to the table with a great deal of ceremony. A piper ushers in the Haggis and all raise a glass of Scotch whisky and "brrreath a prrayerr for the soul of Rrrobbie Burrrns!" It is then served with "neeps and nips," mashed turnips and nips of whiskey. I think you have to drink a lot of Scotch before you can truly enjoy this dish. But a party of Scots without a Haggis is simply not heard of.

I prepared this recipe for the Medinah Highlander Pipe and Drum Band of Chicago. They piped the Haggis into the dining room, the boiled sheep's stomach being carried on a silver tray by Craig, my assistant. The Pipe and Drum Major cut the Haggis in the sign of the Cross and the party began. These pipers ate everything in sight . . . so I am willing to offer you *my* version of Haggis.

1 pound beef heart, cut into 2-inch-wide strips	1½ cups peeled and finely chopped yellow onion
1 pound beef liver	4 tablespoons Scotch whisky
½ pound lamb stew meat, cut in 1-inch pieces	2 cups toasted oatmeal (toasted on a cookie sheet in a 375° oven for 10 minutes)

SEASONINGS

2 teaspoons salt	½ teaspoon dried rosemary
½ teaspoon freshly ground black pepper	¼ teaspoon freshly grated nutmeg
1 teaspoon dried thyme, whole	

THE CASING

3 beef caps (Talk to a sausage shop about these.)

1 cup distilled white vinegar

½ tablespoon salt for soaking

Place the beef heart in a 4-quart covered pot and just cover with cold water. Simmer, covered, for 1 hour and 10 minutes. Add the beef liver and lamb stew meat, and cover and simmer for 20 minutes. Remove the contents of the pot and cool. Reserve 1 cup of the liquid. Grind everything coarsely.

In a large bowl mix all the ingredients, except for the beef caps, vinegar, and salt for soaking. Mix well and set aside.

Rinse the beef caps in cold water. Turn them inside out and soak them in 2 quarts of cold water with the salt and vinegar for ½ hour. Drain them and rinse very well, inside and out.

Divide the meat mixture into three parts. Fill the beef caps with the meat mixture and tie the ends off with string. Two will have to be tied on just one end, but the third piece will be tied on both ends. Prick the Haggis all over with corn holders or a sharp fork. Place in a steamer and steam for 1 hour and 20 minutes.

Serve the Haggis, sliced, with beef or lamb gravy.

FINNAN HADDIE

Serves 3–4

Finnan Haddie is the proper name for a wonderful smoked haddock, or cod, that comes from Scotland. It is basic to Scottish cuisine and certainly to Scots history, since it is a method of preserving food for the winter. The word "haddie" is the Scottish name for haddock and "finnan" refers to Findon, the region where this great method of smoking fish originates. Real Finnan Haddie from Scotland can be purchased frozen from any good fishmonger. It is not expensive, and it is much more lightly smoked than regular smoked cod.

2 tablespoons butter

1 medium yellow onion, peeled and thinly sliced

1 pound smoked haddock (Finnan Haddie), skinless, cut into small serving pieces

Freshly ground black pepper to taste

1 tablespoon cornstarch

1 cup half-and-half

GARNISH

Chopped parsley

Heat a large covered frying pan and add the butter and onion. Sauté for a few minutes and add the smoked fish, along with the pepper. Cover and cook for 5 minutes. Mix the cornstarch with ¼ cup of the half-and-half. Blend with the remaining half-and-half, and stir into the frying pan. Simmer gently while the sauce thickens, and then cook the fish until very tender, about 10 more minutes. Garnish with the chopped parsley and serve.

SCOTTISH BROTH

Serves 6–8

When I was very young I would always request Campbell's Scotch Broth when I was sick. My mother always had some in the house. However, now that I know what the real thing tastes like, I cannot go back to the can. This soup is easy to prepare and wonderful on a cold winter night. If someone will play the bagpipes for you while you cook, so much the better.

1 pound lamb breast, cut into ½-inch-wide strips (Use a cleaver. Do not remove bones.)

1 pound lamb steak, diced (Save the bone for the pot.)

½ cup pearl barley

2 bay leaves

1 teaspoon dried thyme, whole

2 tablespoons chopped parsley

4 tablespoons butter

3 carrots, diced

1 cup peeled and diced turnips

2 medium yellow onions, peeled and diced

2 medium leeks (white parts only), rinsed and chopped

2 stalks celery, chopped

1 cup finely chopped green cabbage

Salt and freshly ground black pepper to taste

½ cup frozen peas

GARNISH

2 tablespoons chopped parsley

Place the lamb and bones in a 6-quart pot and add 2 quarts of water. Bring to a boil, reduce the heat, cover, and simmer for 20 minutes. Skim off any scum that appears.

In the meantime, boil the barley in 2 cups of water for 10 minutes, then drain and set aside.

Add the bay leaves, thyme, and parsley to the pot.

In a large frying pan melt the butter and sauté all of the vegetables, except the peas, until the onion is tender. Add the vegetables to the pot and simmer for 45 minutes, covered. Add the drained barley to the pot and cook, covered, for another 15 minutes. Add salt and pepper to taste, along with the peas. Bring to a boil and serve. Garnish with parsley.

BARLEY AND MUSHROOM CASSEROLE

Serves 6–8

This is another dish that shows the ingenuity of the Scottish cook. Barley is not expensive, and it swells to six times its size, not twice, like rice. By itself it is tasty, but in this dish it becomes a joy. A great replacement for potatoes at your house.

- 6 tablespoons butter
- 2 cloves garlic, peeled and minced
- 2 yellow onions, peeled and minced
- 1 pound mushrooms, thinly sliced
- 1 cup pearl barley
- ½ tablespoon dried basil
- 3 cups Chicken Stock (page 74) or use canned
- Salt and freshly ground black pepper to taste
- ¼ cup chopped parsley

Preheat the oven to 375°.

Melt the butter in a 2-quart stove-top covered casserole. Add the garlic and onion and sauté over moderately low heat until onion is translucent, about 5 minutes.

Add the mushrooms and sauté over moderate heat until mushrooms are golden, about 5 minutes.

Add the barley and basil to the mushroom mixture, and toss lightly, then pour in the Chicken Stock and season to taste with salt and pepper.

Slowly bring the casserole to a boil, then remove it from the heat. Cover the casserole and bake in the oven until the barley is tender, about 45 to 50 minutes.

Before serving, add the chopped parsley and toss gently. Serve piping hot.

SCOTTISH EGGS

Makes 8 eggs

I do not like the remark about the Scots being cheap. They are not cheap, they are *frugal*. They waste nothing, a trait that Americans should certainly admire. In this dish a fine breakfast or lunch is prepared from sausage and eggs, but this old favorite raises the mixture to new heights. You must try this one.

8 hard-cooked eggs, peeled, at room temperature

¼ cup all-purpose flour (See Hint, page 423.)

1½ pounds bulk pork sausage

1 cup dry bread crumbs

½ teaspoon ground sage

¼ teaspoon salt

2 eggs, beaten

6–8 cups peanut oil for deep-frying

Coat each hard-cooked egg with flour. Divide the sausage into 8 equal parts. Make a patty out of each bit of sausage, and use it to coat each egg completely. Mix the bread crumbs, sage, and salt. Dip the sausage-coated eggs into the beaten eggs; roll in bread-crumb mixture.

Heat the oil to 375° for deep-frying. Deep-fry the eggs, 4 at a time, 7 minutes' minimum. Drain. Serve hot or cold.

SHORTBREAD

This is rich, and I mean rich! Real Scottish shortbread is a wonderful thing, and you certainly cannot get this flavor from a tinned product, even if it is from Scotland. Try making your own. It is great.

2 cups all-purpose flour   ½ pound butter, softened
   (See Hint, page 423.)

1 heaping tablespoon
   cornstarch

½ cup sugar

Place all of the dry ingredients in a mixing bowl and blend well. If you have a heavy-duty electric mixer, cut in the butter with the machine. If not, do it by hand with a pastry blender.

Knead the dough by hand for just a moment and form it into a circle ¾ inch thick on a nonstick baking sheet, and flute the edges. Prick the whole circle with a fork. Bake in a preheated 325° oven for ½ hour, or until it just begins to turn a light golden brown. Allow it to cool for a few minutes, and then remove it to a rack for the final cooling. When cool, the cookie can be cut, but the Scots simply break it up into pieces and serve it with tea. Wonderful!

NOTE: If you wish to form smaller cookies from this recipe, just remember to watch the baking time. Smaller cookies will cook more quickly.

THE SPANISH
IMMIGRANTS

SPAIN

Immigrants from Spain have totaled more than a quarter of a million since 1820. When one considers that Spain was the first European power to establish an empire in the New World and to impose its language, religion, and customs on the people there, it is surprising that we are not more aware of the descendants of those great explorers. During the sixteenth century they ruled the Western world, largely due to their power on the seas. Pedro Menéndez de Avilés entered Florida during this time and took twenty-five hundred Spanish with him up the rivers into the Carolinas. You can still find Spanish communities in these places. And under the Spanish flag Columbus claimed Puerto Rico and Jamaica. Later, the Spanish took on Mexico.

The Spanish heritage included the language, the Roman Catholic religion, and Spanish customs and architecture. One of the most blessed gifts was the wine that was necessary for the worship services of the Church. It was a Spanish priest who really got the California wine business going.

During the Spanish Civil War (1936–1939) a large group came to this country from Spain. Unlike many other immigrant groups, about 57 percent of all Spaniards who came to the United States between 1899 and 1952 either returned to Spain or moved on to another country, usually in Latin America. The group that arrived here following the civil war, however, included many intellectuals who stayed, such as philosopher George Santayana, cellist Pablo Casals, and biochemist Severo Ochoa, along with many literary figures.

The dishes that these Spanish immigrants brought to America remain very close to those you still find in Spain. The tortilla of the Spanish is not a fried corn or wheat pancake but an omelet, and the paellas of rice and seafood rank, in my estimation, among the great dishes of the world. So, chill the dry sherry and set out the tapas. A Spanish dinner party will be a delight!

CODFISH PIL PIL

(Dried Cod in Garlic Mayonnaise)

The Spanish, the Portuguese, and the Basques all love this dish. I admit that it might take some getting used to, since it is based on dried cod, a winter staple. However, I must include it because it kept a lot of our immigrant ancestors alive, and now their children eat it to remember their heritage. Use the recipe for Codfish Pil Pil found on page 87. It will tame any Spaniard.

SPANISH CHORIZO SAUSAGE

Makes 4½ pounds sausage

This wonderful sausage is important to the Spanish kitchen. Please do not confuse it with the stuff that is sold under this name in Mexican American markets. The meat that is used in the Mexican type of chorizo is generally worse than "trimmings," so you really are paying too much for too little. Find a good Latin market you can trust or make your own sausage and really enjoy it!

2½ pounds pork butt, cut into pieces

1 pound lean beef chuck, cut into pieces

1 pound fresh pork fatback, cut into pieces

1 cup boiling water

2 cloves garlic, peeled and chopped

½ tablespoon cayenne pepper

1 ounce large dried mild red chile pods, such as ancho, pasilla, or Anaheim (Mexican or Latino markets will have these. Weigh the peppers first and then stem and seed them.)

1½ tablespoons salt

2 tablespoons paprika

2 tablespoons red wine vinegar

Sausage casings for stuffing (page 45)

Grind the meats and fat coarsely. Mix together and refrigerate, covered.

Place the cleaned dried peppers in a stainless-steel bowl and soak them in 1 cup boiling water. Cover the bowl with a plate and allow them to soak for 1 hour.

Place the peppers, along with the soaking liquid, in a food processor, and add the garlic, cayenne, salt, paprika, and wine vinegar. Purée to a pulp and blend this mixture with the meat. Mix well. Allow to stand at room temperature for 1 hour and then stuff the mixture into casings (see

Hint below). Form the sausage into rings, as in Polish sausage, tie with string, and hang them in a cool, dry place for 2 days. It's best to make this sausage in the cooler months. I put mine on a wooden stick and hang them in a corner of the kitchen, then use an electric fan to dry them. After drying, place them in plastic bags in the refrigerator.

If you want, you can simply form the sausage into patties and fry them rather than using casings. I prefer using the casings.

HINT: ON STUFFING SAUSAGE. This job is really quite simple if you use a mixer such as a KitchenAid with a sausage-stuffing attachment. Or you can do it by hand with a sausage funnel. (See the illustration on page 30.) Most meat markets can supply you with the casings. Order "Polish sausage size," and they will know what you mean. Cut the casings into 3- or 4-foot lengths, and wash in fresh water, rinsing the insides by putting the casings directly on the end of the faucet. Drain well and stuff. Do not pack too much into each casing or the sausages will split while cooking. Remember to poke tiny holes in the sausages before cooking them. I use a corn-on-the-cob holder for this. Prick them well.

SPANISH CALDO GALLEGO

Makes about 3 quarts, or 12 servings

There are many versions of this wonderful soup, but its roots seem to be in Spain itself. It is a classic combination of beans, meats, and vegetables. One reading of the recipe will help you understand why our immigrant Spanish grandmothers made this often. It is delicious and cheap!

½ pound dried white beans, soaked in water overnight and drained

1 pound chicken thighs

½ pound Spanish Chorizo Sausage (page 452) or Mexican chorizo from a good market, cut into ½-inch pieces

½ pound smoked ham, cut into ½-inch dice

¼ pound salt pork, chopped

1 medium yellow onion, peeled and chopped

3 cloves garlic, peeled and crushed

2 teaspoons Worcestershire sauce

Few shots of Tabasco

2½ quarts water

In an 8-quart stockpot simmer all of the ingredients, covered, for 45 minutes, or until the chicken is tender. Remove the chicken from the pot. Debone the chicken, chop the meat, and reserve.

Add to the pot:

½ pound potatoes, peeled, quartered, and sliced

½ pound green cabbage, thinly sliced

2–3 cups kale (tough stems removed), thinly sliced

½ pound turnips, peeled, quartered, and sliced

Simmer, covered, for 25 minutes longer. Return the boned chicken to the pot and add:

Salt and freshly ground black pepper to taste

Simmer a few more minutes until all is hot, and serve. The soup keeps well for a few days in the refrigerator.

NOTE: Chopped fresh dill makes an excellent garnish for this dish.

TORTILLA OF POTATO AND ONIONS

Serves 4 as a light dinner, 8 as tapas

No, this is not a Mexican dish. In Mexico a tortilla is a fried cornmeal or flour pancake. In Spain a tortilla is an omelet, turned once in the pan, and then served in wedges like a pie. Any number of fillings can be used once you master the trick of turning the tortilla.

This dish is common in the tapas bars of Madrid. Our Spanish immigrant ancestors ate them often in the early days, and their descendants still do.

½ pound red-skinned potatoes, cooked but still firm, unpeeled and sliced

1 medium yellow onion, peeled and sliced

2 cloves garlic, peeled and chopped

3 tablespoons olive oil

6 eggs

Salt and freshly ground black pepper to taste

Heat a 10-inch SilverStone-lined frying pan and sauté the potatoes, onion, and garlic in the oil. Beat the eggs with a bit of salt and pepper and pour over the hot vegetables. Using a wooden spatula, raise the edge of the omelet so that the uncooked top can flow under the omelet. Cook for about 5 minutes on medium heat. Place a plate over the top of the pan and invert both plate and pan so that the omelet comes out upside down. Slide it back into the hot pan to cook the second side. Cook for about 2 more minutes.

PAELLA VALENCIA

Serves 6–8

The Spanish love this rice dish. Anything in the way of meat and sausages, seafood, and vegetables, can be added to it. The name "paella" simply refers to the big round pan in which the dish is cooked. This particular recipe is done in the style of Valencia, and it contains a little bit of everything. Since it is so versatile, you can understand why our immigrant ancestors brought it with them to the New World.

In Spain they use an Arborio-style rice for this classic dish. I much prefer Uncle Ben's Converted Rice. You can use either.

1 pound mussels, in the shell

1 pound small clams, in the shell

½ cup olive oil, or more if needed

2 pounds chicken thighs

½ pound boneless pork butt, cut into ½-inch cubes

2 yellow onions, peeled and sliced

2 cloves garlic, peeled and finely chopped or crushed

1 cup cubed smoked ham (½-inch cubes)

1 cup sliced Spanish Chorizo Sausage (page 452) or Mexican chorizo from a good market

1 red bell pepper, seeded, cored, and thinly sliced

2 cups Uncle Ben's Converted Rice

3 cups Chicken Stock (page 74) or use canned

⅛ teaspoon crushed saffron threads (page 52) (optional)

2 tablespoons Annatto Oil (page 134)

1 teaspoon paprika

Salt to taste

½ cup peas, defrosted if frozen

½ pound large shrimp, peeled

1 cup dry white wine

GARNISH

Lemon slices

With a paring knife or a pair of pliers trim or pull off the fuzzy beards from the mussels. Rinse the clams and mussels well and soak them in cold water for 1 hour. Drain, leaving any sand behind.

Heat a 15-inch round paella pan or a large frying pan. Add the ½ cup olive oil and brown the chicken until brown on all sides. Remove the chicken from the pan and set aside. Brown and cook the pork in the same way. Remove the pork to the chicken plate, leaving the oil in the pan.

Reheat the pan and add the onion, garlic, ham cubes, and chorizo slices. Sauté until the onion is clear and then add the red bell pepper. Cook for a moment and remove from the pan, leaving the oil behind.

Reheat the pan and add the rice. Stir over medium heat until the grains begin to color just a bit. You may need additional oil at this point. Now, add the reserved chicken and pork, along with the cooked vegetable mixture.

In a saucepan bring the Chicken Stock to a boil and add the optional saffron, the annatto oil, paprika, and salt. When ingredients are hot add to the paella pan or frying pan. Heat until all comes to a boil. Reduce the heat to medium and cook the dish, covered, rotating it now and then on the burner, for about 8 minutes. Stir in the wine. Add the shrimp, clams, and mussels to the pan, being sure to push the clams and mussels down into the rice, hinged sides down. Sprinkle the peas on top and continue to cook, covered, until the clams and mussels are open and the rice is just tender.

Garnish with the lemon slices and serve.

TAPAS

This is the highest form of "grazing" that I know. In Spain tapas bars sell drinks along with little dishes of everything you can imagine, all seasoned with lots of garlic and fine olive oil. These are not really recipes but simply suggestions that will get you going on making your own tapas table. Craig, my assistant, and I tasted all of the dishes below at the fabulous tapas bars in Madrid.

Place each of the following in small dishes and set up your own tapas bar. Your guests will need toothpicks to serve themselves on their own plates. Provide lots of good dry sherry.

Cheese slices marinated in garlic and olive oil

Mushrooms grilled with garlic and olive oil with thin ham slices. Prosciutto is the closest thing that you will find to a good Spanish ham unless you live near a Spanish deli that carries Serrano ham.

Pork steak in small chunks fried with garlic, oil, and salt

Pigs' ears, thinly sliced crosswise, fried in garlic and oil, salt and pepper, and parsley. Add a little broth to the pan and simmer covered until tender. Then add parsley garnish.

Mussels in tomato sauce with lots of garlic, olive oil, and parsley

Chorizo sausages, cooked in the oven, then sliced, and deep-fried

Shrimp fried in garlic and olive oil

"Papas a la machina," deep-fried sliced potatoes. All right, they are potato chips, but they are called a la machina because the machine they use cuts the spuds into little waffle-patterned slices. You can find such a slicer, called a mandoline, in a gourmet shop, or you can buy waffled potato chips. The Borner company of Germany makes this type of slicer, which you can find in many gourmet shops. Be sure to get the safety guard.

Olives

Anchovies in oil with bread for dipping

THE SWEDISH
IMMIGRANTS

SWEDEN

Modern-day Sweden is an affluent and prosperous nation. It is also an egalitarian nation (in 1984 a Swedish cabinet minister enjoyed a salary only twice as great as that of a factory worker), which through high taxes provides one of the most comprehensive systems of social services in the world.

Sweden is large—the fourth largest European nation—and richly endowed. The natural resources include some 96,000 lakes and thousands of rivers, enough water to feed Europe's largest softwood timber reserves. It is also a nation rich in mineral resources, especially iron. Centuries before Christ, amber—fossilized tree resin forty to sixty million years old—was gathered on the shores of the North and Baltic seas to be traded with Greece and Rome via a network of overland and river routes. Amber was regarded as a rare and wondrous substance and is still very much prized by the peoples of Lithuania and Latvia.

Sweden was and remains a place of beauty, but it was not seen in this way by most of the peoples of the ancient world. The Greeks and Romans regarded Sweden, and the rest of Scandinavia for that matter, as a cold and mysterious territory inhabited by "an unhappy race whom endless night invades" (Homer). The Greeks called the region Thule, meaning "the beyond," and today American soldiers speaking of the backcountry will still refer to it as the "thulies." Potential invaders were repelled by the remoteness of the area and the harshness of its climate. Consequently the people retain a homogeneous ethnic identity.

In the very early days Sweden was the land of two major tribes, the Svear (from which the country derives its name) and the Gotar (Goths). These people were great seamen and fishermen and for generations Sweden ruled the northern seas. In 1638 the nation decided to establish itself overseas and thus the Swedish Mercantile Company founded the colony of New Sweden in North America at the mouth of the Delaware River. It is believed that the Swedes and Finns of New Sweden introduced America to the technique of dovetailing used in building log houses.

Between 1850 and 1930 over 1.2 million Swedes immigrated to this country. America needed people to settle its vast frontier territories and to provide labor for developing industries. At the same time events in Sweden made the trip to the New World very desirable. Sweden had enjoyed a lengthy period of peace, the smallpox vaccine had been made available, and potato cultivation had been very successful. So population rose; indeed, the land became overpopulated, so the best a young man might find would be work as a hired hand on someone else's farm, without hope of advancement. Crops failed on the west coast several times during the nineteenth century, giving rise to the description of Sweden as "one great poorhouse." So, off to America. By 1910 one out of every five Swedes lived in America.

The Swedes who came to America tended to continue the occupations they had practiced in the old country. Farmers headed to the homestead states, ironworkers went to Massachusetts, miners and quarry workers found themselves in upper Michigan, lumbermen in the Pacific Northwest, and fishermen in San Francisco. Many went to Minnesota, but my Washington State still has the second largest percentage of Swedish Americans.

With the presence of so many Swedes we can boast of some fine Swedish food. The following recipes are gifts from friends and the results of experiments in our own kitchen. Don't put off trying the Jansson's Temptation. Your junior high kid will read the recipe and yell "Yech!" But, if you make the dish the young person will suddenly decide to be Swedish!

THE SWEDISH FORMAL BUFFET, OR KALAS

The concept of the Swedish Formal Buffet, or Kalas, is very different from the more commonly talked about smörgåsbord in this country. "Smör" refers to butter and "bord," of course, is bread. So a smörgåsbord is really a sandwich buffet, but the Kalas is a table filled with traditional dishes, some hot, some cold; breads; cheese; desserts. It is a mouthful! And it is eaten in several courses, or tables.

The following list of dishes will help you design your own Kalas. I have provided a recipe for each of the starred dishes.

THE COLD TABLE

Gravlax*

Cold Poached Salmon with Mustard Sauce*

Pickled herring in wine sauce

Pickled herring in sour cream

Herring Salad, Swedish Style*

Tossed green salad

Liver paste or pâté

Pickled beets

Cucumbers with sweet and sour dressing

Cucumbers with red onions and sour cream

Assorted sliced Scandinavian cheeses

THE HOT TABLE

Jansson's Temptation*

Baked Brown Swedish Beans*

Swedish Loin of Pork*

Potato Sausage*

Swedish meatballs

THE BREADS

Swedish rye

Caraway rye

Pumpernickel

Crisp bread (Knäckebröd)

THE DESSERTS

Swedish Pancakes with Lingonberries*

Cookies

Fresh fruit

* Recipes follow

GRAVLAX

Serves 8–10 as part of a Kalas

This quickly cured salmon is the Swedish version of what the New Yorker calls lox. So many Swedish immigrants turned to fishing in places like the Pacific Northwest that this dish has become well-known to us but it is still delightful.

2½ –3 pounds fresh salmon, center cut, cleaned and scaled, skin left on, cut into 2 fillets, small bones removed

THE CURING SALT

⅓ cup kosher salt

⅓ cup sugar

Freshly ground black pepper to taste

½ teaspoon saltpeter (page 45)

GARNISH

1 bunch of fresh dill, chopped

THE DRESSING

¼ cup vegetable oil

Pinch of sugar

2 teaspoons distilled white vinegar

½ teaspoon Dijon mustard

Tell your fishmonger what you are making and he will help you prepare the fish. Be sure that there are no small bones in the fish (see **Hint**, page 464).

Mix all the ingredients for the curing salt in a bowl. Lay the two fillets side by side, skin side down, on a plastic tray and sprinkle with the curing salt. Place the dill on top of one of the fillets and put the other fillet on top, like a sandwich. Wrap the entire fish with plastic wrap and then with aluminum foil. Place a small wooden board on top and put a clean brick on top as a weight. Place the whole works in the refrigerator to cure for 2 days.

To prepare for serving, slice each fillet into very thin pieces across the grain, thus removing the slice from the skin. This will take a very sharp knife.

Mix together the ingredients for the dressing. Arrange the slices on a platter and top with the dressing.

This can be served with any of the breads listed on the *Kalas* menu.

HINT: TO REMOVE TINY BONES FROM FISH simply use a pair of small, long-nose pliers. Gently rub your hands along the cut flesh of the fish, in both directions, and you will discover the tiny bones. Pluck them out, one by one, with the pliers. Simple.

MUSTARD SAUCE FOR COLD POACHED SALMON

Makes about 1 cup

This is a light and delicious sauce that is perfect for cold poached salmon. Remember not to overcook the fish!

2 tablespoons Dijon mustard	6 tablespoons olive oil
1 tablespoon sugar	6 tablespoons sour cream
1 tablespoon distilled white vinegar	2 tablespoons finely chopped fresh dill, or more to taste

Mix the mustard, sugar, and vinegar in a bowl. Beat in the oil a little at a time until well blended. The sauce will thicken rapidly and must be stirred vigorously. Finally, add the sour cream and plenty of finely chopped dill.

Serve on the side with cold salmon.

HERRING SALAD, SWEDISH STYLE

Serves 8 as part of a Kalas

This pickled herring, beet, meat, and potato salad is so very close to what the Latvians enjoy as Rosolos (page 281). It points to the influence that the enormous nation of Sweden had on the rest of northern Europe. In the Swedish version of this dish, which was brought to the New World, whipping cream is used in the dressing rather than mayonnaise.

- 1 1-pound can pickled beets, sliced and diced small (Drain and reserve liquid.)
- 2 6-ounce jars wine-flavored pickled herring pieces, drained and diced small
- 1 green apple (unpeeled), cored and diced small

- ½ pound new potatoes (unpeeled), cooked and diced small
- ½ cup finely diced cooked beef or veal
- 2 tablespoons yellow onion, peeled and diced small
- ⅓ cup finely chopped dill pickle

THE DRESSING

- 6 tablespoons reserved beet liquid
- 2 tablespoons distilled white vinegar
- 1–2 tablespoons sugar

- Pinch of freshly ground black pepper
- Salt to taste
- ½ cup heavy cream

GARNISH

- 2 hard-boiled egg yolks, chopped or grated

Mix all of the ingredients for the salad in a salad bowl. Blend all of the dressing ingredients except the whipping cream. Stir the dressing into the salad. Whip the cream and gently fold into the salad. Garnish with the chopped or grated egg yolk.

JANSSON'S TEMPTATION

Serves 8

This is a bit unusual, to say the least. Though I am half Norwegian, I had never heard of this dish until it was served to me by my dear Swedish friend, Joanne Klein. "Potatoes baked with onions, anchovies, and cream. Wonderful!" she said. I was pessimistic, and now I long for the stuff. Norwegians are not supposed to long for Swedish dishes!

2¼ pounds russet potatoes, peeled and cut into julienne strips, about 2 inches by ¼ inch (I use a mandoline, page 29.)

1 tablespoon salt

1 10½-ounce jar Swedish sweet pickled anchovy fillets (page 36) (found in any Scandinavian market), drained, the juice reserved

5 tablespoons butter

2 medium yellow onions, peeled and thinly sliced

Freshly ground black pepper

1¼ cups heavy cream

Place the potatoes in a bowl of water along with the salt. Chop the drained anchovy fillets coarsely and set aside. Melt 2 tablespoons of the butter and sauté the onion slices for a few minutes.

Melt 1 tablespoon of the remaining butter in an 8 × 8-inch glass baking dish; grease the bottom and sides. I melt the butter in the baking dish in the microwave.

Drain the julienned potatoes very well.

Place one third of the drained potatoes in the bottom of the buttered baking dish. Top with half of the sautéed onion, half of the chopped anchovies, and black pepper to taste. Top with another third of the potatoes, the remaining onion, anchovies, and more black pepper. Add the remaining potatoes. Pour the cream and reserved anchovy juice over all, and add more black pepper. Melt the remaining 2 tablespoons of butter and drizzle on. Bake in a preheated 375° oven for 1 hour.

BAKED BROWN SWEDISH BEANS

(Brüna Bonor)

Serves 8

These beans are a bit different from our regular baked beans. They came from Sweden with the immigrants, and were grown here for many generations. Today they are imported from Sweden and can be found in Swedish food shops as well as on the buffet of many a Swedish church social.

2 cups dried brown beans (available in specialty stores) (page 38)

6 cups water

1½ teaspoons salt

½ cup distilled white vinegar

½ cup dark corn syrup

3 tablespoons brown sugar, packed

2 tablespoons butter, melted

1 small cinnamon stick

Pick over and rinse the beans. Add the water and soak the beans at least 12 hours.

Bring the beans and soaking water to a boil. Cover the pan and simmer for 1½ hours.

Add the salt, vinegar, syrup, brown sugar, butter, and cinnamon stick. Stir to mix. Simmer, uncovered, for 1 hour, or until the beans are tender. The liquid should be as thick as a sauce at the end of the cooking period.

If the liquid is not thickened, turn up the heat for 10 minutes, or until the liquid is reduced. Remove the cinnamon stick. Serve hot.

SWEDISH LOIN OF PORK

(Fläskkarre)

Serves 6–8 as part of a Kalas

This is a dish offered in the home of my Swedish friend, Joanne Klein. She is a terrific cook and adds dried fruits to get the characteristic sweet "Swedish" flavor in this dish. Your family will become very fond of this one.

15 dried prunes, pitted

12 dried apricots, pitted

1½ cups water

1 3-pound loin of pork, almost all visible fat removed

1 teaspoon salt

¼ teaspoon freshly ground black pepper

Cover the prunes with the water; bring to a boil. Turn off the heat, add the apricots, and let cool. Drain and reserve the liquid. With a sharp knife make slits the length of the pork loin. Rub the roast with salt and pepper and insert ½ the cooked prunes and apricots in the slits. Tie the meat up into a roast. Insert a meat thermometer. Place the meat on a roasting rack in a pan and place 1 cup water in the bottom of the pan. Additional water may have to be added to prevent drying. Roast in a preheated 325° oven for 1½ to 1¾ hours. Remove the meat when the thermometer registers 155°.

SAUCE FOR PORK LOIN

Reserved prunes and apricots with juice from above recipe

1 cup dry white wine

1 cup Chicken Stock (page 74) or use canned

Pan drippings

Place all of the ingredients in a small saucepan and bring to a simmer. Cook for 5 minutes. Purée in a food blender until smooth. Return the sauce to the pan. Bring to a simmer before serving. You may want to thicken the sauce with 1 tablespoon of cornstarch dissolved in 2 tablespoons of water, stirred into the sauce while simmering.

POTATO SAUSAGE

Makes about 8 pounds of sausage

This sausage was obviously filled with potatoes in order to stretch out the meat that our Swedish immigrants could afford when they first came here. Today the hardworking Swedes do not need such fillers, but they love this sausage anyhow. It is unusually good. I like lots of allspice and black pepper in mine.

4 pounds peeled potatoes, coarsely ground (Use ascorbic acid dissolved in a bowl of water to prevent blackening. See Hint, below.)

2 pounds ground beef, cut into pieces

2 pounds ground pork (pork butt is good), cut into pieces

Freshly ground black pepper to taste

2 medium yellow onions, peeled and quartered

1½ –2½ tablespoons salt to taste

2 teaspoons ground allspice

Beef casings for stuffing

Coarsely grind (¼-inch chop) the potatoes, beef, and pork in a meat grinder. Cut into 1-inch pieces first if grinding in the food processor. Soak the potatoes in the water with ascorbic acid. Grind the onions the same way. When ready to mix the sausage, drain the potatoes well and combine all ingredients in a large bowl. Mix well.

Stuff casings loosely (page 453). Cut in appropriate lengths and tie with a string. Pierce the casings in several places, then simmer the sausage in water to cover about 40 minutes.

NOTE: I use a corn-on-the-cob holder as a sausage piercer. Works great.

HINT: TO PREVENT CUT POTATOES FROM DISCOLORING soak them in water that contains an ascorbic-acid product called Fruit Fresh. Add 1½ tablespoons of Fruit Fresh to 1 quart of water. Works terrific for potato sausages, potato pancakes, etc. This is a perfectly safe and natural product; it is simply vitamin C.

SWEDISH PANCAKES WITH
LINGONBERRIES

(Plätter)

Makes about 80 3-inch pancakes

You really should find a Swedish Plätt pan for this. It makes small pancakes, about 3 inches in diameter, which are very much enjoyed by the Scandinavian community. You can certainly make them in a larger form, but these little ones are so cute.

2 eggs	1 tablespoon sugar
3 cups milk	1 teaspoon salt
1½ cups all-purpose flour (See Hint, page 423.)	Butter or oil for frying

GARNISH

Butter	Confectioners' sugar
Lingonberry preserves	

Beat the eggs and add the milk and flour gradually along with the sugar and salt. Heat a plätt pan or small frying pan over low heat and brush with oil or butter. Stir the batter well and cook thin and light pancakes. Serve with butter, lingonberry preserves, and a bit of confectioners' sugar.

THE THAI
IMMIGRANTS

THAILAND

Thailand is one of the very few countries in Asia to have escaped colonialism. Even the name of the country means "The Land of the Free." While they do have a monarch, the king really remains as a symbol of the continuity of the country's independence, and he is revered and esteemed.

Thailand is a Buddhist nation, and that certainly helps one understand why the people are so very gracious, dignified, and kind. Buddhism in the way it is practiced in Thailand seems to instill such virtues.

The Thai people probably originated in southwestern China. They migrated toward the region that is now Thailand during the first thousand years A.D. By the thirteenth century several small Thai states had emerged. The greatest of these was the kingdom of Ayutthaya, founded in 1350. It was known as Siam to the outside world and claimed all the territory that makes up present-day Thailand, as well as other areas nearby.

In the early 1800s, King Mongkut, the model for the king in Rodgers and Hammerstein's famous musical, *The King and I,* came to rule, followed by his son, King Chulalongkorn, after whom the best university in Thailand is named. They accelerated modernization and brought in a number of important reforms that forestalled European empire builders.

The people of Thailand continue to hold the monarchy in highest regard and the current king, Bhumibol Adulyadej, and his beautiful queen are beloved and revered.

Siam was renamed Thailand in 1939. It was the first Asian nation to belong to the United Nations, having joined in 1946. And Thailand remains the world's fifth largest producer of rice and the largest exporter of rice.

Channing, my older son, was traveling in Thailand a year or so ago. He was so taken by the beauty of the Thai people that he returned home and told his mother and me that he wanted to marry a Thai woman, adopt Chinese children, and live in Italian clothes. That is possible in our time, so I simply replied, "Perfect. All you need is a job!" Well, he thought he could get around to that. Can you imagine the cost of the life-style to which he aspires?

Today there are Thai restaurants in most major cities in this country. Americans have really taken to Thai cuisine. So have I! The following recipes are easy to prepare at home and you will find several classics that appear on most menus. I see no reason why you cannot become a fine Thai cook. *"Sa Wa Dee Khap!"* "A very respectful thank you."

THAI PORK WITH GARLIC AND BLACK PEPPER

(Moo-Gra-Teiam)

Serves 4–5

This recipe is so simple that when you read it you will think that I have forgotten something. Good cooking really need not be complex.

Monora's Thai restaurant in San Francisco does a fine job on this dish, but then Monora does a fine job on every dish.

- 3 tablespoons peanut oil
- 4 tablespoons peeled and finely chopped garlic
- 1 pound boneless pork roast, butt or loin, very thinly sliced
- 2 tablespoons Thai fish sauce (page 40)
- 1 teaspoon freshly ground black pepper or more to taste (I like lots!)
- 1 tablespoon chopped fresh coriander stems (page 49)

Heat a wok and add the peanut oil. Sauté the garlic for a moment and add the pork. Cook for 3 to 5 minutes and then add the remaining ingredients. Chow (page 32) or stir for another minute or so and serve.

Shrimp and Fish Cakes

(Tod-Mon)

Makes about 16 patties

While it is true that the Thai immigrants have opened thousands of restaurants in this country, the quality of these establishments varies greatly. When I go into a Thai eating house, I order this particular dish and use it to judge the rest of the menu. This is a Thai classic, and to see it prepared poorly breaks my heart. You may be better off to make this one at home.

1 pound large shrimp, peeled, chopped in food processor to a coarse paste

1 pound whitefish (cod, whitefish, halibut), boneless and skinless fillets, chopped in food processor to a coarse paste

¼ pound fresh green beans, trimmed and cut into ½-inch pieces

2 teaspoons peeled and chopped garlic

2 eggs

2 teaspoons Thai red curry paste (page 44)

¼ cup Thai fish sauce (page 40)

4 tablespoons cornstarch

½ teaspoon sugar

½ teaspoon freshly ground black pepper

2 tablespoons chopped fresh coriander (page 49)

3 cups peanut oil for deep-frying

Combine all of the ingredients except for the cooking oil. Mix well and form into 3-inch round patties, ¼ inch thick. Setting the thermostat to 360°, heat an electric skillet, placing about 1 inch of oil in the pan. Fry each patty, turning once, until golden brown.

Serve with the Cucumber Condiment that follows.

CUCUMBER CONDIMENT

Makes 1 cup

You will find yourself using this condiment with many Thai dishes. It is at once flavorful, cool, and refreshing. Perfect!

- 1 firm medium-sized cucumber
- 2 tablespoons distilled white vinegar
- 2 tablespoons sugar
- 1 teaspoon salt
- ¼ teaspoon ground white pepper

- ½ small yellow onion, peeled and sliced lengthwise into paper-thin slivers
- 12 paper-thin lengthwise slivers of seeded hot fresh red chile peppers, about ¼ inch long

GARNISH

- ½ cup dry roasted unsalted peanuts, coarsely chopped

Julienne the cucumber. I use a mandoline to do this (page 29).

In a deep bowl stir the vinegar, sugar, salt, and white pepper until well blended. Add the remaining ingredients, except the peanuts, and toss with the marinade. Top with the peanuts just before serving. Serve at once or cover and chill for no longer than 2 hours before serving.

THAI BEEF SALAD

Serves 4 as part of a Thai meal

Such a creative and clever way to serve beef. The fresh mint and the fish sauce have a flavor that is so refreshing that I am having trouble staying at my computer. I want to go cook! This will become a favorite.

2 tablespoons peanut oil

2 cloves garlic, peeled and finely chopped

¾ pound beef flank steak, sliced thinly across the grain

THE MARINADE

½ cup peeled and thinly sliced yellow onion

¼ cup lime juice, freshly squeezed

¼ cup Thai fish sauce (page 40)

10 fresh mint leaves, coarsely chopped

½ teaspoon sugar

½ teaspoon red chili paste with garlic (page 44)

GARNISH

2 cucumbers (unpeeled), sliced paper-thin

Chopped scallions

Fresh coriander leaves (page 49)

Heat the oil in a wok and chow (page 32) the garlic for just a moment. Add the beef slices and sear just until they lose their pink color, 1 or 2 minutes. Do not overcook! Place the meat in a bowl and add the ingredients for the marinade. Mix well and chill for ½ hour.

Make a bed of cucumber slices on a platter. Put the meat and marinade on top and add the remaining garnishes. Chill again before serving.

PAD THAI

Serves 4–6 as part of a Thai meal

This is probably the most popular noodle dish from Thailand, at least it is so in many Thai restaurants here in America. It takes a bit of doing, but it is worth the effort.

Have all ingredients ready to go before you begin to chow (page 32). Otherwise, you will overcook the noodles.

½ pound Thai flat rice noodles (*bahn pho*) or rice sticks (found in Thai or Oriental markets)

Oil for deep-frying
½ pound fresh firm bean curd, cut into tiny cubes

¼ cup peanut oil
½ tablespoon garlic, chopped
½ cup very thinly sliced skinless and boneless chicken breast
¼ pound shrimp, peeled and cut in half the long way
2 eggs, beaten
1 tablespoon dried shrimp powder (page 46)
¼ teaspoon freshly ground black pepper

3 tablespoons finely chopped dry-roasted salted peanuts
2 tablespoons lime juice, freshly squeezed
1 tablespoon sugar
6 tablespoons Thai fish sauce (page 40)
¼ cup Tamarind Sauce (page 478)
2 teaspoons red chili paste with garlic (page 44)
2 cups fresh bean sprouts

GARNISH

2 limes, quartered
⅓ cup fresh coriander leaves (page 49)

3 chopped scallions
4 tablespoons finely chopped dry-roasted peanuts

I suggest you start this dish by preparing the Tamarind Sauce from the recipe on page 478. Set it aside to cool.

Soak the noodles in ample warm water until supple, about 15 minutes, drain and set aside. Place the noodles in boiling water and cook just until the water returns to the boil. Drain again. Heat the oil for deep-frying to 375° and deep-fry the cut bean curd. Be sure to pat the bean curd dry on a paper towel first so that it will not spatter fat on you. Drain the bean curd and set aside.

Heat a large wok and add the peanut oil, garlic, and chicken. Chow for a few minutes and then add the shrimp, drained noodles, beaten eggs, and deep-fried bean curd. Toss well and chow for 3 to 4 minutes over medium-high heat. Add the remaining ingredients, except the garnishes, and chow or stir for a few more minutes until the noodles are hot and tender.

Place on a serving platter with the garnishes, which are an integral part of the dish.

TAMARIND SAUCE

Makes ¾ cup

1 ounce dried tamarind (page 47)
10 tablespoons hot water
1 teaspoon salt

¼ cup sugar
6 tablespoons rice wine vinegar (page 45)

Soak the tamarind in about 5 tablespoons of hot tap water. Stir until you have a paste. Strain the juice from the pulp, squeezing the pulp in a small strainer. Discard the pulp.

Place another 5 tablespoons of water in a small saucepan. Add 2 tablespoons of the tamarind juice, along with the remaining ingredients. Bring to a simmer and cook, uncovered, for about 10 minutes, stirring often. The color should look like a light brown syrup. You should have ¾ cup liquid. If not, add additional water and heat again for just a moment.

Store, covered, in the refrigerator for up to 2 months.

THAI SQUID SALAD

Serves 4–5 as part of a Thai meal

I know people who claim that they hate squid. I know, I can't under-stand it either, but they are adamant. However, they change their tune when I offer them this Thai jewel. Do not overcook the squid and you will be most pleased.

1 pound squid pieces, cleaned (See Hint, page 480.)

1 quart water

THE DRESSING

1 stalk fresh lemongrass, peeled and the bottom 4 inches chopped (page 42)

2 dried Kaffir lime leaves, finely chopped (page 41)

½ cup peeled and thinly sliced yellow onions

1½ tablespoons freshly squeezed lime juice

1 tablespoon Thai fish sauce (page 40)

½ teaspoon sugar

1 teaspoon chili oil (page 41)

½ teaspoon finely chopped garlic

2 scallions, finely sliced

10 fresh mint leaves, cut into thin strips

8 sprigs chopped fresh coriander (page 49)

1 small jalapeño pepper, seeded and thinly sliced

GARNISH

Bed of leafy green lettuce

Sliced cucumber

Lime wedges

Cut the cleaned squid into 1½-inch squares and score in a diamond pattern on the outside of the flesh. (See the illustration on page 480.)

Bring 1 quart of water to a boil and blanch the prepared squid pieces for 1 minute. Drain the squid and plunge it into cold water to stop the cooking. This is the most important step in this salad! Do not overcook the squid. Drain the squid again and set aside.

Mix together the ingredients for the dressing. Toss with the squid pieces and place on a bed of lettuce leaves. Garnish with the cucumber slices and lime wedges. Chill before serving.

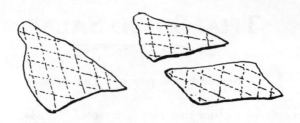

HINT: ON CLEANING SQUID. Buy frozen or fresh squid that are about 5 to 6 inches long. Pull off the head and set aside. Squeeze out the filling from the tube and discard. Rinse the tube and remove the clear plastic-like backbone of the creature. I save the tentacles, but not the head, for other dishes.

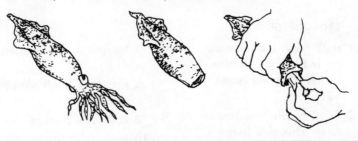

THAI BASIL BEEF

Serves 4 as part of a Thai meal

This is close to a hot beef salad. The Thais have the most amazing ability to put together herbs and spices in blends that no one else seems to have thought of. This is one of my favorite Thai dishes.

4 tablespoons peanut oil	1 tablespoon soy sauce (Kikkoman is best here.)
3 cloves garlic, peeled and finely chopped	1 teaspoon sugar
3 jalapeño peppers, seeded and sliced	¼ teaspoon ground white pepper
1 pound beef flank steak, thinly sliced across the grain	½ cup coarsely chopped fresh basil leaves
4 tablespoons Thai fish sauce (page 40)	

Heat a wok and add the oil and garlic. Chow (page 32) or stir for just a moment and then add the peppers and meat. Chow again for just a couple of minutes so that the meat sears to medium rare, just a bit pink inside. Quickly add the remaining ingredients and toss for a moment.

THAI CHICKEN IN RED CURRY AND COCONUT

Serves 6 as part of a Thai meal

You need to find a Thai or Vietnamese market to make this dish. The secret is the wonderful Thai red curry paste. It comes in a can and a little goes a long way.

- 2 tablespoons peanut oil
- 2 cloves garlic, peeled and finely chopped
- 4 whole chicken breasts (about 2 pounds), bone in, hacked (page 33)
- 1 yellow onion, peeled and sliced

- 1 14-ounce can coconut milk (page 38)
- 2 tablespoons Thai red curry paste (page 44)
- 1 teaspoon salt
- 1 tablespoon Thai fish sauce (page 40)

GARNISH

Chopped fresh coriander leaves (page 49)

Hack the chicken, leaving the bones in. Heat a wok and add the oil and garlic. Chow or stir the chicken pieces until they are well browned. Add the onion to the pan and cook just until the onion is clear. Set the wok aside.

In a 6-quart stove-top casserole heat the coconut milk, red curry paste, salt, and fish sauce. Bring to a simmer and add the chicken and onion. Cover and simmer until the chicken is tender, about 15 minutes.

Garnish with coriander.

THAI CHICKEN AND LEMONGRASS SOUP

Serves 7–8 as part of a Thai meal

I have included this dish for Channing, my oldest son. Oh, I love it too, but Channing is not only in love with Thai soup, but with Thai women. He hopes that if he marries a Thai woman, she will find the time to make this soup whenever he desires it. But this is America, so you had better have me make the soup, son, or learn how to make it yourself.

6 cups Chicken Stock (page 74) or use canned

4 slices dried galangal root (page 50)

1 slice fresh ginger, the size of a 25-cent piece

2 cloves garlic, peeled and sliced

3 shallots, peeled and sliced

7 dried Kaffir lime leaves (page 41)

3 stalks lemongrass, peeled and the bottom 5 inches chopped (page 42)

1 teaspoon Thai red curry paste (page 44)

1 tablespoon sugar

1 14-ounce can coconut milk (page 38)

3 tablespoons Thai fish sauce (page 40)

¾ pound thinly sliced skinless and boneless chicken breasts

2 small jalapeño peppers, seeded and thinly sliced

2 tablespoons freshly squeezed lime juice

Salt and freshly ground black pepper to taste

GARNISH

Chopped fresh coriander leaves (page 49)

Place the Chicken Stock in a 6-quart kettle and add the galanga root, ginger, garlic, shallots, Kaffir lime leaves, lemongrass, and red curry paste. Bring to a simmer and cook for 10 minutes. Drain the stock and discard the solids.

Return the stock to the pot, add the sugar, coconut milk, and fish sauce, and bring to a simmer. Add the chicken and bring to a simmer again. Cook for 5 minutes. Add the remaining ingredients, except the garnish, and bring to serving temperature. Garnish with the coriander and serve.

NOTE: Many Thai cooks prefer to leave the solids in the soup stock and do not drain it at all. This gives a bit brighter flavor, if you wish.

THE VIETNAMESE
IMMIGRANTS

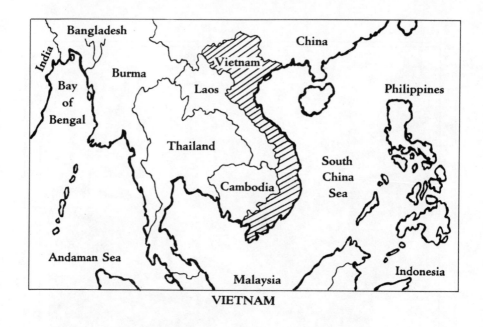

VIETNAM

Vietnam differs considerably from the other mainland countries of Southeast Asia, namely, its neighbors Laos, Cambodia, and Thailand. Vietnam has been much more influenced by China than have these other countries, which have responded more to the Hindu culture to the west. As you travel from India to Vietnam you find that it is in Vietnam that the people use chopsticks, the women wear pants instead of sarongs, and the life-style reflects the teachings of Confucius in addition to Buddha.

The original inhabitants of Vietnam were overcome by the Chinese about 100 B.C. The Chinese ruled Vietnam for a thousand years. The Vietnamese adopted Confucianism, the Chinese system of government, Taoism and Buddhism, and many agricultural and cooking practices. Throughout this time, however, the Vietnamese preserved their own culture and greatly resented the Chinese.

Successive Vietnamese dynasties ruled after the Chinese were driven out. Western penetration began in the sixteenth century and among the newcomers were the French. In the 1860s attacks were made on Catholic Vietnamese and French Catholic missionaries. The French responded by seizing the southern provinces and establishing the French colony of Cochin China. By the 1880s the remaining Vietnamese court fell and the French assumed complete control over Tonkin in the north and Annam in the central district in addition to Cochin China. The French dominated the country, except during a period of Japanese occupation during World War II, until 1954.

Bitter fighting had broken out in 1946 between the French and a coalition of Vietnamese Communists and nationalists, the Viet Minh, led by Ho Chi Minh. In 1954 the French lost to this coalition following the Battle of Dien Bien Phu. An international conference met in Geneva and arranged for a temporary partition of the country at the 17th parallel, thus creating the Democratic Republic of Vietnam in the north and the Republic of Vietnam in the south. The plan called for the reunification of Vietnam to be achieved by elections in 1956.

In 1956 the president of South Vietnam, Ngo Dinh Diem, canceled the elections and with the help of the United States tried to create an anticommunist bastion in Southeast Asia. The National Liberation Front, the Vietcong, then began a campaign of guerrilla warfare, backed by Ho Chi Minh, to topple Diem and reunify Vietnam. Despite U. S. intervention, the Republic of Vietnam fell in 1975 and the country was reunified under a Communist government. Many nations suffered tremendous political and social upheaval including the United States, Cambodia, and Laos.

Thousands of Vietnamese fled and many came to this country. From 1975 to 1977 another wave of Vietnamese left for political or economic reasons. These were the original "boat people." The third wave of immigration began in 1978 when large numbers of ethnic Chinese living in Vietnam fled the country. By 1989 over 450,000 Vietnamese had come to the United States.

The Vietnamese are very family oriented. It is not unusual to find three or four generations living together under one roof, as they have brought their living and eating habits with them. The food has been influenced by both the French and the Chinese. The French popularized strong coffee, pastries, asparagus, French bread, and meat pies. The Chinese influenced the use of chopsticks, stir-frying in a wok, and serving long-grain rice separately at the meal rather than mixed with the other dishes. Salads are popular and an extensive selection of fresh herbs adds a delight that you will find nowhere else.

The recipes that we have chosen for this section are really quite typical of the whole cuisine. It is not complicated cooking but you must find fresh herbs, and find them all the year around. Please don't miss the Lemongrass Chicken or the Rare Beef with Lime. They are both culinary classics!

VIETNAMESE MEATBALL
ON A STICK

Serves 6 as part of a Vietnamese meal or enough to fill 12 8-inch rice wrappers

These tiny meatballs on a stick are just the most juicy and delicious tidbits you can imagine. Cook them on charcoal and serve them in rice paper wrappers, and you are in business. The Vietnamese immigrants brought the rice wrappers and the works to these shores.

1½ pounds lean ground beef

1 egg white

2 tablespoons soy sauce

2 tablespoons *nuoc mam* (fish sauce) (page 40)

½ teaspoon salt

½ teaspoon ground white pepper

1 tablespoon sesame oil

2 cloves garlic, peeled and crushed

2 tablespoons dry sherry

½ teaspoons liquid smoke (I prefer Wright's.)

1 teaspoon sugar

1 tablespoon cornstarch

Place all of the ingredients in an electric mixer and blend until very smooth. Mold all of the meat mixture into walnut-size meatballs and place on metal or bamboo skewers. Broil in the oven, turning once, or on the charcoal grill, much preferred. Serve with chopped fresh coriander or mint, lettuce leaves, and moistened rice paper wrappers (see **Hint**), and Vietnamese Dipping Sauce (page 488).

HINT: ON PREPARING RICE PAPER WRAPPERS. These round rice wrappers can be found in large Oriental or Thai/Vietnamese markets. They come dried. *To serve:* Place a moistened kitchen towel on the counter and put a few sheets of rice paper on the towel. Do not let them overlap. Spray them on both sides with a plant sprayer and allow them to soak up the water for a few minutes. Prepare only the amount you need. They are not reusable. Do not let them sit too long or they will become soggy. When they are soft they are ready to serve. The wrappers come in several sizes, so choose the one that is the most convenient for a particular dish.

VIETNAMESE COLD SHRIMP ROLL

Makes 1 roll

Once you have assembled your ingredients, these colorful rolls are simple and fun to make.

1 rice paper wrapper (12-inch) (See Hint.)	Pork strips, chowed (page 32) with oil and garlic
Large shrimp, peeled, cooked, and split lengthwise	Green lettuce leaves
Bean sprouts	Fresh mint leaves
Fresh coriander leaves (page 49)	Basil leaves (optional)

Have all of the ingredients ready, including the dressing and dipping sauce that follow (page 488). Lay out the moistened rice paper noodle (see **Hint**) and fill with a bit of each of the ingredients. Sprinkle some dressing over the ingredients, roll up like a burrito, and enjoy. Dip rolls in the dressing below.

DRESSING

1 tablespoon sesame oil	1 tablespoon rice wine vinegar (page 45)
2 tablespoons light soy sauce (not "Lite"—see page 46)	1/4 teaspoon sugar

Mix all ingredients together well before using.

NOTE: This roll can be prepared up to 3 hours ahead of serving time. Keep at room temperature.

VIETNAMESE DIPPING SAUCE

Makes about 2½ cups

½ cup *nuoc mam* (fish sauce) (page 40)

2 tablespoons rice wine vinegar (page 45)

2 teaspoons sugar

1 cup water

¼ cup grated carrots

¼ cup grated *daikon* radish (page 39)

1 clove garlic, peeled and crushed

Juice of ½ lime

Chili oil (page 41) to taste

Mix all the ingredients together well and chill a bit before serving.

VIETNAMESE PORK ROLLS

(Cha-gio)

Makes 8 servings

These are the Vietnamese version of Chinese spring rolls, although I much prefer them to the American-Chinese variety. You can serve these with lettuce leaves for folding and wrapping, along with fresh herbs, and you have a full meal.

2 tablespoons peanut oil

2 cloves garlic, peeled and crushed

½ pound lean ground pork

¼ pound shrimp, cooked, peeled, and coarsely chopped

Pinch of salt

4 scallions, chopped

¼ cup finely grated *daikon* radish (page 39)

2 tablespoons *nuoc mam* (fish sauce) (page 40)

2 ounces *sai fun* noodles (page 38), soaked in warm water for 15 minutes

Freshly ground black pepper to taste

8 lumpia wrappers (page 42), frozen, 10-inch diameter

Peanut oil for deep-frying, about 6 cups

Heat a wok and add the oil and garlic. Chow (page 32) or stir for a moment and add the ground pork. Chow until the pork falls apart and then add all the remaining ingredients except the lumpia wrappers and frying oil. Chow for just a few minutes, transfer to a bowl, and let the mixture cool.

Heat the deep-frying oil to 375°. Place one eighth of the filling in the middle of a lumpia wrapper and roll up like a burrito. Seal the seam with water. Roll all 8 wrappers. Deep-fry the rolls, 2 or 3 at a time, until they are golden brown. Serve them with Vietnamese Dipping Sauce.

VIETNAMESE LEMONGRASS
CHICKEN

Serves 4–6

This quickly prepared but terrifically flavorful dish is great served with rice paper wrappers (page 487). I love it with a few leaves of mint and basil. This one you must try. It is easily done in a wok.

1 3-pound frying chicken

4 stalks lemongrass (page 42), minced, about ½ cup

3 scallions (green and white part)

1 teaspoon salt

¼ teaspoon freshly ground black pepper, plus more to taste

2 tablespoons peanut oil

2 small fresh red chile peppers, seeded, cored, and chopped

2 teaspoons sugar

½ cup Chicken Stock (page 74) or use canned

GARNISH

½ cup chopped dry-roasted peanuts

2 tablespoons *nuoc mam* (fish sauce) (page 40)

Chopped fresh coriander leaves (page 49)

Hack the chicken into small serving pieces (page 33), chopping through the bones with a sharp cleaver. Remove the outer leaves of the lemongrass and finely slice the tender white part at the base of the stalks. Bruise with a mortar and pestle or the handle of a cleaver. Finely slice the scallions, including the green tops. Mix the chicken with the salt, ¼ teaspoon pepper, the lemongrass, and scallions and set aside for 30 minutes.

Heat a wok, add the oil, and when oil is hot add the chicken mixture and stir-fry for 3 minutes. Add chile peppers, and stir-fry on medium heat for 10 more minutes, or until chicken no longer looks pink. Season with sugar and pepper and add the Chicken Stock. Chow (page 32) or stir for a few minutes. Garnish with the peanuts, *nuoc mam*, and coriander. Serve with rice, if desired.

VIETNAMESE BEEF SOUP

This is a very common dish among our Vietnamese immigrant ancestors, and it is easy to prepare. I will just describe the dish for you and you can go at it. It is that simple.

Heat a pot of stock, half Chicken Stock (page 74) and half Beef Stock (page 78) or use canned. Allow at least 1 cup of stock for each person. When the stock is boiling, add a pinch or 2 of sugar and some ground allspice (very little). Add a thin slice of raw beef for each person and cook for just a few seconds so that the beef remains very tender and not overcooked. Garnish the soup with fresh coriander leaves. Often cooked noodles and sliced yellow onion are served on the side. Each person can add either or both to his or her soup bowl.

VIETNAMESE RARE BEEF
WITH LIME

Serves 6, as it is very rich

The title on this one is a little misleading since the beef is not just rare, it is raw. Marinating the meat in the lime juice almost cooks it, and the result is fresh-tasting and delightful. Do not be reluctant to try this dish. It is even better than steak tartare.

**1 pound sirloin-tip roast,
sliced paper thin**

Slice the meat *very* thin. For easy slicing, I freeze a boneless roast until it is very firm but not hard. Or have your butcher do it.

MARINADE

½ teaspoon peanut oil

2 tablespoons dried minced
onion flakes

2 tablespoons oyster sauce
(page 43)

3 tablespoons freshly
squeezed lime juice

½ cup peeled and thinly
sliced yellow onion

1 jalapeño pepper, seeded
and thinly sliced

GARNISH

Chopped scallions

Chopped dry-roasted
peanuts

Fried onion flakes

Fresh coriander leaves
(page 49)

Lime wedges

First, prepare the fried onion flakes for the marinade and the garnish. Heat a small frying pan and add ½ tablespoon peanut oil. Put in 2 tablespoons of dried onion flakes and toast over medium heat until the onions are a light brown. Drain on paper towels and place in a sealed jar. They will keep in the refrigerator for several days and they make a great garnish.

Combine the ingredients for the marinade in a large bowl. Mix well and add the meat. Toss a couple of times, cover, and place in the refrigerator to chill for 2 hours. Arrange the meat on a cold platter and top with the garnishes. The dish can be eaten with rice paper wrappers (page 487) or with rice.

THE WELSH
IMMIGRANTS

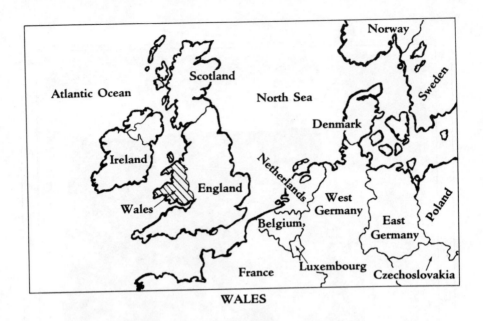

WALES

The absolutely charming people called the Welsh are descended from two ethnic groups: Celtic invaders who arrived around 500 B.C. and the earlier tribes who came from the Iberian peninsula, perhaps as early as 8,000 B.C. When the Anglo-Saxons launched their invasions against these people in the fifth, sixth, and seventh centuries A.D., they called these people "Welsh" meaning "foreigners." Most of the Welsh were absorbed into the general population of England and southeastern Scotland. The Cymry ("fellow countrymen") who held out in the mountainous west continued to speak their own Celtic language (Cymraeg) much longer. In 1536 a political union between England and Cymru, or Wales, was achieved. And Wales has been increasingly influenced by English culture ever since.

After the Norman invasion in 1066, William the Conquerer built a series of towns in Wales. During the fifteenth century Henry the VII of England seemed proud of his small amount of Welsh blood and he became quite popular with the Welsh, though he did not seem to do much to improve the life of the people. He died in 1509 and his oldest son, who became Henry the VIII, a very determined man, took the throne. He united Wales with England and worked for improvements in the relationships between the Welsh and the English. The Welsh were allowed the same rights as Englishmen but anyone of importance had to speak English, not Welsh. That became the law! Welsh was allowed only in the home and sometimes in the marketplace. You can imagine what that must have done to the spirit of the Welsh. But they were determined to maintain their culture, and they have.

During the seventeenth century many Welsh came to America, some of them Puritans who were campaigning for reform of the Anglican Church. Welsh Baptists joined with English Quakers and traveled to the New World. Thus we had the Puritans in America. The Welsh continued to come for generations and many wound up working in the coal mines of Pennsylvania just as they had worked in the coal mines of Wales.

Today there are few communities in America that can actually point to Welsh immigrants. Scranton, Pennsylvania, is such a place. We joined in a Welsh hymn sing, a Welsh tea party, and had a grand time of sharing with a men's chorus who had flown in from Wales for the occasion.

My love for the Welsh has not come about because of the food, though it is enjoyable. My love for the Welsh has come about because of their hymn singing! John Wesley, the founder of Methodism, of which I am a part, loved to sing with the Welsh miners before they went down into the coal mines . . . and he joined them in singing at 5:00 in the morning!

This culture has produced some great intellectuals, among them, the actor Richard Burton and the poet Dylan Thomas. The cooks of Wales have never gained international fame . . . and, to be honest with you, I suppose they don't deserve it. The following recipes will let you taste some very fine things from Wales, and if the menu does not fill you up, then I suggest you attend a Welsh hymn sing. That will fill you up for sure!

WELSH CREPES

(Ffrois)

Serves 4–6

This is a lovely little currant crepe that is served for dessert or at a fancy tea. Mrs. Ceinwen Hughes, from Wales, gave us this recipe.

1 cup all-purpose flour (See Hint, page 423.)

Pinch of salt

3 eggs

1¾ cups milk

Salad or peanut oil for pan-frying, or use Crisco

6 tablespoons dried currants

½ cup sugar

Juice of 2 lemons

Put the flour, salt, eggs, and milk in a bowl and beat at medium speed until blended. The mixture will be a thin batter.

Prepare a SilverStone-lined pan of desired size by melting a small amount of oil or Crisco to cover the bottom (the fat should be hot). Pour a scant 3 tablespoons of batter into the pan, tipping it so that it coats the bottom. Sprinkle all over with ½ tablespoon currants. Cook the first side until it is a golden brown. Turn the crepe with a spatula and cook the other side. Turn the crepe out onto a large plate, sprinkle with sugar and lemon juice, and roll up. Crepes can also be piled up and sliced in portions like a cake. Continue with remaining batter. Keep crepes warm in a 200° oven.

This recipe will make a dozen or more.

WELSH MEATBALLS

(Faggots)

Serves 8

I spiced this dish up a bit, as Welsh cooking tends to be a tad bland. These meatballs are very popular with the Welsh immigrants who came to this country.

2 pounds pork or beef liver, cut into large pieces

1 pound pork butt, cut into large pieces

1 pound fresh pork fat, cut into large pieces

1 egg

2 cups bread crumbs

2 large yellow onions, peeled and minced

2 teaspoons crumbled dried sage

1 teaspoon dried thyme, whole

2 teaspoons salt

½ teaspoon freshly ground black pepper

In a meat grinder, grind the liver, pork, and fatback finely. Mix all of the ingredients together well and mold into 1½-inch meatballs. Place them in a greased pan and add 1 cup of water. Bake for 40 minutes in a preheated 350° oven.

WELSH RAREBIT

Serves 3–4 as a snack or light course

I was pleased to find that Welsh Rarebit really is Welsh. It is simply a sumptuous cheese sauce that is served over toast, so it is great for a light evening supper or for a Sunday brunch.

½ pound sharp Cheddar cheese, grated

1 teaspoon butter

1 tablespoon Worcestershire sauce

¼ cup beer

2 teaspoons all-purpose flour

1 teaspoon dry mustard

Salt and freshly ground black pepper to taste

Place all of the ingredients, except the beer, in a double boiler and cook, stirring often, until a smooth sauce is obtained. Add the beer and continue to heat for a few moments. Serve over toast.

LEEK PIE

Serves 6 as a vegetable and starch course

The leek is the national symbol of Wales. It is also one of the favorite foods of the Welsh. This vegetable keeps well over the winter in the ground, and it is used to flavor wonderful soups and stews—and, in this case, a pie. The recipe is simple so I will just describe the dish.

Slice about 8 large leeks (white part only), washing them first very well. Pan-fry them in a bit of butter until they are tender. Place them in a pie shell and top with lightly cooked bacon. Add salt and freshly ground black pepper to taste. Top with another layer of pie dough, and, using a fork, poke a few holes in the top of the dough. Bake in a preheated oven at 375° for 30 to 45 minutes.

You may wish to use the recipe for Basic Easy Crust on page 501.

WELSH CAKES

Makes about 5 dozen, depending on size of cutter

This is a very important Welsh recipe. When I first met my Welsh friend, Tom Gable, of Scranton, Pennsylvania, he agreed to meet me at my hotel and talk about the community in his area. "I'll bring some Welsh cakes," he said proudly. I thought a cake was a cake, but in Wales this sweet-currant fried biscuit is called a "cake." The recipe comes from another Welsh friend, Gladys Davis.

7 cups all-purpose flour
(See Hint, page 423.)

2 tablespoons baking
powder

2 teaspoons salt

½ pound lard

½ pound margarine

2½ cups sugar

1 tablespoon ground
nutmeg

1½ cups currants

3 eggs

¾ cup milk

Blend the flour, baking powder, and salt together. Using a pastry blender, cut in the lard and margarine until the mixture is grainy. Stir in the sugar, nutmeg, and currants. Beat the eggs and mix with the milk. Blend the liquid into the solids, stirring with a fork to form a soft dough.

Roll out the dough about ½ inch thick and cut into rounds of desired size. A round cookie cutter works well for this.

Bake on an electric nonstick, griddle, with thermostat set between 325° and 350° (griddle should be ungreased), on one side until the edges are firm (golden brown) then turn only once to cook the other side. Do not undercook.

To ensure uniform thickness, a ½-inch-thick wooden form can be made and the cookies rolled out inside the form with the rolling pin resting on the wood.

SCONES

Makes 12 scones, depending on size of cutter

I owe deep thanks to Kitty Jenkins of Scranton, Pennsylvania. She and her husband came here from Wales and settled in the beautiful Pennsylvania hills. She was most helpful in setting up a meeting and television shoot in Scranton, and she presented us with a formal Welsh tea party. This is her recipe. It will convince you that a good rich Welsh scone is not to be confused with the mild biscuits made in the rest of this country.

- 4 tablespoons (½ stick) butter
- 1¾ cups all-purpose flour (See Hint, page 423.)
- ¼ teaspoon salt
- 5½ tablespoons sugar
- 1 teaspoon baking soda
- 2 teaspoons cream of tartar
- 2 eggs
- ⅓ cup milk

Using a pastry blender, cut the butter into the flour and salt. Mix until the mixture resembles coarse cornmeal. Add the sugar, baking soda, and cream of tartar. Mix well.

Beat the eggs with the milk and add to the flour, using a wooden spoon, to make a spongy mixture. Place the dough on a well-floured plastic countertop or board and pat it out to ½-inch thickness. Cut dough into rounds with a biscuit cutter. Flour your hands and place the rounds on a nonstick cookie sheet and leave for 10 minutes to settle.

Bake in a preheated oven at 450° for 8 minutes.

These should be served with butter and/or jam, or with cream and jam for special occasions.

VARIATIONS

Cheese scones: Add ¼ cup grated Cheddar cheese. *Fruit scones:* Add currants or raisins.

COLD PORK PIE

Serves 6

This may sound strange to some of our American minds but in Wales a cold pork pie always seems to be sitting about and waiting for you. The local bakeries in Wales all sell them, and I practically lived on the things when I was there in 1960. Our Welsh immigrant ancestors brought the recipe with them, of course.

1½ pounds lean pork, coarsely ground (Best to grind your own.)

1 yellow onion, peeled and chopped

2 eggs, beaten

¼ teaspoon cayenne pepper

¼ teaspoon ground sage

2 tablespoons Worcestershire sauce

Salt and freshly ground black pepper to taste

½ recipe Basic Easy Crust (See below.)

Mix all of the ingredients together, except the crust, and place in an 8-inch deep-dish pie plate. Bake, covered, in a preheated oven at 375° for ½ hour. Remove from the oven and pour off the accumulated fat. Cover with the crust and return to the oven for 45 minutes, or until the crust is golden brown and flaky.

Allow to cool completely before serving.

This is great for a first course, a midnight snack, or a luncheon dish.

BASIC EASY CRUST

3 cups all-purpose flour (See Hint, page 423.)

1 teaspoon salt

½ cup (1 stick) margarine

½ cup Crisco

1 egg

1 tablespoon distilled white vinegar

3–4 tablespoons ice water

In a medium-size bowl stir the flour and salt together. Cut in the shortenings, using a pastry blender. Keep working the flour and shortening until the mixture is rather grainy, like coarse cornmeal. Mix the egg and vinegar together and, using a wooden fork, stir the mixture into the flour. Add enough ice water so that the dough barely holds together. Place on a marble pastry board or a plastic countertop and knead for just a few turns, enough so that the dough holds together and becomes rollable.

I roll out my dough on a piece of waxed paper. It is easy to handle that way. If you have a marble rolling pin, it will be even easier. If you use a wooden rolling pin, be sure to dust a teaspoon of flour on it a couple of times when you are rolling out the dough.

NOTE: This recipe will make enough dough for one 9-inch pie with two crusts, top and bottom.

LEEK AND POTATO SOUP

(Cawl Cennin)

Makes about 2½ quarts

The Welsh leek, a national symbol, is a way of remembering who you are in a new land. Henry V of England was very proud of his Welsh blood and therefore used the leek as a symbol of his reign. I will bet that he loved this soup! And you thought it was French!

1 pound potatoes, peeled and sliced or diced	1 teaspoon salt
1 pound leeks (white and green parts), sliced thinly	Freshly ground black pepper to taste
7½ cups Chicken Stock (page 74) or use canned	1 cup heavy cream

GARNISH

Chopped parsley

Slice or dice the potatoes, slice the leeks thinly, being careful to wash off any dirt or sand. Simmer the potatoes and leeks together with the Chicken Stock, salt, and pepper for 40 to 50 minutes. Mash the vegetables or purée them in a food processor. Check the seasonings and reheat, adding the cream. Garnish with parsley. Serve warm or chilled.

THE
YUGOSLAVIAN
IMMIGRANTS

YUGOSLAVIA

Yugoslavia: one country with two alphabets, three religions, four (main) languages, five (principal) nationalities, six republics, and a border with seven nations. Given this conglomeration, Yugoslavia is a miracle of twentieth-century unity and as such has earned respect as a small non-aligned power.

Yugoslavia has borders with Italy, Austria, Hungary, Romania, Bulgaria, Greece, and Albania. For centuries this area assumed different shapes and proportions as the Turkish Ottoman Empire and the Austrian Hapsburgs argued over the territory. Even the Venetians got in on the act.

Yugoslavia means "land of the southern Slavs." The six republics are Slovenia, Croatia, Serbia, Bosnia-Hercegovina, Montenegro, and Macedonia.

The Serbs make up about 40 percent of the population. They celebrate their own particular form of Eastern Orthodox Christianity and use their own alphabet, an alphabet developed by two brothers, the monks Cyril and Methodius, in the ninth century in Macedonia. The ethnic church and the unusual alphabet were brought to the United States by these people, and these two characteristics seem to have helped keep the Serbian community together.

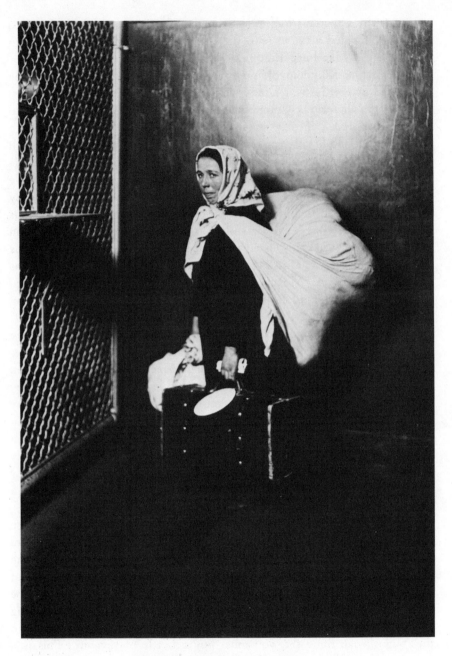

A Slavic mother, Ellis Island

The Croatians make up about 22 percent of the nation, the second-largest group. They are members of the Roman Catholic Church and use the Latin alphabet. You can understand that they had an easier time assimilating here than did the Serbs. During the tenth and eleventh centuries the Croatians had an independent kingdom, but from 1102 to 1918 they formed a union with the Kingdom of Hungary, and through Hungary, the Hapsburg Empire.

In 1929 the Kingdom of Yugoslavia was formed but it came to be dominated by the Serbs, a situation that was unsatisfactory to the Croats. In 1945 the victorious Communist-led partisan forces headed by Tito reconstituted the Yugoslav state with Croatia as one of its republics.

The Croatians first began coming to this country in the seventeenth and eighteenth centuries, a handful of sailors, merchants, craftsmen, adventurers, and missionaries, most from the Dalmatian coast. In the early nineteenth century ships came here regularly from Dalmatia and many sailors jumped ship in New Orleans or San Francisco. Later, Croatians came here in response to reports of gold in California and the expansion of copper and coal mining in a variety of states. At the beginning of this century thousands came as a result of everything from farming problems to political problems. Most wound up as unskilled laborers in America.

In the late 1940s and 1950s thousands of Croats came here following the Communist revolution in Yugoslavia. These twentieth-century immigrants were better educated than their predecessors. Today there are between 500,000 and 700,000 Croatian-Americans.

There are also about 300,000 Slovenian Americans. Most are Roman Catholic and in the old days lived under the rule of the Hapsburgs. They came here as a hardworking and frugal lot, having left their own country due to diminishing land resources.

Other groups should be discussed as well, and I expect to hear from your group if I did not talk about you in depth. This article simply points to the fact that what we now call Yugoslavia is made up of many different groups and traditions, and the nation can certainly boast of a varied history.

The many influences that affected the political history of Yugoslavia also affected the cuisine of the nation. In the following recipes you can see the influence of the Hungarians, the Germans, even the Turks. None of the recipes are particularly complex . . . not like the history of Yugoslavia. You must try the Duck Sauce with Dried Cherries and the Cevapcici. You will also find yourself using the Serbian Pork Seasoning regularly. Finally, when you serve the meal and want to really get into the Yugoslavian mind-set, you must buy a bottle of slivovitz. This is a favorite plum brandy that has been aged 10 years or more from Yugoslavia and it is so strong that after four sips you will think that you understand Yugoslavian history.

YUGOSLAVIAN BUREK

Makes 18–20

These phyllo-rolled meat pies look like snails, but they taste like heaven. The only secret to this dish is found in handling the phyllo dough (see **Hint,** below).

1 tablespoon olive oil

1 medium yellow onion, peeled and chopped

1 pound ground beef

1 teaspoon ground allspice

2 teaspoons Hungarian paprika

Salt and freshly ground black pepper to taste

1 box phyllo dough sheets (12 inches by 17 inches)

¾ cup butter, melted

Heat a large frying pan and add the oil. Sauté the onion until soft, and then add the beef, spices, and salt and pepper to taste. Cook until the meat is crumbly but not dry. Allow to cool completely before continuing.

Lay 1 sheet of phyllo dough on the counter. Brush with some of the butter. Place a heaping ⅓ cup of meat mixture across the sheet along the long side, 2 inches from the edge. Fold the bottom over the meat mixture and roll into a snake. Cut the roll in half and coil each roll into a snail shape. Place on a nonstick baking sheet and butt the end up against the edge of the pan to prevent uncoiling. Brush with additional butter. Bake in a preheated oven at 375° for 15 to 20 minutes, or until just golden.

Keep remaining sheets of phyllo dough covered with plastic, and work quickly to prevent it from drying out.

HINT: ON HANDLING PHYLLO DOUGH. Be sure the dough is at room temperature before you open the box. Place the sheets of dough on a large cookie sheet and cover them with plastic wrap and then a heavy towel. In this way they will not dry out while you are working with them. Work fast for best results and do not have the butter too hot when brushing the dough.

Cevapcici

(Yugoslavian Sausages)

Makes 25–30 sausages

My cousin-in-law John Sarich is Yugoslavian, the son of immigrants from the region of Dalmatia on the Adriatic Coast. He tells me that years ago when we first met he was fascinated by the fact that I loved cooking so much. He began to study his own family recipes and opened a Yugoslavian restaurant. He is now the chef at Château Ste. Michelle Wineries here in Washington State. What a trip!

1 pound ground lamb

1 pound ground veal

1 pound ground pork

1 large yellow onion, peeled and grated (Use a food processor.)

3 cloves garlic, peeled and crushed

3 tablespoons *hot* Hungarian paprika or sweet paprika and a little cayenne

2 tablespoons freshly ground black pepper

Salt to taste

Pinch of freshly grated nutmeg

Olive oil for basting

Mix all the ingredients, except the oil, thoroughly and roll the mixture into little "cigars" about 1 inch by 3 inches. Rub lightly with olive oil and grill or broil until done. These are great on the barbeque.

Serve with Yogurt Sauce (recipe follows).

1 pint Homemade Yogurt
(page 428) or yogurt
from the market

½ cucumber, peeled,
grated, and drained 1
hour

2 cloves garlic, peeled and
crushed

Juice of ½ lemon

Salt and ground white
pepper to taste

Pinch of cayenne pepper

Mix all the ingredients together and serve with Cevapcici as a dip.

NJOKI

**Serves 4–6. Can also be served as a pasta or starch dish
with almost any meal.**

John Sarich, my Yugoslavian cousin-in-law, is willing to stand in the
kitchen for hours to make these potato dumplings. I admit they are
worth it. You can see a kinship in the name *njoki* and the Italian, *gnocchi*.

2 pounds baking potatoes
(unpeeled), washed

2 tablespoons butter,
melted

1 egg yolk

1 cup ricotta cheese

1 teaspoon Hungarian
paprika

¼ teaspoon ground nutmeg

½ teaspoon salt

Ground white pepper to
taste

Pinch of cayenne pepper

2 cups all-purpose flour
(See Hint, page 423.)

Boil the potatoes until they are fork tender. Drain them well and allow to
cool just so that you can touch them. Peel and run through a potato
ricer.

Place the potatoes in the bowl of an electric mixer and add the melted
butter, egg yolk, ricotta cheese, and seasonings. Blend about 30 seconds.
Add the flour and blend until a smooth dough is achieved.

Roll the dough into long cylinders the thickness of your finger. Cut
into ½-inch thick pieces. Press with a fork to give the dumplings some
texture. Set on a lightly floured tray to dry. (Flouring the dumplings
before you put each on a tray will help keep them separated when they
cook. Allow them to dry for about 3 hours.)

Bring 8 quarts of water to a boil and add about ¼ of the *njoki*. Boil
gently until they float to the top. Continue to boil for 1 minute and then,

using a strainer, remove them from the pot to a warm bowl. Be careful not to overcook. Continue cooking until all are done. Serve with Duck Sauce with Dried Cherries (below).

DUCK SAUCE WITH DRIED CHERRIES

Serves 4

This is really much more of a very heavy gravy than it is a normal duck dish. I find it delightful, and it is just as good on pasta as it is on John's Njoki (see above).

- 1 3- to 4-pound duck, cut into 4 serving pieces
- 1 cup olive oil
- 2 cups yellow onions, peeled and thinly sliced
- 4–6 cloves peeled and chopped garlic
- ¼ cup chopped Italian parsley
- ¼ cup chopped celery leaves
- 3 cups chopped ripe tomatoes
- ¼ cup dry marsala
- 1¾ cups dry red wine
- 2 whole cloves
- 2 bay leaves

- ¼ teaspoon freshly grated nutmeg
- 2 sprigs of fresh rosemary or ½ tablespoon dried rosemary
- 2 teaspoons Hungarian paprika
- 1 cup dried sour cherries, pitted if possible, soaked in ½ cup warm brandy for 1 hour, reserving the brandy (Cherries can be found in Middle Eastern markets or in fancy food shops.)
- Salt and freshly ground black pepper to taste

Heat the olive oil in a large skillet over medium-high heat. Place the duck pieces in the skillet and brown well to melt off the fat. Remove the duck and drain off most of the fat and oil, reserving ¼ cup.

Add the reserved oil to a 6-quart covered ovenproof casserole and sauté the onion and garlic until tender. Add the parsley and celery leaves and sauté for a few more minutes. Add the tomato and simmer for 15 to 20 minutes.

Add the marsala, red wine, and seasonings and bring to a boil. Add the duck pieces, cover, and cook in a preheated oven at 375° for 2 hours or until the duck meat falls from the bones.

Remove the casserole from the oven and place it on the stove top to cool enough to remove all the bones from the duck quarters. Be careful for the little bones! Return the meat to the pot and add the cherries, along with the brandy. Simmer, uncovered, until the sauce reduces and thickens, about 15 minutes. Salt and pepper to taste.

Serve over *Njoki* (page 509), pasta, or rice.

STUFFED SQUID

Serves 4–5

These are simple to make and wonderful to eat. No, they will not look like squid when you are finished with them. Yugoslavians love squid and octopus. We should eat more of it.

3 pounds cleaned squid (page 480), bodies intact and tentacles finely chopped	⅛ pound prosciutto, chopped
¼ cup chopped parsley	¼ cup grated Romano cheese
4 cloves garlic, peeled and finely chopped	Juice of ½ lemon
3 large shallots, peeled and finely chopped	Salt and ground white pepper to taste
	¼ cup olive oil

GARNISH

Lemon wedges

Mix together the chopped squid and all the other ingredients well, except the olive oil and garnish. Stuff the mixture into the bodies of the squid and, using a toothpick, seal the ends. Do not fill them too full because they shrink when cooking and too much filling will prove to be a problem.

Sauté the stuffed squid gently in the olive oil, about 3 minutes per side. Serve with lemon wedges.

MIXED PEPPER AND TOMATO SALAD

Serves 4–6

This one is quick to make and very colorful. John, my Yugoslavian cousin-in-law, reminds me that the Yugoslavians love peppers of every form. So be it!

1 yellow bell pepper

1 green bell pepper

1 red bell pepper

1 red onion, peeled and sliced

3 firm tomatoes

2 tablespoons chopped parsley

Salt and freshly ground black pepper

¼ cup red wine vinegar

½ cup virgin olive oil

Pinch of sugar

Core, seed, and slice the peppers. Chop the tomatoes into a large dice. Mix together all the cut-up peppers and tomatoes with the remaining ingredients and let stand 1 hour. Serve at room temperature.

SERBIAN PORK SEASONING

The Serbs are a major ethnic group in Yugoslavia and many have come to this country. One of my students from my days as a college chaplain gave me this recipe years ago. I have lost her name, but I bet she will call me when she sees this recipe from her grandparents.

¼ cup fennel seeds

3 tablespoons salt

2 tablespoons sugar

1 tablespoon *each* of ground white pepper and freshly ground coarse black pepper

Whirl the fennel in a blender until coarsely crushed, or crush it in a mortar and pestle. Blend with salt, sugar, and peppers and store in a covered jar.

Use this mixture to sprinkle on in the inside of a boneless pork loin roast and then roll up the meat and tie it on the outside with string. Rub some of the seasoning on the outside also. Place the pork roast on a rack in the oven and roast for 30 minutes per pound in a preheated oven at 325° or until a meat thermometer registers 165° when inserted in the center of the roast.

This seasoning is a very delicious addition to pork.

FRIED PEPPERS YUGOSLAVIAN

Serves 4–5 as a side dish

Since Yugoslavia and Hungary border each other, it is plain to see why the Hungarians' love for peppers is shared by the Yugoslavians. Choose Cubanelle peppers for this dish as they are the closest to Hungarian peppers. Green Anaheim peppers will do, but they are a bit hotter.

1½ pounds Cubanelle (page 39) or Anaheim green peppers (page 36)

4 tablespoons olive oil

3 cloves garlic, peeled and finely chopped

Salt to taste

2 tablespoons white wine vinegar

Cut the peppers in half lengthwise and remove the stems and seeds. Heat the oil in a large frying pan and sauté the garlic for a moment. Add the peppers to the pan and toss them in the oil. Cook to desired tenderness. (I like mine to still be just a bit crisp.) Salt and place the peppers on a serving platter. Sprinkle with the vinegar. This dish may be served hot or cold.

SERBIAN PORK AND BEANS

Serves 4 as part of a meal

This is a simple bean dish that you have probably seen before, but the addition of paprika and hot red pepper flakes probably points to a bit of Hungarian influence. It is a good bean dish, and our Yugoslavian immigrants must have eaten a lot of this in their early days in this country.

1 pound dried white beans, rinsed and drained

1¾ pounds smoked pork hocks, cut in 1-inch pieces

2 medium yellow onions, peeled and chopped

2–3 garlic cloves, peeled and crushed

3 tablespoons freshly rendered lard (page 168) or olive oil

2 tablespoons Hungarian paprika

1 teaspoon crushed hot red pepper flakes (optional)

Put the beans in a heavy casserole and cover with water. Bring to a boil; boil for 2 minutes. Remove from the heat and let stand, covered, for 1 hour. Add the smoked pork and cook slowly, covered, for 1 hour. Meanwhile, sauté the onions and garlic in hot lard or oil until tender. Stir in the paprika and cook for 1 minute. Add the mixture to the beans and pork; continue to cook until the beans are tender, about 40 minutes. If desired, sprinkle with hot red pepper flakes. Salt and pepper to taste. The final dish should have a very thick sauce.

OCTOPUS APPETIZER

Serves 5–6 as a first course

When John Sarich, my Yugoslavian cousin-in-law, cooks this dish, he puts 4 used wine corks in the boiling water for cooking the octopus. I asked him why. He said, "Because that's the way Yugoslavians cook octopus." Sometimes one does things for the sake of tradition, and the original reason is lost. The reason for this tradition is certainly lost on me.

1 large fresh octopus leg, about 2 to 3 pounds	1 medium yellow onion, peeled and cut in half
4 quarts boiling water	Handful of celery leaves
1 bay leaf	3 cloves garlic, peeled and crushed
6 peppercorns	
2 whole cloves	4 wine corks
	2 tablespoons salt

Make sure the water is boiling and add all ingredients, except octopus. Let boil for 15 to 20 minutes. Add the octopus and bring back to a rolling boil. Cook for 25 minutes if you like the creature a bit firm or, for a bit more tender dish, try 1½ hours or until octopus pierces easily with a fork.

Remove the octopus and cool. Strip off its outer skin and tentacles. Trim the tentacles and save for the salad. Cut the leg into ⅛-inch slices and marinate for 2 hours.

THE MARINADE

¼ cup white wine vinegar	½ red onion, peeled and thinly sliced
½ cup olive oil	
2 cloves garlic, peeled and chopped	2 tablespoons parsley
	Salt and ground white pepper to taste

Mix all the ingredients together and toss with the octopus slices. Chill before serving.

EPILOGUE

There you have it! The point of this book is simple. If we do not understand our ancestral table, I doubt that we can understand our history. If we do not understand our history, it is doubtful that we can understand our future.

When our immigrant ancestors came to these shores they brought with them many customs, memories, and traditions, and the table seems to be the place where those traditions have been held most firmly. Alan King, the great comedian, told my family a story one night, a story from ancient Jewish traditions. His parents had come through Ellis Island, his mother from Lithuania and his father from Warsaw. King spoke about the necessity of the old man of the house to have his own chair at the table. At first I thought the story had to do with the integrity of the older person in the house not feeling out of touch with the family. Now, after completing this cookbook and study, I realize that the story referred not just to the old man but to the meaning of our own history. If the old man does not have a special chair at our table, then our own history has no special place either. An old line from the Seder Eliyahu Rabba says it well: "A table is not blessed if it has fed no elders." Our immigrant ancestors continue to bless our tables.

The author Gertrude Louise Cheney, at age nine, observed: "All people are made alike. They are made of bones, flesh, and dinners. Only the dinners are different."

Leaving Ellis Island, 1912

I am convinced that the dinner table is the best way to understand these glorious differences in our backgrounds, and the table is surely the place to relish such differences. The Jews have another old saying: "Only from your own table can you go away full." In other words, if you are eating fast foods and not dining with your "ancestors," you really do not have a table . . . and you will never be full or satisfied.

Eating with your ancestors is a most profound event!

Surely America is a grand place for the celebration of this truth of the table. Given the nature of the American food stores, you no longer can say that you do not know the tastes of the old countries because you cannot get the food products. The world is becoming smaller, and America is becoming better equipped, through wonderful ethnic markets, to satisfy the real hungers that plague us: Who am I and where did I come from? Why did my ancestors come here?

If you have not eaten with your ancestors, even in symbolic form, you have not been to table. That historical table is a part of the American dream that was shared by all immigrants who came here.

Now, to the kitchen and to cooking for your children or grandchildren that dish that your grandmother brought here. Otherwise, the kids may never understand their past, their present, or their future.

COOKBOOK
BIBLIOGRAPHY

*THE FOLLOWING COOKBOOKS MAY BE HELPFUL TO YOU
IN YOUR QUEST FOR MORE RECIPES FROM A PARTICULAR
ETHNIC GROUP*

Alejandro, Reynaldo. *The Philippine Cookbook.* New York: Putnam Publishing Group, 1982.

Amatyakul, Chalie. *The Best of Thai Cooking.* Hong Kong: Travel Publishing Asia Ltd., 1987.

Andoh, Elizabeth. *An American Taste of Japan.* New York: William Morrow and Company, 1985.

Anthony, Dawn, and Elaine and Selwa Anthony. *Lebanese Cookbook.* Secaucus, NJ: Chartwell Books, 1978.

Antreassian, Alice. *Armenian Cooking Today.* New York: St. Vartan Press, 1975.

Azarian, Tomas. *Recipes from Armenia.* Farmhouse Press, RFD 2, Plainfield, VT 05667, 1985.

Batmanglij, Najmieh. *Food of Life.* Washington, D.C.: Mage Publishers, 1984.

Bayless, Rick, with Deann Groen Bayless. *Authentic Mexican.* New York: William Morrow and Company, 1987.

Benghiat, Norma. *Traditional Jamaican Cookery.* (Harmondsworth, England: Penguin Books, 1985.

Bezjian, Alice. *The Complete Armenian Cookbook Including Favorite International Recipes.* Fairlawn, NJ: Rosekeer Press, 1983.

Bourne, Ursula. *Portuguese Cookery.* New York: Penguin Books, 1973.

Brennan, Jennifer. *The Original Thai Cookbook.* New York: Putnam Publishing Group, 1981.

Cabanillas, Berta, and Carmen Ginorio. *Puerto Rican Dishes.* Rio Piedras, Puerto Rico: Universidad de Puerto Rico, 1974.

Cameron, Sheila MacNiven. *The Highlander's Cookbook: Recipes from Scotland.* New York: Gramercy Publishing, 1966.

Chateau Ste. Michelle. *Tastes of Liberty: A Celebration of Our Great Ethnic Cooking.* New York: Stewart, Tabori & Chang, 1985.

Chirinian, Linda. *Secrets of Cooking: Armenian/Lebanese/Persian.* New Canaan, CT: Lionhart, 1987.

Choe, Ji Sook, and Yukiko Moriyama. *Quick and Easy Korean Cooking for Everyone.* Tokyo: Joie, 1986.

Corum, Ann Kondo. *Ethnic Foods of Hawaii*. Bess Press, Box 22388, Honolulu, HI 97822, 1983.

Cost, Bruce. *Bruce Cost's Asian Ingredients: Buying and Cooking the Staple Foods of China, Japan, and Southeast Asia*. New York: William Morrow and Company, 1988.

Culinary Arts Institute. *Polish Cookbook*. New York: Consolidated Book Publishers, 1978.

Dauzvardis, Josephine J. *Popular Lithuanian Recipes*. Lithuanian Catholic Press, 4545 West 63rd Street, Chicago, IL 60629, 1974.

Donato, Marilyn R. *Philippine Cooking in America*. Circulation Service, PO Box 7306, Shawnee Mission, Kansas 86207, 1972.

Dorcas Guild. *Hungarian Recipes*. The Dorcas Guild of The Magyar United Church of Christ, 119 West River Street, Elyria, OH 44035, 1960.

Farah, Madelain. *Lebanese Cuisine*. Lebanese Cuisine, PO Box 66395, Portland, OR, 1972.

Fitzgibbon, Theodora. *A Taste of Ireland in Food and in Pictures*. London: Pan Books, 1970.

Gow, Rosalie. *Traditional Scottish Recipes*. Pelican Publishing, 1101 Monroe Street, Gretna, LA 70053, 1980.

Harris, Paul. *A Little Scottish Cookbook*. San Francisco: Chronicle Books, 1988.

Hogrogian, Rachel. *The Armenian Cookbook*. New York: Macmillan, 1971.

Kaplan, Anne R., Marjorie A. Hoover, and Willard B. Moore. *The Minnesota Ethnic Food Book*. St. Paul, MN: Minnesota Historical Society, 1986.

Khayat, Marie Karam, and Margaret Clark Keatinge. *Food from the Arab World* (Beirut: Eastern Art, 1959).

Koehler, Margaret H. *Recipes from the Portuguese of Provincetown*. Riverside, CT: Chatham Press, 1973.

Ladies Auxiliary of the Polish Museum of America. *Favorite Recipes of The Ladies Auxiliary of the Polish Museum of America*. Fundcraft, 410 Highway 72, PO Box 340, Collierville, TN 38017, 1984.

Lang, George. *The Cuisine of Hungary*. New York: Bonanza Books (Crown), 1972.

Latvian Evangelical Lutheran Church-Sunday School. *Latvian Recipes*. Latvian Evangelical Lutheran Church-Sunday School, 11710 Third N.E., Seattle, WA 98125, 1984.

Law, Ruth. *The Southeast Asia Cookbook*. New York: Donald Fine, 1990.

Mallos, Tess. *The Complete Middle East Cookbook*. Sydney, Australia: Lansdowne Press, 1979.

Mazda, Maideh. *In a Persian Kitchen*. Rutland, VT: Charles E. Tuttle, 1960.

Mesfin, Daniel J. *Exotic Ethiopian Cooking*. Ethiopian Cookbook Enterprise of Falls Church, VA, 3800 Powell Lane, Suite 404, Falls Church, VA 22041, 1987.

Mitchell, Jan. *Lüchow's German Cookbook*. Garden City, NY: Doubleday, 1952.

Nelson, Kay Shaw. *The Eastern European Cookbook*. New York: Dover, 1977.

Omae, Kinjiro, and Yuzuru Tachibana. *The Book of Sushi*. Tokyo: Kodansha International, 1981.

Polanie Club Editorial Staff. *Treasured Polish Recipes for Americans*. Minneapolis: Polanie Publishing, 1948.

Polvay, Marina. *All Along the Danube: Classic Cookery from the Great Cuisines of Eastern Europe.* Englewood Cliffs, NJ: Prentice Hall, 1979.

Rabade, Raquel. *The Cuban Flavor.* Miami: Downtown Book Center, 1979.

Reno Zazpiak-Bat Basque Club. *From the Basque Kitchen.* Zazpiak-Bat Basque Club, PO Box 7771, Reno, NV 89502, 1973.

Roden, Claudia. *A Book of Middle Eastern Food* (New York: Alfred A. Knopf, 1972.

Sahni, Julie. *Classic Indian Cooking.* New York: William Morrow and Company, 1980.

Schmitz, Puangkram C., and Michael J. Worman. *Practical Thai Cooking.* New York: Harper & Row, 1985.

Searl, Janet Mendel. *Cooking in Spain.* Fuengirola, Spain: Lookout Publications, 1987.

Shalimov, S. A., V. A. Lysenko, and A. I. Veresiuk, *Ukrainian Cookery Recipes.* Kiev, USSR: Technika Publishers, 1989.

Sheridan, Monica. *The Art of Irish Cooking.* New York: Gramercy Publishing (Crown), 1965.

Shulman, Jason, A. *Grandma's Kitchen.* New York: Blue Cliff Editions, 1985.

Silverstein, Fanny. *My Mother's Cookbook.* New York: Carroll & Graf Publishers, 1985.

Singh, Balbir. *Indian Cookery.* New York: Weathervane Books, 1976.

Solomon, Charmaine. *The Complete Asian Cookbook.* Sydney, Australia: Summit Books, 1976.

Valldejuli, Carmen Aboy. *Puerto Rican Cookery.* Pelican Publishing, 1101 Monroe Street, Gretna, LA 70053, 1975.

Van Gilder, Kerstin Olsson. *Splendid Swedish Recipes.* Penfield Press, 215 Brown Street, Iowa City, IA.

Vollmer, Susan. *Authentic Mexican Cooking.* Nitty Gritty Productions, PO Box 2008, Benicia, CA 94510, 1987.

Wade, Lee. *Lee Wade's Korean Cookbook.* Seoul, Korea: Pomso Publishers, 1974.

Wales Tourist Board. *Blas Ar Gymru: A Taste of Wales.* Cardiff, Wales: Wales Tourist Board, 1984.

Wolfert, Paula. *Couscous and Other Good Food from Morocco.* New York: Harper & Row, 1973.

Xan, Erna Oleson, and Sigrid Marstrander. *Time-Honored Norwegian Recipes.* Decorah, IA: Norwegian-American Museum, 1984.

Zane, Eva. *Middle Eastern Cookery.* San Francisco: 101 Productions, 1974.

IMMIGRANT HISTORY
BIBLIOGRAPHY

Adams, Edward B. *Korea Guide*. Seoul, Korea: Seoul International Publishing (Charles E. Tuttle), 1983.

Alford, Harold J. *The Proud Peoples*. New York: David McKay, 1972.

Bernstein, Joanne E. *Dimitri: A Young Soviet Immigrant*. Merlin, OR: Clarion Books, 1981.

Blunden, Godfrey. *Eastern Europe*. New York: Life World Library, 1965.

Brennen, Lenni. *Jews in America Today*. New York: Lyle Stuart, 1986.

Budreckis, Algirdan, ed. *Lithuanians in America, 1651–1975*. Dobbs Ferry, NY: Oceana Publications, 1976.

Diamond, Arthur. *The Romanian Americans*. New York: Chelsea House, 1988.

Dinnerstein, Leonard, and David M. Reimers. *Ethnic Americans: A History of Immigration*. New York: Harper & Row, 1987.

Ehrlich, Paul R. *The Golden Door*. New York: Ballantine Books, 1979.

Fradin, Dennis B. *The Republic of Ireland*. Chicago: Children's Press, 1984.

Fodor, Eugene. *Fodor's Korea*. New York: Fodor Travel Publications, 1983.

————. *Fodor's Yugoslavia*. New York: Fodor Travel Publications, 1988.

Friedman, Thomas. *From Beirut to Jerusalem*. New York: Farrar Strauss Giroux, 1989.

Galbraith, C. A., and R. Mehta. *India Now and Through Time*. New York: Dodd, Mead, 1971.

Gary, D. H. and Lord Kinross. *Morocco*. New York: Viking Press, 1971.

Goodwin, M., C. Perry, and N. Wise. *Totally Hot*. Garden City, NY: Doubleday, 1986.

Haddox, John. *Los Chicanos*. El Paso, TX: University of Texas at El Paso Western Press, 1970.

Halliday, Jon, and Bruce Cumings. *Korea: The Unknown War*. New York: Pantheon Books, 1988.

Haverstock, Nathan A. *Cuba in Pictures*. Minneapolis: Lerner Publications, 1987.

Herberg, Will. *Protestant, Catholic, Jew*. Garden City, NY: Anchor Books, 1960.

Hinkley, H. *The Land and People of Iran*. Philadelphia: J. B. Lippincott, 1964.

Hintz, Martin. *Morocco*. Chicago: Children's Press, 1985.

———— *Norway*. Chicago: Children's Press, 1982.

Hitti, Phillip. *The Arabs, A Short History.* London: MacMillan, 1965.

Hoffman, Mark. *The World Almanac and Book of Facts, 1990.* New York: Pharos Books, 1989.

Horizon Concise History of Scandinavia, The. New York: American Heritage Publishing Company, 1973.

Hotchkiss, Caroline. *Home to Poland.* New York: Farrar, Strauss and Cudahy, 1958.

Hunte, George. *The West Indian Islands.* New York: Viking Press, 1972.

Kaiser, Robert C., and Hannah Jopling Kaiser. *Russia from the Inside.* New York: E. P. Dutton, 1980.

Karklis, Maruta, Laimonis Streips, and Liga Streips, eds. *The Latvians in America.* Dobbs Ferry, NY: Oceana Publications, 1974.

Keon, Michael. *Korean Phoenix.* Englewood Cliffs, NJ: Prentice Hall, 1977.

Kim, H. Edward. *Decade of Success.* Harry Young Publications, 1980.

Kim, Warren Y. *Koreans in America.* Seoul, Korea: Po Chin Chai Printing Company, 1971.

Kittler, Pamela, and Kathryn Sucher. *Food and Culture in America.* New York: Van Nostrand Reinhold, 1989.

Korbowski, Stefan. *Warsaw in Exile.* New York: Praeger, 1966.

Korean Overseas Information Service. *This Is Korea.* Seoul, Korea: Seoul International Publishing (Charles E. Tuttle), 1986.

Kurtz, Seymour. *Jewish America.* New York: McGraw-Hill, 1985.

Lacey, Robert. *The Kingdom.* New York: Harcourt Brace Jovanovich, 1981.

Library of Nations. *Eastern Europe.* New York: Time-Life Books, 1986.

———. *Japan.* New York: Time-Life Books, 1985.

———. *Scandinavia.* New York: Time-Life Books, 1985.

———. *The Soviet Union.* New York: Time-Life Books, 1984.

McCarthy, Kevin. *Saudi Arabia.* Minneapolis: Dillon Press, 1986.

MacVicar, Angus. *Let's Visit Scotland.* Burke Publishing, 1984.

Mannetti, L. *Iran and Iraq.* New York: Franklin Watts, 1986.

Matley, Ian. *Romania.* New York: Praeger, 1970.

Melendy, H. Brett. *Asians in America.* Schenectady, NY: Twayne Publications (New College and University Press), 1977.

Meyer, K. A. *Ireland.* Minneapolis: Dillon Press, 1983.

Naff, Alixa. *The Arab Americans.* New York: Chelsea House, 1988.

National Geographic. "Gloucester Blesses Its Portuguese Fleet" (July 1953, vol. civ); "Life in the Land of the Basques" (February 1954, vol. cv); "New England's Little Portugal" (January 1975, vol. 147, no. 1); "Revolution in the Ancient Empire" (May 1983, vol. 163, no. 5.)

Newsweek. "A Troublesome Exodus" (September 26, 1989).

Pap, Leo. *The Portuguese Americans.* Schenectady, NY: Twayne Publications (New College and University Press), 1981.

Pariser, Harry S. *Guide to Jamaica.* Chico, CA: Moon Publications, 1981.

Rogerson, Barnaby. *Morocco.* Chester, CT: Globe Pequot Press, 1989.

Russell, Francis. *The Horizon Concise History of Germany.* New York: American Heritage Publishing, 1973.

Sarin, Amitra Vohra. *India.* Minneapolis: Dillon Press, 1985.

Schoener, Allen. *American Jewish Album, 1624 to Present.* New York: Rizzoli, 1983.

Shapiro, William E. *Lebanon*. New York: Franklin Watts, 1984.

Shenton, James P., ed. *Ethnic Groups in American Life*. Salem, NH: Arno Press, 1978.

Simpson, John. *Inside Iran*. New York: St. Martin's Press, 1988.

Simon, Julian L. *The Economic Consequences of Immigration*. Cambridge, MA: Basil Blackwell, 1989.

Slater, Mary. *The Caribbean Islands*. New York: Viking Press, 1968.

Spieler, Marlena. *Hot and Spicy*. Los Angeles: Jeremy P. Tarcher, 1985.

Thernstrom, Stephan, ed. *Harvard Encyclopedia of American Ethnic Groups*. Cambridge, MA: Harvard University Press, 1980.

Thomas, William I., and Florian Znaniecki. *The Polish Peasant in America*. Chicago: University of Chicago Press, 1918.

Vardy, Steven Bela. *The Hungarian Americans*. New York: Chelsea House, 1990.

Watts, J. F. *The Irish Americans*. New York: Chelsea House, 1988.

Winder, Viola, H. *The Land and People of Lebanon*. Philadelphia: J. B. Lippincott, 1965.

Wooley, A. E. *Persia/Iran*. Radnor, PA: Chilton Books, 1965.

SOURCES FOR UNUSUAL INGREDIENTS

This list of places will enable you to get some of the harder-to-find ingredients used in this book. They are listed alphabetically by city within each category, and mail-order sources are indicated by an (*). Many of these stores also have catalogues they will send you, which is fun because then you can browse through the pages of exotic foreign ingredients.

General Ingredients

These four stores have a huge selection of ingredients, both fresh and prepared, from all over the culinary map. They all have mail-order catalogues, and you can get a wide variety of ingredients from a single source if you so desire.

*Rafal Spice Company
2521 Russell Street
Detroit, MI 48207
(800) 228-4276
In Michigan: (313) 259-6373

*Balducci's
Mail-order Division
424 Sixth Avenue
New York, NY 10011
(800) 247-2450
In New York: 212-673-2600

*Dean & DeLuca
560 Broadway
New York, NY 10012
(800) 221-7714
In New York: (212) 431-1691

*G. B. Ratto, International
  Grocers
821 Washington Street
Oakland, CA 94607
(800) 325-3483
In California: (800) 228-3515

**Mexican/Latin American/
  Caribbean Ingredients**

India Tea and Spice, Inc.
453 Common Street
Belmont, MA 02178
(617) 484-3737

Tropical Foods, Inc.
2101 Washington Street
Boston, MA 02119
(417) 442-7439

El Coloso Market
102 Columbia Street
Cambridge, MA 02139
(617) 491-1361

La Casa del Pueblo
1810 South Blue Island
Chicago, IL 60608
(312) 421-4640

El Original Supermercado
  Cardenas
3922 North Sheridan Road
Chicago, IL 60607
(312) 525-5610

*La Preferida, Inc.
3400 West 35th Street
Chicago, IL 60632
(312) 254-7200

Hernandez Mexican Foods
2120 Alamo Street
Dallas, TX 75202
(214) 742-2533

Johnnie's Market
2030 Larimer Street
Denver, CO 80205
(303) 297-0155

Algo Especial
2628 Bagley Street
Detroit, MI 48216
(313) 963-9013

La Colmena
2443 Bagley Street
Detroit, MI 48216
(313) 237-0295

Hi-Lo Market
415 Centre Street
Jamaica Plain, MA 02130
(617) 522-6364

The Grand Central Market
317 South Broadway
Los Angeles, CA 90013
(213) 622-1763

Casa Sanchez
2778 24th Street
San Francisco, CA 94110
(415) 282-2400

International Groceries and Meat
  Market
5219 Ninth Avenue (39th and
  40th Streets)
New York, NY 10018
(212) 279-5514

Latin American Products
142 West 46th Street
New York, NY 10036
(212) 302-4323

Americana Grocery
1813 Columbia Road N.W.
Washington, DC 20009
(202) 265-7455

Casa Peña
1636 17th Street N.W.
Washington, DC 20009
(202) 462-2222

Asian Ingredients

Ming's Market
85-91 Essex Street
Boston, MA 02111
(617) 482-8805

*New England Food
225 Harrison Avenue
Boston, MA 02111
(617) 426-8592

· Sun Sun Company
18 Oxford Street
Boston, MA 02111
(617) 426-6494

*Star Market
3349 North Clark Street
Chicago, IL 60657
(312) 472-0599

Tan Viet Market
10332 Ferguson Road
Dallas, TX 75228
(214) 324-5160

*Bangkok Market, Inc.
4804-6 Melrose Avenue
Los Angeles, CA 90029
(213) 662-9705

Yee Sing Chong Company, Inc.
977 North Broadway
Los Angeles, CA 90012
(213) 626-9619

Keesan Imports
9252 Bird Road
Miami, FL 33165
(305) 551-9591

*Southeastern Food Supply
400 N.E. 67th Street
Miami, FL 33431
(305) 758-1432

*Kam Kuo Food Corporation
7 Mott Street
New York, NY 10013
(212) 349-3097

*Kam Man Food Products
200 Canal Street
New York, NY 10013
(212) 571-0330

*Katagari & Company, Inc.
   (large Japanese selection)
224 East 59th Street
New York, NY 10022
(212) 755-3566

*The Chinese Grocer
209 Post Street at Grant Avenue
San Francisco, CA 94108
(415) 982-0125 or
   (800) 227-3320

*Da Hua Market
623 H Street N.W.
Washington, DC 20001
(202) 371-8880

**Greek and Middle Eastern
Ingredients**

*Sahadi Importing Company,
Inc.
187 Atlantic Avenue
Brooklyn, NY 11201
(718) 624-4550

*C & K Importing Company
2771 West Pico Boulevard
Los Angeles, CA 90006
(213) 737-2970

**Indian Ingredients and Exotic
Spices**

Indian Tea & Spices
453 Common Street
Belmont, MA 02178
(617) 484-3737

*Bazaar of India
1810 University Avenue
Berkeley, CA 94703
(415) 548-4110

*International Grocer
3411 Woodward
Detroit, MI 48201
(313) 831-5480

*House of Spices
76–17 Broadway
Jackson Heights, NY 11373
(718) 476-1577

*Annapurna
126 East 28th Street
New York, NY 10016
(212) 889-7540

*Aphrodisia Products, Inc.
282 Bleecker Street
New York, NY 10014
(212) 989-6440

Market Spices
85A Pike Place Market
Seattle, Washington 98101
(206) 622-6340

Scandinavian Ingredients

IKEA
1000 Center Drive
Elizabeth, NJ 07201
(201) 223-4488

*Ingebretsen's
1601 East Lake Street
Minneapolis, MN 55407
(612) 729-9331

*Maid of Scandinavia
32-44 Raleigh Avenue
Minneapolis, MN 55416
(800) 328-6722

Nyborg and Nelson
Citicorp Building
153 East 53rd Street
New York, NY 10022
(212) 223-0700

Miscellaneous Ingredients

Sausage Casings, Curing Salts, Sausage-Making Equipment

*The Sausage Maker
177 Military Road
Buffalo, NY 14207
(716) 876-5521

*Aidell's Sausage Company
1575 Minnesota Street
San Francisco, CA 94107
(415) 285-6660

A Variety of Hardwoods and Hardwood Charcoals

*Don Hysko
People's Woods
55 Mill Street
Cumberland, RI 02864
(401) 725-2700

Hot Chile Peppers to Grow Yourself

The Pepper Gal, Dorothy L.
  Van Vleck
10536 119th Avenue North
Largo, FL 34643

Roswell Seed Co.
115-117 South Main
P.O. Box 725
Roswell, N.M. 88201
(505) 622-7701

Latin Vegetables to Grow Yourself

J. A. Mako Horticultural
  Experience
P.O. Box 34082
Dallas, TX 75234

Asian Vegetables to Grow Yourself

Mellinger's
2310 West South Range Road
North Lima, OH 44452
(216) 549-9861

PERMISSIONS

RECIPES

Grateful acknowledgment is made to the following for permission to reprint their recipes:

Armenian Hand-Rolled Sausages from *Armenian Cooking Today* by Alice Antreassian, St. Vartan Press, New York, 1975.

Cauliflower and Scallions with Black Mustard Seeds and Tandoori Game Hens from *Classic Indian Cooking* by Julie Sahni, William Morrow and Company, New York, 1980.

Peach Chutney with Walnuts and Raisins from *Moghul Microwave: Cooking Indian Food the Modern Way* by Julie Sahni, William Morrow and Company, New York, 1990.

Dublin Coddle and Scallop and Mushroom Pie from *A Taste of Ireland in Food and in Pictures* by Theodora Fitzgibbon, Pan Books Ltd., London, 1970.

Takuan from *Ethnic Foods of Hawaii* by Ann Kondo Corum, Bess Press, PO Box 22388, Honolulu, Hawaii 96823, 1983.

Honey Cake from *My Mother's Cookbook* by Fanny Silverstein, Carroll & Graf/Quicksilver Publishers, New York, 1985.

Stuffed Peppers in Egg from *Lee Wade's Korean Cookbook* by Lee Wade, Pomso Publishers, 18–4 Kwancholdong, Chong-ku, Seoul, Korea, 1974.

Cucumber Condiment from *The Cooking of the Pacific and Southeast Asia,* Foods of the World Series, Time-Life Books, New York, 1969.

Moroccan Red Pepper Sauce from *Middle Eastern Cookery* by Eva Zane, 101 Productions, San Francisco, 1974.

Lamb and Cabbage Stew from *Northwest Orient Magazine,* May 1985.

Chelo and Kateh Rice Cake from *The Complete Middle East Cookbook* by Tess Mallos, McGraw-Hill, New York, 1979.

Advieh from *Food of Life* by Najmieh Batmanglij, Mage Publishers, Washington, D.C., 1986.

Vietnamese Lemongrass Chicken from *The Complete Asian Cookbook* by Charmaine Solomon, McGraw-Hill, New York, 1976.

Polish Lazy Dumplings from *Favorite Recipes of the Ladies Auxiliary of the Polish Museum of America* by Smacznego, The Ladies Auxiliary of the Polish Museum of America, 984 Milwaukee Avenue, Chicago, Illinois 60622.

Polish Noodles and Cabbage from *Polish Cookbook* by Culinary Arts Institute, Consolidated Book Publishers, 1975 North Hawthorne, Melrose Park, Illinois 60160.

Blini and Caviar from *Russian Cooking* by Helen Waite Papashvily, Foods of the World Series, Time-Life Books, New York, 1969.

Basque Bread (Sheepherder's Bread) from *Sunset Magazine,* June 1976, pp. 66–67.

Knishes from *Sunset Magazine,* January 1977, pp. 78–79.

PHOTOGRAPHS

Grateful acknowledgment is made to the following for use of the photographs included in this book:

Author's personal collection: 2

Brown Brothers Photography: 15

Lewis W. Hine Collection, United States History, Local History and Genealogy Division, The New York Public Library, Astor, Lenox, and Tilden Foundations: 57, 60, 63, 144, 249, 301, 505

The Library of Congress, Washington, D.C. From *Ellis Island: Echoes from a Nation's Past,* Susan Jonas, ed. (New York: Aperture Press): 517

William Williams Collection, United States History, Local History and Genealogy Division, The New York Public Library, Astor, Lenox, and Tilden Foundations: 17, 56, 64

INDEX

lamb brewats, 331–332
lamb stew (tagine), 329
preserved lemons, 333
red pepper sauce, 325
roasted lamb, 328
MSG, 273
mujadarra (lentils and rice), 432
mulligatawny soup, 202–203
mung bean(s):
 noodles, chicken with, 162
 pancake, 262
 with pork, 136
mushroom(s):
 and barley casserole, 446
 and barley soup, Polish, 370
 and cabbage pierogi, 372–373
 Polish chicken with, 371
 and sauerkraut pierogi, 372–373
 and scallop pie, 218
 shiitake, filling for sushi, 244–245
 and wine sauce, Basque leg of lamb with, 89–90
mussels:
 paella Valencia, 456–457
 shellfish and rice, 88
mustard sauce for cold poached salmon, 464

nan (Indian bread), 198–199
Napa kimchee, 265
 stir-fried pork with, 266
navratna chutney, 195
nigiri-zushi (sushi with fish), 245–246
njoki, 509–510
noodle(s):
 chicken with long rice, 162
 haluski, 417
noodle(s), egg:
 egg barley, 253
 kugel, 250
 Lebanese rice pilaf, 297
 Polish cabbage and, 369
noodle(s), rice:
 Cambodian fried, with beef and bean curd, 102–103
 Filipino pansit, 140
 pad Thai, 477–478
Norwegian dishes:
 cream sauce, 339
 fish pudding, 338
 lamb and cabbage stew, 340
 potato lefse, 344
 rice pudding, 345
 rommegrot, 346
 rullespulse, 341–342
 sylte, 343

octopus:
 appetizer, 514
 sushi with, 245
okra:
 crisp fried, 187
 and lamb stew, 296
olives, chicken and, 330
omelets:
 kuku eggplant, 351–352
 kuku sabzi, 350–351
 tortilla of potato and onions, 455
onion(s):
 and dill bread, 421–422
 Hungarian hand-rolled sausage with, 180
 Persian salad, 362
 pie, 151
 potato knishes, 252–253
 potato soup, Irish style, 211
 salad, 182
 tortilla of potato and, 455

oxtail(s):
 Basque, 86
 kare kare, 135
 stew, Jamaican, 224
oysters, sushi with, 246

pad Thai, 477–478
paella Valencia, 456–457
pagach, 424
pancake(s):
 blinis and caviar, 419–420
 Bokolgny style, 174–175
 with chocolate syrup, 182
 mung bean, 262
 Polish potato, 375
 potato lefse, 346
 Russian potato, 418
 Swedish, with lingonberries, 470
pans and pots, 22–23
pansit, Filipino, 140
paprika gravy, 167
 sauerkraut cooked in, 180
peach chutney with walnuts and raisins, 194
pepper(s):
 fried, Yugoslavian, 513
 green, and beef, 269–270
 green, sausage with tomatoes and, 181
 Lebanese shish kebab, 295
 mixed, and tomato salad, 512
 piri piri, 382
 sauce, Moroccan red, 325
peppers, stuffed, 256
 Armenian tomatoes and, 76–77
 in egg, 274
 Hungarian red bell, 169–170
Persian dishes:
 advieh, 359
 chelo kebab, 355–356
 eggplant salad, 357
 ghee, 356
 kateh rice cake, 354
 kuku eggplant, 351–352
 kuku sabzi, 350–351
 lamb tongues, 358
 lentil and rice soup, 361
 rice (chelo), 352–353
 salad, 362
 spinach borani, 360
 steamed plain rice, 353–354
phyllo dough, handling of, 507
pickled:
 beef roast, German, 147–148
 pork hocks, 145–146
pickle(s):
 cucumber namasu, 239
 daikon kimchee cubes, 273
 lemon, 204
 Napa kimchee, 265
 shredded daikon kimchee, 272
 spinach with sesame and miso, 239
 takuan (pickled daikon), 241
picon punch, Basque, 97
pierogi (Polish dumplings), 372–373
 leniwe (lazy), 368
 low-fat, 373
pigeon peas, Puerto Rican rice with, 397
pil pil, codfish, 87, 451
pine nuts, fraykee with, 431
piragi, Latvian, 278–279
piri piri, 382
 roast chicken with, 382
plantains:
 fried, 116, 394
 monfongo con caldo, 393

cornmeal mush with cheese, 403
fried cornmeal mush, 404
mashed beans, 404–405
mixed vegetables and veal stew, 406–407
sausages, 402
stuffed cabbage, 405
walnut crescents, 409–410
rommegrot, 346
ropa vieja, Cuban, 111–112
rosolos potato salad, 281
rotkohl (red cabbage), 150
rullespulse, 341–342
Russian dishes:
  beef stroganoff, 414–415
  blinis and caviar, 419–420
  borscht, 420–421
  cauliflower fried in butter, 417
  dill and onion bread, 421–422
  haluski, 417
  kasha, 416
  pagach, 424
  potato pancakes, 418
  radish and egg salad, 418
  round bread, 422–423

salads:
  Cambodian beef, 103–104
  Cambodian raw fish, 101
  eggplant, 357
  green banana, 394
  Hanna's guacamole, 313
  herring, Swedish style, 465
  Indian spinach yogurt raita, 191
  Irving's cucumber, 255
  Japanese cucumber and crab, 240
  Latvian herring, 282
  Lebanese yogurt and cucumber, 294
  lomi lomi salmon, 160
  mixed pepper and tomato, 512
  onion, 182
  Persian, 362
  radish and egg, 418
  rosolos potato, 281
  Saudi Arabian bean, 430
  sauerkraut, Hungarian, 182
  tabouleh, 288–289
  tahini, 433
  Thai beef, 476
  Thai squid, 479–480
  tomato cucumber raita, 192
salmon:
  aku poke, 159
  cold poached, mustard sauce for, 464
  gravlax, 463–464
  lomi lomi, 160
  in miso, 237–238
salsa, homemade, 312
salsa roja, 315
  enchiladas, 314
salsa verde, 317
  enchiladas con queso, 316
salt, sesame, 268
saltibarsciai (cold beet soup), 306–307
samosas, 205–206
sandwiches:
  Cuban, 115
  falafel, 436
  rullespulse, 341–342
sauces:
  Basque tomato, 92
  berbere, 123
  cream, 339
  green pepper and tomato, 181

homemade salsa, 312
Korean barbecue, 263
leban, 435
lumpia, 138
Moroccan red pepper, 325
mushroom and wine, 90
mustard, for cold poached salmon, 464
salsa roja, 315
salsa verde, 317
tamarind, 478
Vietnamese dipping, 488
yogurt, 509
Saudi Arabian dishes:
  baba ghanoush with acorn squash, 429
  bean salad, 430
  falafel, 436
  fraykee with pine nuts, 431
  homemade yogurt, 428–429
  leban sauce, 435
  lentils and rice, 432
  sesame candy, 432–433
  stuffed vegetables, 434–435
  tahini salad, 433
sauerbraten (German pickled beef roast), 147–148
sauerkraut:
  and bean soup, 172–173
  cooked in paprika gravy, 180
  German, 146
  and mushroom pierogi, 372–373
  Polish, 367–368
  raw, with caraway, 307
  salad Hungarian, 182
sausage(s):
  Armenian hand-rolled, 75–76
  Dublin coddle, 212
  fresh, 304
  with green pepper and tomatoes, 181
  hand rolling, hint for, 402
  Hungarian, 179–180
  Hungarian hand-rolled, with onions, 180
  potato, 469
  Romanian, 402
  Scottish eggs, 447
  smoked Polish or Lithuanian, 305, 367
  stuffing, hints for, 453
  Yugoslavian (*cevapcici*), 508–509
  see also chorizo sausage
scallions, cauliflower and, with black mustard seeds, 188
scallop and mushroom pie, 218
schmaltz, 253
scones, 500
Scottish dishes:
  barley and mushroom casserole, 446
  broth, 445
  cock-a-leekie, 440
  cullen skink, 441
  eggs, 447
  finnan haddie, 444
  haggis, 442–443
  shortbread, 448
seaweed:
  aku poke, 159
  Korean crisp laver, 267
  Korean eggfolds with, 268
  rolled sushi, 243–245
semmelknödel (potato dumplings), 152
Serbian pork and beans, 513–514
Serbian pork seasoning, 512
sesame:
  candy, 432–433
  salt, 268
  spinach with miso and, 239
  sushi balls in, 245